Mando
Enjoy this book. I
learned stuff I forgot.
This will help you as it has
helped me remember
                        Jose Romero

Sonny Montes

*and Mexican American Activism
in Oregon*

Armando,
thank you for your support
throughout the years. Keep
up the good work
        Con Cariño
        tu Amigo
        Sonny Montes

Sonny Montes

and Mexican American Activism in Oregon

Glenn Anthony May

OREGON STATE UNIVERSITY PRESS • CORVALLIS

Publication of this book was made possible in part by a subvention from The Oregon Humanities Center and the College of Arts and Sciences at the University of Oregon. The Oregon State University Press is grateful for this support.

The paper in this book meets the guidelines for permanence and durability of the Committee on Production Guidelines for Book Longevity of the Council on Library Resources and the minimum requirements of the American National Standard for Permanence of Paper for Printed Library Materials Z39.48-1984.

Library of Congress Cataloging-in-Publication Data
May, Glenn Anthony, 1945-
  Sonny Montes and Mexican American activism in Oregon / Glenn Anthony May.
       p. cm.
  Includes bibliographical references and index.
  ISBN 978-0-87071-600-3 (alk. paper)
 1. Montes, Sonny, 1944- 2. Mexican Americans--Oregon--Biography. 3. Political activists--Oregon--Biography. 4. Mexican Americans--Oregon--Politics and government--20th century.
5. Colegio Cesar Chavez (Mount Angel, Or.) 6. Oregon--Race relations. I. Title.
  F881.35.M66M39 2011
  305.868'720795092--dc22
  [B]
                                          2010053106

First published in 2011 by Oregon State University Press
Printed in the United States of America

Oregon State University Press
121 The Valley Library
Corvallis OR 97331-4501
541-737-3166 • fax 541-737-3170
http://oregonstate.edu/dept/press

For my children:

Lizzie, Rachel, and Benjamin

Contents

Acknowledgments

During the eight years I have worked on this book, I have received much assistance from individuals and organizations. Research was funded, in part, by generous support from the University of Oregon in the form of a faculty summer research award and a research fellowship in the Oregon Humanities Center. I also acknowledge with gratitude publication subventions provided by the University of Oregon's College of Arts and Sciences and the Oregon Humanities Center. My greatest personal debts are to my family (Helen Liu, Lizzie May, Rachel Liu-May, and Benjamin Liu-May), who endured with remarkably good cheer my preoccupation with this project, and the many people, most of them Mexican Americans, who shared their memories with me in sometimes lengthy interviews. The three interviewees who indulged me most, and cannot be thanked enough, are Sonny Montes, John Little, and Jose Romero. They and all the other people I interviewed in connection with my research are listed in the Note about Sources. Without them, I would not have been able to write this book.

In addition, archivists have helped me to locate important manuscripts; librarians have brought relevant books and published documents to my attention, expeditiously handled my interlibrary loan requests, and assisted me in countless other ways; colleagues at the University of Oregon and other institutions have answered my queries, given me valuable leads, and provided feedback on earlier formulations of my ideas; undergraduates in my History 407 (Oregon history) seminar at the University of Oregon have taught me much about the history of the state's Mexican Americans (and the research papers of four of them are cited in the notes); Mexican American friends in the Pacific Northwest have shown an interest in my work and prodded me to finish the book. Belatedly, let me express my gratitude to the following individuals: Barbara Altmann, Rev. Robert C. Antonelli, Margaret Bean, Marianne Bobich, Patrick Burk, Mary Ann Casas, David Evans, James Fox, Shawna Gandy, Mario García, Matt Garcia, Chuck Grench, Joanne Halgren, Kevin Hatfield, Shawn Helm, Ellen Herman, Marie Hernandez, Julia Heydon, Max Hill, Michael Hussey, Marianne Keddington-Lang, Rita Kester, Linda Long, Alfred McCoy, Noreen Saltveit

McGraw, Suzanne McKenzie, Jack Maddex, Ruthann Maguire, Oscar Martínez, Leon Mitchell Jr., Jim Mohr, Scott Montanaro, Angus Nesbit, Jeff Ostler, the late Peggy Pascoe, Riley Peck, David Peterson del Mar, Daniel Pope, Kay Reid, Aurora Richardson, Bill Robbins, John Russell, Rosanne Rutten, Rudy Saenz, Katie Sloan, Tom Stave, Lynn Stephen, James Strassmeier, Quintard Taylor, Tamara Vidos, Gwen Walker, Timothy Wallace, Janis Wiggins, and Aimee Yogi. I am grateful, too, for the very helpful comments provided by the two anonymous readers of my book manuscript for Oregon State University Press.

I found it extremely challenging to assemble the photographs that appear in this book and could not have done so on my own. The following people assisted me in locating, reproducing, and obtaining permission to use them: Jo Alexander, Christian Boboia, Bill Church, John Little, Helen Liu, Sonny Montes, Jose Romero, and Drew Vattiat. My debt of gratitude to them is great. It is likewise great to Alethea Steingisser of the University of Oregon's InfoGraphics Lab, who created the map.

Finally, I want to single out for thanks my terrific editor at Oregon State University Press, Mary Braun, and my gifted copyeditor, Stacey Lynn. It has been a privilege to work with them.

AWOC: Agricultural Workers Organizing Committee
CAA: Community Action Agency
CAP: Community Action Program
CISCO: Chicano-Indian Study Center of Oregon
CORE: Congress of Racial Equality
CSO: Community Services Organization
D-Q University: Deganawidah-Quetzalcoatl University
ESL: English as a Second Language
GAO: General Accounting Office
GED: General Equivalency Diploma
HEP: High School Equivalency Program
HUD: Department of Housing and Urban Development
LULAC: League of United Latin American Citizens
MAYO: Mexican American Youth Organization
MCHA: Marion County Housing Authority
MEChA: Movimiento Estudiantil Chicano de Aztlán (Chicano
    Student Movement of the Southwest)
NAACP: National Association for the Advancement of Colored
    People
NFWA: National Farm Workers Association
OCC: Oregon Council of Churches
OCR: Office of Civil Rights
OEO: Office of Economic Opportunity
OJT: On-the-Job Training
ORO: Oregon Rural Opportunities
PAVLA: Papal Volunteers for Latin America
PCUN: Pineros y Campesinos Unidos del Noroeste (Northwest Tree
    Planters and Farmworkers United)
PPS: Portland Public Schools
SB 677: Senate Bill 677 (Oregon Legislature)
SCLC: Southern Christian Leadership Conference
SNCC: Student Nonviolent Coordinating Committee
UFW: United Farm Workers (United Farm Workers of America, AFL-
    CIO)
UFWOC: United Farm Workers Organizing Committee
VISTA: Volunteers in Service to America (an OEO program)
VIVA: Volunteers in Vanguard Action (a Hillsboro organization)
VML: Valley Migrant League
WVIP: Willamette Valley Immigration Project

Introduction

In the mid-1970s, after a decade of intense activity and considerable accomplishment, the Chicano movement, the Mexican American struggle for civil rights and social justice, appeared to be losing steam.[1] Cesar Chavez's well-known union, the United Farm Workers, was engaged in an endless, enervating battle with the Teamsters over the right to represent agricultural laborers in contract negotiations. The New Mexican activist Reies López Tijerina, after several lengthy periods of incarceration, had lost much of his following. The Brown Berets were disbanded. The one concerted effort by Mexican Americans to create a national political party had seemingly failed, crippled by conflict between its two leaders, Corky Gonzales and José Angel Gutiérrez. While not all the signs were unfavorable and, as subsequent developments would reveal, a great deal of creative work by Chicano activists lay ahead, the energy and relentless forward movement of the mid- and late-1960s were more difficult to detect.

There were, however, exceptions to the general trend, and one could be found in Oregon's Willamette Valley, hardly a hotbed of Chicano activism up to then. There, for about four years, Celedonio Montes Jr.—Sonny Montes, as he was generally known—a former migrant farmworker from South Texas, mobilized the state's nascent Mexican American community and mounted a social movement. The movement's goal was to save the Colegio Cesar Chavez, a small, besieged, financially challenged college that catered to a largely Mexican American student body. The collective-action movement led by Montes—which featured sit-ins, protest marches, rallies, prayer vigils, and a consistently high level of Chicano support—received a plethora of media attention at the time. Sonny Montes himself became a very visible public figure.

This book tells three related stories. The first is Sonny's. It recounts the process by which a person born to a family of migrant farmworkers became the leader of a social movement. In 1966, at the age of twenty-two, Sonny Montes traveled to Oregon intending to pick the crops and somewhat by chance came into the orbit of—and went to work for—an Oregon-based War on Poverty agency called the Valley Migrant League (VML). Providing educational opportunities, vocational training, and other services to Mexican American migrant farmworkers who came to Oregon's Upper Willamette Valley, the VML helped many of them to leave the migrant stream and settle in Oregon. Furthermore, at a time of widespread prejudice and discrimination against Mexican Americans, the organization empowered those people to solve their own problems. Due to the efforts of Montes and others, the VML was transformed from an Anglo-run agency created to serve Mexican American migrants into an organization run by and for Mexican Americans. One result of that process of empowerment was the emergence of a Mexican American political elite in the area. In the 1970s working as chief administrative officer for the Colegio and faced with a formidable combination of adversaries, Montes enlisted that elite in his campaign to keep the college alive.

A prominent theme in this first story is *asymmetry*—a problem that remains at the heart of the Mexican American experience in the United States.[2] Over the years, most Mexican Americans in the United States, Sonny included, have suffered disadvantages based on five human variables: skin color, ethnic background, level of income, religion, and language. What is more, lurking beneath the surface has been another reality that has set the Mexican-origin population apart: large numbers of them have resided illegally in the country. One unfortunate consequence of that reality has been a tendency on the part of many Anglos to view suspiciously all Mexican-origin people, legal and illegal alike.[3]

The situation that confronted Sonny and his people was historically constructed. It resulted in part from mid-nineteenth-century U.S. imperialism, which brought the region that became the states of Texas, California, New Mexico, Colorado, Nevada, and Arizona under U.S. control. One consequence of that conquest was the progressive socioeconomic decline of the Mexican population in that region.[4] But, in truth, the system of Mexican American subordination did not reach full-blown proportions until the twentieth century. Beginning in the 1890s and continuing until the Great Depression, a massive number of Mexicans—the estimates run upward of a million—entered the United States, escaping destitution and political disruption in their homeland and drawn northward by the opportunity to earn a better living. In that period, Mexicans found work not only in agriculture, which was expanding rapidly in the Southwest, but also in railroad construction, mining, and other industrial lines. As new immigrants flooded into the Southwest, increasing numbers of already established Mexican American families moved beyond the confines of the Southwest in search of better wages, with tens of thousands of them settling in Detroit, Chicago, and other cities in the Midwest. Although living and working conditions varied considerably from place to place, one constant was that most Mexican Americans endured many kinds of discrimination, experienced segregation in the schools, could not participate in the political process, and otherwise were subjected to second-class citizenship.[5]

Much of this book examines Sonny Montes's efforts to cope with the problem of asymmetry, both in his own life and in the lives of other Mexican Americans. Born into a family that spent much of its time following the crops, Sonny entered his adulthood believing that his future lay only in farmwork. But a serendipitous encounter with a man named Jose Garcia diverted him from that path and brought him to the VML. Taking a job with that organization in 1966, Sonny entered an extended period of addressing and wrestling with the problem of Mexican American asymmetry.

The second story concerns the development of a Mexican American community in Oregon. In 1965, the year the VML began operations in Oregon's Upper Willamette Valley, only a few thousand Mexican Americans resided full-time in the state, although at least ten thousand more arrived annually during the harvest months to work as migrant farm laborers. By 1980, the state's Mexican American resident population had increased to more than 45,000 and even more explosive growth was about to occur. One impetus for that expansion was the VML, which provided migrant and seasonal farmworkers with educational and vocational tools that made it possible for them to leave the migrant stream if they chose to do so. Its adult education programs both improved English-language skills and helped many to earn high school degrees; and its vocational training programs gave people new job options. Due

3

in large measure to those programs and other types of assistance provided by VML personnel, large numbers of longtime migrant families opted to settle in Oregon.

But, as I have already suggested, the community development work of the VML went well beyond settlement assistance. The league also worked to give Mexican Americans a political education; these efforts became a priority after May 1967, when a new executive director, John Little, took charge. Under Little, who was both a mentor to and friend of Sonny, the VML pursued a policy of involving the people it served in the running of the organization. It hired hundreds of migrants and former migrants to administer programs, placed dozens more on the agency's board of directors, and involved many people in towns scattered around the Upper Willamette Valley in determining the institution's priorities and assessing its performance. In a sense, the VML served as a school of democracy for many of the Mexican Americans who came in contact with it, and the practical education they received there prepared them to assume positions of leadership in their emerging ethnic community. An important by-product of this political education project was the creation of a Mexican American network in Oregon. For, in addition to training a political elite, the VML was producing a closely related community, one whose shared experience with the VML provided a connective tissue. The Mexican American community in Oregon was being built on strong associational foundations.

The book's third story describes the development of a Chicano movement in Oregon. To some degree, of course, that social movement, which coalesced around the Colegio Cesar Chavez's struggle for survival in the mid-1970s, was a continuation of the second story: it could not have occurred without the earlier substantial increase in Oregon's Mexican American population and the strong bonds, created largely by the VML, among the political elite of that growing ethnic community. These conditions made it possible for Sonny Montes to launch and sustain the social movement he directed.

There is a David-versus-Goliath quality to this third story. On the one side, we find Sonny and his allies, attempting to save a college that has few students, nonfunctioning furnaces, and crippling debts.

On the other, we find two federal agencies—the Department of Housing and Urban Development (HUD) and the Department of Health, Education, and Welfare (HEW)—and an academic accreditation organization, all sharing serious doubts about whether the tiny Chicano college should be allowed to continue its operations. Sonny and his group initially tried to reach an accommodation with those organizations, but the arrangements agreed to did not last, primarily because the college's financial situation continued to deteriorate. The Colegio then turned to collective action and to legal remedies—approaches that wore down its adversaries and kept the college going for a while. But in the end, the school's underlying financial weakness could not be overcome, and the Colegio quietly passed out of existence in the early 1980s.

The key objective of my examination of the protest campaign that developed around the college is simply to understand it. My effort to do so has been influenced by the analytical insights of a number of well-known students of modern social movements—among them, Sidney Tarrow, Doug McAdam, Charles Tilly, and Mario Diani. I devote particular attention to four variables that have played significant roles in modern social movements: the combination of political opportunities that helped to spawn collective action, the repertoire of collective-action techniques adopted by the participants, the ways in which protesters framed their protests, and the mobilizing structure of the movement.[6] This discussion will, I hope, help to explain how, at a time when Mexican American activism was flagging in major Chicano population centers, the Chicano movement in Oregon was becoming more contentious, and also why the momentum of Oregon Chicano's activists was ultimately arrested.[7]

Overview of the Book
In the text that follows, I begin by looking at Sonny's life up to the age of twenty-two—his socialization in Weslaco, Texas, a segregated community just north of the Mexican border, and subsequently in Fort Worth and the San Joaquin Valley; his entry into the migrant worker stream (a stream that included huge numbers of Mexican Americans in that era); and his family's asymmetric interactions with Anglos. My chief aim here is to convey a sense of what it was like

to grow up in a migrant farmworker family, living six months of the year in a home base and the other six in distant labor camps. Following the prologue, the first chapter sets the stage by discussing developments in three overlapping geographical theaters (the Upper Willamette Valley, Oregon, and the United States) in the years preceding Sonny's arrival in Oregon.

Chapters two to four look at Sonny, the VML, and the VML's role in community formation during the period 1966–71. Although Sonny began work with the VML as a program aide, he rose quickly through the ranks. He also underwent a process of radicalization, influenced to some extent by the culture of protest in the mid-1960s but even more by an Anglo supervisor and mentor, John Little, who had just returned from five years of community organization work in Latin America. In 1967 and 1968, Sonny played a major role in transforming the VML into a Mexican American–run organization. While continuing to work at the VML for the next three years, he became involved in a variety of Chicano causes.

The next three chapters cover the period 1971 through 1978. In 1971, Sonny Montes entered a new phase of his life, accepting a job at Mt. Angel College, a small liberal arts college in Mt. Angel, Oregon, that was experiencing financial problems. Hired to recruit minority students to the campus, he also took courses at the college and was able to earn a degree. Meanwhile, his influence on the campus grew steadily. In 1973, with the college close to bankruptcy, he brokered an arrangement by which it became a Chicano-run institution with a new name, Colegio Cesar Chavez, and in the next year, he became its chief administrative officer. After that, with the college besieged from all sides, Sonny, the college community, and its Mexican American supporters battled valiantly to keep the college in operation, mounting a long-term collective-action campaign. In 1978, despite formidable odds, the Colegio worked out an arrangement with HUD, the holder of the bulk of the school's unpaid loan notes, to pay off the debt. For the moment, it appeared to have survived.

A final chapter focuses on three developments in the thirty-plus years after Sonny left the Colegio: the closing of the college, Sonny's vocational history, and the relentless growth of Oregon's Mexican American community.

A Note about Accents and Terminology

Over the past fifty years, Mexican Americans have varied widely in their use of Spanish-language accents—particularly, in the spelling of names. On the whole, I have not included accents in the names of the people discussed in this book. There are, however, exceptions— for example, historical actors such as Reies López Tijerina and José Angel Gutiérrez, whose names have consistently been rendered with accents in the historical literature, and authors whose names appear with accent marks on the title pages of their books. I have also included accents in the names of organizations that have used them consistently and in any book titles in which they have appeared.

The terms "Mexican American" and "Chicano/a" both refer to Mexican-origin U.S. residents. But, since the second term did not come into public discourse until the mid-1960s, I have done my best to avoid using it in reference to pre-1960s lives and events. Finally, after much internal debate, I have adopted the somewhat problematic convention of using the word "Anglo" to describe the European American whites who appear in these pages.

From Weslaco to Cornelius

In the late spring of 1966, twenty-two-year-old Sonny Montes was living in Reedley, California, with his wife, Librada, and young son, Armando.[1] For the past two years, he had earned a living by assisting an elderly couple in running a thirty-five-acre farm that specialized in grape production. A formidable human presence—physically imposing at six feet tall and about 230 pounds—Sonny was an industrious, powerful, able worker. He repaired the fences, oversaw the irrigation, applied the pesticides and sulfur, prepared the fields, hauled the crops to the packing sheds, and pruned the grapevines after the grapes were picked. He also supervised the grape picking, which was done by workers supplied by a labor contractor. At the outset, a few aspects of the job had been unfamiliar to him. He had many battles with the spraying machine; its defiant starting mechanism sometimes defeated his efforts to spray the crops evenly. He also made mistakes in preparing the fields for irrigation and applying the water to them. Still, in time he mastered the techniques. Agricultural work was Sonny's métier, and he was good at it.

Sonny was born on May 24, 1944, in Weslaco, Texas, in the Lower Rio Grande, and that town continued to be his family's base of operations for the first ten years of his life. Weslaco was composed of two entirely separate communities, one inhabited by Anglos and the other by Mexican Americans. As in much of the Lower Rio Grande Valley, the segregation had initially been legally prescribed. In 1921, the newly created municipality of Weslaco passed an ordinance designating the area south of the railroad tracks for Anglo residences and businesses and the area north of the tracks for industry and Mexican American residences and businesses. The two side-by-side communities that emerged over the following decades had little in common but their name. South of the tracks, the streets were paved, a modern sewer system was in place, many of the houses were well constructed, and English was the spoken language. North of the tracks, roads were unpaved, there were no sewers, most of the houses were tiny and cheaply made, and Spanish was spoken almost exclusively. According to the U.S. Census of 1950, the population of Weslaco was 7,514. Of that number, about two-fifths were Anglos, almost all of them residing south of the tracks; about three-fifths were people of Mexican descent, most of them living north of the tracks; and exactly 72 were African Americans, also living in the northern part of town. The situation that prevailed in Weslaco could be observed throughout the Lower Rio Grande Valley: Anglos were favored and dominant; brown-skinned people like Sonny were, by and large, disadvantaged and subordinate.[2]

As a child growing up in Weslaco, Sonny had almost no contact with Anglos, except for his teachers at the North Ward School, one of four elementary schools on the north side of town. No Anglos attended the school he went to. He had no Anglo friends, and outside of school, he rarely spoke to Anglos. While some Mexican Americans in Weslaco ventured into the Anglo part of town and a few Mexican American families even lived there, almost all of them headed by World War II veterans, the members of Sonny's family were not among them, even though his father had served in the U.S. Army late in the war. The restaurants, bakeries, hardware stores, gasoline stations, grocery stores, clothing stores, pharmacies, barber shops, and beauty parlors they patronized; the churches, schools, dances, picnics, barbecues, and baseball games they attended; the places they swam in the summer months; the cemeteries where they buried their dead—all of these were located on the Mexican American side of the tracks.

Sonny's parents—Celedonio Armendadez Montes and Margarita Gonzales Jasso Montes—owned a house on Los Torritos Street in the Mexican American section of Weslaco. That one-storey structure, still standing today, was modest and small, with only about 300 square feet of living space. It was divided into two rooms—the kitchen, which also served as the dining room, and the living room, which also served as the bedroom for the entire family. The Montes home had no indoor toilet: a small outhouse was located on the back lot. It also had no fixed bath or shower. When it was time to bathe, Sonny's mother heated several pots of water on the stove, poured that hot water and several more pots of cold water into a large portable metal tub, and family members took turns bathing in the tub.

Sonny Montes with his parents, Margarita and Celedonio Montes, August 2003. Photograph by Glenn Anthony May.

Sonny's days in Weslaco revolved around family, especially the many members of his father's family who lived nearby. Next to Sonny's parents, the most important person in his life was his paternal grandmother, Maria Armendadez Montes, widowed in 1948, whose house, somewhat larger than his own, was located just across Los Torritos Street. Until 1954, the year Sonny's family left Weslaco for Fort Worth, except for the months when he was following the crops, Sonny saw his grandmother every day. An accomplished cook, Maria Montes made all of her dishes from scratch. Every morning she rose early to prepare the day's tortillas, grinding the corn with *metate* (a curved grinding stone) and *mano* (hand). An extremely devout Catholic, she went to Mass daily and spent many additional hours each week at the parish church doing volunteer work. Maria Montes required all her grandchildren to attend church regularly, whether they wanted to or not. On Sundays and many other days, Sonny walked with her from Los Torritos Street to the parish church, St. Joan of Arc Catholic Church. Although the actual distance covered was no more than half a mile, the walk seemed interminable to Sonny because, from start to stop, his grandmother had a firm grip on the little finger of his left hand to insure that he would keep up with her.

For the Montes clan of Weslaco, Maria Montes's house was the central meeting point. Wedding receptions and holiday dinners were held there; at some point during each day, all the members of the family passed by the house to pay their respects and to chat.

On many evenings after dinner, most of the Monteses, parents and children alike, assembled there to listen to Maria's radio. Often they all sat outside in the dark, their attention fixed on the Spanish-language programs. Sonny's favorite was a cowboy show called *Espuelas de Plata* (Silver Spurs). Sonny still remembers the sound of jingling spurs coming from his grandmother's radio.

As a young child, Sonny played with his sisters Gloria and Estella (born in 1946 and 1947, respectively) and about a dozen cousins of approximately the same age who lived near his Los Torritos Street home, all of them the children of his father's brothers and sisters. The Mexican American parents of postwar Weslaco had no need to search out activities to fill their children's days, nor did they buy their children toys and games. Even if they had been able to afford them, the children didn't require them. The play activities of Sonny and his companions were organized into seasons. First, there was kite season, when the children flew homemade kites constructed out of available materials—paper sacks, sticks, string, pieces of cloth for the tails, and paste made of flour and water. Second, there was tops season, when Sonny and his playmates would endlessly spin tops, most of which were homemade. Third, there was marble season, when the kids played every known marble game and some of their own invention. On very hot days, the boy cousins would hike to one of the nearby citrus farms, climb over the fence, and swim in the nude in one of the concrete irrigation canals. None of them knew how to swim properly, but they would flail away and, by sheer persistence, manage to propel themselves from one bank to the other. In the citrus season, the boys might steal a few oranges and grapefruits from those farms.

Such were the rhythms of life in Weslaco's northern district during the period 1944–54—but for only half of each calendar year. Weslaco's Mexican American families, including Sonny's, resided in the town from November to May, hardly ever for longer stretches. During those months, most of the male heads of households found jobs in the agricultural sector, often working for local farms that produced crops of oranges, grapefruits, and tomatoes. For several years, Celedonio Montes was employed by Weslaco-based La Bonita Company, which processed and packaged fruits and vegetables. He started as a warehouse worker and later became a forklift operator.

Unfortunately, once the citrus and tomato crops had been harvested, Weslaco's Mexican Americans could find few job opportunities in the area. Faced with that reality, most of them left the Lower Rio Grande Valley for the remainder of the year and entered the migrant stream, traveling around the Southwest, and sometimes beyond, in search of farmwork.[3] Those months of following the crops had very different rhythms. Summer after summer, the Monteses were transported in the back of trucks to distant locations, lived in cabins provided by the growers, and spent most of their days laboring in the fields. They picked cotton in at least half a dozen Texas communities (Lamesa, Lubbock, Waxahatchie, El Campo, Sinton, Victoria) and several places in Arkansas, harvested mint and potatoes in Indiana, and gathered onions and tomatoes in the Chicago area. Initially, Celedonio and Margarita did all the picking, but as soon as Sonny, Gloria, and Estella were able to work, they participated, too. By the age of five Sonny was performing simple tasks in the fields, and by the age of eight he was doing a full day's work, often performing the job of an adult.

As soon as there was enough light to see, the Monteses began picking in the fields. They always wore old clothes, since new ones would be ruined after only a few days. For Sonny, the standard outfit was a long shirt, trousers, and sturdy work shoes. He and every other member of the family brought hats and scarves to protect their heads and backs of their necks from the sun. Both Sonny and his father occasionally wore kneepads, especially when they were picking cotton in West Texas, where some of the cotton plants were small. They began their work standing up and focusing on the taller

Sonny Montes and his sister Gloria Angulo, August 2003. Photograph by Glenn Anthony May.

plants, but when their backs began to ache, they got down on their knees and turned their attention to the smaller plants. Some of the workers used gloves, because the picking was often brutally hard on their hands, but the cloth gloves of those days were not very useful in harvesting the difficult-to-pick crops such as cotton and oranges. The stickers on those crops tore the pickers' gloves to shreds. Invariably, the hands of most of the pickers, gloved or ungloved, were covered with cuts.

Despite the fact that cotton was so challenging to harvest, the Montes family preferred to pick it because they could make the most money doing so. The work required the picker to grab the entire cotton boll with both hands and muscle it from the plant. Both of Sonny's parents did the harvesting. After the bolls were picked, they deposited them in twenty-foot-long white sacks that were provided for that purpose. Celedonio's sack was attached to his shoulders, and he dragged it along as he worked his way through the fields. But, strong though he was, he was not strong enough to pull both his own sack and Margarita's. When Sonny reached the age of eight and was deemed old enough to participate fully in the cotton harvest, his mother's sack was placed on his back and he was given the responsibility of dragging it along and keeping up with his mother. Once the sacks were filled, father and son pulled them to the weighing station, where they were weighed and their contents dumped onto waiting trucks. Then, the family members could take advantage of the opportunity to drink water at the only water tank in the cotton field. They usually had to take turns drinking, because the growers provided only a dipper or two for the use of the entire work crew.

By the early 1950s, Sonny's father became increasingly concerned about the family's finances—specifically, about his declining earnings during the six months they spent in Weslaco. Part of the problem was the rise of corporate farming and the attendant mechanization of agricultural operations in the region, reducing the farmers' labor needs.[4] In addition, nature contributed to the woes of the regional workforce. In January 1950, the Rio Grande Valley was hit by an unusual winter storm remembered in the region as the "Great Freeze," an event that, in the words of a local historian, "dealt a near-death blow to the area's citrus industry."[5] La Bonita, lacking crops to process, closed its doors, and for several years the entire valley experienced an economic downturn. After that, Celedonio Montes and many others were left with very poor job prospects during the November-May period. Sometimes Celedonio left his family behind and traveled around the valley looking for work. At one point, having acquired a used Chevy pickup truck, he tried his hand at small business. Early in the morning, he and Sonny would set off from their Weslaco home in the truck to purchase large blocks of ice. They scraped the ice into fine pieces, poured the scraped ice into paper cups, covered it with syrup, and sold the sweetened ice concoctions (their homemade version of snow cones) to workers in the Weslaco area during their rest breaks.

Finally, in 1954, tired of his bleak vocational prospects in Weslaco, Celedonio Sr. decided to move the family to Fort Worth, where, for the next seven years, the Monteses lived year-round. The move brought major changes in their lives. Celedonio was employed first as bricklayer's assistant, moved on to other types of construction work, and then found a job in 1959 as head of maintenance at the Fort Worth Holiday Inn.[6] Soon afterward, Celedonio arranged for Margarita and Sonny, now a junior high school student, to work at the Holiday Inn as well. Margarita held a part-time position in the laundry room. Sonny started in the laundry room and later was promoted to a position as busboy/dishwasher in the hotel's restaurant. On weekdays, immediately after school, Sonny traveled by public transportation to his place of work, situated in the extreme western part of the city, far from the family's rented residence. On school days, he began work at 4:30 p.m. and finished at midnight. He usually worked on weekends as well.

In the late spring of 1961, the Montes family, which had now grown to seven (Lupe was born in 1955 and Diana in 1960), returned to the migrant stream. Hearing from a *compadre* that there was a lot of money to be earned in agricultural work in California, Sonny's father decided to check out the situation. At the end of May, right after the Fort Worth school year had ended, he piled the entire family into his used Chevy sedan and began driving to San Jose. The Monteses spent most of that summer in the vicinity of Morgan Hill, to the south of San Jose, where they picked cherries, strawberries, plums, apricots, and garlic. The next summer, the

Monteses returned to California, this time to Fresno County in the San Joaquin Valley, about a hundred miles southeast of where they had picked crops the previous year. They resided most of the time in Parlier, a small agricultural community southeast of Fresno, picking plums, peaches, walnuts, cotton, and several varieties of grapes.

Although the summer agricultural work in California was financially rewarding for the Monteses, there were costs. When Celedonio had made the decision to take his family to California in 1961, he had realized that the manager of the Holiday Inn would likely replace him in his absence. He assumed, though, that he would be able to find another job in Fort Worth without much difficulty, possibly with the Holiday Inn. But, whereas the hotel's manager was willing to rehire Margarita and Sonny, he made no job offer to Sonny's father. Thereafter Celedonio struggled vocationally in Fort Worth. The job he held longest was as a meat processor at the Swift and Company meatpacking plant, where he was forced to work long hours in a refrigerated building. On some days, for some unexplained reason, his skin turned a bright shade of yellow. For a man who had spent most of his life working outside under the sun, the job at Swift was akin to torture.

In the meantime, Sonny was making steady progress toward completing his high school degree. He had entered Technical

Sonny Montes, summer of 1962, in the vicinity of Sanger, California. Photograph courtesy of Sonny Montes.

High School in South Fort Worth in the fall of 1960. Although the school's name suggested that it focused on vocational education, the student body, numbering about 1,500 in the early 1960s, was composed of both vocational students and those on a traditional academic track. The students were a mix of Anglos and Mexican Americans, since unlike Weslaco and most other towns in the southern part of the state, Fort Worth did not require Mexican Americans to attend segregated schools. African Americans were not so fortunate; they were not admitted to Technical until 1964, the year after Sonny's graduation.[7]

At Technical High, Sonny was an average student—arguably, a commendable performance, given that his job at the Holiday Inn left him little time to study, and he missed several months of classes in his junior and senior years because of his family's late return from their migrant farmwork. For all three years of high school, he signed up for strictly academic classes: English, world history, U. S. history, government, biology, mathematics, and the like. He did fairly well in English, receiving a grade of B on two occasions, and performed even better in his U.S. history class, earning an A in the fall 1961 semester. (Sonny was especially interested in the U.S. Civil War, and in his limited spare time, he enjoyed reading books about it.) His worst showing was in biology; he failed the course in his first semester of high school and received grades of C and D in the following two semesters. Not once during his high school years did any of his teachers, including those who had given him good grades, ever suggest that he should consider college. The subject of college did come up in another context. Sometime in Sonny's junior or senior year, he and his fellow students were subjected to a battery of tests designed to assist them in choosing a career. Shortly afterward, Sonny met with a guidance counselor to discuss the results. The tests showed, the counselor told him, that Sonny was "not college material" and that he would be better advised to pursue a career in which he used his hands, since he had received above average scores in "finger dexterity." For many years thereafter, the words Sonny heard in that meeting remained stuck in his mind. Not college material. Finger dexterity. Not college material. One can only speculate how many other Mexican Americans in Forth Worth public high schools received a similar kind of guidance. Without doubt, institutionalized prejudice against them was widespread. Even so, as Sonny and his family realized, the situation confronting Mexican American students in Fort Worth was markedly better than in South Texas, where segregated education for Mexican Americans was still in place. Sonny graduated from Technical High School in late May 1963, ranking 239th in a class of 498.[8]

Sonny did not see a high school diploma as a ticket to an appreciably better life. Rather, he saw a future for himself that differed very little from his past. Aware that his parents intended to return to California as soon as he had received his diploma, he planned to accompany them. When he thought about how he would earn money for the rest of his life, he imagined that he would do agricultural work. As he explained to me in an interview: "Aside from working at the Holiday Inn, that's all I knew."

Shortly after Sonny's high school graduation, the Montes family left Fort Worth again for Fresno County. At the time of their departure, they assumed that they would work in California only through early fall. As the summer wore on, however, it became clear to Celedonio and Margarita Montes that there was no compelling reason to return to North Texas, and the family decided to stay. In the meantime, Sonny had become engaged to Librada Arce, born in Mexico and raised in Edinburg, Texas, whom he had met at a dance in Fresno County the previous summer. Like Sonny, she came from a family that had long followed the crops during the summer months, but the Arces had graduated from field labor to supervisory work. Librada's brother, Horacio, was *mayordomo* on a farm in Cornelius, Oregon, a small agricultural community west of Portland, and he had taken up year-round residence in the town. During the summer and early fall months, Librada's parents resided in Cornelius, helping Horacio run the farmer's labor camp.

Sonny and Librada were married in Edinburg in January 1964, and, right after the wedding, the newlyweds took up residence in Parlier. Not long after that, Sonny went to work on the grape farm in Reedley, and in November 1964, Armando was born. Step by step, Sonny and Librada began to take on the trappings of a lower-middle-class existence. They bought a small house in Reedley and owned a reliable used car.

Then, out of the blue, in the late spring of 1966, Librada suggested to Sonny that they spend the coming summer in Oregon. She described the venture as an "experiment." Sonny and she would pick crops on the farm in Cornelius where her brother Horacio Arce did supervisory work, and she, Sonny, and Armando could live in the labor camp located on the farm. Librada believed that the family could make more money over the summer in Cornelius than it could make in Reedley. An added bonus would be that they would be able to spend more time with Librada's parents, who, as in past summers, would be living at the same labor camp. "Let's try it," she urged Sonny. "Let's see how it works out." She wasn't suggesting that they leave California permanently: they were committing themselves to go north for only three or four months.

During their discussions about Librada's proposed experiment, one issue Sonny and Librada wrestled with was Sonny's existing job. Obviously he would have to quit, and doing so was risky. But, like his father, who had given up his Holiday Inn position in Fort Worth for the opportunity to make money in California, Sonny was a risk taker. He believed that he might be able to return to his job in Reedley after the summer in Oregon, because the elderly couple he worked for, the Worrels, held him in high regard. And even if that position were no longer available, he was confident that he could find some agricultural work in central California, perhaps doing piecework in the fields. Sonny agreed to his wife's proposal.

In early June 1966, not long after the strawberry harvest had begun in Oregon's Willamette Valley, Sonny, Librada, and Armando arrived in Cornelius, at the farm of Lloyd Duyck, the grower who employed Horacio. A small agricultural community in Washington County, Cornelius was named after Colonel T. R. Cornelius, a pioneer who had come to Oregon in 1845, participated in military campaigns against the local Native Americans, and served in the Oregon legislature. A sizable percentage of the town's residents were, like Lloyd Duyck, people of Dutch extraction. Duyck's neighbors included Leo van Domelen, Victor van der Zanden, Fred van de Berg, Fred Meeuwsen, William van de Coevering, and Leslie Verboort.[9]

More than forty-five years have passed since the arrival of the Monteses in Cornelius, and the changes that have occurred in the interim have been substantial. Located along Oregon State Highway 8, which connects it and other towns in northwestern Oregon to the city of Portland, Cornelius has in recent years been integrated to some degree into the Portland metropolitan complex. Today much of the twenty-mile stretch of Highway 8 between Portland and Cornelius is lined on both sides with shopping malls, small factories, fast-food restaurants, and other business establishments that serve the needs of the growing suburban communities of Beaverton and Hillsboro. Back in 1966, a person traveling to Cornelius by car from downtown Portland would have seen, on both sides of Highway 8, a succession of cultivated fields and little else. In 2008, according to an official head count, the population of Cornelius was 10,955; forty-two years earlier, it had 1,460 residents.[10]

One of the leading farmers in Washington County, Oregon, Lloyd Duyck had about 850 acres under cultivation; his fields yielded large crops of strawberries, raspberries, boysenberries, cucumbers, bush beans, and yellow beans. Duyck paid a decent wage, dealt fairly with his workers, and provided them with above-average housing. His labor camp, which was adjacent to one of his largest cultivated fields, had twenty-six cabins, capable of housing 110 people. Sonny, Librada, and Armando were assigned one of the cabins. Another was occupied by Librada's parents, who were then too old to work in the fields but made their money by other means. Librada's mother was in charge of cleaning the labor camp and assigning the housing units to the migrant families who worked there. She also sold soda pop, candy, and other items to the laborers. Librada's father used to go to the local slaughterhouses during the week to buy fresh meat, which he would then sell to the camp's residents on Saturday, when the workers were paid. Librada's brother, Horacio, assisted Duyck in running the farm and supervised the work in the fields.[11]

A few weeks after Sonny and Librada had arrived in Cornelius, a group of strangers paid an evening visit to the labor camp.[12] They introduced themselves to the camp's residents as employees of the Valley Migrant League, a nonprofit organization created for the explicit purpose of serving the needs of migrant and seasonal farmworkers in Oregon's Upper Willamette Valley. Funded by the Office of Economic Opportunity, the VML was a component of President Lyndon Johnson's War on Poverty program. The leader of the VML delegation was Jose Garcia, the director of the VML's office (or "opportunity center," the term used by the organization) in the neighboring town of Hillsboro. Garcia explained that he and his co-workers wanted to make a presentation about the VML's programs.

Some of the farmworkers decided to hear what the VML employees had to say. In an open area on the grounds of the labor camp, they gathered in a circle around Garcia and his companions. Sonny spotted the meeting from a distance, was curious about what was going on, and walked over to see and hear for himself. Garcia told the camp's residents that the VML offered a range of free services and programs to migrant and seasonal farmworkers. He talked about adult education classes, which were offered in spoken English (for migrants who had limited English-language skills), basic education (for those with adequate spoken English who had little formal schooling), and GED preparation (to enable migrants to earn a General Equivalency Diploma). Vocational training programs were also available to adults who were interested in learning new ways of earning a living and perhaps leaving the migrant stream. The VML offered stipends to people enrolling in adult education and vocational training classes to compensate them for income lost when they were in school. During the summers, children of migrant families could attend summer school classes and child-care programs. The opportunity centers also offered job counseling and assisted families in getting housing and health care.

Sonny had never heard about the VML before. He listened intently to the presentation, and at one point he asked a question. At the end of the meeting, Garcia approached him and struck up a conversation. Learning that Sonny was a farmworker and that he had not thought about doing anything else in life, Garcia inquired if Sonny would consider applying for a job as a program aide for the VML. Sonny asked Garcia to describe the job, and, after hearing the description, he said that he was not interested. "It sounded too complicated," he recalls. Besides, the pay was only $300 a month, "which wasn't a bad salary in those days, but it really wasn't that much, because we could make more in the fields." Undeterred, Garcia urged Sonny to give some more thought to the matter and said that he would return to discuss the job possibility with Sonny again.

About a week later, Garcia reappeared and renewed his request. When Sonny again expressed reservations, Garcia did his best to respond. He was both persuasive and persistent, and after a long discussion, Sonny came up with a formula that would allow him to take the position: he would pick crops in the fields from sunrise to noon, return to the camp to shower and change his clothes, and then report for duty with the VML, working from about 1:00 p.m. to 10:00 p.m. By holding both jobs, he would have a chance to find out if the VML work appealed to him without sacrificing any income. Garcia had no objections to Sonny's proposal—the program aides did much of their work in the evenings, because most of the farmworkers could not go to the opportunity centers or attend meetings at the labor camps until they had finished working for the day. The two men reached an agreement. Sonny Montes became a foot soldier in the War on Poverty in late June 1966.

Contexts: The Upper Willamette Valley, Oregon, and America ca. 1965

A fact that distinguishes the United States from most other modern world powers is that the bulk of its empire building has occurred internally, rather than externally. For much of its history, large sections of the South and the West have served as internal economic colonies of the United States, producing staple crops, tropical goods (e.g., cotton, sugar, tobacco), dietary supplements, and basic raw materials for the more commercial and industrial North and East, for urban/industrial pockets in the colonial regions themselves, and for the world market. In 1965, and for most of the previous century, Oregon functioned as such an internal colony.

The state's two chief economic engines were the lumber industry and agriculture. In the mid-1960s, Oregon was the nation's leading lumber-producing state, as it had been every year since 1938. Forest-based plants produced goods worth close to $1.5 billion; workers in the industry numbered about 75,000, constituting slightly less than half of Oregon's total manufacturing workforce. Appearances, and even statistics, can be deceiving, of course. With the benefit of hindsight, we now know that Oregon's lumber industry was in the early stages of decline in the 1960s, as overharvesting was taking a toll on the timber stands. While the state's annual income from timber was still increasing, that would not be the case for long.[1]

Agriculture, the state's second largest industry, yielded cash receipts totaling close to $450 million in 1965. Although, unlike the timber industry, there were no hints that Oregon's agricultural sector was in decline in the decades following World War II, it was experiencing important changes. For one, Oregon agriculture was undergoing consolidation, as was the case throughout the United States. Between 1945 and 1964, a period in which the total acreage devoted to agriculture in Oregon remained stable, the number of farms in the state decreased by 37 percent. For another, as in other states, many farmers were beginning to mechanize harvesting operations—to the extent that it was possible to do so, since not all crops could readily be harvested by machines.[2]

Among the many crops grown in Oregon in the mid-1960s, wheat, barley, oats, and other field crops generated the greatest returns, but the state was perhaps best known for the niche agricultural markets in which it dominated. Oregon produced about 35 percent of the nation's grass and legume seeds, and its crops of tree fruits, berries, nuts, and vegetables were also significant. The *Oregon Blue Book*, an official publication produced by the office of the Secretary of State, boasted:

> We rank first in the nation in snap beans for processing,
> filberts, holly, winter peas, tame blackberries, black raspberries,
> boysenberries, loganberries and youngberries; second in
> strawberries, red raspberries, peppermint, all pears, walnuts,
> prunes, broccoli for fresh market; third in sweet cherries, hops,
> green peas for processing, onions.[3]

The Upper Willamette Valley

One region in Oregon that participated actively in those niche agricultural markets was the Upper Willamette Valley—the area surrounding the northern branches of the Willamette River system. Compared to many colonial agricultural zones, the Upper Willamette Valley was atypical in that it was fairly densely populated. The land area of the six counties constituting its core (Washington, Multnomah, Yamhill, Clackamas, Polk, and Marion) was 5,648 square miles, or slightly less than 6 percent of Oregon's total. Its population, according to the 1960 decennial census, was 907,977, a bit more than 50 percent of the entire state's population of 1,768,687. Whereas population density in the state as a whole was 18 people per square mile, in the six core Upper Willamette Valley counties, it was 161 per square mile. That same census classified close to 80 percent of the region's population as urban, which meant at the time that they lived in communities of more than 2,500 people. Two of those communities contained considerably more than 2,500 residents—Portland, the state's largest city, with a population of 372, 676, and Salem, the capital and the third largest city, with 49,142 inhabitants.[4]

While the Upper Willamette Valley's urban sector was substantial and rapidly expanding, once one left the cities and large towns and ventured into the surrounding countryside—to places such as Cornelius, for example—the ambience was unmistakably rural and agricultural. In 1964, a year in which the federal government conducted an agricultural census, the census takers counted 14,181 farms in those six counties—or about 36 percent of the total number of farms in the state. On the whole, although there were exceptions, such as Lloyd Duyck's operations, Upper Willamette Valley farms were small in size: on average, about 94 acres, or less than a fifth the size of the average farm in the state, 515 acres.[5]

That had not always been the case. In the early stages of white settlement in Oregon, farms in the Upper Willamette Valley were quite large, thanks to the generous land grants available to settlers in Oregon. The Donation Land Law of 1850 had granted 320 acres of land to male white settlers over the age of eighteen who were already cultivating land in Oregon and a similar amount to their wives, and had provided further that white males over twenty-one who settled in Oregon afterward would receive 160 acres, and their wives would be granted a like amount. Up to about 1880, the farms of the Upper Willamette Valley that resulted from these grants tended to concentrate on wheat cultivation and livestock, although some acreage was devoted to fruit trees and vegetables. By then, however, an important transformation was taking place. As a direct result of railroad construction in the region, the valley was linked to the national market, and local farmers put increasing amounts of acreage into horticultural crops, which could yield substantial profits. The process of change was accelerated by local land companies, which bought up sizable plots of land from existing farms, planted fruit trees on them, and sold them in 5- to 15-acre tracts. The Oregon Fruit and Land Company was involved in such activities in Marion County in the 1890s, as was the Churchill-Matthews Company in the next decade in Yamhill County. Between 1880 and 1920, many farms in the Upper Willamette Valley were subdivided, and much of that acreage was devoted to the production of orchard fruits, nuts, berries, vegetables, and hops. Some of that produce was sold locally, some was shipped by rail to distant markets, and some was processed, either by drying or canning, and then either sold locally or shipped.[6]

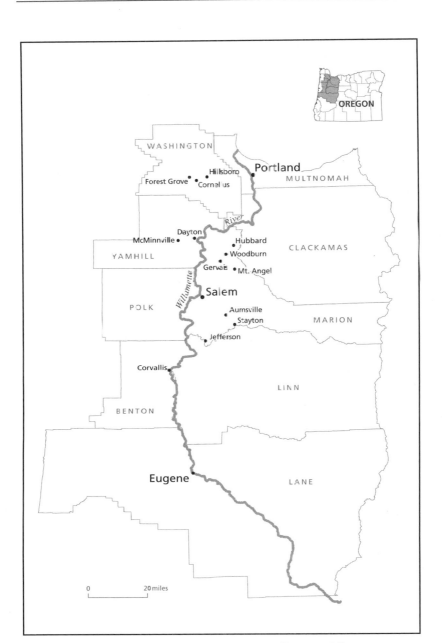

Map of northwestern Oregon, showing the Upper Willamette Valley.
Cartography: UO InfoGraphics Lab. Data Source: ESRI.

As of the mid-1960s, although a variety of crops were grown in the Willamette Valley, the bulk of the income earned by its farmers came from vegetables, berries, and nuts. Marion County, which had the largest number of acres of cultivated farmland in the region, also generated the most farm income. The principal vegetable-growing county of the state, with substantial crops of sweet corn and snap beans, it had annual vegetable sales of about $8.5 million in 1964. Marion County farms also harvested for sale the largest crops in Oregon of both strawberries (29 million pounds out of a statewide total of 90 million) and blackberries (13 million pounds out of the state's 22 million). Washington County was the state's largest producer of filberts and its second largest producer of strawberries. Clackamas County specialized in raspberries, yielding close to half of the state's total. Polk County harvested the most cherries, while Yamhill County produced sizable amounts of several crops—strawberries, cherries, and filberts.[7]

The Upper Willamette Valley's agricultural production provided work not only to people who labored on the land; close to 10,000 Oregonians were employed by the state's canning and freezing plants, which were concentrated in the vicinity of Salem. One of the largest food processing complexes in the country, it handled more than forty different fruits and vegetables and was responsible for about 10 percent of the country's frozen food production in the mid-1960s.[8]

Migrant Farm Laborers in the Internal Colony
Since the early decades of the twentieth century, when Oregon's farms began to grow fruits, nuts, and vegetables in large quantities, the state's agricultural sector had relied on a combination of local seasonal labor (including school-age children and housewives) and migrant workers to pick the crops. For the period 1900–1940, we don't have hard data on the size of the migrant workforce, but it is clear that it included Anglos, Asians, and Mexican-origin people. During World War II, Mexican contract workers were added to the labor pool, as a result of the federal government's *bracero* program, intended to meet labor needs that could not be satisfied by Americans alone. Between 1943 and 1945, 3,000 to 5,000 *braceros* worked on Oregon farms; the numbers were somewhat smaller in 1946 and

26

1947.[9] For the next seventeen years, the state continued to import several hundred Mexican nationals each harvest season through a modified version of the *bracero* program, which was terminated in 1964, but an overwhelming majority of the migrant agricultural workers in the state were Anglos from various states and Mexican Americans, most of them from South Texas. Initially, the former outnumbered the latter, but by the late 1950s and early 1960s, when the number of interstate migrant farmworkers in Oregon grew to about 18,000 at the apex of the harvesting season, Mexican Americans began to predominate.[10]

In post–World War II Oregon, the living and working conditions of migrant farm workers, whether Anglo, Mexican, or Mexican American, were often deplorable. Much of the housing provided by growers was shoddily constructed. Sanitation, both in the labor camps and in the fields, was frequently deficient. The health of migrant families was poor, and the educational level of migrant children was low. Labor contractors cheated many migrant workers out of their wages. The situation in Oregon was, in short, not appreciably different from that prevailing in Texas, California, Arkansas, and every other state in which migrant farmworkers followed the crops and attempted to earn a living.[11]

To its credit, Oregon had begun in the late 1950s to improve the lot of the migrants who labored in its fields. The driving force behind the initiative was a coalition of concerned citizens and organizations that championed the interests of the disadvantaged. One key player was the Oregon Council of Churches (OCC), an interdenominational agency for cooperation founded in 1935 that included most of the Protestant churches in the state. In August 1956 the OCC called upon the Oregon legislature to conduct a formal investigation into the "serious problems" of the migrants who came to Oregon each year. Due in large measure to the OCC's urging, in May 1957 the legislature brought into existence the Legislative Interim Committee on Migratory Labor, which was charged with producing a report on migrant conditions and making recommendations for remedial legislation.[12]

The dominant figure on the Interim Committee, and also its chairman, was Don Willner, an attorney and freshman member of the Oregon House of Representatives. Born in New York City in 1926, Willner had earned his bachelor's and law degrees from Harvard. Willner considered himself to be a liberal of the Hubert Humphrey variety—which meant that he was committed to promoting the interests of labor unions, racial and ethnic minorities, and the poor. Arriving in Oregon in 1952, he had opened his own law office and devoted most of his time to representing unions and civil rights groups. Winning a seat in the Oregon legislature, Willner had focused on civil rights in the 1957 legislative session. One of his allies was Mark Talney of the OCC, a driving force behind the creation of the Interim Committee. Talney persuaded Willner to seek a position on that committee and successfully lobbied the eight other committee members, four of them farmers, to choose Willner as chairperson.[13]

Willner recognized from the outset that, if a report in favor of migrant farmworker legislation were to emerge from his committee, he had to win the support of the farmers on it. Between August 1957 and October 1958, he arranged for the committee to tour the state to examine migrant labor camps and hold hearings about migrant living and working conditions. The tours had a powerful impact on the farmers on the committee, who, according to Willner, were "amazed" at conditions in some of the labor camps. Religious people with strong moral beliefs, they were won over.[14]

Willner also received help from government agencies. In December 1957, Oregon's governor, Robert Holmes, had created the Inter-Agency Committee on Agricultural Labor, which was to assist the Interim Committee in gathering data about migrants. Eight state agencies took part. Professor Don Balmer of Lewis and Clark College, who had been hired by Willner as the Interim Committee's research director, coordinated the data collection. The Bureau of Labor conducted the most extensive survey, under the supervision of Assistant Labor Commissioner Tom Current, a native of Minnesota and a strong supporter of migrant legislation. Current enlisted scores of volunteers to interview migrants and crew leaders and later coauthored a lengthy "preliminary report" that provided the Interim Committee with massive amounts of data and sensational descriptions of deficient migrant housing and abuses committed by contractors.[15]

The Interim Committee's own report, prepared by Balmer and published in October 1958, included some of that information. Balmer also relied on the raw data furnished by other agencies and the testimony taken at the committee's sixteen public hearings. Balanced and straightforward, his report presented both a detailed description of the problems that needed to be addressed and the drafts of six pieces of recommended legislation (on labor contracting, housing, and other matters). All nine members of Willner's committee supported the report.[16]

Having secured a favorable committee report, the friends of the migrants now faced the challenge of getting the legislature to pass the necessary legislation. That task was rendered more difficult by the fact that, during the 1959 session when migrant worker legislation was being considered and debated, Willner was no longer a member of the legislature, having been defeated in a campaign to gain a seat in the Oregon Senate. To improve their chances of succeeding, Willner and his allies created a lobbying organization known as the Oregon Committee on Migrant Affairs, which was to work for passage of the bills. Among the charter members were Talney and other figures in the OCC, some Catholic leaders, Tom Current, and Tom McCall, the future governor who was then a popular television journalist and a prominent Republican. Over the following months, Willner, the OCC, and members of the lobbying group spent a lot of time talking to newspaper editors across the state, winning the support of many, and traveling to Salem to press legislators to pass the bills.[17]

Ultimately they prevailed. In 1959, the legislature passed five out of the six bills recommended by the Interim Committee. One piece of legislation, written for the purpose of stopping the often unscrupulous practices of labor contractors, required the licensing of contractors by the state and regulated their activities. A second launched a pilot summer program for the education of migrant children. The others attempted to improve the quality of housing used by farm laborers, sanitary conditions in the fields, and the safety of vehicles used to transport workers. On paper, Oregon appeared at the time to be one of the most enlightened states in the country in protecting migrant interests.[18]

This is not to say that the laws, however laudable in the context of the times, addressed all migrant ills, nor that they were carried out to the letter. Over the next several years, the Oregon Bureau of Labor, charged with licensing contractors, was able to eliminate a large number of operators who mistreated migrant farmworkers. Still, the bureau often pointed out that crew leaders, who were not covered by the 1959 legislation, committed some of the worst offenses.[19] Working together, employees of the Oregon Board of Health and the Bureau of Labor inspected hundreds of labor camps and harvesting fields. In 1960 alone, out of the 307 camps visited by the Board of Health, 45 were closed and the owners of 99 others were required to make improvements. Many unlivable housing units were repaired or replaced. Less successful were efforts to improve sanitary conditions in the fields, the Bureau of Labor reporting in 1964 that about half of the farms inspected continued to have "substandard sanitation facilities." Frequently toilets were either broken or unclean, and workers on their breaks all drank water from the same drinking cup, as Sonny had regularly done when he was picking cotton in Texas and Arkansas.[20]

The state's summer school program for migrant children operated for six summers (1959–64), until state funding was cut off. To direct the project, the Oregon Department of Education chose Ron Petrie, an idealistic, energetic twenty-five-year-old principal, who had set up a bilingual education program for the Spanish-speaking migrant children who used to attend his school in St. Paul, Oregon, in the spring and early fall. Beginning in 1959 with schools at three large migrant labor camps, all in the Upper Willamette Valley, the project expanded in subsequent summers, but at no time encompassed more than four communities. Enrollment grew from 109 in 1959 to 573 in 1962, and then tapered off considerably in the last two years. The schools were able to develop a range of instructional techniques that, as Petrie put it, were "tailored to the needs of the migrant," and most of the children who attended the summer courses were able to advance about half a year in their grade levels. School attendance, however, was consistently irregular—a problem that is inherent in all educational efforts targeting the children of migrant families. In the summer of 1963, when a total of 335 children were enrolled in the schools, average daily attendance was 181. In a report about migrant education written in 1964, the Oregon Department of Education concluded somewhat pessimistically that "the value received" from the summer school program "may not be appropriate to the expenses involved."[21]

Beyond the activities mandated by the legislation of 1959, concerned groups implemented a variety of programs in the early 1960s to help Oregon's migrant workers. The OCC expanded its migrant-related activities, its chief instrument of expansion being the "camp adoption program," in which member churches forged relationships with and delivered services to farm labor camps. Church volunteers organized English classes for adults as well as recreational activities and devotional services for all the camp residents; in some cases, too, they helped migrant families to settle in the state, providing financial help and arranging for vocational training for the family's breadwinners.[22] Assistance to migrant workers also came from Stella Maris House, a Catholic social work organization in Portland that was staffed by three members of the Madonna House Apostolate. In collaboration with the OCC and several agencies in Multnomah and Clackamas Counties, Stella Maris House organized health clinics at three migrant labor camps, a day-care center for children of migrant families, and a clothing center at which migrants could buy items at minimal cost. Irene Chauvin of Stella Maris House, a trained nurse, oversaw the well-baby clinic at the day-care center and coordinated the health clinics in the camps.[23]

Furthermore, in 1963, the Oregon State Board of Health was awarded a $62,000 federal grant for the Oregon Migrant Health Project aimed at improving the health of migrants in three Oregon counties (Washington and Polk in the Upper Willamette Valley and Malheur in eastern Oregon). In addition to providing funds to monitor sanitary conditions in labor camps and harvest fields, the project delivered medical attention to families that had rarely received it in the past. Renewed in subsequent years with sufficient funding to increase the number of counties covered, the grant allowed project nurses to hold clinics, immunize children, and conduct thousands of health screenings every year; to refer people requiring further attention to physicians, dentists, and hospitals; to assist them in getting medication; and to promote the use of health records in migrant families. During the summer months, thanks to another U.S. Public Health Service grant, fifteen college students were assigned to work under the supervision of the project nurses and sanitarians, assisting them in conducting clinics, filling out health records, and disseminating health education materials to migrant families.[24]

As was the case in 1958–59, when cooperative activity had helped to bring about the passage of migrant-related legislation, organizations supportive of the migrants continued to work together to develop legislative initiatives. In 1963, a newly created "Friends of the Migrants Committee" attempted to push several pro-migrant measures through the Oregon legislature. Among its members were Rev. Kent Lawrence, a member of the OCC Board and chairman of the Oregon Migrant Ministry; Sarah Hall Goodwin, director of both the Oregon Migrant Ministry and the OCC's programs in Oregon and part of Idaho; Mary Kay Rowland of Stella Maris House; and Don Willner, now a member of the Oregon Senate. In October 1964, a considerably larger organization known as VOCAL (Volunteer Oregon Citizens for Agricultural Labor) was established for the purpose of supporting migrant legislation in the next legislative session. Its membership list included a familiar cast of characters—Lawrence, Goodwin, and others from the OCC, Rowland from Stella Maris House, several priests, Willner, Balmer, and Petrie.[25]

By the mid-1960s, therefore, Oregon had made headway in addressing many of the problems faced by migrant workers. Important legislation had been passed and programs of various kinds had been introduced. Still, it must be recognized that the work done thus far had been unsystematic and seriously underfunded. Good works had been done, but not necessarily good work. The resources at hand were inadequate. The situation would begin to change only when the national government and the VML, which received funding from it, entered the picture.

Oregon's Resident Mexican Americans
Up to now, Mexican Americans have made only token appearances in this chapter—as members of the large migrant farmworker army that came to Oregon in the summer months to pick the crops. But not all

Mexican-origin people in Oregon were migrants. By 1965, around the state, small groups of year-round Mexican Americans resided.

It is difficult to determine the size of Oregon's resident Mexican American population with any precision. The census of 1960 did not attempt to provide counts of Mexican Americans, nor did it, like recent censuses, enumerate all U.S. residents of "Hispanic" heritage. To estimate the number of Oregon's Mexican Americans, we are obliged to look for hints in various census tables, particularly those with data on "foreign stock" people, a census category that included foreign-born residents as well as residents with one or more foreign-born parents. In 1960, out of the 301,048 Oregonians of "foreign stock," a total of 3,119 of them identified their country of origin as Mexico. Exactly 1,000 had been born in Mexico and the other 2,119 had one or more parents who were Mexican born. Of those 3,119 "Mexican stock" Oregonians, slightly fewer than half (1,361) resided in the Upper Willamette Valley.[26]

But, without question, more than 3,119 Mexican Americans resided in Oregon in 1960. That figure does not include people with grandparents or great-grandparents (or more distant ancestors) who were born in Mexico, since the census made no effort to count them. Furthermore, even the numbers for Mexican-born Oregon residents and Oregonians with Mexican-born parents are surely too low, given the fact that undercounting of the Mexican American population has been a persistent problem in U.S. censuses, in part because large numbers of them have been involved in seasonal agricultural labor. What can we conclude about the size of Oregon's Mexican American population? At the very least it was 3,119 in 1960. But to that figure should be added the number of uncounted grandchildren and great-grandchildren of Mexican-origin people plus the number of Mexican American residents who were not counted by the census enumerators. Most likely, then, there were at least 4,000 to 5,000 Mexican American residents of the state in 1960. By 1965, the year in which the VML came into existence, the figure had perhaps grown to 6,000.[27]

The number of Oregon's Mexican American residents was unquestionably small—less than 0.3 percent of the state's population in 1960, even if we use the upwardly adjusted figure of 5,000 for the Mexican American total. Still, at the time, no ethnic or racial minority in the state was large. According to the 1960 census, only 36,650 people (or 2.1 percent of Oregon's population) were nonwhites. The largest nonwhite group was African Americans (18,133), followed by Native Americans (8,026), people of Japanese descent (5,016), and people of Chinese descent (2,995). The lack of diversity was a direct result of the state's history of racial intolerance. Oregon's constitution, adopted in 1859, had denied voting rights to both African Americans and Chinese Americans. Although the document was subsequently amended, both groups had been subjected to a wide range of discriminatory practices over the decades. Japanese Americans had fared somewhat better up to the 1930s, but they, like other Japanese Americans in the western United States, had been interned during World War II. Native Americans had fared worst of all: huge numbers of them were killed in the nineteenth century as a result of warfare with whites and exposure to white people's diseases; throughout both the nineteenth and twentieth centuries, their cultures had been relentlessly attacked; and they had been stripped of most of their lands, first by treaties and later by federal legislation.[28]

In light of that history, it is not surprising that the Mexicans and Mexican Americans in Oregon, both permanent and temporary residents, experienced more than a little animosity from whites. During and after World War II, *braceros* in Oregon encountered a host of problems. Hospitals refused to provide treatment to sick or injured Mexicans. In 1947, in the vicinity of Medford, five young Anglos attacked a Mexican national without provocation. The local police threw the battered Mexican in jail. Furthermore, despite the good works of the Oregon legislature, as the number of Mexican-origin farmworkers increased in the late 1950s and 1960s, there were persistent complaints about mistreatment by Anglo growers.[29] Still, it would be hard to make the case that the level of Anglo prejudice and discrimination against Mexican-origin people was higher in Oregon than elsewhere. One mitigating factor was the presence of activists such as Willner and Current, who were continuing to work to improve the lot of disadvantaged groups in the state.

Mexican Americans settled in Oregon for a variety of reasons, as a brief review of the life experiences of three families and one unmarried man who came to the Upper Willamette Valley will illustrate. Joseph

Hernandez Gallegos, a native of San Antonio, had served in the U.S. Army during World War II and had been discharged early for medical reasons. Suddenly out of work, Gallegos became intrigued by reports he heard from others that good jobs were available at the Portland shipyards. But the prospect of remunerative employment wasn't Joseph Gallegos's only reason for considering relocation: apparently unaware of Portland's history of race relations, he also hoped to escape the racism and ethnocentrism that existed in the Southwest. In 1943, Gallegos, his wife Elouise, and their three children left San Antonio for Portland, where both Joseph and Elouise found work in the shipyards. After the war, they remained in Portland, occupying a succession of rented houses. Gallegos made a living by dividing his time between two types of activities: for half the year, he was employed as a semiskilled laborer in the lumber mills, and in the summer months, he and his family worked as farm laborers in the Pacific Northwest. Later, he and his wife did janitorial work in Portland, and then, beginning in the late 1950s, they went into the restaurant business, first operating a Mexican restaurant on West Burnside Street and, after that, another one on Union Avenue (today Martin Luther King Boulevard).[30]

Ruben Contreras, born in Mexico City in 1921, took a different route to Oregon. From a well-to-do family—his father had served in the Mexican Congress—Contreras initially wanted to become a medical doctor and enrolled in medical school in Mexico City. But in 1944, feeling that he needed more adventure in his life, he joined the *bracero* program that sent large numbers of Mexicans to work in the United States. The decision shocked most of his family, since *braceros* usually were recruited from the lower classes. Contreras spent the summer of 1944 doing agricultural work in the Midwest and returned to the United States as a *bracero* the following summer, when he repaired tracks for the Southern Pacific Railroad in Oregon. Toward the end of his second contract period, after World War II had ended, he followed the crops to McMinnville, a town in Yamhill County with a population of about 5,000 at the time. There he met a local girl named Alberta Schmauder. Although Contreras was required by the terms of his contract to return to Mexico later that year, he came back to the United States in 1947, this time as an immigrant. He took college classes in Los Angeles and renewed his acquaintance with Alberta Schmauder. They married in 1948 and a year later took up permanent residence in McMinnville, where they raised their five children. Beginning in the early 1950s Contreras worked as a refrigeration technician and in his spare time served as a volunteer for the OCC, assisting the organization in its efforts to improve the lot of migrant farmworkers.[31]

A chance encounter brought Emilio Hernandez to Oregon, and another one enabled him to remain there. In 1963, Hernandez, a forty-four-year-old truck driver and World War II veteran from South Texas, took a leave of absence from his job and, along with his wife and several of his children, visited his sister in Fresno, California. One day during that visit, a Japanese American named Ike Iwasaki arrived at his sister's house to discuss a business matter with her husband. As Iwasaki was leaving, he struck up a conversation with Hernandez, who was sitting on the porch. One of three brothers who owned a farm and a thriving nursery business in Hillsboro, Oregon, Iwasaki told Hernandez that he and his family could make good money by picking strawberries on Iwasaki's farm. He encouraged Hernandez to travel there and even offered to provide free lodging for Hernandez, his wife Hortencia, and his children after the harvest season so that Hernandez could look for a permanent job in the area. Hernandez considered the offer for a day, accepted it, and promptly drove to Hillsboro with his family.

After the harvest season, Hernandez began his search for year-round work in the area. One day he went to a barber's shop in the nearby town of Forest Grove for a haircut, and, while he waited his turn, he began talking to another customer. Learning that Hernandez needed a job, the man asked if Hernandez could drive a tractor. "Of course," Hernandez replied. "I can drive anything. I used to be a semi driver." That conversation led to full-time employment for both Emilio and Hortencia Hernandez at the man's farm in Forest Grove. After working there for two years, Hernandez landed a position as a machine operator at Tektronix Corporation in Beaverton, commuting there every weekday from his home in Forest Grove.[32]

Like Joseph Gallegos and Emilio Hernandez, Santiago Amaya came to Oregon from Texas. Born in 1920 and married in 1942, he had served in the U.S. Army Signal Corps during World War II and afterward had gone into the construction trade. Living and working in Edinburg in South Texas, he had specialized in pipe laying and cement work and eventually rose to the position of foreman of a construction company. But in 1960 he had lost his job, and finding no suitable employment close to home, he signed an agreement with a labor contractor to do agricultural work in Oregon. In April 1961, he, his wife Crescencia, and their nine children arrived in the small town of Independence, where they did farmwork until the early fall, and then returned to Edinburg. Having enjoyed their stay in Oregon and finding that the family could make enough money from the seasonal labor to pay the bills, the Amayas came back to Independence the following spring and decided to stay. Thereafter, Santiago Amaya continued to do agricultural labor, earning enough money to build a house in Independence. Even so, he held out hopes that he might eventually get a job in a machine shop.[33]

In the ranks of the Upper Willamette Valley's Mexican Americans, we see a range of experiences. A certain number of them had lived in the area for more than twenty years. A larger number had arrived more recently, often as members of the seasonal migrant army that by the late 1950s and early 1960s was composed predominantly of Mexican Americans. By and large, the more recent arrivals, while no longer in the migrant stream, had not yet left the agricultural sector.[34] One experience, however, was shared by all: once settled in Oregon, none of them had access to an ethnic community remotely comparable to that which they had left behind. Growing up in Portland, the Gallegos family's only son, also named Joseph, interacted rarely with Mexican Americans. His parents socialized with about five other Mexican American families in the city, but they tended to get together only on holidays. Young Joseph had no Mexican American friends and was encouraged by his parents to speak only English and to assimilate into Anglo society. When Ruben Contreras settled in McMinnville in 1949, he was not only the first Hispanic to live permanently in the town, but he was the first one to reside permanently in Yamhill County. And when Emilio Hernandez and his wife came to Forest Grove fourteen years later, they were the third Mexican American family in the vicinity. Jimmy Amaya, the second oldest child of Santiago Amaya, was a few months shy of seventeen when his parents settled in Independence, Oregon, in 1962. At the time, only a handful of Mexican-origin families resided year-round in the town, and Jimmy felt isolated. "I wanted a life," he told me, explaining that there were no restaurants or stores in Independence that catered to people like him. Occasionally, he and other members of his family went to Woodburn, where there was a grocery store owned by a Mexican American and a movie theater that showed Spanish-language movies. As of 1965, despite the fact that Oregon's Mexican American residents numbered about 6,000—with perhaps 2,500 to 3,000 of them living in the Upper Willamette Valley—there was nothing yet resembling a Mexican American community.[35]

The National Context

Let us turn finally to the national context. The 1960s was a decade of turmoil in America, a fact that can be gleaned merely by perusing a few titles of books written on the period: *Fire in the Streets, America Divided, Years of Discord, The Unraveling of America, America's Uncivil Wars, An American Ordeal.* One constant of the decade was social protest. The country was being challenged to address a complex of issues that up to then had been either ignored or incompletely addressed—racial prejudice, ethnocentrism, segregation, gender discrimination, gender orientation discrimination, poverty, inequality, American military intervention abroad.[36] Even though Oregon itself was not a major locus of social protest in the decade, the environment of protest in the nation would have important impacts on the residents of the state, including the Mexican Americans.

Serious social protest in post–World War II America began in the mid-1950s with the emergence of the civil rights movement. Consigned to second-class citizenship for too long, African Americans demanded rights that had been denied them—the right to ride in the front of buses, to be served at lunch counters, to vote, to go to better schools, to live in better neighborhoods, to get better jobs. That they wanted such things is not difficult to fathom, but why did their protest campaign occur at that particular historical juncture?

A compelling explanation is provided by the historical sociologist Doug McAdam, who argues that the emergence of African American protest in the 1950s was the direct result of a favorable "structure of political opportunities." According to McAdam and others, modern social movements tend to develop in periods in which the political system is destabilized (as a result of war or rapid economic change, for example) and the leverage of potentially contentious groups is elevated. In the case of the civil rights movement of the 1950s and 1960s, McAdam finds its origins in the migration of millions of blacks from the rural South to urban places in both the South and North—an exodus that took on steam after 1910. Out-migration alone amounted to more than 4 million people between 1910 and 1960. Both kinds of migration were directly responsible for a combination of developments: a substantial increase in black electoral power, particularly in the northern states to which so many African Americans migrated; the growth of African American churches and colleges, which benefited from the increasing urbanization of the South's black population; and the rapid expansion of NAACP membership in the South, likewise a result of urbanization.[37]

Taken together, these developments insured that African American protest against denials of civil rights would be able to gain a large following in black communities around the country as well as considerable support from national political leaders, particularly in the Democratic Party, who could no longer ignore the African American vote. The result was a cognitive shift. Whereas black protest in the past had generally been doomed to defeat, that was no longer the case by the late 1950s and early 1960s, when national political alignments had been restructured and formidable organizations had emerged within the black community (the NAACP, CORE, SNCC, and SCLC) that could direct the protest campaigns. According to McAdam, the apogee of African American protest was reached in the period 1961–65, when the level of institutional cooperation was very high and the national political climate was particularly favorable.[38] Among the movement's tangible achievements were three landmark pieces of legislation early in the presidency of Lyndon Johnson: the Civil Rights Act of 1964, the Economic Opportunity Act of 1964, and the Voting Rights Act of 1965, all of them intended primarily to alleviate the problems of America's African Americans.[39]

But African Americans were not the only Americans to engage in social protest in that period. By the mid-1960s, the student movement was beginning to gain momentum, and there were some early manifestations of what came to be called the Chicano movement. Women, Native Americans, and other groups were not far behind. What accounts for the emergence of these social movements at this time? Undoubtedly, long-standing grievances played a role, as did new provocations—such as, in the case of the student movement, the decisions of the Johnson administration to escalate the level of U.S. involvement in Vietnam in 1965, which led in turn to a major escalation of student protest against the war. In addition, the civil rights movement itself served as a catalyst for other types of protest. For one, it was a training ground. The student movement, the women's movement, and an important element in the Chicano movement (Cesar Chavez's campaign to organize Mexican American farmworkers) were filled with individuals who had participated earlier in African American protest—as marchers and demonstrators, members of SNCC, and volunteers for the Freedom Summer of 1964.[40] Second, and more important, the development of these social movements was, to a significant degree, a direct consequence of the success that had been achieved by the civil rights movement. That success offered hope to other disadvantaged groups in U.S. society, suggesting that the adoption of social movement tactics might enable them to promote their own agendas. The result was something that social scientists call a "cycle of contention," a period in which there was "heightened conflict across the social system." Sidney Tarrow describes the process by which such cycles occur: "The demonstration effect on the part of a group of early risers triggers a variety of processes of diffusion, extension, imitation, and reaction among groups that are normally more quiescent and have fewer resources to engage in collective action."[41]

There is, however, a significant difference between a social movement that takes to the streets at a time when the structure of political opportunities is propitious and one that does so at a time when (and in some measure because) gains have already been achieved by other aggrieved groups. In the latter case, the political environment may not favor social action. Cycles of contention are a bit like investment bubbles: when others are making outsized gains, it is difficult to stay on the sidelines even though a prudent assessment of the pros and cons may dictate caution.

These observations apply in particular to Mexican American protest in that period of generalized unrest. The truth of the matter is that as of 1965—the year in which, according to most scholarly accounts, the Chicano movement began—the structure of political opportunities for Mexican Americans was not particularly favorable, especially if we compare the situation to that which African Americans faced a decade earlier when they launched the civil rights movement. On the national level, Mexican Americans had limited political clout. Although the Mexican American population was growing at an impressive rate, it still was small—slightly more than 3.8 million in 1960, or about a fifth the size of the African American population; and unlike African Americans, Mexican Americans were largely concentrated in only two states, Texas and California.[42] That concentration had both positive and negative political consequences. On the one hand, it meant that in the tightly contested presidential election of 1960, Mexican Americans could make a difference: thanks in some measure to Mexican American support (as evidenced by the formation of Viva Kennedy Clubs in many Mexican American communities), John Kennedy had been able to carry the crucial state of Texas.[43] On the other hand, it also meant that there were few representatives and senators in Congress from states outside the Southwest who had electoral reasons for promoting legislation favored by Mexican Americans.

The geographic concentration of the Mexican American people was a limiting factor in other ways. Because the Chicano movement was largely a phenomenon of the Southwest, it could not attract anything comparable to the national media attention that the civil rights movement did, since the media centers of the day were in the East. And so too were the country's major philanthropic organizations, potential sources of financial support. Even at the height of Mexican American protest, then, Chicano organizations had difficulty in getting a hearing from audiences that mattered. Although some initiatives might occasionally capture the public's attention—and, in the case of Chavez's movement, even attract a considerable amount of national sympathy—there was never the kind of broad-based support that enabled the civil rights supporters to translate their dreams of equal rights into major pieces of national legislation.

Indeed, by 1965, even for the civil rights movement, the political climate in America was no longer so favorable for successful protest. Part of the problem was internal: within the African American coalition, severe disagreements were surfacing over ideological and tactical issues, contributing to a fall-off in protest activity. Beyond that, following the riots of the mid-1960s in many American cities, a conservative reaction set in. Over the next several years, both political parties devoted considerably more attention to courting the supporters of George Wallace, whose third-party candidacy for the presidency ultimately decided the presidential election of 1968, than to appealing to black voters. While African American protest did not end in the period 1966–70, the changed circumstances definitely weakened the movement.[44]

And if the national political climate in the mid-1960s did not necessarily favor the development of the Chicano movement, the chances for success also were reduced by the fact that Mexican American protest had nothing approaching the institutional support system that had sustained the civil rights movement. Whereas by the 1950s and 1960s there were scores of established black colleges, there were no equivalent institutions of higher education for Mexican Americans. Although many Catholic and Protestant activists would provide assistance to and funding for Chavez's struggle to organize farmworkers, other components of the Chicano movement received relatively little support outside the Mexican American community. And while there were two sizable Mexican American organizations—the League of United Latin American Citizens (LULAC), founded in 1929, and the American G.I. Forum, which came into being in 1948—that had attacked segregation and other violations of Mexican American civil rights and had even scored some important victories in the courts, both of them had adopted a largely nonconfrontational approach and chose to work within the system rather than to challenge and disrupt it. Besides, despite their size, both of them had relatively limited financial resources compared to the major African American organizations.[45] Whereas the NAACP, SNCC, CORE, and SCLC would direct and sustain the civil rights movement, LULAC and the American G.I. Forum would play only supporting roles in the Chicano movement.[46]

As of 1965, two Mexican American social movements had surfaced that would in time become core elements of the Chicano movement.[47] One was Cesar Chavez's aforementioned campaign to organize California's farmworkers. Of all the components of the Chicano movement, this one had the greatest national appeal, largely because the plight of farmworkers bore certain similarities to that of the nation's African Americans, and some of the groups who supported the latter could easily gravitate to the cause of the former. As John Gregory Dunne has written: "Civil rights agitation in the South had stirred eddies of guilt in the nation's psyche about its economically and culturally dispossessed, and as the ripples widened, they naturally began to take in California's Mexican American minority."[48]

Furthermore, the movement led by Chavez, based in California, benefited from a combination of *farmworker-specific* political opportunities that helped it to grow and score some significant early victories. One factor working in its favor was the end of the *bracero* program, which, for more than twenty years, had undercut all efforts to organize farmworkers in the state. Because growers now lacked preferential access to a foreign labor pool, California wages were no longer artificially depressed, and, because farmworkers no longer faced the threat that Mexican nationals would take over the available jobs, they were more inclined to articulate their grievances. A second factor was the U.S. Supreme Court's recent reapportionment decisions that ended rural domination of state legislatures. In California, the principal result of reapportionment was, as one labor union leader put it, to get rid of "the cows-and-acres senators." The balance of legislative power in the state shifted from rural growers to urbanites in southern California—to areas where unions and minorities had particular strength. Even so, it would be a mistake to underestimate the formidable problems faced by Chavez. Farmworkers were incredibly difficult to organize: farmwork was seasonal; farmworkers were often migratory, and there was considerable tension among the ethnic groups involved in farmwork.[49]

Himself a former migrant farmworker, Chavez had worked for a decade as a community organizer for the Community Service

Organization (CSO), helping the poor. But in the spring of 1962, frustrated when a CSO convention rejected his idea of organizing a farmworkers' union, he resigned his job and decided to start a union on his own. Setting up shop in Delano in California's San Joaquin Valley, he and a few colleagues—among them, his cousin Manuel Chavez and his former CSO co-worker Dolores Huerta—drove to every town and labor camp in the valley, speaking to workers and attempting to convince them to join a union. Gradually, they made headway, and the National Farm Workers Association (NFWA) was born. Its first convention was held at an abandoned movie theater in Fresno on September 30, 1962. By 1964, the association had approximately a thousand members, and in the spring of the following year, the NFWA organized its first strike, undertaken to increase the wages of flower workers in McFarland, California. The growers eventually agreed to the increase.

Then came the Delano grape strike, a farm labor action that became a headline story around the country. Since 1959, the AFL-CIO had been financing its own farmworkers' union, the Agricultural Workers Organizing Committee (AWOC), which had made some headway in attracting Filipino vegetable and grape workers, especially those based in the town of Delano. One of AWOC's leading organizers was a Filipino named Larry Itliong. On September 8, 1965, AWOC members under Itliong's leadership launched a strike against grape growers in the Delano area, demanding better wages and other concessions. Asked to join the strike by Itliong, Chavez put the question to a vote of the NFWA, and at a meeting on September 16, the members decided unanimously to join. Following the vote, the two unions—which eventually merged in 1966, forming the United Farm Workers Organizing Committee (UFWOC)—cooperated in running the strike, attempting to stop the grape harvest. Union members and volunteers joined the picket lines; local police harassed the picketers; television and print reporters gave extensive coverage to the strike. Even when his opponents inflicted injury on the picketers, Chavez, who admired Gandhi's writings and achievements, advocated nonviolence. In December 1965, to apply further pressure to the farmers, the unions initiated a boycott of the Schenley Corporation, one of the largest growers of table grapes in the San Joaquin Valley and also the producer of some well-known liquor brands. As the year 1965 came to a close, a boycott of Schenley products was beginning in cities around the country, and Chavez was considering new collective-action techniques to bring the farmers to the negotiating table.[50]

Not yet so well known as Chavez's farmworkers' movement was the New Mexico-based La Alianza Federal de Mercedes (the Federal Land-Grant Alliance), an organization created by Reies López Tijerina. Born in Falls City, Texas, to a family of migrant farmworkers, Tijerina initially chose a religious vocation, serving as an Assembly of God minister for several years and then becoming a Pentecostal preacher. In the 1950s, during a brief stay in rural New Mexico, he became fixated on two apparent historical injustices— that, in the aftermath of the Mexican War, the Mexican-origin people of the region had lost the communal lands that had been granted to their ancestors and that, as a result, their descendants had become progressively impoverished. Research on the subject in Mexico convinced him that the New Mexicans had been deprived of that land illegally—in violation of the Treaty of Guadalupe Hidalgo of 1848. Thus began a crusade that preoccupied Tijerina for the rest of his life.

In February 1963, in Albuquerque, Tijerina and thirty-seven associates founded the Alianza, an organization that had one major objective: to recover from the United States the territory that had been lost by Mexican Americans over the previous 115 years as a result, according to Tijerina's analysis, of the conspiratorial, illegal actions of a combination of Anglos, rich Hispanic collaborators, and the U.S. government. To bring attention to the movement, Tijerina took to the airwaves, buying radio time to broadcast his message. A compelling speaker, he attracted a large audience. His message also had considerable appeal in a region where there was widespread poverty and more than a little resentment because of recently adopted policies by the U.S. Forest Service that appeared to discriminate against Mexican Americans. As of September 1965, the Alianza claimed to have more than 20,000 members.[51]

Hence, by 1965, Chicanismo was clearly in the air in the United States. Mexican Americans were joining social movements, protesting against perceived injustices, and receiving national media coverage for those activities. Over the next decade, as we shall see, this activity would markedly increase: a host of community and student groups would be created; Chicano political activists would launch major initiatives, especially in Texas, California, and Colorado; and Chavez and his followers would record several major victories. But it must be emphasized that, however great the level of involvement and expense of energy, however creative the initiatives undertaken, and however much attention the U.S. press and public would pay to the various manifestations of Chicanismo, political realities—insufficient numbers, lack of institutional support, and no electoral strength—placed limitations on what the protesters could ultimately accomplish. The structure of political opportunities of the day was working against the Chicano movement, a latecomer in a cycle of contention. Important victories would doubtless occur, but in the end Chicano activists would find it difficult to maintain the momentum.

The Valley Migrant League

Shortly after announcing his desire to "cure" and "prevent" poverty in America in his 1964 State of the Union Address, President Lyndon Johnson charged Sargent Shriver, the late President Kennedy's brother-in-law and the director of the Peace Corps, with developing a national poverty program and fashioning a piece of legislation to put the program into operation. The bill, drafted by a task force assembled by Shriver, became the Economic Opportunity Act of August 1964, which created the Office of Economic Opportunity (OEO), appropriated approximately $1 billion for its first year of operation, and set in motion a number of programs offering opportunities to America's poor. The Job Corps gave vocational training, education, and work experience to poor young men and women. Other programs targeted adult illiteracy and rural poverty. The act created the VISTA (Volunteers in Service to America) program, which assigned volunteers to poor communities to assist in implementing poverty programs. Last but not least, there was the Community Action Program (CAP), intended to stimulate urban and rural communities "to mobilize their resources to combat poverty." The program provided funding to public and private nonprofit agencies to undertake projects that aimed to eliminate poverty. Communities were expected to identify the problems to be addressed, to draw up and carry out their own programs, and to do all that "with the maximum feasible participation of residents of the areas and members of the groups served." The legislation aimed to give agency to the poor, and the Community Action Program, in particular, was seen as an instrument of community development.[1]

With the passage of the Economic Opportunity Act, a substantial amount of money was made available to local governments and nonprofit organizations to assist the poor. But the amount available, however large, could not fund every conceivable project. To receive funding, public and private agencies had to develop compelling grant proposals in which they made the case for the projects they wanted to carry out. The principal author of the proposal that launched the VML in Oregon's Upper Willamette Valley was Tom Current.

Beginnings

A longtime friend of Oregon's migrant workers, Current had left his position in the Oregon Bureau of Labor in 1961 and taken a job with the Area Redevelopment Administration, a federal agency that addressed economic problems in areas of high unemployment. Based in Portland, he supervised the agency's work in eleven states. For long stretches, though, there was little work to do because the Area Redevelopment Administration was poorly funded. During one such stretch, toward the end of 1964, Current's superiors loaned him to the OEO, where he was asked to review proposals relating to migrants. Unfortunately, the initial batch of submissions was "dreadful," according to Current, and none was deemed worthy of funding. The OEO then directed Current to return to Oregon to see if he could generate a "decent" proposal.[2]

Back in Oregon, Current called a meeting of some of the people who had been heavily involved in Oregon's migrant-assistance projects over the years—Don Willner, influential people in the OCC, the staff at Stella Maris House, and others. Then, in preparation for the meeting, Current drew up a five-page sketch of a migrant-assistance organization he called the Valley Migrant League, which was to operate in Oregon's Upper Willamette Valley. That sketch contained, in embryonic form, all the key elements of the organization that ultimately received OEO support—opportunity centers, summer schools, day-care programs, adult education.[3]

At the organizational meeting, which was held on January 16, 1965, Current's ideas were received enthusiastically. Irene Chauvin of Stella Maris House wrote afterward: "The cry over the years had been a lack of money with which to do anything concrete. This appeared to be the breakthrough we needed, money-wise, to implement our dreams for helping the migrant." In short order, Willner prepared the papers of incorporation of the VML, providing for a large "representative" board of directors and a smaller executive committee. A board was then elected, and Kent Lawrence of the Oregon Migrant Ministry was chosen as chairman. Meanwhile, an ad hoc committee prepared the formal application for a CAP grant from the OEO. Many times longer than Current's original draft, the submitted proposal was essentially an elaboration of that earlier document. The only significant addition was a request for money to publish a bilingual newspaper. In mid-March 1965, the OEO approved a grant of $681,000 to cover the VML's expenses through the end of the year.[4]

Over the following months, the VML began to take shape. Sarah Hall Goodwin, who had done fieldwork for the Migrant Ministry for twelve years, was hired to oversee adult education. Sam Granato, a career social worker who had served as supervisor of day-care services for the Oregon State Public Welfare Commission, was placed in charge of the VML's day-care programs. Area directors and assistant area directors, who would be based at the VML's five opportunity centers (initially, Woodburn, Stayton, Dayton, Hillsboro, and Independence), were also hired. The center at Independence opened its doors in the first week of May, and the one at Woodburn, housed in the same old church building where the VML headquarters was located, held an open house later in the month. Finally, on May 29, 1965, the board announced its choice for executive director: Will Pape, a longtime employee of the YMCA, most recently in Portland.[5]

By early June 1965, with the arrival of many migrants in the state, the VML moved into action. Over the next two and a half months, thirteen VML summer schools were operating in the Upper Willamette Valley, with total daily attendance averaging about 500. Twelve day-care centers were opened as well, with daily attendance close to 300. All five of the opportunity centers offered an adult education program, organized clubs and recreational activities, and assisted migrants with health, vocational, and housing problems. Each week thousands of copies of the *Opportunity News*, the VML's bilingual newspaper, were distributed to migrants and seasonal farmworkers. The OEO initially assigned forty-six VISTAs to the VML (the number was later reduced), and they were given a range of jobs, which included visiting migrant camps.[6] In that first summer of the VML's operation, local newspaper coverage of the organization's activities was celebratory. VML employees were depicted as selfless and committed; migrants and seasonal farmworkers who participated in their programs were seen as fortunate and grateful. "Valley Center Helps Enrich Lives of Migrants" was the title of one front-page story in the Salem *Capital Journal*. The *Oregon Journal*, a Portland daily, featured a five-part series documenting the VML's efforts. In one of them, Ruben Contreras, the Mexican-born assistant director of the Dayton Opportunity Center, discussed the VML's positive impact. "Migrants feel that someone really cares about them, someone considers them more than just field workers," he said. "They are beginning to realize someone is trying to help them achieve a better status in life." Assessments of the VML by the funding agency were uniformly positive. "I think this is an overall excellent program," asserted one OEO evaluator in August 1965.[7]

As the summer of 1965 came to a close and most of the migrants left Oregon, the VML's level of activity decreased accordingly. Day-care programs and schools for migrant children were closed. More than a hundred employees were laid off, leaving on the payroll only the core staff of about sixty people. Still, adult education classes continued for the seasonal farmworkers who remained in the region, as did recreational activities and counseling sessions at the opportunity centers.[8]

The next year began promisingly. In early January 1966, the OEO awarded the VML a grant of $609,000, allowing the organization to add two more opportunity centers in Salem and Sandy, bringing the total to seven. A week later, an OEO evaluator wrote another favorable report on the VML, concluding that it was a "well-run organization." More awards were announced in the spring, increasing the amount of federal funding in that year to more than $1.2 million and adding a new job training and job placement program. At the end of May 1966, as the VML geared up for a summer of intensified activity, Pape reported to the board of directors that the editor of a new bimonthly magazine to be published by the OEO was preparing a feature story on the VML.[9] The stock of the organization was very high, and all signs indicated that it was going higher. Or so it seemed at about the midpoint of 1966, when Sonny Montes was recruited to work at the Hillsboro Opportunity Center.

Signs of Discontent
Out of the seven opportunity centers operating in the Upper Willamette Valley in June 1966, the one at Hillsboro had given the VML central administration the most trouble.[10] The first opportunity center director (or "area director," as the position was often called)

in Hillsboro had been a dynamic, combative woman named Ruby Ely, the estranged wife of a Los Angeles judge, who had worked with migrants for many years and also served in the Peace Corps in Honduras. Ely took seriously the notion that the people helped by VML programs should participate in their planning and execution, and she had nurtured the development of the Washington County Mexican-American Club, made up of Mexican-origin people who were residing in the area. She was especially close to its leader Emilio Hernandez of Forest Grove. "She was the smartest woman I ever met," Hernandez told me.

Increasingly, Ely found herself at odds with the VML administration. She believed that the VML was not doing enough to assist migrants in settling in Oregon; VML administrators at the Woodburn office, sensitive to growers' concern that VML programs might deprive them of their workforce, maintained that the organization should provide resettlement assistance only to migrants who had already made an independent decision to leave the migrant stream and criticized Ely for encouraging them to leave. Ely complained that the VML was not doing enough to involve farmworkers in decision making; her critics asserted that she favored Mexican American migrants while ignoring Anglo migrants and had created a cleavage between the two groups in Hillsboro and other communities in Washington County.

In the context of the times—which is to say, in the early days of the Johnson administration's War on Poverty—the kind of criticism Ely and her Mexican American allies in the Hillsboro area were leveling at the VML was hardly unique. Throughout the United States in 1965 and 1966, there were complaints, especially from the ranks of America's racial and ethnic minorities, that many of the organizations funded by the OEO's Community Action Program—known as Community Action Agencies (CAAs)—did not give sufficient attention to the concerns of the communities served and included only a token representation of poor people and members of racial and ethnic minorities on their governing boards. The criticism was most intense in the case of CAAs administered by local governments, a majority of the approximately 1,000 CAAs created in the first few years of the OEO's existence. White political elites—in particular, the mayors of large cities—insisted on having control over the money given to local governments and resisted the idea of sharing power with the poor. But, as the events unfolding in Hillsboro in 1965 demonstrate, even CAAs that were free of local governmental control, such as the VML, might fall short of the goal of "maximum feasible participation" and become the sites of conflict.[11]

In fact, the specific criticism leveled by Ely at the VML administration bore a striking resemblance to the attacks made on CAAs controlled by urban political machines. The VML, like many urban CAAs, was portrayed as unsympathetic to the interests of the population served, unduly concerned about offending powerful whites, and adamantly opposed to the idea of giving the poor a significant role in the making and implementation of agency policies. Furthermore, there was a certain amount of truth to Ely's critique of the VML. As we shall see, while the organization's leaders undoubtedly had good intentions, they were not prepared, either by training or inclination, to consider seriously the sort of approach that their critics considered essential.

At the end of May 1966 the VML fired Ely, but that action only made things worse. In June, Ely, Hernandez, and her other allies created an organization called Volunteers in Vanguard Action, or VIVA, with Hernandez as its president. Six out of the eight VISTAs who had been working at the Hillsboro Opportunity Center promptly announced that they were leaving the VML and going to work for VIVA. Hernandez launched an all-out assault on the VML, charging even more stridently that its leaders were not serving the interests of Mexican American migrants. Meanwhile, VIVA announced its intention to assist any migrants wanting to settle in Oregon and appealed for federal support to fund its activities. Such developments suggested that the VML under Will Pape's leadership was not meeting important migrant needs.

To replace Ely, the VML had chosen Jose Garcia, the man who was to recruit Sonny to the organization.[12] Garcia had started work in June 1966, only a short time before his first meeting with Sonny. Twenty-eight years old, he was a former seminarian. In 1963, he had entered the liberal arts college at Mt. Angel Seminary (in Mt. Angel, Oregon), preparing for the priesthood, but had withdrawn from school in 1966, during his junior year, shortly before taking a position with the VML, having decided against becoming a priest.

Well-read and a fascinating conversationalist, Garcia impressed Sonny and almost everyone else he met.

Garcia was also, unknown to most of the people he worked with at the VML, a troubled man. Born into a family of Mexican American farmworkers and raised in California, he was embarrassed about his past as well as his ethnicity. To many of the Anglos he met, he was Joe Garcia or Joseph Garcia, and the story he told them in perfect English was that he was of Portuguese descent. To Mexican Americans, he was Jose; he communicated with them in Spanish, which was the language he had spoken at home. Garcia's inner turmoil extended to his choice of vocation. He had chosen to study for the priesthood to please his mother, a deeply religious woman. But the priesthood was anything but a calling for him; Jose was good-looking and something of a lady's man.

Even for someone who did not bring so much emotional baggage to the office, the job of area director at Hillsboro would have been difficult enough. Like other area directors, Garcia was expected to enroll migrants and seasonal farmworkers in VML programs. But, unlike the others, he would have to do that in the face of constant public criticism from a segment of the target population, the members of VIVA. He would also have to deal with a large number of growers who, because of VIVA's presence in the area, were not keen on opening their labor camps to visitors, and he would have to hire and train three new opportunity center employees (one of whom was Sonny), the openings being created by the turmoil of the previous months.

A New Line of Work

During his conversations with Jose Garcia prior to accepting the VML job, Sonny had expressed concerns about his qualifications. He was a young, inexperienced, unworldly farm laborer, he told Garcia. For most of his twenty-two years, he had given little consideration to doing anything but agricultural work. As an adult, he had not paid a great deal of attention to current events and politics, since such concerns had seemed irrelevant to his life. But they would not be irrelevant to his new job. Sonny feared that his lack of experience and basic knowledge would be serious handicaps in working for the VML. Furthermore, he was unfamiliar with Oregon, having spent less than a month in the state. To alleviate Sonny's concerns, Garcia agreed to help.

For the first month of Sonny's employment in Hillsboro, he and Garcia met together almost every day for several hours, usually in the early afternoon. The two of them would leave the opportunity center office, located in the city center, and walk across the street to a public park, where they would sit down and talk at the base of a large old apple tree. The subjects varied, but the content was always germane to the work Sonny was expected to do—the objectives and programs of the VML, the abusive labor practices that existed on farms in the area, the techniques that Sonny might use in explaining VML programs to farmworkers, the things he might say to families when he discussed the possibility of leaving the migrant stream. On that last subject, Sonny remembers that Garcia advised him never to "promise something that you won't be able to deliver." He should be absolutely truthful about the difficulties the migrants might encounter.

Those meetings with Jose Garcia under the apple tree in Hillsboro, which amounted to an intensive, individualized training program, helped Sonny considerably in his work for the VML. They also affected his approach to community development, making him aware of the necessity of providing basic information to people so that they could feel confident enough to participate in the political process. To this day, Sonny considers Jose Garcia to be one of the most important influences on his life. Ironically, this man who could not find direction in his own life was able to give it to another.[13]

As a program aide, Sonny's principal responsibility was to inform migrant and seasonal farmworkers about VML programs. Although program aides were among the most poorly paid VML employees, they were also the most indispensable ones, since at the time, aside from the program aides, janitors, and a few other employees who were Mexican Americans, the organization was staffed with monolingual Anglo professionals who were incapable of communicating with the people they served. On most days, Sonny held evening meetings with migrant families at the labor camps. He arrived at a camp after the farmworkers had eaten their evening meals, knocked on cabin doors, and invited the people to come outside and participate in a discussion about VML programs. Sonny conducted the meetings in Spanish, since there were virtually no Anglos in the labor camps of Washington County. His presentations were similar to the one Garcia had given at Duyck's labor camp, informing the migrants about the VML's programs and encouraging them to visit the opportunity center. He discussed the pros and cons of leaving the migrant stream and settling in Oregon. He also let the people know that, if they decided to settle down, "they would not be alone." While there would be difficulties along the way and success was not guaranteed, the VML would provide assistance.

While camp meetings occupied much of his time, Sonny had other responsibilities as a program aide. Over the summer, he and other VML employees organized recreational programs for children at some of the labor camps in Washington County. He also attended staff meetings with the other opportunity center employees, where he and his colleagues discussed their work and thereby learned more about the VML's operations. At those meetings, staff members who supervised specific VML programs (the day-care centers, the adult education classes, and so on) were expected to bring up-to-date lists of program participants. Sonny scanned the lists to see if any of the people he had spoken to at the camp meetings were taking advantage of the programs he had brought to their attention. He spent time in the opportunity center itself, where he and other employees dealt primarily with former migrants who had settled in the area. There he furnished information to drop-ins about adult education classes and vocational training and offered emergency assistance (gas money, food money, transportation to doctors or hospitals). In addition, like program aides at all the opportunity centers, he ran errands and even washed the leased automobiles and vans that were used by the center staff.

During his first few months on the job, at Jose Garcia's direction, Sonny traveled to other opportunity centers to meet other Mexican Americans who worked for the VML. On one occasion he drove a VML-leased Ford Galaxie to Salem to receive a briefing from Sam Hernandez, an assistant area director, about developments in the Salem area. He met with Ruben Contreras in Dayton and Juan Ruiz in Woodburn. At the time, Garcia was vague about the purpose of the meetings, and since Garcia died many years ago, we can only speculate about what he had in mind. But the benefit of these meetings to Sonny is indisputable. He was becoming part of an emerging network of Mexican American VML employees.[14]

At the end of August 1966, Sonny was promoted to the position of assistant job counselor, and his salary increased to $333 a month. The promotion came as a result of the new grant received by the VML from the OEO to fund a job-development and job-training program. For the first fifteen months of the VML's operations, there were no job-counseling and job-placement specialists in the opportunity centers. When people appeared at the centers looking for employment, they generally found sympathetic listeners, but no one with special knowledge about job placement. Sometimes area directors met with the job seekers, and sometimes the responsibility fell to assistant directors or program aides. Between May 1965 and August 1966, through hard work and sheer persistence, VML employees succeeded in placing 365 seasonal farmworkers in year-round jobs. About half the jobs were in the agricultural sector—generally, as farmhands and employees of local nurseries. The other jobs were in a variety of businesses.[15]

The new grant expanded and regularized the VML's job-counseling and job-placement efforts. Thereafter, each of the opportunity centers was to be staffed with a job counselor and an assistant job counselor. The counselors were expected to be "professionals," and, predictably, Anglos were hired for those positions. At the Hillsboro center, Ken Kimmel was the choice. The assistants, on the other hand, were supposed to be farmworkers. Most of the people hired were Mexican Americans like Sonny.[16]

For his first few weeks on the new job, Sonny worked side by side with Kimmel, his supervisor. Although some of their time was devoted to interviewing (and determining the skills and interests of) the migrant and seasonal farmworkers who came to the opportunity center office looking for work, most of it was spent in attempting to convince business owners in the Hillsboro area to hire people who, up to that point in their lives, had done nothing but agricultural labor. At first Sonny simply shadowed Kimmel, observing his discussions with potential employers at their places of business. After a while, Kimmel asked Sonny to make the pitch, and, finding that his assistant was skilled at speaking with the employers, Kimmel let

Sonny operate on his own. Sonny made his first successful placement fairly quickly, finding a job for a hardworking Mexican American at a company that manufactured chemically treated wood products.[17]

As Sonny was mastering his new job, Hillsboro's center director Jose Garcia was doing his best to navigate through the minefield of Washington County politics. Growers in the area were becoming increasingly upset with VIVA, which circulated a newsletter critical of their operations and whose representatives entered the labor camps without the farmers' approval and, according to the farmers, encouraged the workers to leave before the end of the harvest season. VIVA also continued to attack the VML as insufficiently assertive, claiming that its programs aimed merely "to make better migrants out of the migrants." Garcia's approach was to continue attracting farmworkers to VML programs, to coexist with both VIVA and the growers, and to attempt to reduce the level of tension in the county. While critical of VIVA's rhetoric and some of its actions, he praised its objectives and counseled its critics to be more understanding. "A lot of times we don't have the patience we need," he told a newspaper reporter.[18]

Although Sonny had initially been ambivalent about going to work for the VML, his reservations had by now disappeared. He enjoyed helping people, giving them options that they had never had before. He had even begun to think seriously about remaining in Oregon after the summer and continuing on at the VML. He had discussed the matter a bit with Librada, but they hadn't made any firm decision about whether or not to return to Reedley. They had more important things on their minds at the time: Librada was pregnant and the baby was due in October.

Then, at the end of September, Sonny received the disturbing news that Jose Garcia was leaving the VML. Explaining to colleagues that he had decided to pursue a legal career, Garcia said that he was returning to school in California. Sonny felt abandoned, even betrayed, since it had been Garcia who had recruited him. He also became apprehensive about the future. Who would the new area director be? Would he get along with him or her as well as he had gotten along with Garcia? Shortly after learning the news about Garcia's resignation, Sonny shared his concerns with Librada, telling her that he was not sure if they should stay in Oregon. There were too many unknowns—"too much darkness," as Sonny puts it.

The crisis passed. On October 9, 1966, Librada gave birth to the couple's second child, Raquel, at a Portland hospital. A few days later, the VML hired John Patrick Little, a forty-year-old Portland native, as the new area director for Hillsboro. During his first weeks on the job, Little met often with Sonny, and those meetings helped to allay the younger man's apprehensions. Fluent in Spanish, Little seemed to enjoy dealing with people from a non-Anglo culture. Little treated Sonny as an equal and seemed interested in his observations and opinions. Sonny again became comfortable with the idea of remaining in Oregon.[19]

In November, he and Librada began to look for a better place to live in the Hillsboro area. They were still residing in a cabin at Lloyd Duyck's labor camp, and even though they could remain there indefinitely because of Horacio Arce's close relationship with Lloyd Duyck, they needed more space, with a new baby in the family. Eventually, they located a well-maintained one-bedroom rental house in Hillsboro, only a few blocks from the opportunity center and approximately the same distance from the house occupied by John Little, his wife Pat, and their children. Just after Sonny and Librada moved in, John and Pat Little, knowing that the Monteses had no furniture for their new residence, appeared at the door with some mattresses and box springs and an assortment of other useful items. "It was a lot," Sonny recalls, and it was greatly appreciated. "We didn't have the money. I mean, $333 a month was nothing."

Starting in December 1966, Sonny's work as assistant job counselor changed considerably. As a result of a supplementary eighteen-month grant from the OEO, the VML launched a program to provide on-the-job training (OJT) in nonagricultural work to 200 migrant and seasonal farmworkers. The job counselors and assistant job counselors at the opportunity centers were charged with finding farmworkers willing to be trained and employers willing to do the training and to pay a reasonable wage during the training period, which would vary in length depending on the nature of the work. (In practice, the hourly wage paid to the trainees averaged about $2.00.) To induce employers to agree, the VML offered them a payment of up to $25 a week for every trainee for a maximum of twenty-six weeks.[20]

Some of Sonny's work for the new program was familiar. As before, he spent long hours at business sites, speaking to employers and trying to overcome their objections to hiring workers with no experience outside the agricultural sector. In addition, Sonny tried to identify farmworkers who might make satisfactory trainees. He found some of them among the people who dropped into the opportunity center looking for work, but to enlarge the pool, he was proactive. Even during the winter months, hundreds of migrant farmworkers remained behind in Washington County, many of them living in labor camps that were open for the winter. Sonny held meetings at those camps to inform the people about the OJT program and urge them to apply. Once Sonny or Ken Kimmel placed a trainee with an employer, they were required to visit them at specified intervals and, after the visit, write a report about their job performance. If problems were detected, more frequent visits were required and more reports had to be written.

The work was not without its difficulties. Even with financial incentives at their disposal, Sonny and Ken Kimmel had to work overtime to find enough suitable positions for the migrant and seasonal farmworkers who signed up. Some of the employers did not take seriously the responsibility of training the workers, viewing them as cheap labor and laying them off as soon as the VML stopped paying the weekly subsidy. A few of the workers were persistently tardy or otherwise unreliable. More than a few found it difficult to adjust to nonagricultural work. Sometimes there was tension at the workplaces because of cultural misunderstandings between the trainees and Anglo co-workers or Anglo supervisors.[21]

Sonny's supervisors at the VML, John Little in particular, were impressed with his work. On January 1, 1967, Sonny's salary was increased to $390, the top pay level for an assistant job counselor. At about this time, Little praised Sonny effusively in a merit rating report:

> His development as a leader and administrator has shown real promise. . . . He has conducted himself with dignity and courage demonstrating the judgment so necessary to good leadership.

. . . [He] works untiringly many extra hours and weekends because of his fine sense of dedication and commitment to his people. He is very perceptive and the people respond to his direction.[22]

Unfortunately, the many "extra hours" he was devoting to the job meant that he was unavailable to help out around the house. Librada assumed most of the burden of caring for the couple's two young children, Armando and Raquel. Her burden increased by at least 50 percent in March 1967, when the Monteses decided to adopt a newborn child, a girl named Olivia. Sonny was still two months shy of his twenty-third birthday and his family had grown to five.[23]

The Crumbling of the Pape Regime

Meanwhile, the VML was experiencing serious problems, which had been foreshadowed in the tensions between Ruby Ely and the VML leadership. The key area of concern was the participation— to be precise, the lack of participation—of farmworkers in the running of the organization. Despite the fact that CAAs such as the VML were expected to be mindful of the "maximum feasible participation" clause of the Economic Opportunity Act of 1964, the VML under Will Pape did little to include the poor in decision-making and governance.

From the early days of the organization's existence, VML policy statements had identified three different methods of including migrants and ex-migrants in program planning and execution. First, they could serve as members of the VML board of directors, the chief policy-making body of the organization. Second, they could hold positions on the VML staff. Third, at the local level, they could be members of area advisory boards, groups that were supposed to be organized by the opportunity centers to provide input about programmatic needs.[24]

But more than a year after the VML had begun operations, it had made limited progress along all three tracks. In the case of the area advisory boards, nothing was done. Furthermore, while farmworkers were represented on the VML board of directors, their participation was minimal. According to a policy adopted in June

1965, eighteen seats on the forty-six-person board were to be held by seasonal farmworkers. In theory, then, the VML was in compliance with an OEO guideline that at least a third of all board members of OEO-funded nonprofits be representatives of the groups served. In practice, only a handful of those farmworkers attended the meetings because they were held at times and places inconvenient to the workers and were conducted entirely in English, a language many of the Mexican American board members could not understand. Pape and his associates made no effort to accommodate the farmworkers on the board.[25]

In hiring staff members, the VML did only marginally better. For the first fifteen months of its existence, it gave no jobs in the central administration to former migrants. Moreover, it initially appointed only Anglo professionals to the position of area director. Although two ex-migrants, Ruben Contreras and Juan Ruiz, were asked to serve as assistant area directors during the VML's first summer of operations, some of the farmworkers viewed the former as a "Tío Tomás" (Uncle Tom), since he was on close terms with members of the Anglo establishment, and they had even stronger reservations about the latter, who had become a labor contractor. Ruiz eventually became the VML's first Mexican American area director in February 1966. Two other Mexican Americans were appointed to that position later in that same year—Contreras and Sonny's boss Jose Garcia (who, as we know, often disguised the facts that he was a Mexican American and that he came from a family of farmworkers). Meanwhile, most migrants and ex-migrants employed by the VML, Sonny Montes among them, held the lowest-paying positions in the organization: program aide, assistant job counselor, and janitor.[26]

The VML did not place power in the hands of farmworkers for the simple reason that Will Pape and his allies in the central administration did not want to do so. A career social worker and a longtime employee of the YMCA, Pape was disposed neither by training nor vocational experience to allow migrants and former migrants a significant role in the organization. His approach was paternalistic in the extreme. Pape often likened the migrants and seasonal farm served by the VML to "sick people" and he likened VML employees to "doctors," whose job it was to cure the sick. The migrants had the illness; the VML had the medicine. The migrants had the problems; the VML had the solutions. In the world according to Pape, there was little room for migrant agency and "maximum feasible participation." Pape's approach was more or less what might have been expected from a social worker of that period. As James Leiby writes in his history of social welfare and social work: "In general, the professionals conceived of their method by analogy with that of the physician: they made a *diagnosis*—a systematic assessment of a situation—and applied a *treatment* or *intervention*. . . . The idea of diagnosis implied a pathology, and that implied a normal state."[27]

As time passed, some members of the VML board of directors became worried that Pape's paternalistic approach was alienating the people whom the organization was supposed to serve. Tom Current, the founding father of the VML and a member of the board since May 1965, raised the concerns. In the summer of 1966, a board committee chaired by Current initiated a review of VML programs and policies. After meeting with migrants and ex-migrants at several locations and hearing a litany of complaints, the committee filed a report detailing a number of weaknesses in the agency. Chief among them was insufficient farmworker participation "at the Board of Directors level" and "at the area level." In late September 1966, as a direct result of the report, the board instructed Pape and his staff to increase the "participation of recipient groups."[28]

Following the board's directive, over a period of several months, the VML administration held a series of meetings at the Woodburn headquarters to discuss the issue of farmworker involvement in the organization. Pape and his staff took part, as did all the opportunity center directors. The discussions often dealt with specifics: for example, how many farmworkers should be included on the board, whether area advisory boards should be created, and, if so, what powers they should be given. At bottom, though, a philosophical issue was being debated. In one camp were Will Pape and his allies, the most loyal being Bob Wynia, the VML's assistant executive director, and Sam Granato, the head of the VML's day-care program. The key figure in the other camp was John Little, Sonny's boss. Little joined the discussions in Woodburn while they were in progress—the first meetings took place before he came to work for the VML in mid-October 1966. But, once he started attending, and notwithstanding the fact that he was a newcomer, he participated actively, demanding far greater farmworker involvement in the organization.[29]

For John Patrick Little, community development was an article of faith. No one in the VML had more experience with it. Born in Portland in 1926 and a graduate of the University of Portland, Little had spent much of his adult life as an educator. But in 1961, his life had taken a sudden turn, when he and his wife, Pat, had lost their youngest child, only six months of age. That experience caused the Littles to reevaluate their priorities. Both Catholics, they decided to enlist in the Papal Volunteers for Latin America (PAVLA), an organization that sent lay volunteers from the United States to assist Latin American bishops with problems in their jurisdictions. U.S. dioceses paid the expenses of most of the volunteers. Obtaining financial support from the Archdiocese of Seattle, the Littles and their remaining children left for Cuernavaca, where PAVLA had a training school for the volunteers.[30]

The training center at Cuernavaca, then known as the Center for Intercultural Formation, was the creation of Monsignor Ivan Illich, a Vienna-born priest and sociologist. The Cuernavaca center provided trainees with six hours of daily instruction in Spanish followed, after dinner, by lengthy lectures on Latin American culture. The language training was excellent, but in Little's view, the lectures on culture were even better. Illich's approach was iconoclastic and subversive. He brought in a team of Latin American speakers whose lectures had a common theme: the virtual certainty that the Papal Volunteers would fail at everything they tried to accomplish and that the indigenous people would hate them for their efforts. At one point, Illich told Little privately: "You Americans are so culturally chauvinistic. . . . I have brought these people here to test your chauvinism. If you can stand us, you can stand wherever you're going to."[31]

In addition to attending classes, Little did some reading on his own. In the early 1960s, there was much discussion in the United States about community development, but he had read nothing on the subject, nor had he heard much about it at the Cuernavaca center. Thinking that some grounding in community development techniques might be useful, Little went to the center's library in search of reading matter. He found only a single volume on the subject—*The Missionary's Role in Socio-Economic Betterment,* edited by John Considine, a Maryknoll missionary. The chapter Little found most valuable was one titled "Employment of Community Development Techniques." Its two principal themes were that the essence of community development was community self-help and that the role of the community development worker was "catalytic," rather than directive. The goal was to help the community to solve its own problems.[32]

In that chapter, Considine included a lengthy passage from an article by Carl C. Taylor, which described the execution of a community development program as a four-step procedure. The first step involved the identification by the community members of their "common felt needs." Next, the community needed to select and plan its first project. An important consideration in choosing that project was that it be "practically feasible"; it was important to succeed. Third, in executing the project, the community had to mobilize and harness almost completely "the physical, economic and social potentialities of the local community groups." The final, and most important, step was the creation within the community of "the determination to undertake additional community improvement projects." At that point, the development worker was superfluous.[33]

Following the training session, the Littles were assigned to Ecuador, where a bishop needed help with a variety of projects. Over the next four and a half years, John Little spent his time working with carpenters, mechanics, and shoemakers in Ecuador, attempting to improve the quality of the goods they produced and to increase their income. In dealing with them, he put into practice the techniques he had read about in Cuernavaca, acting as a facilitator rather than as a leader. All three groups established cooperatives. The carpenters and the shoemakers decided to build factories and the mechanics a shop. Gradually, Little's role shifted from catalyst to technician. He left the running of the cooperatives to the locals and focused on supervising the construction of the buildings and the installation of machinery. When the Littles left Ecuador in October 1966, the factories and the mechanics' shop were in operation. In the end, as John Little put it, he "had worked himself out of a job."[34]

Given his recent overseas experiences, Little had no doubt that Mexican American farmworkers were capable of identifying their own needs and planning their own projects. So, in the meetings at Woodburn, he pushed vigorously for change within the VML, and over time he prevailed. While Pape and his supporters continued to raise questions about the feasibility of giving more power to the poor, Little's side had the momentum. By the end of November 1966, the VML administration agreed to establish area advisory boards in all the opportunity centers.[35] Meanwhile, the OEO in Washington weighed in, applauding the VML's "efforts to get fuller and more meaningful participation of the farm worker" and urging the organization to place additional representatives of the "target group" on the board and in senior staff positions.[36] In January 1967, when a new board was elected, twenty-seven out of the fifty places went to farmworkers or former farmworkers.[37]

One thing worth noting about the struggle that was occurring within the VML is that, while the issues at stake were of great importance to Mexican Americans, who were thus far underrepresented in the organization, the principal contending parties were Anglos—on the one hand, Pape and his supporters; on the other, Current, Little, and a few other area directors, who were receiving a modest amount of support from OEO bureaucrats in Washington, D.C. This situation was somewhat different, then, from the highly publicized struggles that were taking place at about the same time in Los Angeles and other U.S. cities where the issue of underrepresentation of the target population by local government-controlled CAAs led to prolonged protest by minority groups and, ultimately, to the creation of new CAAs in those cities that were run by those minority groups. One obvious explanation for the difference is that, whereas in Los Angeles, there were substantial numbers of politically active African Americans and Mexican Americans who could and did mobilize to fight for their own interests, in Oregon's Willamette Valley the Mexican American population was, at this juncture, very small and not yet organized.[38] Hence, at the outset, Anglos such as Little would lead the battle—and they would do so by attempting to reform the existing CAA rather than launching a new one. But, in time, that would change, as Little would recruit a cadre of Mexican Americans to the community development campaign.

65

Having been defeated on the issues of the area advisory boards and farmworker representation on the board of directors, Pape and his clique were clearly in retreat. Then, in a seven-week span from mid-January 1967 to early March 1967, two developments raised new questions about Pape's leadership and ultimately led to his resignation. One was a personnel matter relating to a Mexican-born college graduate named Guadalupe (Lupe) Bustos, who ran the VML's adult education program in the Woodburn area.[39] A talented, inspiring teacher, Bustos was an argumentative and temperamental colleague. Bustos also despised his supervisor, the Woodburn area director Juan Ruiz, feeling that he was far better qualified than Ruiz to run the Woodburn Opportunity Center. In January 1967, there had been a flare-up between the two. After attending a VML-sponsored meeting at which farmworkers had charged that local labor contractors had made false promises to migrants in order to lure them to Oregon, Bustos had aired their complaints publicly. Himself a labor contractor and the brother of labor contractors, Ruiz was furious, interpreting the charges as being directed at him and his brothers. He then asked Pape to fire Bustos, which Pape did.

At that point, Bustos contacted local reporters and the VML board, charging that he had been treated unfairly. The board appointed a committee to investigate the charges, and after a few weeks, that committee reported that Bustos's firing had been unjustified, since it stemmed largely from "matters not related to the VML." That report convinced the board to reinstate Bustos and transfer Ruiz to another opportunity center. The decision was a blow to Pape. But when Bustos resumed work a few days later, he returned to his old ways, treating co-workers nastily. In early March 1967, Pape fired Bustos again and reappointed Ruiz as Woodburn area director. All those developments received extensive coverage in the press, conveying the impression that the VML was in disarray.

As the Bustos affair was coming to a head, Pape's administration was under public scrutiny for another matter. On February 28, the *Oregon Journal*, a paper that had given favorable coverage to the VML in the past, published the first of a series of stories about the VML, coauthored by two staff writers, Jim Lang and Marge Davenport. The VML, they wrote, "is a bureaucrat-ridden gravy train which is wasting money by the bundle and steadily alienating many of those it is supposed to serve." The reporters' most serious charges, supported by documents found in the VML's files, related to the organization's leasing of and service agreements for a fleet of automobiles (primarily Ford Galaxies). They asserted that the rates charged for the vehicles were excessive, suggested that the people who had negotiated the agreements were guilty of improprieties, and calculated the money wasted in 1966 at more than $50,000.[40] The articles had an immediate impact. OEO officials were appalled by the suggestion of possibly illegal conduct. In a preliminary report on the matter, an OEO evaluator found that, while the reporters' research was occasionally slipshod, "they have led us to a pattern of developments with sinister overtones." On March 6, 1967, Oregon congressman Al Ullman urged Sargent Shriver to initiate an investigation of the VML.[41]

Two days later, Pape submitted his letter of resignation, to become effective in a month. While he claimed that his leaving had nothing to do with the organization's problems, the truth was that the stress of the job had become too much for him. Just before his resignation, some VML employees had found Pape in a catatonic state in his Woodburn office and had to carry him out of the building. During Pape's last month with the VML, Kent Lawrence, the chairman of the VML board of directors, and Bob Wynia, the assistant director, divided between themselves the work of the executive director. Pape attended a few public functions, said almost nothing, and slipped out of town.[42]

The turmoil that engulfed the VML during the last six months of the Pape regime and the bad publicity that resulted from it should not blind us to the fact that, even during that period of disarray, the VML continued to provide an enormous amount of assistance to farmworkers in the Upper Willamette Valley. At the opportunity center level much valuable work was done by area directors such as Jose Garcia and John Little, job counselors such as Ken Kimmel, assistant job counselors such as Sonny Montes, teachers, and program aides. Data compiled by the VML itself testify to the number and range of the services that were rendered. Between January 1966 and March 1967, a total of 1,737 migrant and seasonal farmworker families were served by the VML. During that period, 2,973 "transportation services" were provided to those families, 2,087 "welfare services," 2,296 referrals to health agencies, and 496 referrals to legal aid agencies. In addition, VML staff members held 1,449 job interviews with members of the target population, enrolled 1,574 people of farmworker background in VML adult education classes, and, during the summer of 1966 alone, accommodated 2,401 children in VML child-care programs (1,412 of them in day-care and 989 in education programs). The VML also claimed to have assisted a total of 343 migrant families in settling in the Upper Willamette Valley.[43]

Such numbers are staggering, but they are also, numbers being only numbers, somewhat unsatisfying. The story of the VML, like the story of the emergence of the Mexican American community in Oregon, cannot be told simply by invoking aggregate statistics. At bottom, that story is about personal experiences and choices, and only from individual life histories can we ultimately gain a full understanding of the processes of social, political, cultural, and attitudinal change. Let us consider, then, the experiences and choices of Tina Garcia, one of the 1,574 people who attended the VML's adult education classes during the period January 1966–March 1967.

Born in Robstown, Texas, Tina Garcia had grown up in a migrant farmworker family that had traveled widely to make a living. By the early 1960s, Garcia's family had begun to spend much of the summer in the Pacific Northwest, going to Idaho to harvest beets, to Washington to pick berries, and to Oregon to pick pole beans. A good student, Tina had started high school in Texas but had not completed her degree. In the fall of 1966, twenty-years old and recently married, she found herself living and working in the Upper Willamette Valley of Oregon with her new husband. Her parents resided nearby and Garcia visited them regularly. During one such visit, her mother revealed that some employees of the VML had come to her house to discuss the organization's programs. Garcia's mother was especially interested in the VML's adult education classes—not for herself but for her daughter. She pressed Tina to contact the organization, telling her that it offered her the possibility of completing her high school degree. After returning to her home in Independence, Oregon, Garcia visited the opportunity center in that town, spoke to some staff members, and began going to an adult education class. In short order, it became clear that Garcia was a first-rate student, and her teacher referred her to the local adult-education supervisor, who gave Garcia a test. After grading it, the teacher announced to her that she was ready to take the GED examination. Three weeks later, in December 1966, Tina Garcia had her high school degree. Even so, she continued going to adult education classes in Independence.

Garcia's decision to contact the VML had already changed her life, but her relationship with the organization was only beginning. A few months after she got her GED, two major events occurred in her life: she and her husband separated and she learned that she was pregnant. Garcia's daughter was born in August 1967. Soon afterward, a VML employee named Esther Nash visited Garcia and asked her if she would consider applying for a position as a bilingual assistant in the VML's adult education program in Dayton, Oregon. Garcia applied for and was offered the job, and she began working for the VML in October 1967. She also resumed her education. The Dayton center had started a college preparation class and Garcia joined it. Then in the spring of 1968 the VML and Linfield College in McMinnville launched an experimental program to provide college classes at Linfield to five members of the farmworker community, with the school and the VML sharing the expenses. Garcia was chosen as one of the participants. She graduated from Linfield in three years and immediately moved on to a career as a teacher and educational administrator in Oregon, focusing on migrant education. From 1999 to 2001, she was associate superintendent of the Oregon Department of Education. Most recently, Tina Garcia has served as the director of the Region 16 Migrant Education Program of the Willamette Educational Service District, overseeing migrant education in six Oregon counties.[44]

The Further Education of Sonny Montes
Sonny had played no part in the debates in Woodburn in the fall of 1966 and the winter of 1967. As a low-level employee of the VML, he was excluded from them, even though he and other opportunity center employees were aware that they were going on. But, during those months and the ones that followed, he had a

series of discussions with John Little that dealt with many of the issues raised in Woodburn.

Most of the meetings took place in Little's office at the Hillsboro center. They were never scheduled; there was never an agenda. Sonny simply entered the office, and then and there he and John Little talked. Very social animals, both of them love to talk, especially Little. If talking were a competitive sport, John Little would be an Olympic champion. He loves to tell humorous anecdotes, and he tells them well, providing neither too much detail nor too little, slowly building up to the climax and, once he reaches it, erupting in a loud, jolly, infectious belly laugh that lasts for half a minute. His stories are works of art. Little loves to discuss religion, philosophy, sports, music, politics, history, sex, literature, child rearing, economics, medicine, law—frankly, there is little that John Little doesn't enjoy discussing. He is well read, well informed, excited by ideas. He is also opinionated, sometimes quite critical of others who disagree with him, and not the least bit shy about sharing his opinions with others. You always know where John Little stands on issues.

In their conversations in Hillsboro in late 1966 and early 1967, Sonny and John Little discussed a wide range of subjects. More often than not, though, at some point in their discussions, they focused on questions related to the governance of the VML. How representative was the VML of the population it served? Were farmworkers and former farmworkers capable of running the programs? Were they capable of being job counselors, and not merely assistant job counselors? Were they capable of being area directors? How much power should be given to area advisory boards? Little was preoccupied with these questions, since at the time he and Pape were wrestling with them in Woodburn. Sonny was interested in them too, since reports and rumors about the Woodburn debates were circulating within the organization.[45]

Reflecting back on those discussions in the Hillsboro center, the two men agree on many points, but their emphases are strikingly different. John Little describes the meetings as a discursive exploration of a number of related issues, culminating in an agreement on certain conclusions. He emphasizes the details of administrative reform. "We concluded that the people ought to be in charge, that they ought to be running the organization," he said at one point. "We concluded that the people were capable of being center directors, job counselors, and so forth," he said at another. "We concluded that the area advisory boards should be doing something, that they should have real power."

For Sonny, on the other hand, the conversations with John Little primarily addressed the single underlying issue of justice and injustice, not the specificities of VML governance. What bothered him most was that the VML was treating Mexican American farmworkers unfairly. As an assistant job counselor, he was doing exactly the same work as the job counselor but was receiving only a fraction of the pay. Virtually all the Mexican Americans in the organization had similar experiences, being assigned to subordinate, even menial positions while the top posts went to Anglos unfamiliar with the culture and language of the people they served. It was not that the administrative details did not matter to Sonny. It was rather that they mattered less than the larger issue, which was a personal and highly emotional one.

These two views of the same series of events are not incompatible. No doubt, the Little-Montes conversations dealt with both administrative reform and the issue of injustice. But, in this telling of the story of Oregon's Mexican Americans, we need to pay particular attention to Sonny's account: we need, in other words, to try to see those meetings not through the lenses of a forty-year-old Anglo community development specialist sympathetic to the poor, but through those of a somewhat unworldly twenty-two-year-old Mexican American former farmworker with special knowledge of prejudice, discrimination, and asymmetry. Once we do, it is readily apparent why the meetings affected Sonny so powerfully. By engaging in a dialogue with his youthful assistant job counselor about the VML, John Little, whether consciously or not, was tapping into a wellspring of resentment and anger that had long lain dormant within Sonny. For Sonny, as for others, the resentment and anger had their origins in life experiences: experiences of living in substandard housing during the months that he and his family engaged in migrant agricultural labor; of receiving an inferior elementary education in the segregated schools of Weslaco; of being excluded from restaurants, restrooms, movie theaters, swimming pools, and other public facilities because of his ethnicity; and of suffering a countless number of other slights, indignities, and humiliations.

Some of those experiences had affected him deeply.[46] There was the time, for example, in the early 1950s, when Sonny, his family, and other farmworkers had been traveling in a truck between Weslaco and Sinton, located in the vicinity of Corpus Christi, where they sometimes picked cotton. The driver of the truck was Sonny's uncle Pedro Jasso, his mother's oldest brother. The road they traveled on passed through the King Ranch, which occupied more than 800,000 acres of land spread out over four Texas counties. At some point along the way, one of the travelers started knocking loudly on the side of the truck to signal that a bathroom break was needed. After Pedro Jasso had brought the truck to a stop, all the passengers filed off, the women going to the right of the vehicle and the men to the left, crossing the road. Sonny's mother and two sisters, Gloria and Estella, joined the women, while Sonny accompanied his father. Since there were no trees or shrubbery alongside the road, he and his father scaled a fence and found a spot where they could relieve themselves.

Right after they had finished, an Anglo woman appeared, pointing a shotgun directly at them and yelling obscenities. Most likely she was an employee of the King Ranch, but to this day, Sonny isn't sure. Celedonio grabbed Sonny and the two of them ran back to the fence, scaling it hurriedly. The woman followed, still aiming the gun in their direction. Meanwhile, Sonny's mother and the other passengers heard the commotion, and when they saw the woman with her gun aimed at Celedonio and Sonny, they began screaming, afraid that the woman was going to fire. Fortunately, she fired no shots. All of the passengers hustled back to the truck and Uncle Pedro sped away.

There were times in high school when Sonny experienced overt prejudice. Back in the early 1960s, male students at Technical High School in Fort Worth had the option of taking physical education classes or participating in ROTC, and Sonny chose the latter. In the spring, the ROTC students held a dance. Sonny was interested at the time in an Anglo girl by the name of Linda Hawkins, and the two of them often interacted at school, walking together from class to class and meeting over lunch. But when he asked her to go to the dance with him, she wouldn't give him an answer. "She kept stalling and stalling," Sonny recalled. In the end, he cornered her and asked her, once and for all, whether she would accompany him. He remembers every syllable of her reply: "I don't know how to tell you this, Sonny, but my parents will not let me go out with Spanish Americans." When Sonny attended the ROTC dance that year, his date was a Mexican American girl.

And there was the time in the summer of 1962 when Sonny and his family were picking grapes on the farm of an old Armenian in the San Joaquin Valley. The farmer used to spend his days sitting in a rocking chair on the back porch of his house and scrutinizing the work of the people who harvested his grapes. He criticized the farmworkers ceaselessly. For his entire life, Sonny's father was an amiable, calm, even-tempered individual, someone who hardly ever showed anger, even when others mistreated him. But on this occasion, after the family was subjected to a barrage of abuse from the farmer, Celedonio decided that he had heard enough. "We're leaving and you are going to have to pay us," he announced to the farmer. The grower wrote them a check, but from the amount that he owed the Monteses he deducted a sum that, he claimed, was intended to cover their Social Security contributions. The Monteses knew that the farmer was lying about the deductions, since he had not asked them to provide their Social Security numbers when they had been hired. Celedonio and Sonny demanded the full amount, but the farmer refused: "Take the check or give it back to me," he said. The Monteses took the check.

The old Armenian was taking advantage of them because, in those days and in that place, he knew that he could get away with it. Political power in the San Joaquin Valley was in the hands of the growers. Most farmworkers, the Monteses included, were either not aware of their legal rights or not inclined to insist on them, recognizing that the authorities would not support them. In time, of course, things would change, thanks in large measure to the union-building efforts of AWOC and Cesar Chavez's NFWA, but in the summer of 1962, those organizations were in the very early stages of mobilizing farmworkers in California.[47] In need of money and faced with an intransigent grower, agricultural workers like the Monteses felt that their only option was to take the check.

The practice of deducting money for Social Security payments and then not making the payments was widespread in California's San Joaquin Valley and elsewhere. Also common was the practice of overcharging agricultural workers for rent and food. During the summer of 1961, Sonny and his family were lodged in a labor camp near Morgan Hill, California, their living quarters being a canvas tent pitched on a wooden platform that served as the tent floor. The camp also housed several hundred Mexican-origin male workers— *solteros* (unmarried men), as they were often referred to—who were crammed together in long wooden buildings that resembled army barracks. The *solteros* slept at night on small cots provided by the camp operator, and during the days, the camp served them simple meals. The amounts charged for those services often approximated the workers' wages. As a result, when the *solteros* collected their pay at the end of the week, they received almost nothing.

From his father, Sonny had learned to deal with such mistreatment by turning the other cheek, ignoring it as best he could, accepting the fact that life was like that, unfair and immutable. Sonny's meetings with John Little, on the other hand, raised the possibility that inequality and injustice did not necessarily have to be endured, that Mexican Americans could stand up for their rights, and that change was possible. When that happened, something appeared to snap in Sonny, and once the snapping occurred, things were never quite the same.

The transformation that took place within Sonny was similar to that which many Mexican Americans and African Americans experienced in that era. In some cases, the precipitating agent was formal education—exposure to new ideas in college courses, involvement in student activist groups, and the like. In some cases, it issued from the rising expectations that accompanied the political, legislative, and economic advances of the times. Among Mexican Americans—who, unlike the African Americans, had no system of colleges and no mentoring system in place—another catalytic agent was mentoring by Anglos, such as Fred Ross's mentoring of Cesar Chavez and John Little's of Sonny Montes. But, whatever the specific causes, the transformation that occurred typically featured two key components: a marked increase in ethnic self-consciousness and a more activist stance on economic, social, and political issues.

In Sonny's case, changes in behavior and attitudes could be detected almost immediately. As in the past, Sonny attended meetings of the opportunity center staff. But, whereas before, during Garcia's tenure as opportunity center director, he tended to be reticent, Sonny now became vocal. And as he became more outspoken, it became clear that he was a remarkably effective speaker. It wasn't so much that he was eloquent, although he could be. It was more that, with his impressive physical presence, the power of his voice, and his newfound conviction, Sonny seemed to command attention. At those VML staff meetings, Sonny focused on a single issue. He demanded that the Anglo professionals on the staff of the VML's opportunity centers be replaced with Mexican American farmworkers. He bore no personal animus toward his Anglo colleagues; in fact, he got on well with most of them. But, having come away from his meetings with Little with a sense of rage about the prejudice, discrimination, and injustice he, his family, and his people had suffered in the past and having also come to the conclusion that the VML was a fundamentally flawed organization, he insisted that immediate corrective action was necessary.

The Revolution

On April 7, 1967, the day Will Pape's resignation went into effect, the VML board of directors began a search for a new executive director. Several internal candidates stepped forward, among them Bob Wynia, the assistant executive director who had been loyal to Pape up to the end and was also on close terms with the OEO program analyst assigned to monitor the VML. Wynia lobbied hard for the job, but the board ultimately offered it to John Little. One important point in Little's favor was that many members of the board were sympathetic to his community development approach. A second was that, since he was fairly new to the organization, he bore no scent of the Ford Galaxie scandal. Little began his new job in Woodburn in the first week of May 1967.[1]

Almost immediately, Little had to turn his attention to preparing the organization for the arrival of the approaching migrant army. Additional staff members had to be hired for the summer months. Plans for the VML's component programs had to be finalized. Little also had to deal with the continuing fallout from the *Oregon Journal*'s exposé of the VML. Following the appearance of those stories, both the federal government's General Accounting Office (GAO) and the OEO had announced that they would conduct investigations into the VML's finances and procedures. The GAO quickly launched an audit, completing its on-site investigation before Little began his tenure as executive director. But the OEO auditors, slower off the mark, hadn't even started. Once they did, Little's workdays became much longer. Auditors peppered him with questions about past operations. Since Little knew almost nothing of the particulars, he found it necessary to immerse himself in the VML's files in order to provide the answers. The experience proved to be both time consuming and frustrating for Little, an investment of much energy in cleaning up a mess left by the former administration.[2]

Then there were personnel matters. As executive director, Little was surrounded by members of the old regime who had been his opponents during the VML's internal struggles in late 1966 and early 1967. The two he considered most problematic were Wynia and Sam Granato. Wynia, he felt, was philosophically hostile to community development. In his campaign to get the executive director's office, Wynia, aware that the board wanted to prioritize the participation of farmworkers, had tried to convey the impression that he had become a convert to community development, but Little doubted his sincerity. Granato was objectionable on two counts: he was not keen on community participation, and he nearly drove Little crazy with his efforts to quantify the VML's performance.[3]

During the Pape regime, the VML had been fixated on quantitative measures of performance. The fixation stemmed to some degree from the organization's dependence on grants from the OEO, an agency that, like most federal agencies, was also fixated on numbers. OEO directives and manuals required grantees to provide a wide array of quantitative data in their reports and grant renewal applications. One number the OEO was particularly interested in—and which OEO-funded agencies were instructed to provide—was the number of the organization's "contacts" with the people served. Neither the OEO nor the VML defined the word *contact* precisely, but, in most manuals and reports, it referred to interviews or meetings of VML employees with one member, or several members, of the target population. Contacts included house meetings, camp meetings, job counseling sessions, and at least a dozen other kinds of interactions. Some of these were transitory, some lasted several hours, but all were supposed to be counted.[4]

Under Pape, the VML's unofficial director of counting had been Granato, who, in addition to running the day-care program,

John Patrick Little, at the time of his appointment as executive director of the Valley Migrant League, May 1967. Photograph courtesy of John Little.

supervised in-staff training. Granato had devised a system of counting contacts, which he explained at excruciating length in the training sessions he conducted. All VML employees, including John Little, were given pads of printed forms called contact slips. The pads were supposed to be attached to the employees' belts, assuming they wore belts. Whenever a VML employee had an interaction with a migrant or seasonal farmworker, he or she was supposed to tear off a contact slip and fill it out immediately. The slips were passed on to superiors, and eventually all the recorded data were reported to VML headquarters, where totals could be calculated and then included in reports and other documents. High as the counts were, they conveyed the impression that sizable numbers of migrants and seasonal farmworkers were benefiting from VML activities.[5] In reality, though, they were more a measure of the amount of energy expended by the VML staff than of the effect of the organization's operations on people's lives.

Little intended to fire both Wynia and Granato but hadn't decided how or when. Sonny provided the impetus to make a decision. Shortly after Little's promotion, Sonny, still the assistant job counselor in Hillsboro, traveled to Woodburn to speak to his boss. The main subject of their discussion was Wynia. Sonny disliked Wynia intensely, considering him to be Janus-faced. "He'd come to us and say all the right things in front of us and then he'd go to the people in power and say 'We cannot allow these ex-farmworkers to take over the organization.'" In his meeting with Little, Sonny insisted that Wynia be dismissed immediately. "Why is this guy still here, John?" he asked. As Little recalls the episode: "I recognized that Wynia was bad news, but Sonny recognized that Wynia had to go right away, that we couldn't fool around with him."[6]

Little asked Wynia to resign, and the assistant executive director reluctantly agreed. The resignation was announced on June 29, 1967. For the record and the sake of appearances, Little reported that Wynia was "taking a position in another migrant project in California." On the same day, Little informed the board that Granato was also leaving the VML for another job opportunity. That departure was engineered by Little alone. Technically, Granato was laid off, not dismissed: his position was eliminated as a result of an administrative reorganization necessitated by a change in the way that the OEO funded the VML's day-care program. Granato moved on to a day-care position in another OEO-funded agency in Portland.[7]

In the great scheme of things, the firing of Bob Wynia was a minor event. In the context of Sonny Montes's story, however, it was significant, for it signaled that Sonny Montes, still a low-ranking employee of the VML, was beginning to play a key role in the organization. The tutorials in Little's office had taken. "Why is this guy still here, John?" Why, that is, have you, John Little, not gotten rid of someone you know to be an obstacle to the achievement of our goals? The student was lecturing the teacher. Having just begun his job as executive director, Little was already working himself out of it.

A Study Night

Another event occurred on June 29, 1967, the day Wynia was fired. Although the VML board of directors was scheduled to hold one of its regular monthly meetings on that date, it held instead, at Little's request, a "study night" in the town of Newberg, Oregon, about eighteen miles from Woodburn. The VML had held a few study sessions in the past, usually in remote communities, for the ostensible purpose of gauging the reactions of farmworkers and ex-farmworkers to VML policies. More often than not, the people in attendance griped about the organization's deficiencies. This time, the stated aim of the session was to give the representatives of the farmworker community an opportunity to discuss with Little and the board "the future direction of the VML." In other words, they were being asked to take part in program planning.[8]

Little had a clear motive in scheduling this meeting so early in his tenure. He wanted to transform the VML into a genuine community development organization as soon as possible, and he envisaged this study night as an important first step in the transformation. Furthermore, to insure that the session would achieve his objectives, he met beforehand with two members of the farmworker community who were also members of the VML staff to discuss how the meeting would be conducted. One of the people he consulted was David Aguilar, the assistant job counselor in the

Aumsville Opportunity Center, and the other was Sonny. While the three of them did not completely script the meeting that was to take place, they worked out most of the details in advance.[9]

Thirty-eight people attended the session in Newberg. About twenty of them were members of the board, including the chairman, Kent Lawrence. All of the VML's area directors were present, as well as Little and a few other members of the central administration. Finally, there were eight people who were described in a board member's report of the event as "farmworkers from Spanish-American clubs." Included in the last category were Sonny and David Aguilar, representing Los Amigos of Washington County and the Club Latino-Americano of Jefferson, respectively, and Ventura Rios and his brother Jose Rios, both members of the Yamhill County Farm Workers Organization. Like Sonny and David Aguilar, Ventura Rios had once served on the VML staff, but he had since turned his attention to organizing a farmworkers' union in Oregon.[10]

Los Amigos, the organization Sonny represented, had been founded in early October 1966. Made up of about twenty Mexican American families in Hillsboro and the vicinity, it began as a social club, holding informal meetings in members' homes and sponsoring social activities. In that sense, it was very different from VIVA, also based in the Hillsboro area and led by Emilio Hernandez, which had an overtly political agenda and saw itself as a rival to the VML. The two leaders of Los Amigos—its president, Eddie Lopez, and its vice president, Margarito Treviño—were favorably inclined toward the VML and uncomfortable with VIVA's continuing opposition to it. Treviño, a former migrant farmworker, had taken and completed the VML's GED preparation class. Lopez was one of the farmworker members on the VML board. Sonny had joined Los Amigos in November 1966, right after he and Librada had moved to Hillsboro from Duyck's camp in Cornelius. He attended the club's sessions regularly and even helped to compose the organization's song at a meeting in December 1966. In April 1967, when Los Amigos sponsored a fund-raising Mexican dinner for a Hillsboro-based migrant-assistance organization called Valley Volunteers, Treviño served as "kitchen chairman" and Sonny was master of ceremonies.[11]

The inclusion of representatives of the farmworker clubs at the study session was a tactical decision by Little, Montes, and Aguilar.

Since the establishment of the VML, one of the stated objectives of the organization had been to foster the development of groups or clubs of "ex-migrant residents." Although the policy had been largely ignored during the Pape regime, as had been evident during the central administration's battles with Ruby Ely and VIVA, Little was intent on nurturing and empowering the clubs, since he saw them as key players in the VML's community development efforts. As of mid-1967, there were nine of them in the Upper Willamette Valley, including VIVA (which was not represented at the June 1967 meeting because it still officially refused to have any affiliation with the VML). They all included between fifteen and thirty-five families.[12]

Since the three planners intended the eight club representatives to be the central players in the Newberg meeting, those eight were positioned at a table in the front of the room, facing the other participants. Sitting together as a panel, they led a discussion with the board members and the VML staff about the organization's problems. Sonny served as moderator, pursuant to a decision reached at the Little-Montes-Aguilar planning session. "The meeting needed a leader," Little explained. "You had to have a guy who could talk. David Aguilar was a bright guy, but he could drone on at a meeting. Sonny could talk." From the outset, the representatives of the clubs adopted a very critical stance toward the VML, faulting it for giving insufficient power and responsibility to the farmworker communities it served. Then they offered concrete suggestions, presenting the board and the VML staff with six resolutions that they had drafted in preparation for the meeting. All were intended to increase the role of farmworkers in the VML.[13]

Two of the six resolutions addressed specific perceived deficiencies. One dealt with the farmworkers' concerns about the quality of day-care provided to migrant children. In the summer of 1967, unlike in the past when the VML mounted a full-fledged day-care program of its own, the VML had been directed by the OEO to contract with local providers for day-care services. According to the panel, most communities could not accommodate the day-care needs of migrant families. It was resolved, therefore, that the VML make a greater effort to encourage farmworker groups and churches to organize day-care centers. A second resolution concerned the stipends paid to people attending the VML's adult education and vocational training classes. Feeling that the stipends were too low and that some stipend recipients were not sufficiently motivated, the farmworkers urged (and it was resolved) that the stipends be increased and that the club representatives assist the VML staff in choosing qualified candidates for the programs.

Three resolutions focused explicitly on the issue of farmworker involvement in the VML. One, echoing a familiar theme, called for the hiring of more ex-migrants by the organization. To expedite the process, the people attending the meeting also urged that the job descriptions for VML positions be revised to make it possible for people lacking academic credentials to be considered for them. Two other resolutions encouraged more frequent contact between the VML leadership and farmworkers—one urging the executive director and area directors to spend more time with migrants, the other calling for regular meetings between the officers of the farmworker clubs and the area directors. A final resolution concerned the VML board of directors, which the farmworkers believed was too large to do its work effectively. The panel suggested that the full board meet only four times a year, that professional interpreters attend those meetings to provide translations so that non-English speakers could understand the proceedings, and that committees shoulder more responsibility.

Over several hours, the club representatives, the board members, and the VML staff debated the resolutions. Although a few board members were defensive about the panel's criticisms of the organization, there was general support for the package of resolutions, including the idea of undertaking a complete reorganization of the board. After making a few cosmetic changes, the group adopted all six resolutions.[14]

The meeting of June 29, 1967, was a turning point in the history of the VML. For the first time, Mexican American farmworkers were setting the agenda. Instead of being an organization that acted in the interest of farmworkers, it was becoming, under Little's leadership, one that responded to the expressed needs of farmworkers. The meeting also confirmed, this time in a public forum, Sonny Montes's emergence as a key participant in both the VML and the Mexican American community. He was involved in the planning session with Little and Aguilar that preceded the study night; he participated in drafting the resolutions that were discussed; he was one of the representatives of the farmworker clubs that ran the meeting; and he moderated the discussion that led to the approval of the resolutions. Sonny was now helping to change the culture of the organization that employed him and developing policies that would improve the lives of the people it served. The role he played at the Newberg meeting suggested that he would not likely remain an assistant job counselor for long.

A Promotion

When John Little took over the leadership of the VML in early May 1967, the Hillsboro Opportunity Center was left without an area director. Typically, it took the VML a month or two to fill such a position, and in the interim, one of the "professionals" already on the staff would serve as temporary area director. In this instance, Chuck Campbell, the area teacher (who was responsible for the adult education program in Washington County), was asked to do that. A bright, friendly, capable man, Campbell made no secret of the fact that he wanted to be the permanent area director in Hillsboro. But the job was not Campbell's for the asking. The VML was required to advertise the opening, review the applications, and interview candidates before making an appointment. As the job search unfolded, several other candidates emerged, Sonny Montes among them.

Sonny was an ambivalent candidate. In the past, when he had talked with John Little about whether someone like himself was capable of serving effectively as an area director, Sonny had stated confidently that a former farmworker could probably do a better job than a professional, since he or she had a better understanding of the needs of the people served by the VML. But, when the theoretical possibility became a real opportunity and Little asked Sonny whether he was interested in applying for the area directorship, Sonny expressed reservations. He worried aloud about how he, with no college degree and administrative experience, would be able to supervise college graduates such as Campbell and his former boss Ken Kimmel. Would they resent his promotion? Would there be friction? Given Sonny's lack of credentials, wouldn't the VML be more inclined to choose someone with more education and experience?

The job search lasted for slightly more than two months. Several candidates were interviewed, including Sonny and Chuck Campbell. As expected, during Sonny's interview, concerns were raised about his lack of formal qualifications and his ability to do the job, but, in the end, the hiring committee chose him, impressed with his work performance and undoubtedly influenced by Little's strong endorsement. By now, it was common knowledge in the VML that Sonny was one of Little's most trusted advisors. "I took some heat because of that decision," Little admits today, but he believed that it was the right one and ignored the criticism. Sonny assumed the post of Hillsboro's area director on July 15, 1967, slightly more than a year after he had joined the VML as a program aide.[15]

Six days later, an article announcing Sonny's appointment appeared in *Opportunity News*, the VML's bilingual newspaper circulated in the Upper Willamette Valley. Beside the two columns of text describing Sonny's life was a striking photograph of him. Viewed in profile, seated at a desk, wearing a starched long-sleeved white shirt and a tie but with his right sleeve rolled up almost to his elbow, he looked the part of an area director, a man whose job involved both supervising employees in the office and doing his own share of work in the community. He appeared to be older than twenty-three, serious, intense. The story itself emphasized Sonny's humble origins, presenting him as the man of the people that he was. "Celedonio 'Sonny' Montes has always been near the fields. As a child he traveled from Texas east to Indiana and Illinois with his

Profile of Sonny Montes at the time of Sonny's appointment as area director of the Hillsboro Opportunity Center. Photograph from Opportunity News, *published by the VML, July 21, 1967, 3; image created from a microfilmed copy.*

family to harvest the crops." The sentences that followed conveyed the message that such a man brought a valuable perspective to the job, since he understood the people he served. A quote from Sonny drove home the point. "My life is much the same as before. . . . I am working with people and workers I have always known. We are in this together—the workers, the community, and the VML."[16]

Little's Ordeal

In the first ten weeks of Little's tenure as executive director, there had been definite signs of forward movement in the VML. Old enemies were dismissed, a young ally was promoted, summer programs were up and running, and steps were taken to increase significantly the participation of farmworkers in the organization. Then, three developments caused the situation to change for the worse for both Little and the VML.

The first concerned the audits. On July 18, 1967, the GAO issued a report of its investigation of the VML's finances. The OEO's auditors filed their own report on August 31. While neither agency determined that illegal conduct had occurred, both concluded that much money had been wasted. John Little and members of the VML board were directed to respond. The auditors' reports, discussed at length by the press, appeared to confirm the thrust if not all the details of the *Oregon Journal*'s exposé.[17]

Second, there were definite indications that federal funding for War on Poverty programs was going to be cut. Around the United States, urban riots and bad publicity about CAP programs had raised concerns about the efficacy of the OEO's efforts. Furthermore, the escalating costs of U.S. involvement in Vietnam had made it clear that the federal government simply did not have enough money both to fight a costly overseas war and to fund fully Johnson's Great Society programs.[18] The situation was especially dicey for a scandal-tainted OEO-funded organization that had already received so much money from the federal government. For the twelve-month period April 1, 1967–March 31, 1968, the OEO had made grants to the VML totaling more than $1.3 million, a slight increase over the amount given in the previous funding cycle even though the VML no longer ran summer schools for migrant children, those

85

having been taken over by the state's Department of Education.[19] In the more hostile funding environment that prevailed by the summer of 1967, a reduction of the VML budget seemed inevitable.[20]

Third, there was tension between Little and the Migrant Division of the OEO—a development that would have been troublesome in flush times, but was potentially crippling at a time when funding cuts were being discussed. The OEO program analyst assigned to the VML, Gene De la Torre, had strong opinions about how the VML should do its job; Little believed that De la Torre, who came from a family of labor contractors, was ill-suited to oversee migrant programs and also suspected that the program analyst was being fed false information about the VML by Bob Wynia, the disgruntled former assistant director. On August 24, 1967, following a six-day visit to the VML, De la Torre wrote a negative evaluation of the organization, asserting that the new executive director "has not been able to get the program off the ground." He directed Little to reduce staff levels, eliminate three of the seven opportunity centers, and increase the level of farmworker participation on the board (a very strange order given the fact that the VML was in the process of doing precisely that). In a follow-up letter to the VML board, Noel Klores, De la Torre's OEO supervisor, endorsed the program analyst's directives and warned that, unless the VML began operating at "peak efficiency," his office could not justify giving it additional funds.[21] Then, on September 13, 1967, De la Torre called Little to tell him that the VML was likely to receive no more than $800,000 in the next funding cycle, with most of it being not new money but rather unexpended funds from previous grants.[22] The projected cut was almost 40 percent. Aware that the organization's future was in doubt, the VML board immediately appointed a task force led by Little and Tom Current to respond to the criticisms from the auditors, the press, and OEO officials and to lead the fight against the budget cuts.[23]

In the end, the organization survived, due largely to the efforts of the task force and help received from an influential ally, Senator Wayne Morse. Morse had only recently become interested in the VML. Shortly after the task force was created, its members determined that they needed friends in high places in order to prevail in the escalating battle with the OEO's Migrant Division. The method chosen was to invite all the members of Oregon's congressional delegation to a "demonstration day" at the Woodburn headquarters to learn firsthand about the VML's programs. One congressman, John Dellenback, and one senator, Morse, agreed to come, but their schedules were so full that it was impossible to arrange a single session at which both could be present. Consequently separate sessions were arranged.[24]

The one with Morse took place at Woodburn on the evening of November 9, 1967. The meeting included presentations by Little and other members of the VML staff about the organization's programs, a discussion of the VML's recent problems by Tom Current, and a question-and-answer session involving Morse and his assistants. One of the presenters on that evening was Hillsboro's new area director Sonny Montes, who was given the assignment of discussing "community involvement." He stood out. "Sonny Montes did a beautiful job of telling about Hillsboro, participation, needs in housing, etc.," commented Mary Kay Rowland of Stella Maris House, a member of the VML task force, who took notes about what transpired. By all accounts, Morse came away with a favorable view of the VML. "Morse listened. He seemed interested and understanding," observed Rowland. The senator said that he wanted to sit in on a few of the VML's adult education classes, expressed an interest in having dinner with the task force at a later date, and, most important, offered to assist the VML in resolving its differences with the OEO.[25]

That offer proved to be invaluable to the VML, as its relations with the OEO continued to deteriorate. By late November 1967 Klores of the Migrant Division was threatening to cut off all funding to the VML:

> The Valley Migrant League, as it is presently constituted, is inadequate to implement a program of the magnitude and complexity for which it has been funded. . . . Whether or not the Valley Migrant League will be phased out entirely as of March 31, 1968, or allowed to continue a portion of present operations will depend entirely on the procedures implemented to strengthen [the] program and administration along the lines recommended.[26]

Little meanwhile continued to endure what he considered bad treatment from De la Torre. Finally, in January 1968, concerned that the OEO was intent on destroying the VML, Little appealed to Senator Morse for the help he had offered. In response, Morse and his staff intervened on the VML's behalf.[27] The OEO immediately removed De la Torre as program analyst for the VML, replacing him with Hank Aguirre, who proved to be more supportive. The tone of the communications between the funding agency and the nonprofit improved as well, and the Migrant Division agreed to allow the VML to operate five opportunity centers, not four as it had previously insisted. There was no longer any suggestion that the VML would be phased out. But, even with Morse's intervention, the OEO, strapped for cash, was unable to fund the VML at a level comparable to that of previous years. On March 15, 1968, Little learned that the organization would receive only $610,000 for the period April 1, 1968–March 31, 1969, with more than 60 percent of that amount being unexpended old money. In the future the VML was to be a pared-down nonprofit, focusing on adult education and job training.[28]

Although John Little prevailed in his battles with the OEO Migrant Division, an enormous amount of time was invested in the effort. "For months, I was under siege," he recalls. "They'd fire memo after memo at us, and I'd have to respond. I was just trying to survive the onslaught from Washington."[29] One consequence of the time investment was that Little and his allies in the organization could not move as quickly as they would have liked in implementing the six resolutions adopted at the study night of June 29, 1967. While there was forward movement, the pace was erratic.

The progress was greatest on the agenda items that were easiest to implement—the setting up of day-care centers, for example, which did not require the cooperation of OEO personnel. In fact, opportunity center directors, Sonny among them, met immediately with farmworker groups and local churches for the purpose of creating day-care centers. In Washington County, this cooperative activity resulted in the establishment of a center in Forest Grove; in other communities, VML employees and local residents achieved similar results. By all accounts, these newly created centers were successful. Even the OEO's Migrant Division, highly critical of most VML operations at the time, had to acknowledge that the organization's day-care program was "functioning effectively."[30]

Contact between the opportunity centers and farmworker groups also increased, and those groups interacted more frequently with the VML leadership. In addition, the VML quickly adopted a new procedure in choosing stipend recipients. After receiving applications for the programs and screening the applicants to make sure they were eligible for funding, the staff of each opportunity center met with an advisory committee of farmworkers to choose the recipients. Throughout the VML, it was generally felt that the new way of doing things was superior to the old. But there was also some frustration, because in this period of cutbacks the OEO balked at raising stipend levels.[31]

Unfortunately, the progress was slower on the two agenda items that were most important—the reorganization of the VML board of directors and the proposed changes in the VML's hiring practices. There were extenuating circumstances. Although there was considerable support on the board for both resolutions, members had different ideas about how to implement them. Initially, committees were given the tasks of debating the merits of the proposals and rewriting the VML's manual of operations, the latter assignment being necessary because, in order to restructure the board and revise the organization's hiring practices, the organization's by-laws and policy statements had to be changed. All that took time, which was at a premium because of the ongoing battles with the Migrant Division.[32]

As a result, the VML's nominations committee, which was charged with working out a plan to reorganize the governance of the VML, did not complete its deliberations until early November 1967. The board held a preliminary discussion of that plan on November 29, and finally, on December 27, it approved a package of new by-laws and related documents that transformed the way that the VML would do business in the future. One of the approved changes increased considerably the percentage of farmworker representatives on the VML board of directors, with each of the farmworker clubs sending two members apiece. Another reduced the number of meetings of the full board to only four a year.

Henceforth, the board's executive committee was to do most of the important work of the organization. That body was expanded from nine to sixteen members, with the added requirement that at least seven of those members were to be farmworkers. Two co-chairmen, one of whom was to be a farmworker, were to preside over it.[33]

In late January 1968, a new VML board was elected according to the new procedures. Mary Kay Rowland, who attended the session, commented afterward: "We were a little surprised in the end to see how many farmworkers were on the Board and Executive Committee, but pleased also." Beginning with that session, interpreters also attended meetings of the VML board and the entire discussion was translated for the benefit of non-English speakers.[34]

The VML made the least progress of all in hiring more staff members from farmworker backgrounds. Between July 1967 and March 1968, a committee of the board devoted many hours to the task of rewriting job descriptions, and the proposed revisions were discussed at a few board meetings. But, as of April 1968, the VML had not changed its hiring policies, and few people from farmworker backgrounds, Sonny being an obvious exception, held responsible positions in the organization.[35]

Sonny as Area Director

Following his promotion to area director in July 1967, Sonny focused on his new job responsibilities. He spent some of his time trying to convince government officials and local investors to build low-income housing in Washington County. As he told the VML board of directors at a meeting in November 1967, the "urgent need" of the seasonal farmworkers served by the Hillsboro Opportunity Center was affordable housing. He devoted attention to the Hillsboro center's migrant camp outreach program, which won praise from the central administration for its "creative use of movies as an attention getting factor." With assistance from Sonny, a legal aid clinic was set up in Hillsboro and the opportunity center also began work with community groups to create a medical clinic for poor families. As before, the center provided job-counseling services and administered its own OJT, adult education, and vocational training programs.[36]

A major requirement of Sonny's new job was attendance at meetings, mostly with farmworkers past and present in Hillsboro and the surroundings towns. Sonny had some experience with conducting meetings, since as a program aide and assistant job counselor he had held many of them at migrant camps. But, in his new position of area director, the purpose of the sessions was not to recruit people to VML programs but rather to assist members of the settled farmworker community in identifying needs and solving problems. In other words, Sonny was serving as an agent of community development.

Most of what Sonny knew about community development techniques was derived from John Little. During the spring of 1967, in the period between Pape's defeat and Little's promotion to the position of executive director, he and Sonny had continued to meet several times a week at the Hillsboro Opportunity Center. One topic that came up often was community development. (As Little put it: "We spent a lot of time rapping about empowering people.") At the time, Little was even more preoccupied than usual with the subject, since he and two other area directors, following up on their victory over Pape, were lobbying hard within the VML to adopt a community development approach in the organization's interactions with farmworkers.[37]

During those sessions at Hillsboro, Little gave Sonny a mini-tutorial on community development techniques, drawing both on the literature he was familiar with (including the book by Considine he had found in the Cuernavaca library) and his own experiences as a Papal Volunteer in Ecuador. They talked at length about strategies that could be used to encourage a community to solve its own problems, the techniques that could be adopted in conducting meetings, and the types of community projects that could realistically be accomplished. A recurrent theme was the notion that the principal responsibility of the community organizer was to assist and enable, but never to dictate.[38]

After Little became executive director, he attended a number of the meetings organized by Sonny with groups in Washington County and had an opportunity to observe Sonny's efforts to put these ideas into practice. "He was a natural at community organization," Little recalled, the proud teacher discussing his prize pupil. Sonny never tried to tell people what to do, never acted like a "caudillo." He kept his comments to a minimum, listening carefully and intervening only for a few limited purposes—to review the practical solutions that had been suggested by the discussants or to challenge the group to make a decision. Little was especially impressed with Sonny's "talent for taking shit." In several sessions attended by the executive director, local residents made personal comments about Sonny, some rather mean spirited, accusing him of being a radical, a Tío Tomás, and so forth. Sonny never responded in kind, always trying to redirect the discussion to the problems at hand and encouraging the people to focus on developing their own solutions to those problems. Sonny "inspired hope," said Little.[39]

In spite of Sonny's promotion to area director, his contributions to the organization, and the high regard in which he was held, his salary at the VML did not increase appreciably. While the advertised starting salary for an area director was $667 a month, Sonny was not automatically entitled to that amount because he was a continuing employee rather than a new one. Instead, his salary was determined by a formula recently adopted by the OEO as a cost-cutting measure, which prohibited OEO-funded organizations from giving salary increases of more than 20 percent in any calendar year to employees already on the payroll. Obliged to apply the new formula to Sonny, the VML set his monthly salary at $468, exactly 20 percent above the $390 he had earned as assistant job counselor. As a result, his monthly pay was $265 less than that of any other area director in the VML; it was even lower than that of several of the staff members he supervised in Hillsboro.[40]

Sonny's supporters in the VML attempted to address the inequity. The same OEO memorandum that placed the 20 percent cap on salary increases permitted the OEO regional office to make exceptions in extraordinary circumstances. So Little and Tom Current appealed to that office to remedy the injustice and to waive the application of the formula. Current wrote: "When a member of the client group shows sufficient potential and achievement to progress and bring himself out of poverty it is most difficult to justify holding that employee at a wage barely above the poverty level." Unfortunately, the upper-level administrators would not budge. "There is no question as to the services Mr. Montes has provided to migrant and seasonal farm workers," Noel Klores acknowledged in a letter to Little in early February 1968, but, in the agency's view, Sonny's "work history" did not warrant a salary comparable to that of other area directors.[41]

By the time Klores had rendered his decision on salary, Sonny had moved on to a new assignment, this time as area director in Woodburn. The change in location was necessitated by the budget cutbacks that the OEO had initially imposed on the VML. Forced in December 1967 to reduce the number of opportunity centers from seven to four, Little closed down the ones in Hillsboro, Independence, and Sandy. Meanwhile, a personnel committee evaluated the seven area directors to determine which four of them should be retained and which three should be let go. Rated second out of the seven, Sonny was asked to stay on. One of the dismissed employees was Juan Ruiz, the area director in Woodburn, the same man whose struggle with Lupe Bustos had contributed to Pape's downfall. Sonny replaced Ruiz in Woodburn in January 1968.[42]

Plotting Revolution

Since he was now working in Woodburn, Sonny was able to interact more often with John Little and to lobby more effectively for the policies he favored. One issue above all preoccupied him and other Mexican Americans in the VML at this time: the fact that the organization had not yet done anything of consequence to promote more farmworkers and ex-farmworkers to staff positions of responsibility and influence. Both in staff meetings and in private discussions with Little, Sonny spoke out insistently and often in favor of replacing the Anglo professionals with Mexican American farmworkers. "Sonny kept pushing me," Little remembers. The young area director was upset that the VML had not made more headway on that front. As was the case with the decision to dismiss Wynia, Sonny was taking the lead, furnishing additional evidence that Little's mentoring had been successful and that the impetus for change was now shifting from Anglo advocates of community development, such as Little and Current, to Mexican Americans such as Sonny.[43]

And as was also the case with the firing of Wynia, the pressure applied by Sonny produced results. By the early spring of 1968, with the organization no longer under attack from the OEO Migrant Division, Little began to meet regularly with Sonny, David Aguilar, a few other Mexican American employees of the VML, and several members of the farmworker community to discuss the issue of VML staffing policies. The meetings soon turned into planning sessions. "Here's what happened," Little explained, using words reminiscent of the ones he used to describe his earlier meetings with Sonny in Hillsboro. "We agreed that we should make changes, that all these positions [in the VML] should be taken over by farmworkers. We agreed on when it was going to happen and how it was going to happen. And we agreed to announce it at a board meeting." In effect, tired of waiting for the VML board to come up with a plan to place more farmworkers in positions of responsibility, this group was going to force the board to implement changes immediately.[44]

Little and the other planners decided that the announcement would be made at the VML board of directors meeting on April 28, 1968, scheduled to be held at the Jason Lee Methodist Church in Salem. The group chose Sonny and David Aguilar to lead the discussion at that session. Beforehand, Little and Sonny did "a lot of politicking" with Tom Current and other like-minded individuals on the board to insure that they would cooperate. Current was enthusiastic, feeling that the proposed change was overdue; a few people raised questions, but they appeared to be willing to go along. On the night before the planned event, Sonny organized an open-air meeting at a park in Dayton, which was attended by a number of Mexican American employees of the VML and members of farmworker clubs from Salem, Independence, Dayton, and Washington County. Following the script of the study night ten months earlier, Sonny wanted to present the board with a package of concrete proposals to discuss. Of the ten resolutions agreed to, two were deemed essential: one requiring the VML to place people from a "farmworker background" in all the key positions in the opportunity centers and one demanding changes in the VML's operations manual that would eliminate "educational requirements for VML employment."[45]

At the board meeting itself, Sonny set the tone in his opening remarks. The key issue, he stated, was who controlled the VML. Was it "a program of the people," or did it belong to the "power structure"? Up to this point, the people had not been in charge. "If you look at the problem realistically, your conscience will bother you. We have been taken advantage of by this organization, by the conditions in the camps . . . , by the wage that is paid to some of the people." The problem, in short, was asymmetry. An organization that was funded to help Mexican American farmworkers was treating them unjustly. Sonny's comments were harsh and combative. As Mary Kay Rowland of Stella Maris House observed after the fact: "He has become fired up for La Raza."[46]

Sonny then addressed the ten resolutions that had been drafted the previous night, focusing on the failure of the VML to place people of farmworker background in charge of the opportunity centers:

> We have had problems for three years. We have been here
> three years and have not had farmworkers as area teachers, area
> directors, job counselors, etc. We are willing to learn and we
> have not had an opportunity to be in these positions. . . . We
> have not been given a chance to prove that we can do these
> things. The majority are tired of asking for things.[47]

Challenged to provide specifics, Sonny cited chapter and verse. Assistant job counselors did the same work as job counselors but received a fraction of the pay. One Mexican American assistant job counselor, who had held the job for several years, had been obliged to train three of his supervisors. "He has been ready to be a job counselor ever since he came into the program and knows the job better than the job counselors."

In the discussion that followed, Little, Current, and most of the other people in attendance endorsed the changes Sonny was asking them to make. Citing the results of staff evaluations, Little supported Sonny's assertion that farmworkers were capable of doing staff jobs that up to then were held primarily by Anglo professionals: "We have found that the most effective contact people with farmworkers are their own people. . . . We have to face the basic problem that farmworkers do not completely trust the middle-class professional people as advisors but would trust their own people."[48] Current admitted that he was disappointed that the VML had not moved more quickly in promoting farmworkers within the organization.

The only disagreement concerned the timing of the proposed staffing changes, with some members of the board arguing that a transition period would be necessary and Sonny pushing for implementation "as soon as possible." Actually, the difference between the two positions was not great. No one on the board even hinted that the transition period should extend more than a few months, and Sonny himself had to concede that the changes could not occur overnight. Even so, Sonny became visibly upset at several points in the discussion. What bothered him most was that the Anglo board members were stating their opinions at all. When Current suggested a procedure for filling the staff positions, Sonny barked: "You are telling us what to do. We want to make our own decisions as to who we want and who is to be the area teacher." When another board member offered some other ideas, he said: "I do not think we want to discuss what you think we should have, but what we want to have." As assertively as he could, Sonny was telling the Anglo-dominated board that, from that day forward, the agenda of the VML was to be set by farmworkers. Even some of Sonny's strongest supporters on the board were unsettled by his remarks. Mary Kay Rowland wrote after the meeting: "'We don't want you telling us anything—We're here to tell you.' [This] is part and parcel of the basic philosophy. But does that mean cutting out everybody?"

In the end, the formula agreed to at the session was that the transfer of authority would take place within two months, with the specifics to be worked out by John Little in consultation with the farmworker community. The other nine resolutions were agreed to as well. Immediately afterward, in an interview with the press, Little pronounced the meeting a success, indicating that he was "pleased" with the discussion and the outcome. The Salem *Capital Journal* reported:

> Little said the change stems from a belief of the migrants that "they can communicate with their people better than our professionals can." . . . Little added that the full participation

by migrants is a goal of the federally financed program and the board's action is in keeping with that objective.[49]

For Sonny and his Mexican American allies, too, the results of the board meeting were satisfying. Three years after it had been funded into existence, the VML was being transformed from an organization controlled by Anglos that served farmworkers into one that was to be largely directed by farmworkers. At the local level, area advisory boards and farmworker clubs were already functioning; within the VML board of directors, farmworkers and their supporters were setting the agenda; and in the opportunity centers, farmworkers were about to take over the key administrative jobs. The VML of Will Pape was dead.

The policy changes adopted by this Oregon-based migrant-assistance organization constituted a clear victory for the principle of "maximum feasible participation." As it happens, such victories were not so commonplace in the War on Poverty's Community Action Program. Although it is perilous to generalize about a program that included so many separate agencies, it is probably fair to say that, over the entire course of the War on Poverty, a majority of CAAs gave only lip service to the notion of involving the communities served in policy development and implementation. Those that did otherwise were primarily stand-alone nonprofits that were not dominated by local political hierarchies and received their funding directly from Washington, D.C. Some of them came into existence because of dissatisfaction with existing local government-controlled CAAs—for example, the Watts Labor Community Action Committee, which was organized because African Americans in Los Angeles felt that the city's official War on Poverty agency was not meeting their needs. Some, like the VML, were the product of initiatives set in motion by the OEO hierarchy.[50] But, as the VML's experience illustrates, direct funding from Washington was no absolute guarantee that community participation would be prioritized. The VML became a farmworker-run organization only after a lengthy period of struggle.

At the time, the local press described the events that transpired in the Salem church on April 28, 1968, as a "revolution." That is also the word that Sonny and his former colleagues have used ever since to refer to the changes they produced. Significantly, there was an ethnic dimension to those developments. Most of the migrant and seasonal farmworkers who labored in Oregon's fields in the mid- to late-1960s—and hence most of the people served by the VML—were Mexican Americans. Many of the people who helped to bring about the transformation of the VML and who subsequently took charge of the organization were Mexican Americans as well. Both to the participants in those events and interested observers alike, it was clear that the revolution of 1968 was not simply an administrative reconfiguration of a visible nonprofit organization. It was also a seminal event in the emergence of a Chicano movement in Oregon.

Sonny Montes played a prominent role in this development. He was a driving force behind the changes introduced. Both in private meetings and public gatherings, he had become an outspoken and effective advocate for Oregon's nascent Mexican American community, demanding greater representation of Mexican American farmworkers on the VML's board of directors, more input by Mexican Americans in VML policies, and more responsible positions for Mexican Americans on the VML staff. Without question, he had become the chief Mexican American voice in the VML administration. But, strange as it may seem, the new VML created by the revolution of 1968 was apparently not going to include Sonny Montes. Toward the close of the meeting of April 28, 1968, after all the resolutions had been approved and while some of the attendees were slipping out of the room, the VML board addressed a few final items of business, one of them involving Sonny. The minutes of the session summarize what took place:

> Members of the Board and staff expressed their feeling of regret because of the resignation of Sonny Montes. Everyone wished him luck in his new venture and appreciated all that he had done for the community and for his tremendous job and dedication as Area Supervisor.[51]

Within days, Sonny had left Oregon.

Activist

Sonny's departure for California was a direct result of marital problems—which, in hindsight, he blames primarily on himself. Immersed in and energized by work at the VML he considered important, he was neglecting his family life. On most days, Sonny left for work early in the morning and arrived home late at night, following a meeting in Woodburn or some other community. Meanwhile, Librada was left to attend to the couple's three young children alone. Understandably, she felt overburdened and unappreciated.

Also contributing to the problems in the Montes home was the social difference that separated Sonny and Librada's families. Although the Mexican American agricultural community of that period is often imaged as an undifferentiated rural proletariat, class divisions—and class conflict—definitely existed within it. Sonny had grown up in a family of limited means, with his father dividing his time between agricultural labor and a variety of menial jobs. Librada Arce's family, on the other hand, was a rung or two above Sonny's on the Mexican American socioeconomic ladder and in the process of going higher. Her brother, Horacio, was an upwardly mobile labor supervisor, who increasingly tended to see the world through the lenses of the growers. The social distance that separated the two families led over time to tension between Horacio Arce and Sonny. Arce had strong objections to Sonny's new line of work, believing that the VML's efforts to move migrant farmworkers out of the migrant stream would damage the regional economy—and his own economic prospects in the process. The two men argued frequently.

Librada, on her part, was never openly critical of the VML. Nor did she openly disagree with Sonny's evolving ideas. But she also did not share his obvious passion for improving the lot of migrant field hands. Furthermore, because Librada was so fully involved in household activities, she was cut off from the life experiences that were transforming Sonny: the tutorials he received from Jose Garcia and John Little, the contacts with Mexican American leaders in other Oregon communities, the planning sessions that led to the revolution of 1968. While Sonny's worldview was changing in important ways, Librada's was not.

The couple's marital problems were hardly unique. In most households of that (or this) day, wives have borne a disproportionately large share of child-rearing responsibilities. During those years of child rearing, husbands and wives have often led parallel lives, involved in very different activities during the daytime hours. For Sonny and Librada, there had been warning signs: communication breakdowns, arguments. Eventually, the arguments escalated and Librada decided to leave. At the time Sonny and his VML colleagues were launching their revolution, Librada took the three kids back to Fresno County. After the Salem board meeting, Sonny went there, too. Acknowledging that he was responsible for the strains in the couple's relationship, he was intent on patching his family back together. It took about four months for the two of them to work out their problems.

By August 1968, they were all back in Oregon, residing again in a small cabin at Duyck's labor camp in Cornelius, since Sonny had given up the Hillsboro rental house when he had left Oregon in pursuit of Librada. Sonny had a new job. He was an "area teacher" for an organization known as the Farm Workers Home that was affiliated with the VML. Soon he and Librada would have a fourth child as well. Their second son, David, was born on December 29, 1968, a very snowy day, which meant that the drive to the hospital in the family's 1963 Chevy was slow and hazardous.[1]

Aftermath of the Revolution

While Sonny had been attending to family matters in California, the VML had been attempting to carry out the decisions made at the Salem meeting. The key task was to place the opportunity centers under the control of farmworkers. The VML administration had no difficulty in hiring able people to staff the positions formerly occupied by Anglo professionals. But many members of the VML board believed that, given the new employees' lack of formal educational credentials, they needed ongoing staff training. Hence, training programs were put in place and the new staff members began attending them. At the same time, aiming to increase the level of community involvement in the VML, the board of directors made changes to the area advisory boards. Under the new arrangement, which was worked out by December 1968, a majority of the members of the advisory boards were to be farmworkers, and those boards were given a significant role in hiring opportunity center personnel and evaluating their performance.[2]

Another event that had occurred during Sonny's stay in California was the creation of the Farm Workers Home, the organization he went to work for. It was the brainchild of the Washington County Farmworkers Committee, a group of about a dozen people affiliated with Emilio Hernandez of VIVA. Since the appointment of John Little as the VML's executive director, Hernandez's criticism of that organization had abated and he had begun to cooperate with it.[3] In May 1968 Hernandez and the other members of the newly formed Washington County Farmworkers Committee approached the VML with the idea of creating an essentially independent migrant-assistance agency in the Hillsboro area—an agency that would perform many of the same functions as an opportunity center but would not be directly supervised by the VML. In the arrangement they envisaged, the Washington County Farmworkers Committee would set the new organization's agenda, choose the staff members, and evaluate their performance. The organization's only connection to the VML would be financial: the VML would provide the funding.[4]

At the end of June 1968, the VML board voted to support the proposal "on a six-month trial basis." Little, who held Hernandez in high regard, was enthusiastic. "Emilio really believed in democracy," Little told me in an interview. "And he had a lot of integrity." The Farmworkers Committee, co-chaired by Hernandez and an Anglo farmworker named Ken Glover, rented an old two-storey house in Forest Grove and renamed it the Farm Workers Home. Several VISTAs soon arrived to repaint and repair the place. Meanwhile, the committee drew up a set of objectives for the Farm Workers Home that bore a close resemblance to those of the VML: to assist farmworkers "in any way possible" while they were harvesting Oregon's crops; to facilitate their resettlement in Oregon if they made a voluntary decision to relocate there; to find employment for resettling migrants; and to "help them improve themselves educationally." The staffing pattern of the Farm Workers Home mirrored that of the VML opportunity center: there was a director, an area teacher, a job counselor, and a secretary/receptionist.[5]

For the position of director, Hernandez's committee chose Lupe Bustos, a controversial choice given his confrontational style and former difficulties with the VML. Since being terminated in early 1967, Bustos had worked for another OEO-sponsored organization in Utah. But it was known that Bustos wanted to return to Oregon, and his supporters in Washington County, who saw him as an uncompromising defender of farmworker interests, lobbied vigorously for his appointment. It is unclear if Hernandez himself had doubts about hiring Bustos; if he did, he was in the minority. "They thought that this guy was going to take them to the end of the rainbow," Sonny told me, recalling the devotion that Bustos inspired among his followers.[6]

The other staff members of the Farm Workers Home were Jose Morales, a former farmworker and a member of the Washington County committee, who held the position of job counselor; Lupe Lopez, the secretary/receptionist; and Sonny, the area teacher, which meant that he oversaw the adult education program in the area. Morales admired Bustos. Sonny was less enamored of the director, but the two men had a satisfactory personal relationship and respected each other. In fact, Bustos had actively recruited Sonny for the area teacher position.[7]

From the outset, the Farm Workers Home did not live up to the VML's expectations. In public statements, Bustos professed to be an advocate of farmworker autonomy and community development. Interviewed by a reporter in August 1968, he described the Farm Workers Home as "a program run by former farmworkers for farmworkers" and decried the fact that many state and private agencies did not believe that migrant workers "can lead and direct if given the opportunity." Bustos's everyday actions belied his rhetoric. "Lupe was elitist," John Little recalls. "He thought he should run everything." Relations between Bustos and Emilio Hernandez, the leading figure in the Washington County Farmworkers Committee, quickly soured. The day-to-day Bustos, the elitist and autocrat, was philosophically at odds with Hernandez, the believer in democratic processes and community empowerment. Hernandez criticized

Bustos's unwillingness to share power with the farmworkers in Washington County. He was also distressed that many of those same farmworkers idolized Bustos and were unwilling to question any of the decisions he made.[8]

Sonny shared Little's and Hernandez's views of Bustos's management style. "He was only good at making people dependent on him," Sonny told me. He became convinced as well that, given Hernandez's dissatisfaction with Bustos, "it was only a matter of time before this damn thing was going to explode." So he adopted the approach of focusing on the work at hand and trying to avoid conflict with Bustos. He organized adult education classes. He also helped out the job counselor Jose Morales, since Sonny had much more experience than Morales with that line of work.[9]

By late February 1969, the Farm Workers Home experiment was failing. Hernandez and Bustos fought constantly. Bustos himself conceded that too little attention had been given to the goals of educating and getting jobs for migrants. Another issue arose: some of the agency's funds were missing and there was suspicion of foul play. In all these matters, Morales, who Sonny describes as a "blind follower" of Bustos, supported the director. Sonny sided with Hernandez, but did not do so openly. Troubled by the turmoil, the VML initiated a review of the Farm Workers Home to decide whether or not to continue funding the agency beyond the six-month trial period.[10]

Finally, on March 2, 1969, during a meeting held by the VML at Pacific University in Forest Grove to discuss the Farm Workers Home, the long-anticipated explosion occurred. In attendance were the staff members of the Home, members of the Washington County Farmworkers Committee, and representatives of the VML, including John Little. From the start of the session, Hernandez attacked Bustos, raising questions about his leadership. There was also some discussion of the missing money. During a break in the proceedings, Morales, furious at Hernandez for criticizing Bustos, followed him into a restroom and punched him in the face. Bleeding from the blow, Hernandez ran back to the meeting room and said to Little: "John, we don't want the program here anymore. You guys should take it back." Later the same day, rallying in support of the bloodied Hernandez, the Washington County Farmworkers

Committee voted to return the county's migrant-assistance program to the VML.[11]

Over the next few weeks, a new arrangement was worked out for Washington County. The VML cut off all support for the Farm Workers Home as of March 31, 1969, created in its place a new opportunity center in Forest Grove, and launched a search for an area director. Bustos announced publicly that he would not apply for the job and severed all connections with the VML. Sonny did apply, and on April 30, 1969, he was appointed to the position.[12]

Los Gatos

In March 1969, while the VML was in the process of ending its sponsorship of the Farm Workers Home, Sonny and approximately thirty-five other Mexican Americans affiliated with the VML attended a conference in Los Gatos, California.[13] John Little had learned about the Los Gatos conference from Jose Garcia, the former Hillsboro area director, who was one of the organizers. At the time, Garcia claimed to be connected to the University of Santa Clara, today known as Santa Clara University, but the exact nature of that connection is unclear.[14] The stated objectives of the meeting were to raise the consciousness of the participants, to reinforce Mexican American cultural identity, and to provide leadership training. Thinking that the experience would be valuable to the Mexican Americans in the organization, Little chartered a bus to transport the VML representatives to Los Gatos and paid all their conference-related expenses.

Among the VML participants were three current area directors—David Aguilar, Concepcion Perez Jr., and Jimmy Amaya (the son of Santiago and Crescencia Amaya of Independence, Oregon). Also in attendance were several other current or former VML employees, such as Ventura Rios, head of United Farm Workers of Oregon, which he had founded in July 1968. Joining them were more than 150 Mexican Americans from other federally sponsored migrant-assistance agencies in Oregon, Washington, and California. All the attendees were male. They were housed in the dormitories of a children's summer camp, the rooms furnished with rows of bunk beds. Much of the time, they attended lectures given in Spanish by a team of instructors. The topics discussed were the status of Mexican Americans in the United States and the emergence of the Chicano movement, especially the latter.

Although Sonny and his colleagues were certainly aware of the existence of the Chicano movement, the truth of the matter is that, before the Los Gatos meeting, few of them had much detailed knowledge of it. Former farmworkers themselves, they were best informed about the activities of Cesar Chavez and his farmworkers' union. But most of them were relatively unfamiliar with the many other faces of Mexican American protest. At Los Gatos, they received a short course on some of the major organizations involved in the Chicano movement and the repertoire of collective-action techniques they employed.

Predictably, there was some discussion of Chavez. Since the first major strike against the Delano grape growers in 1965, Chavez had remained highly visible. In April 1966, the pressure applied by the boycott of the Schenley Corporation had finally paid dividends: Schenley recognized Chavez's union and signed a contract with it. A fiercer battle followed with the DiGiorgio Corporation, one of the largest growers in the state, but Chavez prevailed again. In the meantime, the NFWA and AWOC had merged, forming the United Farm Workers Organizing Committee (UFWOC).

In August 1967, the UFWOC launched another major strike, this time against Giumarra Vineyards, the largest table-grape grower in the Delano area. When the company brought in strikebreakers, Chavez called for a nationwide boycott of Giumarra grapes. Then, after discovering that Giumarra, with the cooperation of other growers, was placing the labels of those growers on the grapes it shipped to supermarkets in an effort to deceive shoppers, Chavez launched a nationwide boycott of all California table grapes in January 1968. Throughout 1968, the grape boycott was an inescapable fact of life for many Americans. Not only did they read about it in the newspapers and see stories about it on the television news; they literally came face to face with it whenever they went to the supermarket. There were many lessons to be learned about successful social protest from the techniques used by the UFWOC and its supporters.[15]

The Los Gatos instruction team talked as well about Reies López Tijerina, who was not well known to the VML group, even though by 1969 he was attracting a great deal of national media attention. The attention was due to Tijerina's increasingly militant public posture. In July 1966, Tijerina had met with New Mexico's governor and asked for a "full investigation" into the land grants issue. The governor gave the state archivist the assignment of looking into the matter, and she reported that there was "little validity" to Tijerina's claims. At that point, Tijerina concluded that he could get no justice by legal means. In October 1966, he and more than 300 other members of the Alianza Federal de Mercedes briefly occupied a campground in the Kit Carson National Forest, claiming it had once been a Spanish land grant. Tijerina and several other *aliancistas* were arrested and later released.

Seven months later, Tijerina announced that the Alianza would again occupy the same site and, to prepare for the occupation, called a meeting of Alianza members in Coyote, New Mexico. Local authorities, led by the district attorney of Río Arriba County, Alfonso Sánchez, prepared to prevent them from holding it. Most *aliancistas* were stopped at roadblocks, but a few of them who had managed to enter Coyote were arrested for unlawful assembly and put in jail in Tierra Amarilla, the county seat of Río Arriba County. On June 5, 1967, angered by the arrests, Tijerina and his followers attempted to enter Tierra Amarilla to rescue the arrested men and to perform a citizen's arrest of Sánchez. They engaged in a shoot-out with local law enforcement officers, wounding two of them in the process, but found neither their friends nor the district attorney. At that point, the *aliancistas* left. A manhunt ensued, and eventually most of the invaders either turned themselves in or were captured. For the next several years, Tijerina spent much of his time in court, fighting to avoid a prison sentence. When not in court, he continued to give fiery speeches and remained in the public's eye.[16]

At Los Gatos, some attention was also given to the Crusada Para La Justicia (Crusade for Justice), an organization established in Denver in 1966 by Rodolfo "Corky" Gonzales, a former professional boxer. Based in an old Denver church, the Crusada offered youth and adult education programs, and encouraged both cultural nationalism and political activism. Gonzales was also a writer; his best-known piece was the powerful, disturbing, poem "I Am Joaquín," written in English and first published in 1967—a work that, as one scholar has astutely observed, "captured for many young Mexicans the cultural schisms that fractured their identity, . . . not only those divisions rooted in the mixture of Spanish and Indian ancestry and culture but also those engendered by the tensions between American and Mexican cultural identities." By exposing the "confusions" at the heart of Mexican American identity, Gonzales's poem had enormous appeal to young Mexican Americans of that era. Gonzales's political program also attracted a following. Among other things, he demanded better education for Mexican Americans, better housing, job development, wealth redistribution, land reform, and an end to police brutality in the barrios.[17]

Sonny and the other conference participants learned something too about the Mexican American Youth Organization (MAYO), the major political organization of Mexican American youth in Texas, which was founded in San Antonio in 1967 and led by José Angel Gutiérrez. MAYO sought some of the same changes that Gonzales's organization sought—economic betterment for the Mexican American population, educational reforms, an end to police brutality. To achieve its ends, it staged many demonstrations and protest rallies and became increasingly involved in the political process, organizing voter registration drives and supporting Mexican American candidates in local electoral contests.[18]

Finally, there were presentations about recent Chicano protests in East Los Angeles. In March 1968, more than 10,000 high school students walked out of their schools to protest the education they were receiving. The deficiencies of East Los Angeles high schools, which had a predominantly Mexican American student body, were many: inadequate funding, poor facilities, overcrowded classrooms, unmotivated, mostly Anglo teachers, and appallingly low graduation rates. In the fall of 1967, disgruntled students began discussing the possibility of staging a walkout (or "blowout," as they called it at the time). A sympathetic Mexican American teacher at Lincoln High School, Sal Castro, joined the discussions, and he helped to line up assistance from the Brown Berets and the Los Angeles chapters of a recently established college student organization called United Mexican American Students. The former was a renamed and much modified version of an organization called Young Citizens for Community Action, formed in 1966, which initially attempted to involve Mexican American high school students in community service activities. But over time its members had experienced harassment from local law enforcement authorities and they had changed their orientation from offering services to promoting a Chicano identity within the community. The Brown Berets also emphasized strict discipline and upright conduct. The East Los Angeles blowouts brought no major improvements in the area high schools, but they did result in a minor epidemic of blowouts in Mexican American communities in Colorado, Arizona, and other states.[19]

There was a hard edge to the lectures given at the Los Gatos conference, the speakers using the inflammatory rhetoric that was common in Chicano meetings, conferences, and rallies of that day. They talked about the unrelenting racism of Anglos and the injustices perpetrated on Mexican Americans by the Anglo-dominated power structure. They denounced the public schools as tools of cultural subjugation, faulting them for celebrating the role of people of northern European ancestry in building the United States while paying almost no attention to the contributions of Latinos in developing Florida and the Southwest. The presentations had a powerful effect on the VML participants: they were both impressed and unsettled by what they heard. Back in the dormitories, after dinner, they talked nonstop. "Some of the speakers really riled us up," recalls Jimmy Amaya. "A lot of anger came out."

In addition to hearing lectures, the conference goers took part in field trips planned by the organizers. On one day, they participated in a demonstration at a local high school where Mexican American students and parents were protesting the administration's unwillingness to incorporate a Chicano studies component into the curriculum—a demonstration inspired by the blowouts of the previous year. On another day, Jose Garcia led the entire VML delegation to a bank, where they tried to cash the checks that had been given to them to cover their conference expenses. The field trips were, in a sense, assertiveness training exercises, undertaken to demonstrate to the participants that, acting collectively, they could even up the odds a bit and stand up to a system that reflexively assigned them subordinate status. Hence, by joining the picket lines at the school, they were attempting to change an educational system that had long been unresponsive to their needs, and, by appearing en masse at the bank, they were making an effort to change the policies of financial institutions that often refused to cash the checks of Mexican Americans while cashing the checks of Anglo customers.

By providing the VML representatives with information about the broad scope of Mexican American protest in the country and instruction in certain collective-action techniques, the Los Gatos conference was a formative event in the development of a Chicano movement in Oregon. It served as a connective link between the surge of Chicano activism then occurring in populous Mexican American communities in the United States and individuals such as Sonny Montes, David Aguilar, and Jimmy Amaya, who were assuming leadership positions in Oregon's comparatively small Mexican American community. Up to then, the principal manifestation of Mexican American activism in Oregon had been a struggle for control within a federally funded nonprofit agency. Furthermore, most of the ideas that had thus far inspired Mexican American action were transmitted to the actors not by the emerging Chicano movement in the Southwest but rather by a middle-aged Anglo community organizer from Portland who had read about them in a book and put them into practice during a five-year stint in Ecuador with the Papal Volunteers—the very same Anglo who arranged for Sonny and his colleagues to attend the Los Gatos meeting. At Los Gatos, exposed for the first time to the broad range of ideological positions and protest techniques of the larger Chicano movement, a select group of Oregon's Mexican Americans experienced something close to an epiphany. "It had a big impact on me and everyone else," Amaya remembers. "It radicalized me. . . . Afterward we made a lot of noise." John Little noticed the change almost immediately, when he had a meeting with his Mexican American area directors right after the conference. "When they got back from California, they all gave me the evil eye."

An Apprenticeship in Collective Action

In Sonny's case, the impact of the Los Gatos experience was immediate and substantial. Whereas in his first stint as an area director he was completely immersed in his VML work, in his second he was increasingly focused on—and hence devoted large amounts of his time to—political and social causes. He became an activist.

One cause that commanded his attention in this period of his life was Cesar Chavez's ongoing campaign against California's agricultural industry. When he had lived in the San Joaquin Valley between 1963 and 1966, Sonny had first become aware of Chavez's union-organizing efforts, and from afar, he had applauded. Sonny's sympathies were easy to understand, given the fact that he had labored in the fields under conditions little different from those Chavez was trying to change. Since arriving in Oregon, Sonny had continued to follow Chavez's activities, and he had also taken an interest in the union-organizing efforts in Oregon of his friend Ventura Rios.[20] Even so, his involvement in the cause was negligible in the years before the Los Gatos conference. When in the summer of 1967 Chavez had launched the boycott against Giumarra Vineyards, Sonny was not among the pickets who assembled daily outside Portland-area Fred Meyer Stores attempting to dissuade customers from purchasing the Giumarra table grapes sold there. Nor could he be found on the picket lines in 1968 when Chavez launched the boycott of all California table grapes and picketing resumed in Portland.[21]

Sonny did not make an appearance on the picket lines until April or May 1969, more than a year into Chavez's national grape boycott. By then, as a result of the boycott, several national grocery store chains had stopped stocking California table grapes. But others stood firm, including Safeway, then the world's second largest supermarket chain, and the UFWOC decided in the early spring of 1969 to target Safeway stores in the western United States. In preparation for the campaign, the Portland organizers, Nick Jones and Ed Chierra, sought new recruits to walk the picket lines. In Portland, as in other major U.S. cities, the UFWOC relied on union allies to recruit pickets, and at this time Sonny received a call from a union official who asked him to participate. Infused with the spirit of Chicanismo from the Los Gatos meeting, Sonny agreed to serve as a picket.[22]

After that, on most Saturdays and sometimes on weekdays after work, he joined the picket lines outside Safeway stores in the Portland area, most often the one at the Lloyd Center in downtown

Portland.[23] Sometimes he took his children along. Whenever he could, he tried to bring John Little and other VML employees with him. "We would stand outside the Safeway stores and pass out information," Sonny remembers. "And then we would do all kinds of things." One action he performed more than a few times was to enter a Safeway store, fill a shopping cart to the top with grocery items, including table grapes, and proceed to the checkout counter. While the checker was ringing up the items in his cart, Sonny would inquire if the grapes being sold in the store were union grapes, and after he received the expected reply, he would ask to speak to the manager. When the manager finally appeared, Sonny would explain that because of Safeway's policy of selling nonunion grapes he could not purchase any groceries at all from the company. Then he would walk out of the store, leaving the filled-up grocery cart behind.

As time passed, and the boycott went on, Sonny took a more prominent role in the picketing. The VML owned several bullhorns that didn't get much use. Sonny borrowed one of them for an extended period of time, brought it to the picket lines, and used it to broadcast the union message to shoppers and passersby. While many people supported the pickets, a number were hostile. "We'd take a lot of harassment," Sonny remembers.

For Sonny, one of the highlights of the grape boycott was the visit of Cesar Chavez to Oregon in December 1969. Chavez scheduled two days of activities in the state, starting with a rally on December 19 at the University of Oregon in Eugene. He then moved on to Hubbard, northeast of Woodburn, where the VML had arranged a meeting with farmworkers in the gymnasium of the elementary school. About 200 people were in the audience. Most were Mexican American farmworkers, but there was also a good turnout of VML staff members, including Sonny and John Little. Slight and soft-spoken, addressing his audience in Spanish and English, Chavez delivered a powerful message, demonizing the agricultural corporations.[24]

By late July 1970, most of the major California grape producers had signed contracts with the UFWOC. In Portland itself, at the end of that month, Nick Jones announced that only union grapes were being sold in the city's stores. The boycott committee held a victory rally on August 1, 1970. But by then the UFWOC's attention was already shifting from grapes to lettuce, and a lettuce boycott would follow. Sonny, bullhorn in hand and children in tow, would participate in that campaign as well.[25]

Other causes competed for his attention. He organized and attended, again bullhorn in hand, demonstrations in Hillsboro against perceived police mistreatment of Mexican Americans.[26] He also helped to establish a Mexican American cultural, educational, and activities center in the Woodburn area, the Centro Chicano Cultural. The idea for the center actually emerged from discussions in the summer of 1969 among John Little, Sonny, David Aguilar, and several other Los Gatos alumni. Aware that Mexican American communities in California and other states had developed centers of that kind, the founders felt that the creation of one in the Willamette Valley would serve the vital need of educating local Mexican-origin people about their cultural heritage. They intended the Centro Chicano Cultural to be an independent nonprofit, separate from the VML. Thanks in large measure to Little's strong connections with the state's Catholic leaders, the Centro's board received sizable contributions from Catholic organizations, allowing it to purchase a sixty-three-acre farm in Gervais, where the Centro would be housed.[27]

Already highly visible due to his VML work and his activism, Sonny attracted further attention thanks to Oregon's governor. In August 1969, responding to complaints from Oregon's Mexican Americans about discrimination and unfair treatment, Governor Tom McCall began holding regular meetings with a group of ten Mexican Americans, one of them being Sonny. In December, McCall formalized the arrangement, creating a body called the Governor's Advisory Committee on Chicano Affairs, consisting of fifteen appointees. Sonny was one of the fifteen. Unfortunately, while McCall was willing to talk, the committee accomplished little.[28]

In this time of protest, the Oregon press began to track more closely Chicano activism in the state. Sonny was one of four Mexican Americans featured in a lengthy September 1969 article in the Portland *Oregonian*, titled "Chicanos Organize to Fight for Mexican-American Citizen-Rights." It began: "There are some new voices in Oregon, the voices of men and women of Mexican descent who, like their black brothers, want to find their rightful place in the sun. They are part of what has come to be known in the West as the Chicano Movement." The section on Sonny, which focused on his farmworker past and his work for the VML, described him as "messianic in his concern over the Chicano Movement."[29]

Sonny also became involved in the antiwar movement. He was not convinced by the government's arguments that U.S. national interests were at stake in Vietnam, and he shared the concern of his people about the disproportionately high number of Mexican American casualties in the conflict. He went to some local protest meetings. Then, on August 29, 1970, he and other Mexican Americans connected with the VML attended the Chicano National Moratorium rally in Los Angeles, a large antiwar gathering sponsored by a coalition of Mexican American organizations. The VML delegation chartered a bus to transport them to that city.[30]

The organizers' plan was for the protesters to march first through downtown Los Angeles and then proceed to Laguna Park in East Los Angeles, where the rally would be held. Sonny and his group joined the march at the starting point and followed the designated route. In all, approximately 20,000 people took part. By 2 p.m. Sonny and his group had reached Laguna Park, and they sat down on the grass to listen to speeches. Suddenly, a disturbance erupted at the opposite end of the park. Sonny and the people near him were not sure what had caused the trouble, but they could see that members of the crowd were throwing rocks at the police and the police were wielding clubs. When the police lobbed tear gas canisters at the crowd, the protesters retreated in disarray, with the police in pursuit. With tear gas canisters now being fired in Sonny's direction, he and the others dashed out of the park and onto the city streets.

In the ensuing battle, hundreds of people were arrested. Three protesters died, one of them Ruben Salazar, a well-known Mexican American reporter, who was struck by a tear gas projectile. In the commotion of that day, two young members of Sonny's group were separated from the others and could not immediately be located. Sonny feared the worst. The next day, the VML group returned to Laguna Park to locate the missing. Eventually they found the two, both of whom had been beaten by the police. With everyone accounted for, Sonny and the others boarded the bus and returned to Oregon.

Still other issues attracted his attention in the spring and summer of the following year. In May 1971, the Oregon legislature passed Senate Bill 677 (SB 677), a controversial piece of farm labor legislation. Strongly supported by Oregon's farm lobbyists, it aimed to halt the development of farmworker unions in the state. One of its provisions would have effectively barred Oregon's agricultural laborers from striking against their employers during the harvest season. After its passage, the United Farm Workers of Oregon and other groups protested against it, demanding that Governor Tom McCall veto the bill. Sonny served on the committee that coordinated the protest activity, and on June 16, 1971, he led a rally in Salem of about 150 people, mostly Mexican Americans. On the steps of the state capitol, speakers denounced SB 677 as "inequitable" and "anti-labor," and Sonny led the protesters in chants of "Chicano power." Later in the month, Cesar Chavez and other UFWOC organizers came to Oregon to lend their support. Under unrelenting pressure from labor groups, church leaders, and a coalition of liberal organizations, McCall vetoed SB 677 in July.[31]

Also in the month of July 1971, Sonny led demonstrations on the campus of Portland State University, protesting the school's failure to educate Mexican American students. By his count, there were exactly three Mexican Americans in the entire student body. Together with one of them, he issued an ultimatum to the university president, demanding that the institution recruit more Mexican Americans, provide tutoring and counseling to those students, and develop a Chicano studies program. "The university should be more sensitive to our needs," he told a reporter. "It's sickening that so few Chicanos are at PSU when we are the largest minority in the state."[32]

By now, Sonny's involvement in protest activities had come to the attention of the Federal Bureau of Investigation, which in the late 1960s and early 1970s was closely monitoring Mexican American activism throughout the country. The bureau was particularly interested in the Brown Berets, which by 1970 had evolved into a paramilitary organization, mimicking in some respects the programs and organizational structure of the Black Panthers. Its membership had increased rapidly as well, with chapters being established in several states. The FBI and police departments considered the Brown Berets subversive, harassed its members, and infiltrated the organization.[33] In November 1970, FBI sources in Oregon reported that a group of approximately twenty Brown Berets were active in the Woodburn area and named Sonny as one of them. The report was only partially correct. In fact, there were a few Brown Berets in Oregon's Willamette Valley at the time and one had even worked briefly for the VML, but Sonny himself was never a Brown Beret.[34]

A well-known characteristic of police intelligence reports is that many (if not most) of them are inaccurate. Human sources of intelligence often provide information in exchange for payments. Sometimes these intelligence providers have useful information at their disposal, and sometimes they don't. But even when they don't, they typically provide something; otherwise, they will not be paid. Furthermore, all police organizations regularly receive tips from individuals who want to besmirch the reputation of enemies, rivals, and other people they simply dislike.[35] As sources, then, police and FBI files must always be read skeptically. In the case of Sonny's FBI file, there is a predictable mixture of truth and fiction—on the one hand, verifiable reports about Sonny's attendance at union meetings and demonstrations, some of which are based on newspaper stories, and on the other, undocumented and unverifiable assertions by unnamed sources that Sonny was a Brown Beret.

As Sonny's FBI file grew in size, agents analyzing the collected data began to suspect that those undocumented assertions were incorrect, since the bulk of the material suggested only that he was a leader of Oregon's Mexican American community and an organizer of demonstrations. In March 1971 a new informant told the FBI that Sonny was "not considered favorably" by the Brown Berets, and later that year another source stated categorically that Sonny was not a member of that organization. Finally, in April 1972, several months after he had left the VML (and a few months before the Brown Berets were officially disbanded), the FBI's Domestic Intelligence Division concluded that Sonny was "not a member of an organization with anti-U.S. objectives." Eleven months later the FBI decided to end its investigation of Sonny, and the surveillance stopped.[36]

Sonny's involvement in Mexican American-related causes, a development set in motion by the Los Gatos conference, had important consequences for the growth of the Chicano movement in the Willamette Valley—which at this point was in its early stages, amounting to not much more than VIVA and the organizations Sonny was affiliated with (the VML, the Centro Chicano Cultural, Rios's union, and so forth). As Sidney Tarrow, Doug McAdam, Mario Diani, and other students of social movements tell us, the effectiveness of these movements depends to a considerable degree on the repertoire of collective-action techniques adopted by the movement and the linkages established between the movement and its members. The techniques adopted by the movement need to be appropriate, and the linkages need to be reliable enough to generate support when required. The underlying truth is that social movements depend on special knowledge learned and social networks already developed.[37]

Sonny's participation in the grape boycott, the Centro Chicano Cultural, the United Farm Workers of Oregon, the antiwar movement, and the demonstrations in Hillsboro, Salem, and Portland was valuable preparation for what was to come. From those involvements, as well as from the instruction given at Los Gatos, he and other Mexican American activists received a basic training in modern-day collective-action techniques. They learned how to set up pickets; organize demonstrations, rallies, and marches; and get coverage from the press. They learned as well how easy it was to lose control of a large gathering of protesters, as had been the case in the Los Angeles rally.

Furthermore, as a result of all those activities as well as from his work at the VML since 1966 and his involvement in social organizations like Los Amigos, Sonny was developing an impressive range of contacts, both organizational and social—a personal alliance system that included other Mexican American activists and leaders, neighbors and friends, members of farmworker clubs, VML staff members past and present, farmworkers and former farmworkers he had helped, labor union members, antiwar protesters, college students, and individuals of all colors and ethnicities. Other Mexican American activists and leaders in the region were developing similar. kinds of connections as well. Slowly but surely, a Mexican American network, one based on a combination of associational and personal linkages, was being established in the region. In a few years, when Sonny became the principal spokesperson for a new Chicano cause, he would be able to draw on the knowledge learned and networks developed during this earlier period of activism.

The Issue of Access

The VML in 1969 was not the same organization it had been in 1966, the year Sonny had joined it as a program aide. Its budget had decreased considerably. The intra-organizational struggles that had absorbed Sonny during his first two years at the VML had been won and farmworkers were firmly in control. While there was still satisfaction to be gained from providing education and vocational training to migrants and seasonal farmworkers, the truth of the matter was that, on most days, the job of a VML area director was routine.

But there were, from time to time, deviations from the routine. An important issue that preoccupied Sonny and the rest of the VML administration in the spring and summer of 1969 was access to farm labor camps. Since the creation of the VML in 1965, a sizable number of farmers in the region had consistently prevented employees of the VML and other federally supported organizations from entering their labor camps, thereby making it next to impossible to inform farmworkers about programs intended to help them. One reason for the denial of access was that the farmers didn't want outsiders telling them how to run their operations. In addition, some of them, aware of the UFWOC's success in organizing farmworkers in California, suspected that the people who sought entry into their camps would try to convince their workers to join the union.[38]

All over the region, farmers posted signs on their property warning visitors that if they tried to enter the camps without authorization they would be prosecuted for trespass. Sometimes the visitors were prosecuted. In July 1968, for example, two VISTAs and a Portland sociologist associated with VISTA attempted to enter a camp south of Hillsboro at the invitation of two adult Mexican American camp residents whose son needed medical attention. The three invitees were arrested at the request of the farmer Al Luttrell. "I still own the place," Luttrell said. "I've got my rights. I'm furnishing people with a lot of jobs." Fortunately for the three visitors, a federal judge later dismissed the charges.[39]

As the 1969 harvest season got under way in Oregon, John Little was intent on solving the problem of camp access. The opportunity for doing so occurred when the VML was able to secure the services of a recent law school graduate who had gone to work for VISTA in Oregon. Born and raised in Atlanta, with a law degree from George Washington University, Marshall Lichtenstein had signed on with VISTA right after finishing law school in order to avoid military service. VISTA's modus operandi was to send the volunteers to parts of the country they were unfamiliar with, the rationale being that outsiders would be more likely to shake things up than people who had roots in the area. So Lichtenstein, a young middle-class Jewish man from the South, was shipped off to the Pacific Northwest. He arrived in Eugene, Oregon, where he and others received training at the University of Oregon. During the training period, federally supported agencies in the region had an opportunity to check out the volunteers and express an interest in getting them assigned to their agencies. When Little, needing an attorney to help him address the camp access problem, learned that Lichtenstein was available, he pushed hard to get him. Lichtenstein started to work for the VML in mid-July 1969.[40]

He immediately focused on camp access. After discussing the situation with Little, Lichtenstein decided that the way to proceed was to bring a "test case" before the courts in which they would challenge the farmers' right to refuse entry to the camps. The legal argument on which the test case would be based was that the farmers' claims of private property rights could not take precedence over the right of poverty workers to inform citizens about federal poverty programs and to deliver benefits to those people. To bring this test case, Little and Lichtenstein needed to orchestrate an incident in which three things occurred: first, employees of a federally supported program would have to attempt to enter a camp; second, the owner of the camp would have to deny them entry; and third, the employees would have to be arrested. The arrest was a crucial precondition. Unless it occurred, the courts would not have the opportunity to rule on the issue of camp access.[41]

In addition to developing those plans with Little, Lichtenstein contacted the Multnomah County Legal Aid Service in Portland in search of assistance. Headed by Charles Merten, that organization employed eleven attorneys and a supporting staff of twelve people, and it was capable of doing several things Lichtenstein could not.

While he had a legal education, Lichtenstein had no practical legal experience and was unlicensed to practice in Oregon. Merten and one of his young assistants, Neil Goldschmidt, who had worked for two years for the Legal Aid Service, gave advice to Lichtenstein about the projected "test case" and agreed to take on the job of securing the release from jail of anyone arrested for trespass.[42]

Meanwhile, Little was lining up people who would be willing to enter a labor camp and be arrested. He approached Sonny and a VISTA worker from New York City named Lois Heinlein. Both were interested in the assignment, and Lichtenstein thought they were good choices. He was very keen on Sonny, whom he viewed as energetic and smart. He still recalls one of his first meetings with Sonny, which took place at the Forest Grove Opportunity Center. Lichtenstein had received a "mini Berlitz" Spanish course during his VISTA training session in Eugene and liked to try out his rudimentary Spanish on any Mexican Americans he encountered. But when Lichtenstein attempted to speak to the opportunity center staff in Spanish, all of them burst out laughing. "What's the matter?" Lichtenstein asked. "Marshall, we understand you," Sonny replied. "But you speak Spanish with a southern accent."[43]

After being recruited for the assignment, Montes and Heinlein met several times with Little and Lichtenstein to plan the attempted camp entry. Goldschmidt sat in on at least one planning session. The plan, as it emerged, was for Montes and Heinlein to visit workers in a migrant labor camp in North Plains, a small town near Hillsboro. The thirty-two-unit labor camp and the seventy-two-acre berry farm on which it was located were both owned and operated by Ron Tankersley, thirty years old and Texas born, himself a former migrant farmworker and one of several members of the Tankersley clan who operated farms in the area. Ron Tankersley represented himself to the press as a model employer. He claimed that he charged nothing for rent, heat, and lights, provided used cars for the migrants' use, and had even paid for a worker's emergency operation. "I would sooner see my workers taken care of than live in a $30,000 home," he told a reporter. But for several years, those same workers had lodged numerous complaints about Tankersley with the VML, maintaining that his recruiters had lured them from the Rio Grande Valley to North Plains by making false promises about the amount of money they would earn and the quality of the housing they would receive. Furthermore, Tankersley and his relatives had a history of doggedly resisting efforts by the VML and other agencies to enter their camps, and they were known to be hotheads.[44]

At the planning sessions, various details of the projected camp visit were worked out. Needing an invitation from someone residing in the camp, Lichtenstein and Little arranged to get a letter from a migrant couple asking Heinlein to visit them to discuss securing permanent housing in the area. The planners decided where Montes and Heinlein were to park their car and what they would say to Tankersley when he appeared. They also decided that Goldschmidt, who had the job of getting Montes and Heinlein out of jail once they were arrested, would be stationed inside a Dairy Queen restaurant a few miles away from Tankersley's farm. Still, what is striking in retrospect is how much was left to chance. Thinking back on the episode, Lichtenstein described the attempted camp entry as a "seat-of-the-pants" operation and admitted that he did not fully appreciate the dangers involved.[45]

The date set for the camp entry was August 8, 1969, a Friday. According to the plan, Montes and Heinlein were to leave the Forest Grove Opportunity Center in a government vehicle and drive directly to Tankersley's farm. Before setting off, however, Sonny did something that had not been planned. Having worked in Washington County for several years, Sonny had developed a good working relationship with the sheriff's office. Just to be prudent, he called that office and informed one of his friends there about the plan to enter the labor camp. "I was concerned about safety," Sonny explains. "I told them: 'We are going to Ron Tankersley's camp. I think there may be trouble.'" His friend told him that a deputy would pay a visit to Tankersley's camp to make sure that things did not get out of hand.[46]

The trouble began shortly after Montes and Heinlein had parked their car at the entrance to the farm.[47] As they began walking toward the camp, Ron Tankersley, members of his family, and a few labor contractors who worked for him emerged from Tankersley's house and screamed profanities at the visitors. Although Sonny was terrified, he tried not to show it. He and Heinlein walked toward the labor camp with the Tankersleys and their associates in pursuit.

When Montes and Heinlein reached the camp, they went directly to the cabin occupied by the couple that had issued the invitation to Heinlein. The woman of the house was reluctant to let them enter, so they talked to her from outside the building. By now, the Tankersley delegation had also reached the cabin. They demanded that Montes and Heinlein leave the farm and, as before, used foul language to convey the message. As calmly as he could, Sonny explained to Ron Tankersley that the couple inside the cabin had invited Heinlein to come. Tankersley replied that he was going to "call the cops."

Sonny did not object to Tankersley's threat—after all, he and Lois Heinlein had come to the camp for the explicit purpose of getting arrested. Still the farmer's words worried him, since he knew that the cops Tankersley was going to contact were not the Washington County officers Sonny had already called but the members of the North Plains police department, who were on close terms with Tankersley. An added cause of worry was that the deputy from the Washington County sheriff's office was nowhere to be seen.

Two North Plains police officers arrived shortly and showed not a bit of sympathy for the alleged trespassers. While the police looked on, Tankersley and his allies pushed and shoved Montes and Heinlein, but no blows were struck. Tankersley also threatened the visitors with arrest. Sonny replied that, in his opinion, he and Heinlein were not trespassing. At that point, Tankersley suddenly turned to the police officers and asked them to leave, adding that he, his family members, and employees would "take care" of the matter. Sonny became even more worried when he heard that statement, fearing that, once the police left, Tankersley and his group would beat them up. To his relief, the Washington County deputy sheriff finally appeared.

Montes and Heinlein were not yet out of danger. The North Plains police officers tried to assure the deputy sheriff that his services were not needed. But Sonny objected strenuously, telling the deputy that he did not "feel comfortable" with the North Plains police. So the deputy remained at the labor camp and took charge of the situation. He explained to Tankersley that he could, if he chose to, have Montes and Heinlein arrested for trespass. Tankersley decided to consult with his group about what to do, and they talked among themselves for a few minutes. Then, to Sonny's surprise, Tankersley announced to the deputy: "I don't want 'em arrested. They can leave."

Many years after the events, Sonny believes that he knows why the grower decided not to press charges. "Ron figured it out," Sonny asserts. That is, Tankersley figured out that Montes and Heinlein wanted to get arrested and sensed that putting them in jail would not be wise. In fact, there is evidence that some of the farmers in the area were aware at the time that the VML and its allies were interested in bringing a test case, and Tankersley himself, in an interview with a reporter after his encounter with Montes and Heinlein, intimated that he was suspicious of the VML's ulterior motives and therefore decided not to have Montes and Heinlein arrested.[48]

Thus ended the incident in North Plains. Thanks to the deputy sheriff's intervention, Montes and Heinlein had escaped physical harm. But, because of Tankersley's decision not to press charges, their effort to enter the camp had not produced a test case for the courts. Immediately after leaving Tankersley's farm on August 8, Montes and Heinlein drove directly to the Dairy Queen where Goldschmidt was waiting and reported to him about what had taken place. Goldschmidt was visibly disappointed.[49]

That reverse did not deter Little and Lichtenstein, however. They developed a new set of plans, and on August 22, 1969, exactly two weeks after the non-arrest in North Plains, three VML-affiliated employees were arrested for entering a camp near Jefferson, Oregon. Little finally had his test case, which then proceeded through the federal courts, with the alleged trespassers being represented by attorneys from the Multnomah County Legal Aid Service. Five months later a federal judge found the alleged trespassers innocent, and Little, claiming victory, announced that the VML would be free to enter labor camps in the future.[50]

The claim of victory was premature. In the 1970 harvest season, many growers continued to refuse entry to VML employees, and the VML was forced to seek help from the U.S. Department of Justice and the U.S. Attorney's Office in Portland. The Department of Justice accepted the VML's contention that camp operators had an obligation to allow reasonable visitation by VML employees, and, following that determination, the U.S. attorney for the District of Oregon, Sidney Lezak, met with both VML officials and a representative of the growers to work out a set of guidelines governing visits by VML workers to the camps. Issued in early November 1970, the guidelines became a precedent for the entire country, effectively guaranteeing access by poverty workers to migrant labor camps. It was one of the most significant accomplishments of the VML.[51]

An Organization in Transition
During Sonny's second stint as area director, changes were taking place in the VML. Some were programmatic. While the VML continued to focus on basic education courses, vocational training, and job placement, it also introduced two new initiatives—a "self-help" housing program and an economic development program.

The self-help housing program was launched to meet a deeply felt need of the communities served by the VML. One problem facing Mexican American farmworkers living in the Upper Willamette Valley (and one that also confronted migrant farmworkers from other states who were considering the possibility of settling in Oregon) was the acute shortage of affordable housing. Decent low-cost rentals and modestly priced homes for sale were both in short supply. Following the revolution of 1968, which put farmworkers in charge of priority setting in the VML, the members of the area advisory boards and the Mexican Americans on the VML board both made it clear to the VML administration that one of their top priorities was addressing the housing shortage. An approach that appealed to many of them was self-help housing. They wanted the VML to introduce projects similar to ones that had been undertaken in other parts of the country in which groups of five to ten families pooled their labor resources and, with some outside assistance, built homes for each of the families in the group. John Little strongly supported the idea.[52]

Perhaps the most outspoken advocate of self-help housing within the VML circle was Pete Collazo, the chairman of the Woodburn area advisory board and a December 1968 addition to the VML board. A former resident of Kerrville, Texas, Collazo was a tall bruiser of a man, who earlier in life had been a semipro baseball player and boxer as well as a political organizer for Henry B. Gonzales, the Mexican American politician from San Antonio who had served in the Texas legislature and was elected to the U.S. House of Representatives in 1961. Although Collazo had not gone beyond the third grade in school, he was bright, well-spoken, and extremely well informed. Having relocated to Woodburn, Collazo, his wife, and several of their children worked in a factory in Canby, Oregon, making onion and potato bags that were used in supermarkets.[53] In January 1969, at a VML board meeting attended by the OEO program analyst Hank Aguirre, Collazo announced to Aguirre that the VML would seek support from the OEO for a new self-help housing program to be launched in the April 1, 1969–March 31, 1970, funding period. The VML's initial request would be for about $19,000, with most of the money going toward the salaries of a housing coordinator and a secretary to administer the program. But the board intended to request much larger amounts in future years.[54]

The OEO approved the budgetary request and the VML's self-help housing program began operations soon thereafter. A housing coordinator was hired. The organization worked out the program basics. Initially, each separate project was to include eight to ten participating families, and each one of them was expected to contribute a minimum of thirty hours of labor a week. The VML was responsible for explaining the program to the community, encouraging families to participate, finding and paying a housing contractor to supervise the work of each team, and arranging loans for potential participants with the Farmers Home Administration to pay for the lots, building materials, and assorted expenses. Little and his staff had high hopes for the program. Their stated goal was to build forty new homes in the first year of the program's operation.[55]

That intention proved to be wildly optimistic. Despite the fact that Sonny and the other area directors were supportive and proactive, immediately holding meetings about the new project with members of the farmworker community, a number of problems surfaced and progress was minimal. It took several months to work out satisfactory arrangements with the local branches of the Farmers Home Administration; to the VML's surprise, relatively few eligible families initially expressed an interest in participating; in many communities, it was very difficult to find buildable lots at affordable prices. During the first full year of funding, not a single house had been built and only the center in Independence was within hailing distance of beginning construction. Staff there had assembled a team of potential home builders, generated a sufficient number of loan applications, and located acceptable lots. Finally, in May 1970 a group of five families began construction of five homes in Independence. Seven months later, when those families moved into their houses, the local press gave prominent coverage to the story. Elsewhere, however, home construction was delayed. When Sonny left the VML in August 1971, no houses had yet been started in Forest Grove. As of January 1974, a total of fifty-seven self-help houses had been built in four of the five areas served by the VML (Jefferson, Independence, Woodburn, and Forest Grove). None had yet been completed in Dayton.[56]

At about the time that the VML launched the self-help housing project, Little and his staff began to promote an economic development program. The basic idea was to interest and assist members of the farmworker community in starting small businesses and cooperatives. The VML helped people to develop their business plans, provided technical advice, arranged introductions, and sought funding from government agencies to support these fledgling businesses and cooperatives. One business started with VML encouragement and help was a gas station cooperative that opened in Hillsboro in September 1969. Sonny and his opportunity center staff played key roles in getting the project started. But, like most of the businesses assisted by the VML—and like most small businesses everywhere—the gas station struggled to make a profit and eventually closed.[57]

In the end, both of these VML initiatives did not live up to the organization's expectations. The self-help housing program, strongly supported by representatives of the farmworker community on the VML board, was responsible for the construction of a modest number of homes. Although those buildings doubtless made a difference to the families that occupied them, the communities served by the VML continued to suffer from a housing shortage. The record of the economic development program was also mixed: on the one hand, it provided some people with useful business experience and, in the short run, generated dozens of jobs; on the other hand, most of those businesses soon disappeared and the program's long-term impact on the region was minimal.

Of greater consequence was another development that occurred during this period—the rise to power of a Mexican American VML administrator named Francisco (Frank) Martinez. Born in 1937, the son of a New Mexico state policeman, Martinez had gotten a college degree, attended a seminary, and become a priest. He spent eight years in parish work in three small communities in rural New Mexico. In 1968, however, having left the priesthood and married, Martinez was looking for new opportunities. He learned that the VML was attempting to recruit an education specialist to assist Lane Williams in running its adult education program.[58]

As it happens, John Little himself was spearheading the recruiting effort, and he was searching for more than an education specialist. Since taking over as executive director, Little had stated repeatedly that he wanted to turn the directorship of the VML over to a Mexican American. Little was hoping to find an education specialist with both administrative skills and formal qualifications who could be groomed to take over the directorship. He had failed in his initial efforts; after identifying several seemingly strong candidates, Little had taken a three-day trip to the Southwest to interview them and had not found anyone suitable. After his return, the director of a migrant program in New Mexico called Little to recommend Martinez. On paper, Martinez had superb qualifications: a strong educational background, a record of accomplishment as a priest. Little and Lane Williams contacted Martinez and conducted a job interview on the phone. Well-spoken, thoughtful, and self-confident, Martinez wowed them. At the end of the phone call, Little offered him the job, and he announced Martinez's appointment at the board meeting on September 29, 1968.[59]

Once on the job, Martinez did not disappoint. In staff meetings, he became a major force, dominating them due to his eloquence (in both English and Spanish) and the power of his arguments. Less than a month after Martinez had started work, Williams reorganized the adult education program, dividing the supervisory duties between Martinez and himself. Nine months later, in July 1969, Williams resigned from the VML to take a position with another OEO-affiliated organization and Martinez was promoted to Williams's former position. One by-product of the promotion was that Martinez, needing an assistant to do the work he formerly had done, hired another New Mexican, Pablo Ciddio y Abeyta. Martinez had first met Pablo Ciddio when the two of them were seminarians, and like Martinez, he had parted ways with the Catholic Church.[60]

In public forums, Martinez at once revealed a combative, demagogic streak. In December 1968, he gave a riveting speech at a "Mexican-American Congress" he organized at Mt. Angel College, which attracted between three hundred and four hundred participants. "This is the time to unite," he told the audience in Spanish. He also urged his listeners to say proudly, "I am a Mexican American." Always articulate and often brutally frank, Martinez became a favorite with local journalists reporting on developments in the Mexican American community. In September 1969, when *Oregonian* reporter Robert Olmos asked Martinez whether public schools in Oregon's Willamette Valley were meeting the needs of the newly settled Mexican American residents, he replied: "There are about five hundred Chicano kids in the valley just hanging around, having dropped out of school. They get disillusioned with what's going on in school. All tests in school are geared entirely to the white community."[61]

This is not to say that Martinez was without flaws or that he was a perfect fit for the VML. Some of his VML colleagues found him formal and pedantic. Although he was no longer a priest, Martinez retained a priestly bearing, aura, and demeanor. Other characteristics set him apart and may help to explain some of the problems he eventually encountered. One enduring reality of the Mexican American community was its heterogeneity. Within the group we call Mexican American, there were a mix of peoples with very different regional, cultural, and social backgrounds. Frank Martinez was a New Mexican, and like many natives of that state, traced his origins to the Spanish settlers of the region. That fact differentiated him from most of Oregon's Mexican Americans, who came from the Rio Grande Valley. Socially, Martinez was far removed from the Mexican Americans he worked with and for. He grew up in a middle-class household with middle-class expectations and aspirations. He was well educated and worldly. Although he had interacted with indigent people during his years of parish work in rural New Mexico, he found those parishioners to be quite different from the Mexican Americans he encountered in Oregon. He was shocked, he told me in an interview, at the "low self-esteem" of the migrants he served at the VML. When members of the "power structure" or farmers spoke to them, "they would bow their heads in fear, in shame." Martinez considered it his mission to convince those people to "believe in themselves."[62]

While it might be overly harsh to characterize Martinez's view of Oregon's Mexican Americans as patronizing and paternalistic, it was arguably closer to Will Pape's view than that of John Little. Little's approach was to empower poor people, trusting in their ability to arrive at good decisions. Martinez harbored reservations about the ability of those people to make good choices and defined his role as raising them up to the point where they could do so. Little was an enabler, Martinez an instructor. Those were significant differences, to be sure, but they were not so obvious during Martinez's first few years with the VML. More obvious were his talents.

By 1970 it was clear that Martinez was the heir apparent to Little. In March of that year, when Little traveled to Washington, D.C., to confer with OEO officials and members of Oregon's congressional delegation, he brought Martinez with him. Two months later, with Little's support, Martinez became chairman of the organizing committee for the Oregon Poor People's Conference, an outgrowth of Martin Luther King's Poor People's Campaign launched in late 1967. The Oregon event was to be held in Salem. The assignment was extremely challenging since little money was available to run the conference, and the participating groups—African Americans, Mexican Americans, Native Americans, indigent whites, even gypsies—bickered among themselves. But Martinez was able to secure a financial contribution from the governor's office and to hold the fragile coalition of organizations together. The conference, which took place in September 1970, received mixed reviews, the local press reporting that, while valid issues were raised, the behavior of some participants left much to be desired. When Governor Tom McCall gave a welcoming address, members of the audience booed him, and at a workshop on legal rights, a resolution was drafted indicting McCall because of his administration's "gross neglect of the needs of the poor." McCall and his staff were furious about the rough treatment, and from that point forward, the governor was cool to Martinez, refusing to provide financial support for follow-up conferences on the issues raised in Salem.[63]

Within the VML, however, the prevailing view was that the Poor People's Conference was a major triumph. In his monthly executive director's report, Little praised Martinez and other participating VML staff members for doing a "tremendous job."[64] Shortly after the conference, Sonny, David Aguilar, Jimmy Amaya, and a few other Mexican Americans in the VML, meeting together, decided that the time had come for Martinez to replace Little as executive director. They spoke with Little, who, pleased that he had at last made himself superfluous, agreed to step down. Little announced his resignation on December 9, 1970 One week later, the board named Martinez to replace him.[65]

Once in charge, Martinez announced that he would not make any major staff or programmatic changes. Even so, there were observable changes in style and tone. Whereas Little was effective at getting results by meeting privately with people and hammering out agreements, Martinez seemed to revel in public confrontation. In speeches and interviews with reporters, he regularly raised questions about the state's treatment of minorities and farmworkers and called for corrective action. Equally confrontational was Martinez's old friend Pablo Ciddio, who became Martinez's principal advisor and also held the position of chairman of the Governor's Advisory Committee on Chicano Affairs. During the period of Pablo Ciddio's chairmanship, the committee sparred constantly with McCall, criticizing his policies and complaining that he ignored their suggestions. Displeased by the criticism, McCall dissolved the committee in March 1971, replacing it with a Commission on Human Rights that was to represent all minorities. Pablo Ciddio described the governor's actions as "extremely tactless." The following month, the VML held a special awards night, honoring organizations and individuals that had made "outstanding contributions" to the people of the state. Various well-known Oregon government officials were nominated for awards, including Congressman Al Ullman and Senators Mark Hatfield (who won an award) and Robert Packwood. Notably absent from the list of nominees was the government official who had sponsored the Poor People's Conference, Tom McCall.[66]

Sonny's Departure

By 1971, as Martinez was beginning to put his own personal stamp on the VML, Sonny was ready for a change. He recognized that he could not remain forever at the organization. For some employees, the VML was a take-off point; for others, it was a way station; but for no one was it a career. The organization's unwritten policy was to encourage people to stay for a few years at most. Almost every person who had been working for the VML when Sonny first joined it in 1966 had moved on. Besides, Sonny no longer wanted to stay. Although his salary problems had by now been solved—in January 1970, having revised its regulations, the OEO permitted the VML to raise Sonny's annual salary to $7,200, making him the highest paid area director in the organization—the job had lost its appeal.[67] He had other ideas in mind for his future.

Over the past two years, taking advantage of the professional development program John Little had set up for VML employees, Sonny had taken a few college courses. To accommodate the employees, who had to work all day, the classroom instruction took place at night at the VML's opportunity centers. The instructors were faculty members from the Oregon College of Education in Monmouth. Sonny took two or three classes. His memory of their content is hazy, but he recalls well that he had no difficulty with the work. He came away from the experience with the belief that he was capable of succeeding in college and he began to think about getting a degree, perhaps even going on to law school. The only problem he faced—and it was a major one—was that, as the head of a household of six, he had to find a way of financing his education while also making enough money to support the family.

A possible solution came to his attention in the summer of 1971. John Little, now working for the migrant education program of Marion County, heard that a local private liberal arts college, Mt. Angel College in Mt. Angel, Oregon, was searching for a director of ethnic affairs. The director had to come from a minority group. One of the director's principal responsibilities would be to recruit minority students to the college. Acquainted with the college's president, Father Christian Mondor, Little contacted him and recommended Sonny for the job.[68]

Intrigued, Mondor arranged to meet Sonny in Mt. Angel, and at that meeting, the two of them worked out an agreement that met the needs of both men. Sonny was most interested in an education. Mondor wanted to hire an effective recruiter. They came up with a formula that bore a certain resemblance to the arrangement Sonny had come up with five years earlier when he had gone to work for the VML: Sonny would split his time between two activities, spending half of it as director of ethnic affairs and the other half as a student. The college would pay him a salary of $7,500 and would waive all tuition and student fees. In September 1971, Sonny resigned from the VML and started work and classes at Mt. Angel College.[69]

The VML After Sonny

After Sonny's departure from the VML, the organization continued to deliver services to the poor. Despite the fact that the Nixon administration slowly dismantled the OEO—it officially ceased to exist in 1975, with several different agencies taking responsibility for funding some of the activities the OEO had previously supported—Martinez managed to secure enough money to fund the key VML programs: education, job training and placement, self-help housing, small business development. Under Martinez's leadership, the VML also launched a bold initiative, gaining control over the delivery of migrant health services in the Willamette Valley in 1973 and opening clinics in Woodburn and Dayton.[70] Martinez continued to work hard, give riveting speeches, and broadcast the message that the state and the country needed to treat Chicanos more fairly. In particular, he opposed several legislative measures—variations of SB 677, which Governor McCall had earlier vetoed—that would have made it much more difficult for Oregon's farmworkers to secure better terms of labor from the growers. The measures were defeated.[71]

But Martinez's record had blemishes. He persisted in adopting an antagonistic stance toward Governor McCall, and in retaliation, McCall and his staff made Martinez's life miserable by repeatedly prodding the federal government into auditing the VML. He also aroused opposition within the local farmworker community by weakening the authority of area advisory boards and consolidating power in the central administration. While he maintained publicly that the VML was a people-run organization, some of the people he served felt that Martinez was not fully committed to the ideal of maximum feasible participation. Ultimately, in early 1974, with regret and several dissenting votes, the VML board let Martinez go. But he landed on his feet, moving on to a successful career in the federal government.[72]

The VML fared worse under Martinez's replacement, Gil Bazan, a Texas-born college graduate who had worked previously in a migrant program in the neighboring state of Washington. Bazan got off to a promising start, winning substantial grants for day-care and manpower training. The organization also began to operate statewide, changing its name to Oregon Rural Opportunities (ORO) in early 1975. After that, Bazan's tenure was disastrous. Management problems surfaced in ORO's health-care operations and other programs, and funding agencies discovered financial irregularities. In December 1978, ORO lost its single largest source of funding, a manpower training grant. One month later, it lost a housing grant. Although Bazan contested the loss of funding in the courts, the judgments went against ORO, and he resigned in May 1979. ORO limped along for a few more months with an acting director and a skeletal staff, and then passed out of existence.[73]

It was a sad end to an organization that, without question, had helped many farmworkers, mostly Mexican Americans. In the fourteen years of its existence, more than 3,000 people had participated in VML/ORO adult education programs, with at least 600 of them receiving GED degrees. More than 1,000 people had signed up for vocational training programs, and at least an equal number had received job placement assistance. During the years in which the organization offered services to children, hundreds of them received summer instruction and thousands more were enrolled in day-care centers run or supported by the VML. Dozens of self-help houses were built. During the Martinez and Bazan years, thousands of people received medical care at the agency's clinics. Year in and year out, moreover, an incalculable number of people—the actual number must be in the tens of thousands—received advice, medical referrals, and various other kinds of assistance from the organization's opportunity centers.[74]

What impact did all those services have on the people served by the organization? Certainly they changed lives. Consider another life story—that of Esther Sanchez, originally from Edinburg, Texas, a woman with a ninth-grade education and poor financial prospects who came to Carlton, Oregon, in the late spring of 1966 to pick strawberries, pole beans, and other crops, accompanied by her third husband, Pedro, and nine children. Hearing about the VML's adult education program and feeling that she should try to get her high school diploma because all her siblings had managed to do so, Esther enrolled in and completed successfully the GED-preparation class at the VML's Dayton Opportunity Center in 1967. Later that same year, having decided that she wanted to become a full-time nurse, she applied to and was accepted by the VML's OJT program, which found her a position as a nurse's aide. The Sanchezes decided to settle in McMinnville. Esther became a major force on the VML's local area advisory board and, after getting a nursing degree at Portland Community College, worked as a nurse in the area for many years.[75] Throughout the Upper Willamette Valley, many similar stories can be told—stories of teachers and school administrators (such as Tina Garcia), attorneys, business owners, farmers, carpenters, factory workers, auto mechanics, furniture makers, store clerks, and tractor drivers, all of whom give credit to the VML for altering the trajectory of their lives. One might hear many more stories told by people who took part in VML programs, and benefited from them, but did not settle in Oregon.

In 1980, a year after the closing of ORO, the Mexican American population of Oregon was still very small—by official count, only 1.72 percent of the state's total (45,170 out of 2,633,105).[76] Even so, the situation had changed considerably since the early 1960s, before the appearance of the VML, when there were fewer than 6,000 Mexican American residents in the state and Jimmy Amaya of Independence had been obliged to travel to Woodburn to buy Mexican food and see a Mexican movie. To what extent was the VML responsible for the growth in Oregon's Mexican American community over the intervening years? There is no simple answer to that question. Even if we knew how many of the new Mexican American residents had participated in VML programs (which we do not), we cannot automatically assume that those programs were responsible for their settling down: invariably a variety of considerations affected those decisions. What we can say for sure is that VML was an important ingredient in the mix not only because its educational and vocational training programs made it possible for farmworkers to leave the migrant stream but also because its presence (and the assistance it provided) made Oregon a more attractive place for migrants to settle down.

The VML also played a key role in nurturing a cadre of Mexican American political leaders in Oregon's Upper Willamette Valley. Due in some measure to the approach and policies of John Little, Mexican Americans in the VML were encouraged to challenge the existing Anglo hierarchy and mount a coup that placed the VML largely in their own hands. After 1968, Mexican Americans dominated the board of directors, held the principal administrative positions, and set the organization's priorities. Given authority, the Mexican Americans of the VML then learned how to exercise it, with the organization functioning as a kind of leadership training institute. In an ethnic community with few college graduates and few established families, the VML served as the place where credentials were established. Many of the leaders of Oregon's Mexican American community in the last decades of the twentieth century and the first decade of the twenty-first had their start in the VML.

Finally, the VML was a place where strong bonds were created among the state's Mexican American leaders. To be sure, the VML leaders-in-training did not always get along—the conflict between Hernandez and Bustos illustrates that point, as does the conflict between Ruiz and Bustos. Social and regional differences did not magically disappear. But by and large cooperation prevailed over dissension in the VML, especially during the period of John Little's directorship. Linkages formed in the VML days—a Mexican American equivalent of the old school tie—persisted for decades, and those were supplemented by other associational ties: affiliation with the Centro Chicano Cultural, involvement with the grape boycott, and so forth. The result was what I have called the Mexican American network, a combination of both personal and associational bonds that could be invoked and mobilized in time of need. As we shall see, the principal occasion for invoking it would occur in the mid-1970s when one of the leaders of the Upper Willamette Valley's Mexican American community, Sonny Montes, led a struggle to save the Colegio Cesar Chavez.

From Mt. Angel College
to Colegio Cesar Chavez

Fifteen miles northeast of Salem, set amid rich farmland in the shadow of Mt. St. Helens, Mt. Hood, and Mt. Adams, the municipality of Mt. Angel, Oregon, was, in many respects, the quintessential American small town, a real-world equivalent of Clark Kent's Smallville, where family and church were the bedrock of the community, where several generations of a family lived in close proximity to each other, and where children were expected to go to school, follow the rules, then go to work, marry, settle nearby, and produce a new generation of children whose lives were expected to follow essentially the same pattern. At its core, the place was conservative, accepting the existing social, religious, political, and economic order and adopting change cautiously.

A white social and political elite was firmly in control of the town. Of the 1,973 residents of Mt. Angel counted by federal census-takers in 1970, 1,941 of them were classified as white, 0 as "Negro," and 32 as "other," a category that included Japanese, Chinese, and various other groups. The 1970 census offered no hints about how many Mexican Americans were in the town—in those days, the census takers included most of them in the total for whites—but it seems likely that there were at least 100 to 200 of them, a not-inconsequential number in a small Oregon town of that day.[1] A sizable percentage of the white townspeople who ran the town traced their ancestry back to German Catholic settlers who had begun arriving in the area in the 1860s, and most of Mt. Angel's officials in the early 1970s came from families with central European origins.[2] In 1966, Mt. Angel began holding an Oktoberfest, a central European tradition, and for four days, visitors were treated to sausages, stuffed cabbage, sauerkraut, strudel, and an assortment of beer and wine. Crafts were displayed, bands played oompah music, and German dances were performed.[3]

Mt. Angel, remote, rustic, and conservative as it was, was a very unlikely setting for the two significant developments that were to unfold there in the 1970s—the creation of a college that was committed to providing an education to Mexican American students, a radical idea at the time; and the waging of a social movement led by Sonny Montes that aimed to save the college from extinction. How was it that this experiment in higher education and this social movement would be launched in such an off-the-beaten-path place? To answer that question, we must first direct our attention to the history of Mt. Angel College, the institution that had hired Sonny in 1971.

A Small College in Trouble
Mt. Angel College had its origins in a girls' school called Queen of Angels Academy, opened in 1888 by a group of Benedictine sisters from Switzerland. The institution underwent a series of name and mission changes over the next decade, and by the turn of the twentieth century, it was known as Mt. Angel Academy and Normal School. The normal school developed a solid reputation as a teacher-training institution, and many of the state's schoolteachers were educated there. In 1947, the normal school was renamed Mt. Angel Women's College, and seven years later, it was accredited as a four-year college, still specializing in teacher training. Up to this point, its students had come primarily from Oregon's Catholic families, and virtually all of its instructors and administrators were Benedictine nuns.[4]

Then came a period of dramatic transformation. In 1958, the college decided to admit men, and its name was changed once more, this time to Mt. Angel College. Enrollment crept above 100 for the first time. New buildings were completed in 1960, financed by loans received from the federal government's Housing and Home Finance Agency.[5] Also in 1960, the college began to offer degrees in subjects other than elementary education. Enrollment continued to climb, and increasingly non-Catholics were admitted. In the 1964–65 academic year, there were 450 undergraduates on campus, and only slightly more than half of them were Catholics.[6]

Another change was structural. In 1965, a decision was made to incorporate the institution as a private college, legally independent from the Benedictine sisters. While a Benedictine nun still served as president and nuns taught most of the classes, laypersons were added to the board of trustees, which made major policy decisions.

At the same time, the college announced a campus-expansion campaign, involving the projected construction of twenty-eight new buildings. The ultimate goal was to triple the enrollment to about 1,200. The first structures to be built were two additional dormitories, and to finance the project, the college took out another federal loan, bringing the total of its mortgage debt to slightly more than $1 million.[7]

Mt. Angel's expansion effort could not have been more badly timed. In the mid-1960s, the United States was in the midst of a massive development of public higher education. As the public sector expanded, private colleges found it difficult to attract students. In 1967, enrollment at Mt. Angel College abruptly fell to 356, and a committee appointed by the board of trustees reported that the college's finances were in a "critical state." Not enough money was coming in to allow the college to make its sizable loan payments. Shortly afterward, the college's president Sister M. Alberta Dieker resigned. She was the last Benedictine nun to head the institution.[8]

From that point forward, Mt. Angel College was in a state of almost constant crisis. The central problem was budgetary. The school did not have a substantial endowment; nor, like some colleges, did it receive large infusions of grant income every year. To pay its bills, it relied primarily on the money received from its students' families in tuition payments. Its campus-expansion initiative had been undertaken on the assumption that enrollment would rise every year, thereby enabling the college to cover its obligations. That did not happen.

The school's financial difficulties led to further changes in the school and, in turn, to a new set of problems. Desperate to keep the ship afloat, the college's new administration, led by Dieker's successor, Brother La Salle Woelfel, attempted to attract out-of-state students. Like many other private schools, the college adopted a permissive conduct code. On the issue of sexual behavior, the student handbook stated: "While the college does not provide contraceptives, it will assume the responsibility of directing inquiring students to competent medical authorities." Also, Mt. Angel refashioned its curriculum, supplementing its degree programs in education, behavioral science, art, and other subjects with a new completely elective liberal arts degree. As a result of the changes, the college attracted a sizable contingent of out-of-state students, some who would have then been described as "hippies." In-state enrollment, on the other hand, dropped sharply, as the college was losing its traditional support base in the state's Catholic population. Other groups were alienated as well. Only a handful of Benedictine sisters still taught at the college, the residents of Mt. Angel kept their distance, and some members of the board of trustees were outraged.[9] Other on-campus developments made things worse. Early in 1969, the chairman of the college's Department of Theology and Philosophy, Father Joseph Biltz, a maverick and social activist, publicly criticized the Catholic Church's positions on the Vietnam War, birth control, and other issues. The local church hierarchy suspended him from his priestly functions, but Biltz stayed on at the college.[10]

These new developments produced more instability. Increasingly concerned by the changes in curriculum, student behavior, and the composition of the student body, and very upset by Brother La Salle Woelfel's refusal to dismiss Biltz, the board of trustees forced Woelfel to resign. For the next eight months, to save money, the college operated without a president, being run by a "management team" of faculty members and administrators. In January 1970, a new president was brought in, but he was fired within a month after a dispute with the board.[11] The board then searched internally for a president, and in February 1970, it chose Father Christian Mondor, a forty-four-year-old Franciscan priest with a varied career as an educator. He had served for several years as vice principal of Serra High School, a Catholic institution in Salem. After Serra had closed, Mondor had resumed his own schooling and earned a doctorate in education from the University of Portland. At the time of his appointment as president, Mondor had been at Mt. Angel College for less than a year, serving as both the chaplain and a faculty member in the Department of Education. Youthful looking, bright, and optimistic, he was popular with students and staff members.[12]

Mondor was a vast improvement over his predecessors, and initially there was a surge of hope. In the first week of his presidency, the U.S. Department of Housing and Urban Development (HUD), the agency that had absorbed the functions of the Housing and Home Finance Agency, agreed to suspend temporarily the school's payments on its outstanding building loans. Enrollment increased slightly. In January 1971, it stood at 305, prompting Father Mondor to remark that the college was doing "quite well."[13]

But within two months it was again in turmoil, as two factions on the campus contended for control. On the left, there was Biltz and a contingent of student activists, the most outspoken being a group of eight African American students who had been recruited to Mt. Angel College and were unhappy with the place. Like African American students at other campuses, they complained that the school did an unsatisfactory job of meeting their educational needs and did not devote enough energy and resources to the recruitment of minority students. Biltz agreed with them and promoted their agenda. As Mondor put it, Biltz "considered himself the voice of the oppressed."[14] On the right, there was the college's board of trustees led by the board chairman August Kalberer, the owner of a Portland restaurant supply company, who wanted to move the clock back to the days when the college offered a more traditional curriculum and educated a very different kind of student. Mondor's impossible mission was to satisfy both factions. Philosophically, he had little sympathy with Kalberer's position. "He didn't understand what Mt. Angel was all about," Mondor recalled. At the same time, while he personally liked and admired Biltz, Mondor found him difficult to work with.[15]

Matters came to a head in March 1971. First, Biltz held a news conference at which he denounced the college as a "white racist institution" and called for its closing. Mondor, who had received no advanced warning of the press conference, was stunned. While publicly acknowledging that some of the criticisms were valid, he pointed out that the college was attempting to recruit more minority students and to hire an African American faculty member.[16] A few days after Biltz's blast, the press reported that Kalberer had written a letter to all Mt. Angel faculty and staff informing them that the college would likely close, alluding vaguely to "various problems involved in the continued operation of Mt. Angel College, not the least of which is financial." Doubtless, the school's finances were shaky, but they were no worse in March 1971 than they had been for the previous four years. Kalberer's real reason for writing the letter was to intimidate the college community. By threatening to close Mt. Angel, he was trying to silence the faculty members and students who were resisting his policies. Mondor reacted immediately, telling the press that the institution would stay open and faulting Kalberer for jeopardizing "the well-being and continued growth of the college."[17]

In the end, the conflict between the activists and Kalberer was resolved in the activists' favor. Following the publication of Kalberer's letter, the student body mobilized and called for his resignation. By the end of the month he and two of his supporters on the board were forced to resign, and in his place, as the new board chairman, was Ivo Bauman, the president of the family-owned private telephone company in Mt. Angel, one of the town's most progressive thinkers, and a strong supporter of Mondor.[18] The working out of the issues raised by Biltz took another two months, largely because Biltz and his group were firm in their views. But eventually, in early June 1971, an agreement was reached that provided for the school to hire an African American professor, to recruit more minority students, to set aside more scholarships for them, and to create a new position of director of ethnic affairs and hire someone from a minority group to fill it.[19] That is how Sonny Montes's job came into existence.

Curiously, Biltz—the person most responsible for creating the position occupied by Sonny—left the college before Sonny arrived there. Over the summer of 1971, Mondor asked Biltz to hire an African American to teach at Mt. Angel. Without consulting the African American students, he chose a man named Ajihad Ra for the job. When the students learned that the hiring had occurred in their absence, they were furious with Biltz and a blow-up ensued. Biltz resigned from the college, left for San Francisco, and later returned to his former diocese in Arkansas.[20]

As this retelling of Mt. Angel College's troubled history should make clear, the institution that hired Sonny Montes as director of ethnic affairs in 1971 was in desperate shape. Its resources were limited and debt load was high. While Father Mondor remained optimistic, press coverage suggested that closing the college was a possibility. In his discussions with me, Sonny has admitted that, at the time he decided to take the job at Mt. Angel College, he knew very little about the institution's recent troubles. Rather, he focused on the positives: the prospect of obtaining a college degree and of

140

assisting other members of minority groups in doing the same. A more risk-averse job applicant might have asked more questions and carefully weighed the costs and benefits of working at Mt. Angel. But, as we know, Sonny, like his father, was not afraid to take a risk.

The New Director of Ethnic Affairs
Sonny began work at Mt. Angel College in September 1971, as a new academic year was beginning. There were now 278 full-time students on campus, a decline of 30 from the previous autumn. The shortfall meant that the college would be operating at a sizable deficit. Still, the situation was not yet so critical as to warrant a new flurry of newspaper stories predicting the college's demise. A fund-raising campaign, launched in the previous spring, had netted several thousand dollars in donations, and the school's summer programs had raised additional income.[21]

From Sonny's first days on the Mt. Angel campus, he was pulled in several directions. Intent on getting his degree, he took as many classes as he could handle. He focused on courses in behavioral science, a department that included faculty members in psychology, sociology, and social work.[22] As before, he had family responsibilities, but he did not have enough time in the day to do justice to them, in part because he was so busy at the college and also because he had a long commute. He and Librada had initially decided not to move the family from Hillsboro, and about a year would pass before they relocated to Woodburn, a much shorter drive to Mt. Angel. Further complicating the situation was the arrival of another child in the Montes household, Javier, who was born on December 27, 1971. With five children to look after and with Sonny so busy, Librada was under an enormous strain.[23]

Then, of course, there was the new job. Sonny had never worked in an academic organization before, and he knew little about American academic culture and mores. As had been the case in the past, he relied on a mentor to provide him with guidance—in this case, Father Mondor, who, despite his own heavy work load, met regularly with Sonny and discussed with him, among other things, the school's financial difficulties, the recent conflicts between the college community and the board of trustees, and the importance of Sonny's job as a recruiter of minority students.[24]

In those early meetings with Sonny, Mondor placed particular emphasis on the goal of increasing the number of Mexican American students on the Mt. Angel campus. He was passionate on the subject. To some extent, the passion had its origins in Mondor's experiences and observations. Having lived and worked in Oregon for more than a decade, he felt that Chicanos "had been treated like dirt" by the largely Anglo populace. Mondor was interested in making amends. But he also was convinced that the country's Mexican American student population offered an important potential source of enrollees for Mt. Angel College. At the time, he estimated that, across the United States, there were at least 50,000 Mexican Americans not then enrolled in institutions of higher education who were capable of doing college work.[25]

Mondor was correct in thinking that the educational needs of many Mexican Americans were not being met. According to a 1971 study funded by the College Entrance Examination Board, in the fall of that year there were an approximately 144,000 Mexican American college undergraduates in the five southwestern states of Arizona, California, Colorado, New Mexico, and Texas (which together included about 85 percent of the country's Mexican American population). But, while that figure was growing steadily, having increased by 14 percent over the previous year, it still was not growing fast enough. As the study's authors pointed out, it "would need to be increased by at least another 100,000 to provide a number comparable to the college-age population." The authors' research turned up other troubling facts: a very large percentage of enrollees went to community colleges, rather than four-year institutions, and financial aid for Mexican Americans was woefully inadequate. Furthermore, about 90 percent of the Mexican American students went to public institutions; access to private colleges was denied many of them due to the limited financial resources of Mexican American families.[26]

One development not discussed by the study's authors was the recent emergence of four small colleges that catered to Mexican Americans: Colegio Jacinto Treviño, based in Mercedes, Texas; Juárez-Lincoln University, also in Texas, which was launched by two leaders of the Colegio Jacinto Treviño who had a falling-out with their colleagues; Universidad de Aztlán in Fresno, California;

and Deganawidah-Quetzalcoatl University (D-Q University), located near Davis, California, which aimed to educate both Native Americans and Mexican Americans. All four schools were still in the process of formation in 1971, all were experiencing serious growing pains, all were experimenting with nontraditional approaches to education, and, as of late 1971, none of them had more than a handful of students on campus. Hence, it would be hard to make the case that these colleges had made significant progress in meeting the needs of Mexican American students in the country.[27]

In Oregon itself, we lack the sort of detailed surveys of Mexican American higher education that were conducted in the Southwest. Census data are at best suggestive, since the census in 1970 did not specifically count Mexican Americans in Oregon. Perhaps the most relevant statistic we can find in the census volumes is that 1,259 "persons of Spanish language" in Oregon were attending college. Unfortunately, however, we don't know how many people in that census category were Mexican Americans, nor do we know how many of them were attending colleges in Oregon.[28] Other hints appear in the sources—the allegations made by Sonny during the 1971 demonstration at Portland State that the university had only three Mexican American students, the documents in the VML records discussing the handful of students the organization supported each year at Linfield College, a story in the *Oregonian* indicating that most universities and colleges in the state had fewer than five Mexican American students, with the exception of the University of Oregon, which had eighty. But, taken together, these fragments do not add up to a complete picture.[29] Such as it is, the evidence indicates that, as of 1971, there were probably not more than a few hundred Mexican American students in Oregon's colleges and universities—that, in other words, the sort of recruiting campaign Father Mondor was considering for Mt. Angel College might possibly yield results.

At this early stage in Sonny Montes's tenure as director of ethnic affairs, Father Mondor, his passions notwithstanding, had fairly modest expectations about the type of Mexican American recruitment campaign that might be conducted by Mt. Angel College. He saw it as a *potentially* valuable initiative. It would help out a group that had been treated badly and might also contribute to balancing the college's budget because, while most of the recruits would not be able to pay the school's high tuition fees, they would qualify for federal financial assistance, and a substantial portion of that money would ultimately be paid to the college. Still, Mondor was far from certain that the Mexican American recruits would be numerous and the financial benefit derived from their attendance would be large. He hoped for progress, but did not expect miracles.[30]

Sonny faced challenges in his new position. As of September 1971, there were exactly two Mexican Americans on campus, a decrease of one from the previous spring. Both were being sponsored by the VML's "head-of-household college program," a slightly modified version of the program that had sent Tina Garcia and several other students with farmworker backgrounds to Linfield College.[31] Given the fact that Mt. Angel had so little experience in educating Mexicans Americans, it would be difficult to make the case to prospective Mexican American applicants that Mt. Angel could meet their needs. The school's remote location was also a negative factor. Even so, if anyone was qualified for the job, Sonny was. He was experienced in recruiting people—to job training programs, adult education classes, area advisory committees, and the like. He also could rely on his personal alliance system, his network of contacts in the VML and other organizations. Some of those people could and would help him to identify good candidates for admission.

Sonny contacted his allies.[32] He asked VML employees, friends in government agencies, and others to recommend prospective students and then got in touch with the people identified. While he spent some of his time recruiting recent high school graduates, he did not focus exclusively, or even largely, on them. He also sought out farmworkers and former farmworkers who had finished their schooling many years before, people who had received their GEDs from the VML's adult education programs, even some who had neither a high school diploma nor a GED but were thought to have academic potential. Sonny describes his approach to the new job as "flexible." His major goal was to "meet a real need out there"—the need of his own people to get college degrees and improve their lot in life.

One of his early recruits was Rito Valdez, who was in his mid-twenties, married, and had several children. A migrant farmworker from Texas, Valdez had followed the crops to Oregon, where he had made contact with VML and enrolled in adult education classes, eventually receiving his GED. Bright and industrious, he had impressed a number of Sonny's former VML colleagues and they had urged Sonny to consider him. A meeting took place, Valdez seemed interested, and Sonny thought that he was a good candidate. Sonny argued his case to the admissions committee and Valdez was admitted.

But, on registration day, Valdez did not show up as planned. Sonny phoned Valdez's home and discovered that his new recruit was still in bed. Woken up and called to the phone, Valdez explained that he was no longer certain about attending college because he had doubts about whether he could support his family while he did so. Such concerns were understandable. Although federal grants would cover a portion of Valdez's college expenses, there were no stipends to reimburse him for the lost income from his job, the cost of additional child care, and other outlays. So Sonny and Rito talked over the financial issues and eventually Sonny persuaded him to register. Valdez did well at college, got his degree, and returned to Texas, where he became a municipal official in the town of Progreso.

The problems Sonny encountered in recruiting Rito Valdez were typical. It took time to identify the right candidates for admission, more time to answer their questions and address their concerns. Invariably money was a key concern—specifically, the impact of college attendance on the family's finances. In many cases, the biggest hurdle to negotiate was to convince the recruit—generally a person who had never given serious thought to the idea of going to college—that he or she was capable of earning the degree. Sometimes Sonny succeeded; sometimes he did not. Initially, the progress was slow.

Over time it sped up. There is a built-in multiplier effect in student recruiting. Once a few students are recruited, it becomes easier to interest the next few. Recruits such as Rito Valdez could be enlisted to identify other potential college students in their communities and assist in recruiting them. Over the course of the 1971–72 academic year, the number of Mexican Americans on the Mt. Angel campus increased from two to a few dozen. With the increase in numbers, Sonny's job changed somewhat. In addition to recruiting students, he served as a counselor to those already on campus, assisting them to make the transition to college, advising them, monitoring their academic progress, and speaking to their instructors about their performance.

On December 22, 1971, three months after Sonny's arrival in Mt. Angel, the FBI made another surreptitious appearance in his life. An FBI agent called on Father Mondor to discuss Sonny. The FBI was still keeping a close watch on Sonny at this point, considering him "potentially dangerous." According to Mondor, the agent explicitly stated that Sonny was a Brown Beret who advocated the use of violence. Mondor had the impression that the agent was trying to influence him to dismiss his director of ethnic affairs. He came to Sonny's defense, asserting that the FBI's views of Sonny were absurd. He characterized Sonny as loyal and hard working, expressed absolute confidence in him, and objected strongly to the agent's assertion that Sonny was a man of violence.[33]

Given the temper of the times, Mondor was not surprised that the FBI was showing an interest in Sonny. He knew that in that era of antiwar protest the FBI was keeping a close watch on college campuses. Nor, for that matter, was he troubled by it. He was sure that there was no factual basis to the FBI's concerns and figured that his strong denials of Sonny's radical tendencies would help to set the record straight. The meeting over, he treated it as if it had never taken place and didn't mention it to Sonny.[34]

A Period of Self-Analysis

Father Mondor was pleased with the new minority student recruitment program. Unfortunately, he did not have much else to be pleased about. Despite the increase in Mexican American students, total enrollment continued to fall at Mt. Angel College. In the winter quarter of 1972, it stood at 259, a drop-off of 19 from the previous quarter. Faced with another budgetary shortfall, Mondor was forced to announce staff reductions and other cost-cutting measures. Asked by the press to comment on the situation, Mondor explained that the college was actively searching for solutions. "We are now engaged in a self-analysis, studying the reasons for this drop in enrollment," he said. "We are in the process of trying to define ourselves in a more limited way."[35]

Such developments affected Sonny's work as well as his relationship with Father Mondor. With the future looking bleak, the president was willing to consider any reasonable proposal that might help save the institution. One idea suggested by Sonny captured his attention—the suggestion that the Mexican American recruitment program be expanded, because it offered the prospect of significantly improving the college's financial health. "I knew," Sonny recalls, "that Latinos were one possible solution to the college's problems. . . . It made sense." In his meetings with Mondor in the winter and spring of 1972, Sonny prodded the president to place greater emphasis on Mexican American enrollments. "He could be a strong advocate," Mondor told me. "And he did push. He did urge us."[36]

This is not to say that overnight Mexican American recruitment became Mt. Angel College's major institutional priority. In this period of self-analysis, which lasted about five months, Mondor and the rest of the college community were meeting frequently, and any proposal that seemed to offer the hope of improving the college's finances was given a hearing. Even so, among the proposals under discussion, the idea of increasing the Mexican American presence on campus received especially serious consideration. Father Mondor's enthusiasm for the idea was in part responsible for the attention it received, but Sonny himself played a key role. During those months he lobbied other members of the Mt. Angel community to gain support for his initiative.

As Sonny lobbied, he fleshed out his proposal. With more Mexican Americans on campus and with the likelihood that their numbers might grow substantially, he argued that the college needed to provide courses and academic programs to meet the new recruits' academic needs. In the winter quarter of 1972, Sonny took the lead in developing a Chicano studies curriculum at Mt. Angel College by organizing a committee for that purpose that included several Mexican Americans living in the area. His principal collaborator was Francisco (Pancho) Loera, who directed the Migrant Education Service Center in Salem and had some familiarity with the Chicano studies programs that were proliferating in California's public colleges and universities. Sonny had become acquainted with Loera in his VML days and was impressed with his intellect. Sonny and he often conferred by phone about program development and Loera traveled from his home in Salem to attend meetings. The work of the committee produced immediate results. In late March 1972, the college announced that a new class, An Introductory Course on Chicano Arts and Affairs, was to be team-taught in the spring quarter by Ajihad Ra, the recently hired black studies specialist, and Adolfo S. Blanco, a college-educated printer living in Dayton, Oregon, who was active in local Mexican American organizations.[37]

A few weeks later, there was another hint that Sonny's initiative was gathering momentum. A Mexican American named Jose Garcia (not the Jose Garcia who had been Sonny's first VML supervisor) joined the college's board of trustees. The holder of a BA from Pan American College and a master's degree from Eastern Oregon College, Garcia worked for the Washington County Intermediate Education District. Not surprisingly, Sonny played a key role in the selection of Garcia. For months, Sonny had been pressing Mondor to add a Mexican American to the board of trustees, and finally the president agreed. When Mondor then asked Sonny for the name of a suitable candidate, Sonny had suggested Garcia, whom he had come to know during his years of working in Washington County.[38]

In June 1972, as the academic year was coming to a close, self-analysis at last gave way to action at Mt. Angel College. The college announced several major curricular and organizational changes. For one, it introduced a College Without Walls program, adopting an academic approach that was receiving some national attention at the time. Students could henceforth enroll in, and receive academic credit for, a wide range of off-campus activities, which were to be coordinated by an academic administrator. Also, a new system of college governance was introduced, reducing the decision-making power of administrators and increasing that of other members of the academic community. Finally, the college committed itself to fostering multicultural awareness. It would schedule more ethnic studies courses, provide minority students with appropriate academic counseling, and attempt to give them enough financial aid so that they could complete their degrees.[39]

Another significant indication of the college's commitment to multiculturalism was the creation of a Chicano studies department, which was announced at the same time and discussed in several newspaper articles. Sonny was featured in all of them, making the case that the new department would be unique. Most U.S. colleges were, in his view, incapable of educating Mexican Americans: "They are still operating on a philosophy of education rooted in the ethnocentrism of white America." Mt. Angel College would, by contrast, provide a "coherent, socially relevant education" to prepare Mexican Americans and others for service to the Chicano community. At the outset, the new department would focus on assisting Mexican American students in making the transition to college. The curriculum would emphasize the "formal study of Chicano culture and society in all of its unity and diversity." The courses to be offered would include the Mexican American Experience, Mexican American History, Economics of the Mexican American Community, and Chicano Contemporary Social Problems. According to the newspaper accounts, the college planned to hire a director of Chicano studies over the summer.[40]

Early in July 1972, the administration provided further confirmation of its decision to prioritize the Mexican American initiative, when it announced the appointment of Ernesto Lopez, a Mexican American, as academic dean. Predictably, Sonny was an active participant in the hiring of Lopez. Early in the search process, Father Mondor had asked Sonny if he could suggest any Mexican American who might be a viable candidate for the deanship. Sonny made some phone calls, learned about Lopez, a doctoral candidate in the School of Education at the University of Oregon, and passed on the recommendation to Mondor. He also helped to recruit Lopez, traveling to Corvallis where Lopez was doing some part-time work and encouraging him to come. At the time, Mondor saw the hiring of Lopez as a masterstroke, believing that it would make the college more attractive to Mexican American students.[41]

The Accreditation Crisis and Its Aftermath
Notwithstanding the announced changes, the college's problems did not abate. In the fall quarter of 1972, enrollment declined to 235, resulting in another substantial budgetary shortfall. As had been the case in 1969, Mt. Angel launched a campaign to recruit new students. Advertisements promoting the college were placed in area newspapers; volunteers visited Oregon's community colleges, attempting to convince students to transfer; recruiters even traveled to Canada, hoping to draw students from private colleges in British Columbia and Alberta.[42]

Then came disaster. In early December 1972, the Commission on Colleges of the Northwest Association of Schools and Colleges, the unit charged with accrediting colleges and universities in Oregon and six other western states, voted to withdraw accreditation from Mt. Angel College, citing deficiencies in its operations. The loss of accreditation, which was scheduled to go into effect on July 1, 1973, had potentially dire consequences. Prospective employers of graduates of Mt. Angel College might not take their educational attainments seriously. Loss of accreditation also meant that Mt. Angel's students would no longer be eligible for many categories of federal financial assistance, a development that was likely to reduce substantially the pool of potential applicants on which it could draw. The impact would be especially severe in the case of Mexican American students, since most of them were dependent on federal funding.[43]

Although the action of the Northwest Association caught Sonny and many other members of the college community by surprise, Father Mondor had been aware for more than a year that the college's accreditation was at risk. In the fall of 1971, an evaluation team from the Commission on Colleges had visited Mt. Angel, the site visit being a required component of the accreditation renewal process. Identifying problems in the college's finances, academic programs, and student services, the evaluators had asked the Mt. Angel administration to address the deficiencies and then to file a report about the steps it had taken. The report was to be delivered to the Commission on Colleges prior to its annual meeting in December 1972, at which time the question of renewal would be formally decided.[44]

In November 1972, Mondor had submitted his report, detailing the progress that had been made—the appointment of Lopez and other faculty members, the clarification of the college's goals, the development of Chicano studies, and the increase in minority enrollment. Unfortunately, he could not report that the college's financial situation had improved. Realizing that an unfavorable decision on accreditation was possible, Mondor attended the commission's December meeting, where he appealed to the voting members to delay their decision on accreditation for a year and grant the college a chance to put its finances in order. They turned him down.[45]

That reverse was a blow to Father Mondor. In public, he vowed to fight on and professed to be optimistic about the college's prospects. "We didn't want the college to roll over and die," he explained to me. Privately, however, he was unsure about the college's chances of survival and began to wonder if it was time for him to move on. Perhaps others might provide better leadership and cope more effectively with the new round of troubles to be faced.[46]

The college's loss of accreditation had immediate negative consequences. The press again speculated regularly about whether the college would survive, and that speculation merely made a deteriorating situation worse. Aware that the college's future was in doubt, the parents of many students decided to make their academic investments elsewhere. When the winter academic quarter began in January 1973, enrollment had dropped to 196. In the spring, it plummeted to about 150. The school's budget in shambles, Mondor was forced to introduce more cost-cutting measures: the faculty was trimmed from thirty to ten, and both the cafeteria and the student union building were closed.[47]

During the twelve-month period following the Northwest Association's decision, the college's administration, faculty, students, and board of trustees made a valiant effort to keep the ailing patient alive. They did so by trying to solve two related problems. One was how to restore the college's eligibility for federal student financial assistance since that was the only way to insure that it would have a large enough student pool to be financially viable. The second was to figure out how to restructure the college so that it could use its limited resources wisely and maximize its chances of attracting students. Mondor and his staff addressed the first problem; the entire college community addressed the second.

Mondor recognized that the college could not easily undo the commission's decision on accreditation. In practice, a college gained eligibility for federal student financial assistance in one of three ways. First, it could apply for full accreditation to a regional accrediting organization such as the Northwest Association. Second, it could apply to such an organization for "candidacy status"—which meant that the school merely had to show promise of meeting full accreditation status in a reasonable time. (Once granted candidacy status, an institution had up to six years to qualify for full accreditation.) The third option might be described as the "three-letter route." A college needed to establish credit-transfer agreements with three accredited institutions and arrange for them to send letters to the Department of Education stating that the agreements were in place.[48]

In light of the fact that the first two options were extremely time consuming, the most appealing one was the third. So Mondor and his administrative staff attempted to conclude credit-transfer agreements with accredited four-year colleges and universities in the state. Over the first nine months of 1973, Mt. Angel officials made overtures to and held face-to-face meetings with administrators from five schools—Oregon State University, Pacific University, Linfield College, Marylhurst College, and the University of Portland. But, while the meetings were invariably cordial and the officials at all five schools expressed sympathy for Mt. Angel, only the University of Portland demonstrated any interest in negotiating a credit-transfer agreement.[49]

Mondor was not out of options, though. Before the Northwest Association had rendered its unfavorable decision, aware that a loss of accreditation was likely, he had begun to investigate an unorthodox way of coping with it: to affiliate Mt. Angel College with a consortium of educational institutions that was then in the process of being assembled. The key player in the consortium was Antioch College in Yellow Springs, Ohio, a liberal arts college with a distinguished past that had begun experimenting in the 1960s with decidedly nontraditional approaches to learning. In this particular experiment, Antioch was attempting to establish a relationship with two of the four recently created Mexican American colleges in the Southwest, both of them unaccredited—Universidad de Aztlán and two branches of Colegio Jacinto Treviño (the main campus in Mercedes, Texas, and another one in San Antonio, Texas). Students at the Mexican American colleges would take their classes on their own campuses, but their degrees would be awarded by Antioch. Since Antioch was accredited, students at the affiliated schools would presumably be eligible for federal assistance too. Additional funding would likely come from private sources, including the Ford Foundation. As soon as he learned that Mt. Angel had lost its accreditation, Father Mondor began discussions with Antioch and the Mexican American colleges about adding Mt. Angel to the consortium. Initial meetings were promising—far more promising than the ones held with the accredited colleges in Oregon about establishing credit-transfer agreements.[50] But as Father Mondor was to discover, the creation of a consortium was a difficult undertaking.

At the same time Mondor was looking into the three-letter and consortium options, the entire college community was engaged in a discussion about institutional reconfiguration. The discussion focused on the idea of changing Mt. Angel from a four-year college into a two-year "institute," offering a small number of specialized academic programs. The institute would issue a certificate, rather than a diploma. An obvious attraction of the institute proposal was that reducing the scope of the institution and the number of courses offered would save a good deal of money.[51] One obvious question raised by the institute idea—a question that was posed at the time but never answered—was exactly how the new institute would mesh with the proposed consortium. By and large, the problems of gaining eligibility for federal funding and restructuring the college were treated on their merits and as independent variables.

From the start, there were major battles on the campus about the two-year institute. Advocates, Father Mondor and Dean Lopez among them, argued that, with the school so short of money and lacking accreditation, it was no longer sensible to operate as a four-year school: the best that could be done would be to offer two years of training in a limited number of subjects. A number of faculty members and trustees doggedly resisted the change, arguing that it was too drastic. Even among the advocates, there was disagreement about what programs to offer. Some wanted to focus on traditional liberal arts subjects; others favored strictly vocational instruction.[52]

By March 1973, it appeared that the advocates of the two-year institute had won. The campus community began drafting plans to establish the institute, and Mondor and Lopez went to Salem to discuss the proposed changes with the Educational Coordinating Council, a state agency charged with assessing and approving new programs in Oregon's colleges and universities. But the drafted plans were very rough, and it was abundantly clear that important decisions had not yet been made. Although the rationale for adopting the institute approach had been to focus on a small number of programs, the documents Mondor and Lopez brought with them

153

indicated that the institute would initially offer classes in six areas of concentration: communication and fine arts, music, women's studies, early childhood development, professional recreation instructor training, and bilingual/bicultural teacher training. It was a curious and much-too-ambitious lineup, a mixture of liberal arts and vocationally oriented programs. What the plans revealed most of all was that, while a majority of the campus community favored the institute, no agreement had been reached about the content of the curriculum.[53]

After the Salem meeting, the discussions about the institute resumed on the Mt. Angel campus. Increasingly, they turned into debates, and tempers flared. Opponents of the institute mounted a rearguard action, again arguing the case that Mt. Angel should remain a four-year college, but they were again defeated. Among the institute's advocates, there were still serious disagreements about which programs to offer and which ones to cut. Alliances were forged and deals were made. Alliances fell apart.[54]

Then, in the months of April and May 1973, in the midst of this seeming chaos, a dominant group within the advocates' camp emerged. Led by Sonny, it consisted of the Mexican American students he had recruited, campus allies he had been cultivating (including Ivo Bauman, the chairman of the board of trustees), and, most important of all, Father Mondor. This group argued that the two-year institute should cater primarily to Mexican American students and offer a curriculum geared to the needs of those students.[55]

How did Sonny's group come to dominate the debate? At the time, among all the contending parties on the Mt. Angel campus, it was the most enthusiastic, energetic, and unified. "You could sense the momentum," Sonny recalls. "We were so involved in what we were doing. We were excited, and we didn't see the difficulties." Whereas most programs on campus were contracting in the aftermath of the Northwest Association's decision about accreditation, the ones associated with Sonny's Mexican American initiative were expanding. In late January 1973, Mt. Angel had received a $30,000 grant for a bilingual/bicultural teacher training program, designed to "produce teachers capable of teaching with equal effectiveness in both English and Spanish"—capable, that is, of dealing more effectively with the growing numbers of Mexican

American pupils in the region. The grant allowed Mt. Angel to offer several new courses in the spring quarter of 1973, including Fieldwork Participant Involvement in the Chicano Community, taught by Dean Lopez. It was also responsible for the inclusion of the bilingual/bicultural teacher training program on the list of the institute's areas of concentration submitted to Educational Coordinating Council in March.[56] And there was more—a marked increase in the number of Mexican American cultural events on campus, the fact that the consortium under discussion involved two other Mexican American schools. In that context, with the Mexican American initiative on the ascendant, Sonny's group pressed the other institute advocates to adopt a Chicano-oriented curriculum. Working behind the scenes, Bauman attempted to convince his fellow trustees to do the same.[57]

By the end of May 1973, Sonny and Ivo Bauman had done their jobs, and the board of trustees rendered its verdict. It decided, first, that in the next academic year the college would operate as a two-year institute and, second, that the new institute would focus initially on only three academic programs: bilingual/bicultural teacher training, Chicano studies, and early childhood development. The second decision represented a decisive victory for Sonny's group, since two of the programs to be offered were intended to appeal to a student body made up largely of Mexican Americans. (In late September 1973, the administration decided to resume its College Without Walls program, adding another option that appealed to Mexican American students.)[58] Further confirmation of their victory came over the next few days. On May 29, reporting a conversation with Father Mondor about Mt. Angel's new look, a reporter commented that "the thrust of the new approach is to provide education [to] and instill pride in [the] Willamette Valley's Chicano community." Two days later, the press revealed that four new members had joined the college's board of trustees. Three were Mexican Americans; the one Anglo was Sonny's former boss, John Little. Naturally, Sonny had recruited all four of them.[59]

Jose Romero

In June 1973, Sonny was given another recruitment assignment. The first director of the Chicano studies program had not worked out, and Mondor asked Sonny to find a replacement. In light of the decision that had just been made to prioritize Chicano studies, the hire was of major importance. Sonny and several Mt. Angel students traveled to the University of Oregon in search of Mexican American graduate students who might be qualified to serve as a program director. One of the people they spoke to was Jose Romero, who had just completed his master's degree in political science.[60]

Born in 1941, Romero had grown up in Moorpark, California, northwest of Los Angeles.[61] Both of his parents had spent much of their lives picking crops in the fields, although by the 1950s Jose's father had landed a job at Lockheed, working as a welder and riveter. Living in a region that produced crops year round, the Romero family did not have to migrate in order to find farm work; they could commute from their home to the fields. All ten of the Romero children were expected to pick the crops or perform other kinds of agricultural labor whenever they were not in school. As a youth, Jose did not give a thought to going to college. His goal was to get a job at the General Motors plant in Van Nuys, about forty miles away, where the pay was good and it was possible for employees to buy a new car or truck at a substantial discount.

After graduating from high school in 1959, Jose landed an assembly-line position at General Motors. Laid off the next year when General Motors temporarily shut down the plant, he found work at Lockheed, where his father was employed. Starting off as a helper in the machine shop, he later became a tool and die maker and was able to earn a reasonable income. Then, one day in 1965, several Peace Corps representatives came to Lockheed, looking for skilled workers to serve overseas. His curiosity aroused, Jose discussed the idea of joining the Peace Corps with his wife, Kathy, who was also interested. From 1966 to 1968, the Romeros served as Peace Corps volunteers in Venezuela.

Back in California in 1968, Jose could have returned to his job at Lockheed, but he wanted to do something else. He had accumulated some savings during the Lockheed years and decided to go to college. Jose enrolled at California State College, Los Angeles, where he majored in Latin American studies and completed his undergraduate degree in two years. At the time, the college was a hotbed of Chicano activism, but while Jose was sympathetic to the activists, he didn't join any of their organizations. He was too busy trying to get his degree and handling family responsibilities: in September 1969, Kathy gave birth to their first child.

Encouraged by one of his professors to consider graduate studies, Jose applied for, and was awarded, a lucrative grant from the Ford Foundation to finance his graduate education. Choosing to enter the political science department at the University of Oregon, he started classes in Eugene in the fall of 1970. Jose did well as an MA student, producing a thesis on the evolution of the farmworker movement in the United States.[62] At that time, he also became involved in political activities, picketing outside Safeway stores in Eugene, attending meetings of activists on campus, and participating in demonstrations around the state. Like Sonny, Jose came to think of himself as a Mexican American activist.

Up to the point that he met Sonny in 1973, Jose had every intention of continuing on in graduate school. The University of Oregon's political science department had accepted him into its doctoral program, and he planned to begin his doctoral studies in the fall of 1973. But the meeting with Sonny and the students from Mt. Angel College caused Jose to rethink his plans. They told him about the growth of Mexican American enrollment at the institution and conveyed to him their commitment to keep the college going. "We can't give up," they explained. "We can't give up on ourselves." To Jose, their enthusiasm was inspiring. "I'll come in a year," he promised, explaining that in that time period he would be able to finish his doctoral coursework and then be in a position to devote his full attention to directing the Chicano studies program. But Sonny urged Jose not to delay his coming; they needed him right away, he said. Jose agreed to discuss the possibility of taking a leave of absence with Kathy and the political science department. Meanwhile Sonny did everything he could to convince Jose to come. He returned twice to Eugene to speak with him, arranged for the Romeros to live rent-free in a house owned by the college that was located beside the campus, and helped to negotiate Romero's salary. Finally, Jose accepted the job. He began work at Mt. Angel College in the first week of September 1973.[63]

The Departure of Father Mondor

As of early September 1973, with a new academic year fast approaching, Mt. Angel College had taken important steps to prevent its closing. A four-year college had been transformed into a two-year institute. The school now focused on attracting Mexican American students, and its reduced curriculum was designed to appeal to them. It had also hired a new director of the Chicano studies program. Mt. Angel had become, to use the descriptive phrase adopted by its administration and picked up by the press, a "largely Chicano-oriented institution." One thing the school hadn't done, however, was to restore its eligibility for federal student financial assistance, which had been scheduled to end on July 1, 1973.

It wasn't for lack of trying. Throughout the spring and summer of 1973, Mondor and his staff persisted in their efforts to establish credit-transfer agreements. In the end, however, only one institution, the University of Portland, concluded an agreement with Mt. Angel College. The others, Mondor concluded, were reluctant to establish a relationship with a struggling unaccredited institution.[64]

Mondor also vigorously pursued the consortium option. On that front, too, there were setbacks. During the early summer of 1973, at an early organizational meeting with representatives from Antioch and the other Mexican American schools, Father Mondor was shaken by the comments of one Chicano college president, a self-proclaimed ethnic militant who spoke approvingly of Hitler's *Mein Kampf* and demanded, among other things, that Mexican Americans be placed completely in charge of the consortium. Still, that unpleasant moment passed, and the group agreed that a Mexican American would be president and Father Mondor would be provost. In August 1973, Mt. Angel College formally committed itself to joining the consortium.[65]

But, within weeks, the consortium had unraveled. The president of Colegio Jacinto Treviño in Mercedes, Texas, was forced out of office by his own faculty and students, and the new leadership expressed reservations about participating in the consortium. At that point, Antioch issued an ultimatum to all the schools, telling them that, unless they committed themselves completely to the arrangement, there would be no further negotiations. Those developments caused Mondor and others on the Mt. Angel campus to reconsider their participation. By the end of September 1973 they had decided to back out, and negotiations never resumed.[66]

As the unraveling took place, Father Mondor and Dean Lopez became resigned to the reality that, for the foreseeable future, the institution was not likely to reach any agreement that would restore its eligibility for federal funding. In other words, they acknowledged that they had done only part of what they needed to do in order to give the college a sporting chance of attracting a respectable number of enrollees in the coming academic year. Although they continued to tell the press that a consortium might be organized and a credit-transfer agreement might be concluded, they also discussed publicly another way of dealing with the accreditation issue: reapplying for accreditation to the Northwest Association. One thing they didn't explain was why, given the college's financial problems, the accrediting agency would be likely to reach a more favorable decision than it had in December 1972.[67]

At this point, on the eve of the new academic year, Father Mondor informed the board of trustees that he intended to step down as president. As we know, he had been thinking about doing so ever since the college had lost its accreditation, but had stayed on to mount a final campaign. When the consortium disintegrated, he felt that there was nothing more he could do. He was mentally and physically exhausted.[68]

Mondor's imminent departure led to a new round of discussions on the campus. A few members of the board of trustees felt that the time had come to close Mt. Angel College, but Lopez, Sonny, and other Mexican Americans argued that they should be given a chance to run the school. Mondor also supported the idea of turning Mt. Angel over to the Mexican Americans. While Ivo Bauman, the chairman of the board, was sympathetic to the idea, he wasn't sure if they had a chance of succeeding. He put the question to the entire board, and the board, urged on by the four Mexican American trustees and John Little, voted to keep the school open and to appoint a Mexican American president.[69]

One obvious candidate for the presidency was Ernesto Lopez, but Mondor had reservations about him. While he admired Lopez's intellect and teaching skills, he felt that Lopez didn't have the desire or even the aptitude to be a college administrator. As Mondor put it, "Lopez was a bit bewildered by the situation." For that reason, he recommended that the board appoint Lopez acting president and launch a search for a permanent Mexican American president. The trustees decided otherwise, appointing Lopez president and forgoing the search. The announcement of the change in leadership was delayed until the start of the school year.[70]

Registration began at Mt. Angel on October 1, 1973. No one knew for sure what to expect, not even Sonny, the school's principal recruiter, who, over the summer of 1973, had been "beating the bushes" to find potential enrollees. If the job of recruitment had been difficult in the past, it now bordered on the impossible, since the college was unaccredited and he could not promise financial aid to prospective students. Sonny cast his net even wider than before, but he hadn't found many people willing to commit to enrolling and that worried him. Ernesto Lopez was more optimistic, telling the press that he expected about a hundred students. Lopez's guess was wide of the mark. When the registration period ended on October 15, the college announced that only 55 full-time students had enrolled.[71]

One small consolation was that the institute received extra income from another source. Thanks to John Little, a group of about 100 teachers from the Marion County Intermediate Education District had signed up to take a course on "cultural awareness." The presence of those teachers had the added benefit of creating the illusion that the number of full-time students was higher than it really was. Over the next few years, the college would receive a small but steady stream of money from similar types of arrangements, many of them organized by Little. A second consolation was that, to the surprise of the college's administration, most of the students who submitted applications for federal financial assistance were able to get it. Apparently, the staff of the Northwest Association had neglected to tell HEW officials that Mt. Angel's accreditation had been withdrawn. Had the snafu not occurred, who knows how few students would have enrolled in the fall quarter? The unexpected windfall of financial aid continued for the rest of the academic year.[72]

The Birth of the Colegio Cesar Chavez

On October 18, Mt. Angel announced Mondor's resignation and his replacement by Lopez. Discussing his decision to leave, Father Mondor explained to the press that, since the college now intended to serve the Mexican American community, it was appropriate that its president be a Mexican American. Mondor kept to himself his reservations about Lopez.[73] The elevation of Lopez to the presidency created an opening for a new academic dean. Jose Romero was appointed to that position about four weeks later.[74] At that point, all three of Mt. Angel's chief administrative officers—Ernesto Lopez, Jose Romero, and Sonny Montes, who now held the job title of director of student services—were Mexican Americans.[75]

Unfortunately for the three of them, the academic institution they administered was unaccredited, unloved, and almost bankrupt. A four-year college that once boasted about 50 faculty members and close to 500 undergraduates had shrunk to a two-year institute with 4.5 paid instructors and a few dozen students.[76] Dormitories that once were full were shuttered up. Many rooms were filled with trash. Every building needed a fresh coat of paint. The entire campus, wrote a local reporter, had "a down-at-the-heels appearance."[77]

And if all that were not enough, on November 15, 1973, with no advanced warning, the deputy director of the HUD office in Portland, Paul Timmons, announced that HUD was considering the possibility of foreclosing on the college's unpaid loans. The total debt owed to the federal agency stood at close to $1 million. According to Timmons, although the college had agreed to make delayed payments to HUD, it had paid exactly nothing for several years. "The situation has not improved," he said, "and it cannot go on like this forever."[78]

Lopez promptly traveled to HUD's regional office in Seattle to meet with agency officials and reassure them that the college would pay off its debts. They asked him to present a plan to HUD, spelling out how Mt. Angel expected to improve its finances and make its payments. If the plan satisfied HUD, the agency would not proceed with the foreclosure. Right after the meeting, Lopez began working on his plan.[79]

But he did not devote all of his attention to it. Lopez and the rest of the college community were busy finalizing arrangements for a ceremony to be held at the college on December 12, a major festival day for Mexicans and Mexican Americans celebrating Nuestra Señora de Guadalupe, a sixteenth-century apparition of the Virgin Mary. The purpose of the ceremony at Mt. Angel on that traditional day of celebration was to rename the college.[80]

As early as the spring of 1973, at a time when the campus community was debating the conversion of the college to an institute, there had been discussions about changing the school's name. No firm decision was made at the time. Then, in October 1973, after the launching of the institute, a student revived the idea. As a result of the governance reforms introduced in the previous year, Mt. Angel had adopted the practice of holding community meetings, attended by faculty members, staff, and students, to debate matters of importance. A meeting was scheduled to revisit the issue of the name change.[81]

At the meeting, the students took the lead, urging the assembly to adopt a more appropriate name for the reconfigured institution. At one point, several of the students went to the blackboard at the front of the room and asked the audience to suggest possibilities. About twenty-five names were suggested and written on the blackboard. Most members of the audience wanted to name the school after an important historical figure of Latino origin. Some consideration was given to Che Guevara. Then, as Sonny remembers it, another young person got up and urged naming the college after Cesar Chavez. The idea appeared to strike a responsive chord in the audience. Sonny himself was strongly supportive, since Chavez was his hero. After a discussion, the group voted unanimously to change the institution's name from Mt. Angel College to Colegio Cesar Chavez.[82]

At that juncture, it was necessary to contact Cesar Chavez to get his approval. Jose Romero wrote a letter to Chavez and sent it to the union's headquarters. Chavez was anything but enthusiastic. He was embarrassed by the honor and concerned that people might think that he had encouraged the school to change its name. Chavez also felt that Oregon's Mexican Americans could serve the Chicano cause more effectively by taking part in boycott activities and helping the union to organize farmworkers than in trying to save a struggling school. Father Mondor and others did their best to convince Chavez otherwise, and in the end he tepidly consented to the use of his name, making it clear that, while he was not promoting the name change, he would not object to it "if that was the wish of the local community."[83]

Having gotten Chavez's approval, college officials and other members of the campus community organized the event at which the name change would be announced. They were secretive. Although they stated publicly that the college's name was to be changed on December 12, they refused to reveal what the new name would be. They asked the Archbishop of Portland, Robert J. Dwyer, to say Mass at the ceremony, and he agreed to do so. As the day approached, there was speculation in the press about the new name.[84]

On December 12, 1973, the ceremony was held, as scheduled, on the Mt. Angel campus. About 100 people attended. Several newspapers covered the event, as did a television crew. Archbishop Dwyer said Mass and gave a sermon. Ernesto Lopez announced that henceforth the school would be known as Colegio Cesar Chavez and shouts and cheers erupted from the audience.[85]

The following day, the administration of the Colegio distributed a news release, explaining their long-term objectives and drawing parallels between their own efforts and those of Cesar Chavez. "Like the farmworkers of La Causa," the release read, "we are struggling nonviolently to bring educational opportunity to students deserving a better chance in life." Also like Chavez and his supporters, they were unwilling to admit defeat: "Many thought the farmworker organization would not last one month. Here it is eleven years later and La Causa persists. Thus we see ourselves. We know that the struggle ahead will be a great one and that there will be much sacrifice over the years. Yet we are committed to survive."[86]

The "Save Colegio Cesar Chavez" Campaign: A Local Manifestation of the Chicano Movement

It would be difficult to make the case that Colegio Cesar Chavez played a significant role in the history of U.S. higher education. Its library was tiny, numbering perhaps 40,000 volumes. Its salaries were uncompetitive, and for a while nonexistent. Most of the time, its core faculty included no PhDs. Its student body was small and shrinking—at no point in its nearly ten years of existence did its full-time enrollment reach 100. Lacking an endowment, it was dependent on outside sources to fund the education of its needy students. For months on end, its furnaces did not work.

As a symbol, however, it was very important. For five years, the Colegio's struggle for survival was a recurring front-page news story in the Pacific Northwest, and its leaders became well known to the public. To many observers, the school assumed the role of David in a battle against a triad of goliaths—HUD, the Department of Health, Education, and Welfare (HEW), and the Northwest Association. The establishment, it seemed, was picking on the downtrodden.

The Colegio's struggle was also an important regional manifestation of the Chicano movement. While there was more to the Chicano movement in the Pacific Northwest in the mid-1970s than the struggle of the Colegio, no other component of that movement attracted as much public attention. One reason it did so was that its leaders, especially Sonny Montes, were skilled in using the tactics available to mobilize support. In addition, Sonny and his colleagues were able to tap into an established network of like-minded people.

The Colegio

The campus of the Colegio Cesar Chavez was modest in size: the total land area was approximately five acres. Although the terrain in that part of Mt. Angel was flat, the college grounds had a fair number of trees, a mix of conifers and deciduous varieties. At one edge of the campus, there was even a small orchard of nut trees. Situated to the south of Mt. Angel's town center, the Colegio was

164

divided into two somewhat unequal parts by South Main Street. On the east side of the street, adjoining the property still occupied by the Benedictine sisters, was Guadalupe Hall, the college's largest building, which housed the cafeteria, a day-care center, and a ballroom that was used for dances, Masses, weddings, and other big events. Across the street were five other buildings belonging to the Colegio. Three were sturdy modern structures: Huelga Hall, which included the Colegio's administrative offices and conference rooms on the first floor and dormitories and classrooms on the upper floor, and two other residence halls, Sala del Sol and Sala de la Luna. The two other structures were weather-beaten wood houses that had been used for art instruction since Mt. Angel College days. One was called Studio San Benito or simply the art building, and the other was referred to as either the studio annex or the pottery building.

In January 1974, at the start of its first full quarter of operations, the Colegio issued a mimeographed handbook titled "Colegio Cesar Chavez: Philosophy, Goals, History, Faculty, Admissions, Financial, Academic and General Information." Not exactly a catalog, since it did not include course descriptions, it still provided important information about the recently renamed institution. For one, it revealed that a change had occurred in the degree plans offered by the school. Students henceforth had the option of pursuing *either* a certificate of competency, which required 60 credit hours in a designated area of concentration, *or* a BA degree, demanding a total of 192 credit hours, with 60 of them in a field of concentration. That section signaled that the decision to change the institution from a four-year college to a two-year institute, one reached after interminable debate, had been modified, with no fanfare or public discussion. The modification is not hard to fathom. Since the Colegio was desperate for income and students, it made little sense to limit the applicant pool to certificate-seeking students and turn away those who wanted a bachelor's degree. For the next eighteen months—until a new catalog was printed and the certificate of competency option was quietly dropped—the Colegio would operate as both an unaccredited two-year institute and an unaccredited four-year college.[1]

Also reflecting the Colegio's need for students, the handbook indicated that the school had adopted an "open admissions policy," replacing the already extremely lenient admissions policy prevailing before. Anyone could enroll in the Colegio so long as he or she completed an application form, provided transcripts of previous educational work, and paid a $10 application fee. The Colegio recommended, but did not require, that applicants take standardized (SAT or ACT) tests. Also not required was a high school degree or a certificate of completion from a GED program or an HEP, but students who did not have such credentials would be required to enroll in remedial courses.[2]

The open admissions policy notwithstanding, enrollment in the Colegio did not increase much in the winter and spring quarters of the 1973–74 academic year. As of March 1974, it stood at approximately 70. About half of those students were enrolled in the College Without Walls program, which meant that they did not necessarily take formal classes. Many did not even reside in the area. College administrators attempted to downplay the importance of the low enrollment figures, asserting that they were a temporary aberration produced by the institution's problems with HUD and the Northwest Association. Antonio Fernandez, who had joined the Colegio in January 1974 as director of planning, told the *Chronicle of Higher Education* in June of that year that, while the college had received 350 inquiries from potential applicants for the following academic year, the administration was reluctant to expand too rapidly. "We would like 150 students next year, and 350 a couple of years later."[3] Those increases did not occur. In January 1975 the press reported that 75 students were attending the college. Three months later another newspaper story indicated that enrollment had fallen to 57.[4]

In the fall of 1975, the Colegio finally published a formal catalog, which spelled out in some detail its nontraditional approach to higher education. Building on the approach of Mt. Angel College, which emphasized the cultivation of the individual, the Colegio had evolved into an institution that essentially tailored its education to the goals of each student. It had only two hard-and-fast graduation requirements: its students had to complete at least the equivalent of 186 quarter units (6 fewer credits than the earlier handbook had called for) and to be bilingual, which it defined as being able not only to converse in English and Spanish but also to "function within two different cultural and cognitive frameworks." The

Colegio left decisions about the content of each student's academic program, including the definition of the major field of study and the development of a plan of study, to the student and a *comité* (committee), a group of four individuals chosen by the student. Each *comité* was to consist of one "core" member of the Colegio faculty (out of the four to six instructors who were hired on a full-time basis), two adjunct faculty members (volunteers, some with academic credentials and some without them, who had experience in the student's field of study and agreed to provide assistance), and one fellow student. The *comité* was supposed to meet frequently with the student and evaluate her or his work. The catalog likened the *comité* to the student's immediate family, and the rest of the college community to the student's extended family.[5]

After developing their study plans, the students turned to their studies. Those in residence and others who lived in the vicinity could sign up for formal classes offered by the Colegio. Each quarter, Jose Romero scheduled about a dozen courses that were of potential interest to the school's enrollees (among them, English as a Second Language, Spanish for Non-Spanish Speakers, and U.S. History). By and large, they were given in the evenings to accommodate students who had jobs or family responsibilities during the days. To an outside observer, many of the classes had the look of those at other small colleges in the country, with ten to twelve students sitting around a rectangular table with open notebooks before them and an instructor at the head of the table, leading the discussion and occasionally standing up to scribble words on the blackboard. When total enrollment numbers were lower, some of the classes could be quite small in size. According to Jose Romero, the classroom discussions were animated, with the students showing no reservations about speaking up and challenging the instructors. One likely reason for their daring was that, as I discuss below, they knew their instructors were not grading them.[6]

Attendance at classes was only one component of the Colegio education, however. Except for the first two quarters of its existence, an overwhelming majority of the students at the Colegio were enrolled in the College Without Walls program, which did not require students to reside on campus and afforded them an extraordinary amount of flexibility in achieving their educational objectives.[7] Students could earn credits by taking tutorials on topics of interest from adjunct faculty members or, as was more common, by participating in activities or holding jobs relevant to their individually structured programs. One student in the basic elementary education program, for example, received college credit for an internship at a migrant education agency.[8]

Students at the Colegio did not receive grades from instructors for their formal classes or from mentors for their off-campus work. Rather, in consultation with their *comités*, they were required to evaluate their own academic performance as well as their progress toward their educational goals. The instrument used to assess student performance was called the "learning portfolio." Each student had to maintain one, which might include "papers, project descriptions, the study plan and statements of learning goals, works of art, video tapes, films, photographs of art works, self-evaluations, personal diaries, evaluations by *comité* members and others with whom the student has worked, and any other information which is representative of the student's learning experience and activities." Students and their *comités* were instructed to review those learning portfolios regularly.[9]

One additional noteworthy feature of the Colegio, which was attractive to older students, was the school's policy of giving retrospective academic credit for life experiences. Initially, the college allowed students to apply for a maximum of thirty hours of retrospective credit, but, when the catalog was issued in 1975, all limits were removed. So, for example, Ricardo Martinez, a thirty-one-year-old student, who was seeking a degree in business administration, was able to earn credit for some of the work he had done as an employee of a state agency. To get the credit, a student was obliged (with the assistance of the core faculty member and the *comité*) to "document" the life experience and explain its relevance to the study plan. The documentation could take a variety of forms. Students might submit tape recordings, written descriptions of the life experiences, collections of pictures and papers, and other evidence of past learning. They were also required to make a formal oral presentation about the life experience.[10]

Unaccredited as it was for long stretches of time and having adopted an open admissions policy, the Colegio attracted an atypical group of students. Most were quite a bit older than normal college students. Some had high school degrees, but others did not. There were housewives with children at home, agricultural laborers who were taking classes during the months when there were no crops to harvest, construction workers who had been laid off. "We are succeeding in providing a college opportunity to a lot of people who otherwise would never attend college," Ernesto Lopez told a reporter in June 1974.[11]

One such student was San Juanita Contreras, who lived in the vicinity of Mt. Angel and whose family did not have the money to send her to a school far away from home. While she was aware that the Colegio was unaccredited at the time she applied for admission, she felt that its curriculum met her needs.[12] Jim Castilla, a graduate of a Washington high school, was a transfer student. He had begun college at Central Washington State and had intensely disliked the school. "It is very hard to attend a traditional school and be able to relate at all to the faculty," he told a reporter for the *Silverton Appeal-Tribune*. "There seemed to be little or no respect for Chicano students—as if we were nothing." It also bothered Castilla that the few dozen Mexican American students at the school tried to "act Anglo" in order to fit in. At the Colegio, he felt completely at ease. "We are free to compete and learn in a comfortable environment. We don't feel on guard and we can express ourselves in Spanish to our instructors when we're . . . you know . . . in a bind. It's just easier to learn in this atmosphere."[13]

Another out-of-state student was Florencia Guillen of Laredo, Texas. She had originally enrolled in Mt. Angel College in the 1972–73 academic year, attracted to it by its new Chicano studies program. Although her freshman year had been disappointing and she had come close to dropping out, her attitude had changed since the Mexican American administration had taken over. "We know our teachers by their first names," she said, "and we all work together. We share a positive feeling about what we are doing."[14]

Like Guillen, Rudy Veliz, an education major, had enrolled in the school when it was still known as Mt. Angel College. Born in Edinburg, Texas, in March 1944, Veliz had spent much of his youth following the crops. Eventually he followed them to the Northwest, and in 1966, now married and with a child, he and his wife,

Candelaria, decided to settle down in the Woodburn area. That is when Veliz came in contact with the VML. Recruited first to the OJT program, he received welding instruction and served as a trainee with a Woodburn company. He then moved on to the VML's adult education program, gained his GED, and was recruited by Sonny to Mt. Angel College. Veliz's decision to pursue a college degree placed an enormous strain on the family. The Velizes continued to live in Woodburn, with Candelaria making most of the money, holding a full-time job at a migrant health clinic in the town. During the school year, Rudy split his time between his studies, internships (including one spent at a nonprofit in Portland that specialized in educational issues, where he and two other Colegio students produced a manual about parental involvement in the schools), and child-care responsibilities in his own household. During the summers, he worked nonstop in the fields. Still, the workload did not stop Veliz from participating in the college's collective-action campaigns whenever he could find the time. He joined in the occupation of the college's administration building, took part in marches, and picketed in Portland.[15]

Cipriano Ferrel, a native of Delano, California, and a graduate of Delano High School, was generally acknowledged to be the school's student leader. Before coming to Mt. Angel, he had worked for several years as a staff member for the UFW (the United Farm Workers of America, AFL-CIO, the name adopted by Chavez's union in the 1970s). Ferrel was bright, well read, and much respected by colleagues and fellow students. A high school classmate and co-worker at the UFW described him as a "quiet, kind, and thoughtful person." But, despite that demeanor, he saw the world through radical Chicano lenses and he had no qualms about speaking up and out if the occasion warranted it. Discussing the Colegio's struggles with HUD, he told a reporter: "We are having an impact on the community, and the government doesn't like that." Ferrel also denounced a host of U.S. government policies—among them family planning, which he likened to a "genocide program" intended to "kill off" Mexican Americans. Interested in learning about how the U.S. legal system actually operated, he spent much of his first two years at the college working as an intern at the Marion County Legal Aid Service. But he also visited the campus a few times a week, kept abreast of the college's problems, and assisted Sonny, Jose, and the rest of the administration in mobilizing student support for collective-active efforts. One of Ferrel's classmates at the Colegio recalls that whenever he was away from the campus for extended periods, he would receive telephone calls from Ferrel providing him with updates on the college's difficulties, and whenever a rally or important campus meeting was scheduled, Ferrel would call him again, urging him to attend.

Ferrel's academic focus shifted somewhat in 1976. At the time, there was growing concern among Mexican American activists in Oregon about the actions of immigration authorities in the state. Ferrel and several of his fellow students decided to form a community-based legal defense group—an organization that came to call itself the Willamette Valley Immigration Project (WVIP), and later, Pineros y Campesinos Unidos del Noroeste (Northwest Treeplanters and Farmworkers United), better known by its acronym PCUN. After the formal launching of the WVIP in the spring of 1977 and Ferrel's graduation from the Colegio at about that time, he went to work for the WVIP and later PCUN, remaining there until his untimely death in 1995.[16]

Keeping track of this diverse group of students, many of whom lived outside the Mt. Angel area, was the time-consuming responsibility of Jose Romero. One thing that added to the difficulty of the assignment was that Jose was himself the mentor of fourteen students who were based in the Yakima Valley and the Columbia Basin in the state of Washington. To oversee their work, he sometimes spent two days a week away from Mt. Angel. Jose Romero was not the only staff member who had to work overtime. All the core faculty members were expected to provide both formal courses and tutorials, assist students in developing study plans and documenting life experiences, and attend conferences with *comités* to evaluate learning portfolios. Adjunct faculty members made important unpaid contributions to the college. Betty Rademaker, who held a doctoral degree in education from the University of Oregon, offered occasional classes and also assisted full-time staff member Jan Chavez in developing the curriculum for the Colegio's education department.[17]

Because most of the Colegio's students were not in residence, it might be thought that the campus resembled a ghost town. The reality was otherwise. After Mexican Americans had gained control of Mt. Angel College in 1973, the administration had made the campus available to members of the local Mexican American community—not only to the Mexican-origin people in Mt. Angel but to the larger concentrations of Chicanos in nearby towns such as Woodburn. Many Mexican Americans in the area frequently attended events held at the college. "That was a no-brainer," Sonny explained. "That's how we were able to generate public support. When you open up the college to the community, you make the people feel as though it's theirs. And the word goes out, and they talk to other people. Before you know it, there's this welling up of support from the community." The college's facilities were used for weddings, anniversaries, and baptisms. Local musical groups practiced there. Maria Luisa Alaniz, who became the Colegio's director of admissions in 1974, held a dance class for young children there. A variety of cultural groups performed there, including, on several occasions, Luis Valdez's Teatro Campesino. On Saturday evenings, dances were held on the campus. There were public lectures and art exhibits. Many groups held conferences at the Colegio, and several Mexican American organizations held weekly or monthly meetings there. As in the past, local school districts, state agencies, and nonprofits scheduled short-term training sessions at the Colegio. The Colegio's students organized campus events. One

Jose Romero, director of academic affairs, Colegio Cesar Chavez, ca. 1975. Photograph courtesy of Jose Romero.

year, a group of them held a monthly film series, featuring movies
on the Chicano movement and the struggle for social justice in
Latin America.[18]

While the Colegio was effectively reaching out to local Mexican
Americans, it had little success in winning over the white elite of
central European origin that held power in the town of Mt. Angel.
Relations between the town and the college had been steadily
declining since the late 1960s, when Mt. Angel College had
gained a reputation as a very liberal school and hippies had first
appeared on campus. The situation worsened when the Mexican
Americans took control, and became worse still when the college's
collective-action campaign began in earnest in the spring of 1975.
Whenever staff members and Colegio students ventured into town,
they were greeted with sullen glares. Rumors circulated frequently
among the townspeople about the school. On one occasion, there
was something of a panic when a baseless rumor claimed that the
Chicanos were stockpiling weapons.[19] During the college's struggle
to reach a negotiated settlement with HUD and restore its federal
funding eligibility, many people from the town and neighboring
communities wrote letters to elected officials urging them not to
support the Colegio. Townspeople even launched a telephone
campaign, and a state official reported that he had received fifty calls
and a letter "opposing the college as it stands now." According to
him, "they oppose it unanimously on the grounds that they feel a
school in Mt. Angel should be an open school for their sons and
daughters—not just one group."[20] The members of the Colegio
community also heard rumors about the allegedly bad intentions of
the townspeople. In the spring of 1975, the college administration
decided to board up the windows of Huelga Hall. When asked about
it, Jose Romero explained: "We are afraid there may be some rocks
thrown at us or something and we don't want flying glass hurting
anyone."[21] Sonny occasionally talked to reporters about the school's
poor relations with the town, asserting that the college community
wanted to improve them. But he got nowhere. "In the 1970s, there
was a lot of racism," he recalled.[22]

The Colegio's staff and students didn't have to leave the college
grounds to encounter hostile treatment. There was ongoing tension
between the school and the Benedictine sisters, a perhaps predictable

development given the legal troubles with HUD and the fact that many of the sisters came from local families and reflected the attitudes of the community at large. For several years, Jose Romero and his family lived in a house owned by the Colegio, located beside the campus. Across the street from the Romeros' house was a day-care center, with a small playground, operated by the sisters. The Romeros had young children, and from time to time, when the center wasn't open, Kathy Romero would take her children across the street so that they could play there. But one day the nuns told the Romeros that they couldn't use the playground and asked them to leave. According to Jose, "They just had it in for us."[23]

This is not to say that there was universal hostility to the college. The town's Mexican Americans supported the college, and Ivo Bauman remained a loyal friend. Ann Keagbine, another resident of Mt. Angel, having read a story in the local paper about the telephone campaign against the Colegio, wrote a letter to the editor, which the newspaper published, expressing her enthusiasm for the institution: "I greatly admire the brilliant and dedicated Chicanos who, having struggled against all odds to get their education, are determined to give their fellow citizens a hand up. I earnestly hope they will succeed in spite of all the obstacles they face." What is more, as we shall see, a number of the state's major newspapers—including the *Capital Journal*, the *Oregon Statesman*, and the *Oregon Journal*—published occasional editorials in strong support of the college. "Give Chicanos a Chance" was the title of an editorial in the *Capital Journal*. "Chavez College Merits Support" was the position of the *Oregon Statesman*. Such evidence, while far from conclusive, suggests that Anglo opposition to the Colegio was primarily concentrated within the town of Mt. Angel—or, to put the point a different way, it was, to a certain extent, a function of proximity. One wonders if this disparity in responses to the Colegio was confirmation of a widely observed reality: that racism and ethnocentrism are typically most intense in communities in which minority groups are most in evidence.[24]

For many members of the Colegio community, the most memorable campus event occurred on May 16, 1974, when Cesar Chavez paid his first visit to the college. At the time, Chavez was traveling through the Pacific Northwest, drumming up support for a new round of boycotts, and he had arranged several meetings in the Portland area, including one at the college named after him. More than 600 people, mostly Mexican Americans, crowded into Guadalupe Hall to see and hear Chavez. Music was played, short plays were performed, and a Mexican American professor from the University of Utah read a poem he had dedicated to the farmworker union leader. Chavez devoted most of his speech to the union's fight with the growers, making his case for the boycott. But he also talked about the Colegio, confessing that, if someone had told him five years earlier that Mexican Americans would have established their own college in Oregon, he "would have thought they were crazy." "Who knows?" he added. "Maybe tomorrow there will be mariachi music in the White House."[25]

Chavez's visit to the Colegio was an important event in Sonny's life. He had seen Chavez in person a few times in the past. He had attended his speech at Hubbard in 1969 and another speech in Salem during the campaign against SB 677. He had even met Chavez briefly in Portland at the home of a union organizer. But that meeting had been inconsequential: a handshake, a few perfunctory remarks, another handshake, and an exchange of good-byes. On this occasion, Sonny had his first extended conversations with Chavez and began the process of establishing a personal relationship with him.[26] Jose Romero also interacted with Chavez during the visit, serving as master of ceremonies of a rally featuring the union leader at Reed College in Portland. At one point in the rally, Jose led the crowd in a familiar cheer:

"What are we boycotting?" he asked.
"Grapes!" the crowd responded.
"What else?"
"Lettuce!"
"What else?"
"Gallo!"[27]

The Presidency of Ernesto Lopez

For the first nine months of the Colegio's existence, Ernesto Lopez led the institution. Lopez had to face a host of problems, but two of them preoccupied and ultimately overwhelmed him—the Colegio's debts to HUD and its loss of accreditation.

The Colegio's debt problems actually involved three separate entities: HUD and the two parties legally liable for the loan notes issued in the 1960s, the Colegio and the Benedictine sisters. In the negotiations that took place, those three pursued very different goals. HUD was intent on getting the government's loans fully repaid or, if that proved to be impossible, extracting as much money as it could from the holders of the debt. The Colegio wanted, understandably, to avoid losing its buildings and landed property. Given its scarce resources, however, there were strict limits to how much it could pay. The sisters were most concerned about their legal obligations as cosigners. Their fear was that, if the Colegio were to declare bankruptcy, the government might hold the sisters liable for the entire unpaid balance of the debt. They were willing to part with money (albeit not a huge amount of it) and small plots of land in order to be released from their legal obligations.

The three parties began discussions in January 1974 and they continued to meet, on and off, throughout Lopez's tenure as president. While Lopez participated in a number of the meetings, he left most of the heavy lifting to the Colegio's able attorney, Don Willner, mentioned earlier, the leading partner in a Portland law firm. James Kenin, an associate in Willner's firm, regularly assisted him. In agreeing to serve as the Colegio's attorney, Willner was fully aware that his client was "indigent" and that his firm would likely receive only token payments for its legal services. But he represented the college anyway, because he believed in the Colegio's mission of providing higher education to a disadvantaged group.[28]

Early in the negotiations, Willner was able to establish a cordial working relationship with the sisters' lawyer, William Paulus. But Willner and Lopez constantly clashed with HUD officials who, while claiming that they were sympathetic to the college and willing to listen to any reasonable offer, did not give serious consideration to the school's proposals. The Colegio's representatives quickly grew weary of HUD's professions of good intentions.[29]

Frustrated at the lack of progress, the Colegio sought to even up the odds a bit. On March 5, 1974, Sonny and a few colleagues organized a meeting in Mt. Angel attended by about 200 representatives of Mexican American organizations in the Northwest. The gathering was the first use of collective action by the college in its struggle with HUD, and the healthy turnout was an early indication that a sizable Mexican American network already existed in the region. Among the people in attendance were David Aguilar, Sonny's former VML colleague and now the director of the Centro Chicano Cultural in Gervais; Amador Aguirre, director of the Centro Cultural in Cornelius, an organization that resembled in many respects the Centro Chicano Cultural in its emphasis on educational and cultural programs; Don Delgado of CISCO (the Chicano-Indian Study Center of Oregon), an organization based in Corvallis that offered vocational, educational, and child-care programs to Mexican Americans and Native Americans; Gilberto Anzaldua, a Mexican American from Harlingen, Texas, who had earlier served with Sonny on the Governor's Advisory Committee on Chicano Affairs; four of the VML's area directors and several leading players in the VML's central administration, including Pete Collazo, then the director of the adult education program, who had joined the VML staff in 1969 after serving about eighteen months as co-chairman of the organization's board of directors; representatives of Mexican American social clubs in the Upper Willamette Valley; three administrators of migrant education programs in the state; and Humberto Fuentes, director of the Idaho Migrant Council.

One action taken on that day was to launch a "Save the College" fund-raising effort, directed by a fifteen-person elected board, to help the Colegio pay off its debt. In addition, Lopez held a press conference at which he announced that he was weighing the possibility of filing a civil rights violation suit against HUD (which, incidentally, he filed three months later), because the government was treating the Mexican American administration of the Colegio differently from the way it treated the Anglo administration of Mt. Angel College. "HUD does not have faith that Chicanos can administer their own institution," Lopez claimed. Sonny spoke too, adding that, whereas the federal government gave a considerable amount of financial support to about thirty African American institutions of higher education, it threatened foreclosure against one of the very few Mexican American colleges in the country. "HUD gave moratoriums to the previous administration," he said. "We were here less than two months when HUD bill collectors were at our door."[30]

The statements made by Lopez and Montes on that day are intriguing. In this public airing of the Colegio's grievances, an event that the school's leaders expected to be covered by the press, they had an opportunity to make their case and, it was hoped, to mobilize support for their cause. In doing so, like collective-action leaders everywhere, they engaged in what some scholars refer to as "framing work"—which is to say, they shaped their specific grievances into "broader and more resonant claims."[31] In this instance, the collective-action frame chosen was a variant of the injustice/unfairness frame, a common one in social movements. Specifically, Lopez and Montes were arguing that an arm of the federal government—an executive department, in fact—was singling out Mexican Americans for unfair treatment. The proof offered was comparative. Both Lopez and Sonny made the point that HUD dealt differently with the Mexican American administration of Colegio Cesar Chavez than it did with the Anglo administration of Mt. Angel College, and Sonny went a step further in asserting that HUD also treated another minority group more generously than it treated the Mexican Americans at the Colegio.

It is worth noting that the frame adopted by Lopez and Montes was different from the one that predominated in U.S. social movements of the 1960s and 1970s—the frame of rights. By and large, African American protesters focused on rights denial, as did Native Americans, women, gays, and, for the most part, other Mexican Americans.[32] But the situation facing the Colegio and its supporters was fundamentally different from that of the others. The Colegio had no "right" to borrow money from the federal government and not repay it. From day one of its protest campaign—and the March 5, 1974, meeting *was* day one—the challenge faced by the Colegio's leaders in mobilizing support was to find collective-action frames that masked, or at least did not draw attention to, the reality that the Colegio's problems with HUD stemmed from the Colegio's failure to meet its financial obligations. Under the circumstances, the injustice/unfairness frame was an appropriate choice.

The local press's response to the March 5 meeting suggested that the Colegio's first efforts at framing were successful. Stories about it were featured prominently in the major newspapers of Salem and Portland. A few days later, an editorial supportive of the Colegio appeared in the Salem *Capital Journal.* "What will be gained if HUD forecloses on the school?" it asked. "It's time for human compassion and less bureaucratic red tape."[33]

The meeting at Mt. Angel demonstrated both that the Colegio was capable of turning out large numbers of the regional Mexican American community and that the Colegio had found a message with the potential of generating support. But, at this point in its struggle with HUD, the tactics adopted on that day were atypical of the college's approach.[34] Lopez relied primarily on the legal skills of Willner and, on a few occasions, the assistance rendered by a political influential. Ivo Bauman, who was still on the Colegio's board but no longer the chairman, had a good friend on Capitol Hill, Oregon congressman Al Ullman, and he periodically prevailed on Ullman to intervene on the Colegio's behalf. One intervention occurred in May 1974, when the discussions with HUD came close to collapsing and HUD threatened to initiate foreclosure proceedings immediately. Contacted by Bauman, Ullman agreed to speak to his contacts at HUD, and the negotiations resumed in late June.[35]

For a while, they even seemed productive. In July 1974, negotiators for the Colegio, the sisters, and HUD's Seattle office worked out a deal involving monthly payments to HUD by the Colegio and the conveyance of assets to HUD by the sisters. "There was great joy!" recalled Bauman. In August, though, the joy turned to dismay when HUD officials in Washington, D.C., reviewed the terms of the arrangement and concluded that the assets to be conveyed by the sisters were insufficient. The deal collapsed.[36]

Meanwhile, the Colegio's accreditation problems were growing more serious. Technically, as we have seen, the federal government should have cut off financial aid to Mt. Angel College in September 1973 but did not, due to an administrative error. As a result, students at Mt. Angel College and, after the name change, the Colegio Cesar Chavez continued to receive federal assistance. On May 30, 1974, however, HEW informed Lopez that the federal funding spigot was going to be turned off.

Oddly, the decision to cut off funds was *not* the result of the government's belated discovery of the error; there is no evidence that the Northwest Association ever informed HEW that Mt. Angel College had lost its accreditation. Instead, it was the indirect result of HEW having learned of the college's name change. When HEW did, one of its units, the Accreditation and Institutional Eligibility Staff, looked into the matter and determined that, in its view, the Colegio was not merely a renamed version of Mt. Angel College but rather "a new four year college" with "a new program." That determination led HEW to the conclusion that this "new" college needed to reapply for accreditation and that, until it was accredited, its students would be ineligible for federal educational assistance.[37]

Lopez and his associates knew that the elimination of federal funding would be crippling. It would likely result in a further reduction of student enrollment at the college. Furthermore, with even less money at its disposal, the school could not possibly make regular payments to HUD. Don Willner immediately wrote a letter of protest to HEW, arguing that the Colegio was not a wholly new institution but rather "the same institution as Mt. Angel College, only with a different corporate name." HEW refused to reconsider its action.[38]

After that, in addition to coping with the HUD negotiations, Lopez had to try to find a way to regain eligibility for federal financial aid. He opted again for the three-letter route. Over the next few months, the school made new overtures to a number of local colleges and universities in an effort to secure the three credit-transfer agreements that were needed. This time around, though, the overtures were even less successful than before, a hardly surprising result given that the college was on life support, with HUD threatening foreclosure. While the University of Portland provided a letter, it included qualifications that made it unacceptable to HEW. A credit transfer arrangement was concluded with D-Q University in California, but, when HEW officials did some research, they discovered that the institution was itself unaccredited.[39] With a new academic year approaching, the Colegio had failed to secure a single letter that might pass muster with HEW.

Having made no progress either with the college's debts to HUD or its accreditation difficulties, as well as being troubled by marriage difficulties, Lopez was exhausted. Toward the end of August 1974, he met with Sonny and explained that "he needed to get away for a couple of weeks, that he was going down to Denver, because he was having some personal problems and he wanted to take care of business." Promising to return in two weeks, he asked Sonny to take over his administrative responsibilities in the interim. Sonny agreed. Lopez never returned.[40]

The Montes-Romero Partnership

With no warning about Lopez's decision to give up the job, the college's board of trustees was unsure how to proceed. The group met with Sonny, Jose Romero, and the other staff members to discuss the options. Toward the beginning of the meeting, both Sonny and Jose were asked if they would be willing to serve as president. Neither man wanted the position. "We realized," Jose recalled, "that one guy was going to go bananas in six months if he had to do the job alone." Someone then came up with the idea of appointing Montes and Romero as codirectors of the Colegio, with each having designated areas of responsibility. Under some pressure, Sonny and Jose agreed. According to Jose, "We didn't want it, but someone had to do it."[41]

The board formally approved the proposal, and the two stepped into their new roles. Sonny, in the position of director of administrative affairs, was responsible for payroll, the business office, legal matters, and the day-to-day operations of the college. Jose held the position of director of academic affairs, overseeing the curriculum, on-campus instruction, the College Without Walls program, financial aid, and student services. On September 12, 1974, the press announced that Lopez was leaving the institution in order to finish up his doctoral dissertation and that Montes and Romero had taken over.[42]

For Sonny, the new title and new portfolio of responsibilities were markers of significant changes that were occurring in his life—changes that could be observed in the lives of many other Mexican Americans of that era. Having been raised in a farmworker family, he had begun his working life in the fields and had lived a working-class existence. Then, through a combination of talent, drive, and good fortune, he gradually ascended the vocational and socioeconomic ladders—rung one, the job in Reedley, where he was responsible for running a small grape farm; rungs two to four, the VML positions, program aide to assistant job counselor to area director; rungs five to seven, his assignments at Mt. Angel, director of ethnic affairs to director of student services to college copresident. Each position brought new challenges, demanded a new set of skills, and drew him further away from the world of limited expectations he had known as a child in Weslaco. This is not to say that he had lost touch with the core values he had grown up with. But he was now a white-collar worker—and an upwardly mobile one at that.

As director of administrative affairs at the Colegio, Sonny was the more visible of the two codirectors; he represented the institution in its dealings with the media and government agencies. But, as Sonny candidly admits, he and Jose operated as equals, always consulting on major decisions. Furthermore, the two conferred frequently with many other members of the college community. When difficult issues arose, they met first with a small group of staff members to discuss the situation and develop a plan.

The group usually included Joseph Gallegos, who held the title of director of planning and research. The only son of Joseph and Elouise Gallegos, the Mexican American couple that had arrived in Oregon from San Antonio in 1943 looking for work in the Portland shipyards, the younger Joseph Gallegos held a master's degree in social work from Portland State University. He had come to Mt. Angel in January 1974 because a student-teacher program he was supervising in the Woodburn area rented office space for him on the Colegio campus. Gallegos soon became a volunteer at the Colegio, helping in the preparation of grant proposals, and then was offered a staff position, continuing to develop grant proposals and playing a major role in the Colegio's effort to regain eligibility for federal funding. Also in that group was Maria Luisa Alaniz, the Colegio's registrar and admissions director. As an undergraduate at the University of Oregon in the early 1970s, she had met and become a close friend of Jose Romero, who was then a graduate student in Eugene. After her graduation in June 1974, at Romero's urging, she had joined the Colegio. Other frequent participants were Jan Chavez, the academic coordinator for the College Without Walls program, who also taught classes on elementary education and early childhood education, and Laney Kibel, who likewise split her time between administrative work and teaching (principally on social science).[43]

After meeting with that core group, the codirectors consulted with the college council, the decision-making body established in Mt. Angel College days, which consisted of staff members, faculty, and students. These meetings tended to be long and discursive; anyone who attended was welcome to offer an opinion. Still the council provided valuable advice, and perhaps more important, the procedure of consulting it served to invest the campus community in the decisions reached. In the battles that lay ahead, the Colegio would present a united front to the public. Finally, Sonny and Jose talked to the board of trustees, which by now was made up largely of Mexican Americans, every one of them recruited by Sonny.[44]

From the beginning of their tenure, Sonny and Jose were overwhelmed with the demands of their new jobs. Their work schedules were extremely demanding. In addition to handling their everyday assignments, they were obliged to attend a plethora of meetings—with each other, the council and the board, federal officials, funding agencies and potential donors, and allies and supporters. Both were obliged to work nights and weekends on a regular basis, and they often had to travel out of town. In addition, for close to a year following Ernesto Lopez's departure, Sonny, Jose, and virtually everyone else employed by the Colegio received no pay. Because of HEW's decision to cut off federal funding to the Colegio's students, the balance sheet was even weaker than it had been before, and the business office was forced to suspend all salary payments to faculty and staff. In the Montes household, to help out, Librada took a job as a nurse's aide at a health clinic in Woodburn. On one occasion during the 1974–75 academic year, Sonny was invited to speak at the University of Oregon and received a fee of $500. When he arrived back in Mt. Angel, he gave the entire amount to the college's business manager, who distributed it equally to every member of the staff.[45]

Everyone who worked for the Colegio had to scramble to pay the bills. The janitor held two jobs, working away from the campus from nine to five and then, in the evenings, attending to his custodial duties with the assistance of his wife and children. Jose Romero sometimes earned extra cash by collecting the cans and bottles left behind after the dances and other social functions held at the

Colegio on Saturday evenings, then taking them to a grocery store, where he received a deposit refund for each one. The ten to fifteen dollars he collected each time enabled him to take his family out for dinner on Sunday night at a Kentucky Fried Chicken restaurant or a pizza place in Woodburn.[46]

Fighting a Two-Front War

When Montes and Romero took over from Lopez in September 1974, neither of the two major problems facing the institution appeared to be close to resolution. Negotiations with HUD were at an impasse. The school was still unaccredited. A new academic year was starting, and the future looked unpromising.

Of the two problems, the difficulties with HUD worried Sonny less. Since he had been included in staff meetings concerning HUD during Lopez's presidency, he felt that he understood the issues well. Based on what he had heard and observed, Sonny had reached the conclusion that, despite HUD's threats of foreclosure, its repeated rejection of Colegio proposals, and its tough rhetoric, it would not ultimately kick the college off its campus. "The whole thing with HUD was fairly simple to me," he recalled. "All of us felt confident that we would prevail, that they would cave in to pressure. . . . I didn't think that HUD had the guts to evict us. My thinking was that sometime, somewhere the whole thing would be worked out." That did not mean he was unconcerned about the effect that HUD's threats of foreclosure and eviction might have on prospective students. But it helps to explain why in the years to come, when press accounts were suggesting that the college's unpaid debts to HUD would result in its closing, Sonny generally seemed unperturbed, expressing optimism that a settlement would be reached.[47]

Sonny was less confident about managing the Colegio's accreditation-related difficulties. Here, he felt, Jose Romero and he were swimming way beyond their depth. Between the two of them, they had only a few years of administrative experience in higher education. Furthermore, not yet the holder of a bachelor's degree, Sonny was a bit intimidated by those he had to deal with at HEW and the Northwest Association. In one of our interviews, he told me about his first meeting with Dr. James Bemis, the executive director of the Northwest Association's Commission on Colleges. During the session, Bemis spoke at considerable length about a document called an "institutional self-study" that all candidates for accreditation were required to prepare. Sonny had no idea what Bemis was talking about.[48]

The Montes-Romero era began with success. In September 1974, with the HUD negotiations at an impasse, the Colegio turned again to its ally in Congress, Al Ullman. Charging that HUD in its recent negotiations with Lopez had "reneged" on the agreement reached in July, Ivo Bauman asked Congressman Ullman to help in restarting the talks. Meanwhile, Sonny directed an appeal to two well-connected Hispanics, Fernando C. de Baca, an assistant to President Gerald Ford, and Roberto Olivas of the National Council of la Raza, a Washington, D.C.–based advocacy organization. These overtures led to a new round of negotiations, and in that round, HUD proved to be atypically accommodating, a development that seemed to provide confirmation of Sonny's analysis of the organization. Finally, at a four-hour negotiating session on October 9, 1974, HUD, the Colegio, and the sisters reached a settlement. The Colegio dropped its civil rights lawsuit against HUD, made an initial payment to HUD of $10,000 to cover its obligations for the next four months, and agreed to a schedule of escalating payments: $2,500 a month for the period February–October 1975 (to be paid out of money deposited in February and June in an escrow account), $3,500 a month for the next year, and the resumption of normal (and much higher) loan payments beginning in October 1976. The sisters turned over two tracts of land to HUD. HUD's foreclosure lawsuit was to be continued until June 30, 1975, but the sisters were dismissed as a defendant in it. Although that did not mean the sisters would be totally absolved of liability if the Colegio couldn't make its payments, HUD would not attempt to recover any money from them until foreclosure proceedings against the Colegio had been completed and the Colegio property had been sold.[49]

Both Willner and Paulus expressed satisfaction with the results. The Colegio was allowed to continue operations and was given time to raise money to pay off the loans. The sisters were able to achieve a degree of separation from the Colegio. HUD itself was hopeful that the legal matters had been resolved. Unfortunately, the settlement was more a reprieve for the Colegio than a victory. While the immediate danger of foreclosure had passed, foreclosure was still a possibility if the Colegio failed to make timely payments to HUD. In his own comments to the press, Sonny sounded a note of caution: "Just because we have reached a settlement, it does not mean that all our problems are settled. The struggle is just beginning."[50]

One problem not yet resolved was the Colegio's accreditation status. Again, it wasn't for a lack of trying. By the time that Lopez had left the Colegio, it was clear that the school had no hope of gaining accreditation through the three-letter route. So in September 1974, the newly appointed codirectors began to explore another route to eligibility for federal funding: seeking candidacy status.

The generally accepted way of achieving candidacy status was to submit an application to a regional accrediting association. But when Sonny, Jose, and their colleagues investigated the procedures for doing that in mid-October 1974, they learned to their dismay that it would be impossible for them to achieve a successful result from the Northwest Association's Commission on Colleges in a relatively short amount of time. It would take months to write the required institutional self-study, a lengthy document covering everything from the institution's academic objectives to the condition of the physical plant. What is more, the Commission on Colleges considered applications for candidacy status only twice annually, and the next deadline for submitting materials was November 1, only a few weeks away.[51]

The Colegio's leaders did not give up, however. At a meeting held to discuss their options, while they were poring over a document titled "Guidelines for Institutional Eligibility for Federal Education Programs," someone suggested that there was, potentially, another way to achieve candidacy status. According to those guidelines, the responsibility for determining whether an institution merited candidacy status—whether, that is, there was "satisfactory assurance" that it could meet full accreditation standards in a "reasonable time"—was actually given not to regional accrediting organizations like the Northwest Association but rather to the U.S. Commissioner of Education. In practice, of course, that option was not what HEW had chosen. Rather than requiring the commissioner to make a judgment call about whether every applicant for candidacy status met the standard, HEW had given accrediting agencies the responsibility for making those determinations. But there was no legal reason the Colegio had to be bound by that practice. Why not send a petition for candidacy status directly to the commissioner?[52]

That is precisely what the Colegio did. Joseph Gallegos composed the petition to Commissioner of Education Terrel H. Bell, asking him to grant eligibility to the Colegio on the basis of its satisfying the applicable criteria. The Colegio, he explained, expected "within a reasonable time" to meet the accreditation standards of a nationally recognized accrediting agency, the Northwest Association. Sonny and the others had no idea how HEW would respond.[53]

A direct appeal to the commissioner was unique, and Bell's office was nonplussed by it. That office passed the petition on to HEW's attorneys, who in November 1974 developed a special procedure to deal with the question of the Colegio's eligibility. The Colegio would be asked to provide further information and documentation (including a self-study), and HEW would then make a determination about the college's eligibility.[54]

The Colegio's staff began to compile the data and documents required by HEW.[55] But time considerations again affected their decisions. To qualify for federal assistance for the 1975–76 funding cycle, the Colegio had to be declared eligible by January 15, 1975. Given that deadline, the Colegio simply did not have enough time to produce a respectable self-study. Sonny decided to go ahead with the direct application to the commissioner without the self-study.[56]

In the first week of January 1975, Gallegos sent HEW all the data and documentation that had been collected. At the same time, aware of the approaching deadline for 1975–76 funding, Montes and Romero contacted Al Ullman, requesting that he urge HEW officials to make a decision before January 15. Ullman's office made some calls, and HEW agreed to extend the deadline for the Colegio and to hold a special January 23 meeting of the Advisory Committee on Accreditation and Institutional Eligibility to consider the Colegio's petition.[57]

The Colegio sent a four-person delegation to Washington, D.C., to meet with the committee—Sonny, Gallegos, Willner's associate

James Kenin, and Pablo Ciddio y Abeyta, who had recently taken a position with the Colegio as director of financial aid. Sonny was uncertain about the Colegio's chances of getting a favorable decision. On the one hand, he felt that the college had "met most of the written criteria." On the other, he was concerned about the failure to include a self-study. The meeting, which lasted an hour, was cordial. When it ended, the committee chairman told Sonny that the committee would give further consideration to the Colegio's application and make a recommendation to Commissioner Bell.[58]

The Colegio delegation returned to Oregon and waited for HEW's response. None was immediately forthcoming. After a while Sonny and his colleagues turned to their friends in high places, asking them to apply pressure to HEW. Ullman did so, as did Oregon's governor, Robert Straub. But their efforts failed to convince the committee to restore the Colegio's eligibility. In mid-February 1975, HEW announced that it had decided to postpone a decision about the Colegio until May, at which time the self-study would be completed. In the meantime, it placed more than $100,000 in scholarship money in an escrow account, to be distributed to the Colegio in the event that HEW ultimately restored the Colegio's funding. The decision to delay a vote on eligibility had serious consequences for the Colegio.[59]

Collective Action

When the Colegio had signed its agreement with HUD in October 1974, Sonny had realized that it would be difficult for the school to make its future payments. "Financially, we were in pretty bad shape," he explained. His hope was that, having received a reprieve, the Colegio might somehow be able to get large infusions of money—through donations, grants, and the restoration of federal financial aid—so that the payments to HUD could be made. Still, that was nothing more than a hope, since the school's financial situation was so dire. "We knew it was going to be hard. We didn't even have the money to pay ourselves. Even if we had received HEW funding, it was going to be tight."[60]

According to the terms of the October 1974 agreement, the Colegio was required to deposit the sum of $10,000 in an escrow account at the First National Bank of Oregon on or before February

3, 1975. The agreement stated further that, in the event that the Colegio failed to meet the payment deadline, it would have to surrender "peacefully" its buildings and possessions to HUD. As the February 3 deadline approached and hope faded that HEW would restore the Colegio's funding eligibility, Montes and Romero became resigned to the fact that the required payment would not be made. And it wasn't. HUD officials did nothing for a while. Then, on March 19, 1975, they demanded that the Colegio's leaders surrender the campus, reminding them of their contractual obligation to turn over the property peacefully.[61]

Again facing the possible loss of the college campus, Montes and Romero had to decide what to do next. As was their practice, they consulted with their core group of advisors, the council, and the board of trustees, and came up with a plan. In dealing with HUD up to now, the Colegio had largely worked within the system. It had hired attorneys, negotiated in good faith, and appealed to elected officials for assistance at strategic moments. The only deviation from that course had been the Mexican American rally at Mt. Angel in March 1974, an effort to rally public support. At this juncture, however, Sonny, Jose, and their colleagues believed that working within the system was no longer sufficient. They felt that it was necessary to adopt tactics that would, as Sonny later put it, "apply extra pressure to HUD."[62]

In effect, they chose to borrow liberally from the repertoire of collective-action techniques that had been used often and, in many cases, effectively in recent years by participants in the civil rights struggle, the farmworkers' movement, the antiwar movement, and other social protest campaigns: sit-ins, picketing, rallies, protest marches, and other types of public demonstration. A number of the people in the Colegio's camp, like Sonny, had firsthand experience with these techniques, having taken part in Chavez's grape and lettuce boycott, antiwar activities, and the demonstrations against SB 677. According to Sonny, the Colegio's decision to change tactics was easily made, because "our strength was in organizing."[63]

In Oregon's Upper Willamette Valley, as we know, a Mexican American network had been in construction since the mid- to late-1960s. By the mid-1970s, it consisted of people who had worked for or had otherwise been affiliated with the VML as well as those

189

involved with ORO (the new name for the VML); members of the Centro Chicano Cultural of Gervais, the Centro Cultural of Cornelius, CISCO, and an assortment of Mexican American social clubs; educational administrators, migrant education specialists, and a variety of others. All of them could potentially be enlisted. Additional support would come from college students, both the Colegio's own and students from other local institutions, who, in that era of protest, were ready to join any demonstration against perceived injustice. Even local high school students could be recruited. Sonny also wanted to arrange demonstrations in Seattle, where HUD's regional office was located. Fortunately, over the years, he had been involved with and participated in meetings at the Northwest Chicano Council and Centro de la Raza in Seattle, and through those contacts he would be able to gain the assistance of Chicano groups in that city.

The Colegio's leaders approached the "Save Colegio Cesar Chavez" campaign with a certain amount of confidence, given their familiarity with collective-action techniques and the existence of a mobilizing structure. But, in reality, the time was anything but propitious for the mounting of a social movement. The underlying problem was the structure of political opportunities confronting the protesters. Recall that the era of successful black insurgency was now long past, and recall too that a decade earlier, at a time when social movements of all kinds were proliferating in the United States, the political climate had not been particularly favorable for Mexican American protest. By 1975, it was even less so. Chavez and Tijerina, leading Chicano figures of the 1960s, had suffered reverses. The Raza Unida Party, founded with great expectations in 1970 and led by two luminaries of the Chicano movement (Corky Gonzales and the talented, ambitious Texas politician José Angel Gutiérrez), had disintegrated by 1973. The Brown Berets had disappeared from the scene.[64]

This was, in short, a very different political context than the one that had spawned black protest in the 1950s and early 1960s. Mexican Americans still could not count on much support from the national political establishment, because they had insufficient national electoral power. Furthermore, the potential resources available to the "Save Colegio Cesar Chavez" campaign were minimal at best. Unlike African American communities in the South that had earlier struggled against civil rights denials, the Colegio in the 1970s did not have access to the help of mass-based organizations such as the NAACP, funded largely by the black community, and CORE, which received large donations from the white community. In the 1970s, the only donor of consequence to Mexican American organizations was the Ford Foundation, which directed its monies to the National Council of La Raza and the Mexican American Legal Defense and Education Fund, which defended Mexican American civil rights in the courts.[65] From the start, then, the Colegio's protest campaign was doomed to remain regional, attracting virtually no outside resources.

The Colegio community decided to begin its campaign with a multifront attack on HUD, combining an occupation of one or more campus buildings with other activities. They also decided that, in the event HUD opted to evict the college and the courts ordered an eviction, the students, staff, and friends of the Colegio would continue to occupy the campus buildings. "They'd have to physically cart us off," Sonny told me. HUD would be faced with the choice of calling in the federal marshals to enforce the eviction order, and, in Sonny's view, HUD didn't have the stomach for that. "It would be bad publicity for them," he explained. "That's why we felt very confident."[66]

On March 26, 1975, a week after the HUD announcement, students and staff members of the Colegio initiated a round-the-clock occupation of Huelga Hall, the school's administration building. At the same time, pickets supporting the institution took up stations outside the HUD offices in Portland and Seattle. At a press conference held on that day, Sonny, Jose Romero, and Jose Garcia, the chairman of the board of trustees, explained that the Colegio's supporters were adopting more confrontational tactics because the federal government was treating the school unfairly. One executive department had negotiated an agreement requiring the Colegio to make periodic payments, whereas another had declared the Colegio ineligible for federal funding, making it impossible for the institution to pay on schedule. The Colegio, they claimed, was being "squeezed" by HUD and HEW. "We are not asking for any

Press conference held at the beginning of the Colegio's collective-action campaign against HUD, March 1975. From right to left: Jose Romero, Jose Garcia (the chairman of the Colegio's board of trustees), Sonny Montes. Photograph courtesy of the Statesman Journal; *image created from a microfilmed copy.*

special favors," Sonny said. "We just want a break."[67] Once again, in presenting his case publicly, Sonny was adopting the injustice/ unfairness frame.

Sonny was also beginning the process of defining his enemies by attaching pejorative attributes to them. In this struggle, they, the enemies, two well-funded bureaucracies of the federal government, were bullies—powerful, demanding, and uncaring. We, a tiny Chicano college, were poor, disadvantaged, well meaning, and set-upon. Simple fairness dictated that this sort of ganging-up should not be tolerated. Sonny also emphasized that the Colegio's protest activities would be entirely nonviolent, adopting an approach made famous by Gandhi, King, and Chavez. "We don't want to hurt anyone, nor do we want anyone to hurt us." Sonny's proposed solution, which he stated at the time, was that the government should forgive the Colegio's debt and award the college to the Chicano community of Oregon.

As the sit-in and the picketing went on, the Colegio announced that on March 29, the Saturday preceding the Easter holiday, it would hold a protest march from the Centro Chicano Cultural in Gervais to the Colegio campus in Mt. Angel, a distance of about seven miles. The choice of tactics was apt. First, a march would call additional attention to the plight of the Colegio in a distinctly nonthreatening way, unlike the occupation of the administration building. Second, a march was a collective-action technique of great symbolic value, again linking the "Save Colegio Cesar Chavez" campaign, without explicitly saying so, to Gandhi (the march to the sea), King (the marches on Montgomery and Washington), and

Chavez (the *perigrinación* from Delano to Sacramento during the first grape boycott).

The march took place on schedule. Sonny and Jose led the marchers, who numbered, according to a press account, "more than 150." Some participants carried Mexican flags; others carried signs. Along the way, the marchers sang to mariachi music and chanted "*vivas*." When the procession reached the Mt. Angel campus, the marchers were given refreshments and a priest from Woodburn said Mass in Spanish. "This is just the beginning," Jose Romero remarked, pleased by the events of the day. "We will continue to generate and increase public support in the intervening weeks to keep our college."[68]

Two days later, the Colegio sent out a mass mailing, requesting assistance from all Chicanos and "persons of conscience" in the school's struggle "to acquire and maintain a viable community-based institution for Chicanos." Asserting that the Colegio was the only institution in the region that addressed the educational needs of Mexican Americans and others who were not being "adequately served by the public school system," the letter called on the school's friends to do two specific things: to send letters or telegrams in support of the school to President Gerald Ford, HUD Secretary Carla Hills, and members of their state's congressional delegation; and to give donations of food, money, and supplies to sustain the individuals participating in the round-the-clock vigil in the school's administration building. The response to the mailing was impressive; President Ford and the others received a flood of correspondence.[69]

The Colegio's collective-action campaign continued into April, as did the press coverage. During that period, many outsiders visited the college. Some were supporters responding to the college's call for help and bringing food and encouragement to the people occupying the administration building; others were simply curiosity seekers. Initially, the Colegio welcomed all of them without qualms or questions, but before long suspicions surfaced. One frequent visitor was an elderly man who was known to everyone as "Stupid." He claimed to be a friend of the Colegio. "Stupid" would wander around Mt. Angel talking to people, ostensibly trying to gather information, which he then reported to the Colegio's leaders. Gradually, though, Jose Romero began to wonder whether "Stupid" was spying on, rather than for, the Colegio. That wouldn't have been difficult, since decisions made at the Colegio were reached openly and collectively. In Guadalupe Hall, there was a table where students, staff, supporters, and even board members would meet to discuss the issues of the day. John Little sometimes stopped there after work and sat with Sonny and Jose, the three of them talking animatedly while John and Sonny puffed nonstop on cigarettes, both men being chain smokers at the time. Anyone could overhear such conversations. A few weeks into the occupation, the Colegio hired a security team to monitor the visitors to the campus.[70]

It was also apparent that law enforcement organizations were watching the Colegio closely. On one occasion, a local television reporter was interviewing Sonny on the grounds of the Colegio. The discussion turned to the "harassment" that, according to Sonny, the Colegio was receiving from the police and the FBI. Suddenly, Sonny pointed in the direction of a van that was parked across South Main Street, in a parking lot owned by the Benedictine sisters. "They're there," he announced. "If you want to, you can go see for yourselves." He and the reporter proceeded across the street and a television cameraman followed, capturing the scene. The reporter knocked on the door of the van, and a man inside the vehicle opened it. When asked who he was, the man replied that he was a deputy sheriff with the Marion County sheriff's office. Inside the vehicle was an impressive array of photographic equipment that was pointed in the direction of the Colegio and was being used to take pictures of anyone entering or leaving the college grounds.[71]

Jose Romero had firsthand experience with an FBI agent, a Mexican American who was based in the Portland FBI office. With the appointment of Clarence Kelley as director of the FBI in 1973, the agency had made a concerted effort to hire more women and minorities, and this Mexican American agent was likely a recent minority recruit.[72] According to Jose, the agent "used to come around and talk to people—to try to find out what was going on." What bothered Jose was that the fellow was always lurking "at the fringes," talking to students and secretaries but never to the people in charge of the Colegio. One day he and three members of the college's security team found the agent in one of the college buildings. "Let's talk about it," Jose said. For about three hours, they had a discussion in Jose's office. "We never threatened him. We never got into a heated argument. We just heard where he was coming from."

It turned out that the agent was from South Texas, with a family history similar to Sonny's. That is where the resemblance stopped. "His idol was J. Edgar Hoover," Jose explained. As a young man he had read a book authored by J. Edgar Hoover and had decided then to model his life on Hoover's. "He swore up and down on J. Edgar Hoover." Jose was incredulous. How could a Mexican American from South Texas identify with an Anglo symbol of law enforcement? "Do you remember the growers, the farmworkers, the Texas Rangers?" Jose asked him. "Do you remember what happened? This is the kind of thing we're trying to address." The FBI agent would not be moved. "That's history," he said. "Now there are new opportunities. . . . We're going to be the law enforcement." The two sides found no points of agreement. Jose summed it up: "Basically he's just stating the company line, and we're saying 'Damn.'"

The truth is that Sonny and Jose never knew the full extent of the spying that took place. They sensed that it was considerable. They heard stories that local sheriffs had files on them. They even heard rumors that one member of the Colegio's staff was an FBI informant. They wondered about every stranger who showed up at the campus. They were always on their guard.

Meanwhile, time was running out on the Colegio. Despite the continuing collective-action campaign and the news coverage, HUD restated its intention to proceed with the foreclosure and take possession of the campus. "We aren't changing our course," commented a HUD official. A hearing on the foreclosure was scheduled for April 28, 1975, in Marion County Circuit Court, and press reports about it suggested that a foreclosure order would be the probable result.[73]

Three days before the scheduled hearing, a midday rally of the Colegio's supporters took place on the mall directly in front of the State Capitol in Salem. The organizers billed the event as a "national demonstration in solidarity with Colegio Cesar Chavez." Newspaper accounts estimated that the event drew about 200 supporters, many of them youthful. In addition to a large group of students and faculty who drove from Mt. Angel that morning, there were a number of people who came from Yakima and Pullman in the state of Washington as well as from Eugene, Portland, and Hillsboro. Signs bearing pointed messages were in evidence: "Stop the HUD Racist Conspiracy," "Hell No, We Won't Go," "Colegio Is for Todos." Two state senators promised to fight for the Colegio. Governor Robert Straub's press aide Ken Fobes also spoke, reporting that the governor pledged his "wholehearted support" to keep the college open.[74]

Under growing pressure, HUD agreed to negotiate with the Colegio and to postpone the foreclosure hearing for a week. Don Willner, representing the Colegio in the discussions, put forward a creative proposal: that the Colegio would agree to turn over its deed to the government, and then HUD would try to get the General Services Administration to declare the land and buildings "surplus property," thereby allowing HUD to give the campus back to the Colegio. But federal officials rejected the idea, saying that they could make no prior commitment about the disposition of the property. HUD went ahead with the court hearing, and on May 5, as expected, the court authorized foreclosure.[75]

After the court's decision, the Colegio escalated the public pressure on HUD. While its supporters continued to occupy the school's administration building, an occupation that had been uninterrupted since late March, they also held sit-down demonstrations at the Portland and Seattle offices of HUD. In announcing the new offensive, Sonny explained that the demonstrations would last two hours on the first day and would increase by one hour on each subsequent day until HUD agreed to negotiate seriously about Don Willner's surplus property proposal. "We want some kind of guarantee that they are serious," Sonny said. While he emphasized again that the demonstrations would be nonviolent, he also stated that the Colegio's supporters were "ready to resist" if any steps were taken to evict the school. "We have worked hard and invested thousands of hours in the Colegio and we will see it succeed."[76]

The Colegio's pressure tactics, combined with the behind-the-scene efforts of Governor Straub and other Oregon politicians, caused HUD to reconsider its course, and the agency invited Colegio officials to Washington, D.C., for a meeting on May 13,

Rally at the capitol, Salem, Oregon, in support of the Colegio Cesar Chavez, April 25, 1975. Photograph courtesy of The Oregonian.

Rally at the capitol, Salem, Oregon, April 25, 1975. Photograph courtesy of the Statesman Journal; image created from a microfilmed copy.

Sonny announces that sit-ins will be held at the HUD office in Portland, Oregon, May 7, 1975. Photograph courtesy of The Oregonian.

1975. Sonny led the Colegio delegation, which included Jose Romero and attorney James Kenin. Many top-level HUD people attended too, among them James L. Mitchell, the second-ranking official in the department. This time, the discussion focused not on the surplus property proposal, but rather on a formula advanced by Willner more than a year earlier, which called for HUD to negotiate a long-term lease with the college once the federal government took possession of the campus. Although Mitchell expressed reservations about leasing the property, he was willing to consider the idea, provided the Colegio could get its finances in better shape. In the end, an understanding was reached that, if the Colegio regained its eligibility for federal funding, HUD would not evict the Colegio and would make an effort to negotiate an arrangement with it, possibly a lease. "I think they're serious about sitting down and working out an agreement," Sonny commented after the meeting.[77]

Thus ended, after forty-eight sometimes-frenetic days, the first phase of the "Save Colegio Cesar Chavez" campaign. Over that period, a group made up of the Colegio community and its network of supporters had occupied and picketed buildings, staged a protest march, organized a rally in the state capital, and attracted a considerable volume of press coverage. By escalating the pressure on HUD, the collective action had accomplished important things— forcing HUD to negotiate when it preferred not to and to consider options it did not like, such as allowing the college to retain control over its campus. But those accomplishments should not obscure the fact that, even after those forty-eight days of collective action, the Colegio's position remained precarious: it had virtually no cash and its staff had not been paid for nine months, a judge had ordered foreclosure, eviction remained a distinct possibility, and the college had not regained eligibility for federal financial assistance. That last reality was especially troubling because, as matters stood after the meeting with HUD on May 13, 1975, unless the Colegio's eligibility was restored, no deal with HUD appeared to be possible.

The Miracle at Twin Falls
During the forty-eight days of nonstop protest, the Colegio's leaders had not lost sight of the importance of restoring the school's funding eligibility. Having failed in February 1975 to convince HEW's ac-creditation committee to make a favorable recommendation to the Commissioner of Education, they still had two opportunities to restore the federal funding. HEW had indicated that it would reconsider the Colegio's application in the spring. The school could also submit a separate application for candidacy status to the Northwest Association's Commission on Colleges, which would be holding its next meeting in June 1975.

In both cases, as Sonny and his colleagues understood, the Colegio's chances of success would depend to a large extent on the quality of its institutional self-study, which had not yet been written. Several months earlier, realizing that the Colegio did not have the human resources to produce that document on its own, Sonny had turned for assistance to a group of old friends from his VML days—the staff members of the Hillsboro Community Action Program, an agency with considerable experience in producing grant proposals and lengthy reports. During the late winter and early spring of 1975, several of those staff members worked on the self-study along with the Colegio's administrators and a few volunteers. (Sonny's involvement was minimal, since he was busy organizing and orchestrating the demonstrations against HUD.) The group was broken up into subcommittees, with each one responsible for generating a particular section of the document. Joseph Gallegos was given the key assignment of editing and polishing the final text. In early April 1975, Gallegos sent the completed self-study to HEW.[78]

HEW's accreditation committee dispatched two consultants to Oregon, their charge being to gather information and then to write a report about the Colegio that was to be used by the government in determining whether to restore its eligibility. They arrived in Mt. Angel on April 22, 1975, at a time when members of the campus community were still occupying the administration building and Bill Walton, the star center of the Portland Trailblazers basketball team and a free spirit who had taken an interest in the "Save Colegio Cesar Chavez" campaign, was visiting the college to demonstrate his support and to bring food to sustain the protesters. The consultants grilled the college administrators for several hours and came away unimpressed, especially with the College Without Walls program, which in their view did not give sufficient guidance to students. They filed a very critical assessment of the Colegio.[79]

Montes and Romero were aware that the visit of the two HEW consultants had not gone well and expected that the HEW committee would not support the Colegio's petition, which turned out to be the case. "These fellows they sent down were not bilingual," Jose would later remark. "They had no understanding of bilingual education. Basically they were traditionalists." The codirectors felt that the school had a better chance of getting a favorable hearing from the Northwest Association's Commission on Colleges.[80]

Six days after the visit of the HEW consultants, Gallegos wrote to James Bemis of the Commission on Colleges, applying for candidacy status and requesting a site visit. Shortly afterward, remembering the Colegio's recent experience with the evaluators sent by HEW, Sonny called Bemis to ask that at least one member of the evaluation team sent by the association be "somebody that was familiar with the Hispanic community and the College Without Walls concept." To Sonny's delight, the commission appointed a two-person team consisting of Charles Flora, president of Western Washington

State College, and Theodore Murguia, president of San Jose City College in California. Murguia was Hispanic. The two men were instructed to visit the campus at the end of May and then to write an evaluation, which the Commission on Colleges would consider, along with the Colegio's application materials, at the commission's June 17–19 meeting.[81]

The site visit took place on May 29, 1975. After touring the campus and examining its records, the evaluators consulted with Sonny and several other officials. Both evaluators appeared to be favorably disposed toward the college, and the visit went remarkably well. Afterward they prepared their report, which, according to instructions provided by Bemis, was to address eight topics. In dealing with the first seven—the institution's educational programs, its governing board, and so forth—the evaluators found little to criticize. They described the self-study as "thoughtfully prepared," displaying "robust enthusiasm and commitment to do something for the Chicano population of our country." Their only reservations, albeit serious ones, could be found in their discussion of the eighth topic, the college's financial condition. They observed that the school's financial records were disorganized, its debt load was heavy, and it had not yet established an "adequate financial base of funding commitments." They also pointed out that the Colegio could not provide "an adequate report on its financial status." That last-mentioned deficiency was significant, since an applicant for candidacy status was required to show evaluators a summary of its latest audited financial statement.[82]

The June meeting of the Northwest Association's Commission on Colleges was held at the Holiday Inn in Twin Falls, Idaho. Composed of twenty-five representatives of member institutions, the commission considered the application of the Colegio on June 18, 1975, the second day of the conference. The representatives began by discussing among themselves the report of the evaluators. Then a delegation from the Colegio was invited to enter the meeting room. Sonny had brought half a dozen people with him, including Jose Romero, Joseph Gallegos, and John Little. After introducing the others, Sonny began his presentation. He focused on the positives, emphasizing the institution's innovative curriculum and its commitment to providing a college education to an ethnic group that had been largely ignored by traditional colleges. He said little or nothing about finances and audits and closed with an appeal: "I said that they, the accredited schools, were like a family—a family that we Chicanos had been excluded from. I asked them to give us a chance, to admit us to the family."[83]

A question-and-answer session followed Sonny's remarks. Several members of the commission raised concerns about the Colegio's financial condition and its failure to provide an audited financial statement. Sonny replied that the school's finances were likely to improve and that the school had hired a new business manager, Bill Cummings, who was getting the business office into shape. He also referred the commission to a letter he brought with him from Cummings asserting that a "current financial statement" would be completed by the end of July 1975.[84] After Sonny and his colleagues had answered all the questions posed to them, the Colegio's delegation was asked to leave the room so that the members of the commission could decide among themselves whether to give candidacy status to the Colegio. Several members were opposed, arguing that the Colegio's financial condition was too weak to warrant the association's endorsement. But, a majority voted for the Colegio, most of them sympathetic to its goals, impressed with the enthusiasm of its leaders, and hopeful that, by restoring the Colegio's eligibility, the institution might be able to survive.[85]

Immediately after the vote, the commission told the Colegio's representatives that the institution had been granted candidacy status. The news was greeted with whoops of joy. Several members of the commission congratulated Sonny, shaking his hand, patting him on the back, and complimenting him on his effective presentation. "You missed your calling, Mr. Montes," one of them said to him. "You should have been an evangelical minister."[86]

It was a stunning victory. Having been granted candidacy status, the Colegio would again be eligible for federal funding. Money would be available to cover staff and faculty salaries, to tend to the grounds, and to pay a few bills. It might also be possible to reach an agreement with HUD, since that agency had indicated that further negotiations with the Colegio could occur if the school regained funding eligibility. "It was as if the Red Sea had opened up," Sonny recalled.[87]

Under Siege

In September 1975, a few days before a new academic year was scheduled to begin at the Colegio, Sonny Montes, Jose Romero, and Jan Chavez met with Bob Pfohman, a reporter for the *Capital Journal*, on the college grounds. The grass on the lawns was freshly trimmed, a visual confirmation of the school's ever so slightly improved financial prospects now that its eligibility for federal funding had been restored, and the mood of the college's administrators was upbeat. According to Pfohman, as he walked beside them and they talked about the school's present and future, all three were "sporting ear to ear smiles." With the Colegio having survived its recent struggles, they expressed thanks for the public support they had received and pride in their own accomplishments. Above all, they acknowledged a sense of relief that those battles were behind them. "At least we can breathe now," Sonny told Pfohman. "We have nobody to fight with."[1]

For about a year after the Twin Falls meeting, the Colegio experienced a period of relative calm. While faculty and staff workloads remained heavy, money was still in short supply, and buildings were often without heat in the winter, there were no threats of immediate eviction, no rallies in the state capital, and no anxiety-producing meetings with HUD, HEW, and the Northwest Association where the stakes were nothing less than the college's survival. With the benefit of hindsight, however, we can see that the calm was illusory. The big problems—the debts owed to HUD, accreditation—had been addressed but hardly solved, and by the fall of 1976, the Colegio would again be struggling for its institutional life.

A New Day, a New Group of Students

Still, for the moment, the situation seemed promising, and the *Capital Journal* was not the only major newspaper in the state to emphasize the positives. A reporter for the *Oregonian* visited the campus on the same day Bob Pfohman did and found a pervasive sense of optimism. "This is a new day for the Colegio," Jose Romero announced at an informal orientation session for new enrollees. "We can forget about demonstrations. The students only have to worry about their studies now, not the existence of the college." Returning student Florencia Guillen expressed her love for the school and her commitment to making it a success. "This is a place where I feel warmth," she said. New students focused on the institution's unique qualities. "Here we are not bound to one individual's ideology," asserted Reynaldo Brown, who was transferring to the Colegio from the University of Washington. "Here we have more freedom to really learn and comprehend."[2]

Perhaps the most significant reason for optimism was the simple fact that new students such as Brown were actually choosing to enroll at the Colegio. Doubtless, the availability of federal financial aid made enrolling in the college more financially attractive than it had been before, but anyone who had been reading the newspapers for the past two years would have been aware that, even with the resumption of federal funding, the Colegio still faced major hurdles. It took a special kind of person to cast his or her lot with the Colegio at this juncture. Those who did, it appears, were often individuals with very unconventional academic backgrounds and/or special reasons for enrolling.

One such student was Ramon Ramirez, who had been born in East Los Angeles and was the son of a former farmworker who had become a house painter.[3] Ramirez had attended a Catholic high school run by the Silesian Order. The Silesians were socially engaged, and at the time they actively supported the farmworker movement led by Cesar Chavez. One day, Chavez came to Ramirez's high school to talk about the problems faced by agricultural laborers and

Jan Chavez, Sonny Montes, and Jose Romero on the Colegio campus, September 1975. Photograph courtesy of the Statesman Journal; *image created from a microfilmed copy.*

his union's organizational efforts. Ramirez was deeply impressed. "He talked about social justice, about how you could do something for your people," Ramirez remembered. "He talked about how, after we got an education, we should come back to the community and contribute to the community." After Chavez's visit, he and some of his classmates organized a march in support of Chavez's union.

After graduating from high school, Ramirez had first attended a small college in Olympia, Washington, and then transferred to the University of Washington. He had not been motivated to study at either place because, in his opinion, the schools didn't provide useful preparation for his chosen life's work—to organize farmworkers and carry on the work of Chavez. During the 1974–75 academic year, while Ramirez was still enrolled at the University of Washington, he heard about the travails of the Colegio and decided to travel to Mt. Angel, both to show his support for the college and to check it out. The place excited him. He liked the flexibility of the curriculum and believed it would afford him the opportunity to learn the skills he considered necessary. He also liked the fact that many of the students at the college were former farmworkers or came from farmworker families. Ramirez transferred to the Colegio in the fall of 1975.

In the two years he spent there, Ramirez thrived. His initial field of study was communications, his goal being to learn how to communicate more effectively with farmworker communities. With the assistance of Tony Gregg, a math instructor and the head of his *comité*, he developed a plan of study, which focused on learning how to put together a newspaper. While he took several classes at the Colegio, most of his instruction took place outside the classroom. As an intern at a community-based printing collective in Seattle, he learned printing and lithography and participated in the production of a newsletter. He next worked on projects in Eugene, helping out an organization called Eugene Coalition that operated a printing press. He also assisted Daniel Desiga, a talented artist and core faculty member at the Colegio, in printing projects on the Colegio campus. While he was obliged to spend weeks, even months, away from Mt. Angel, Ramirez kept in close touch with Tony Gregg, occasionally returning to review his learning portfolio.

After a year at the college, Ramirez switched gears. Along with his close friend Cipriano Ferrel and several other classmates, he helped to establish the Willamette Valley Immigration Project, and the focus of his studies became immigration. Tony Gregg still served as his supervisor. After the formal launching of the WVIP in the summer of 1977, Ramirez became deeply involved in that organization's activities and no longer had the time to update his learning portfolio and meet with his *comité*. Having learned the skills he needed, only a few credits short of the 186 required for graduation, Ramirez moved on to the world of work. He continued to work for the WVIP for several years and, after the name change, for PCUN. Today Ramirez is president of PCUN.

Another student who entered the Colegio in September 1975 was Jimmy Amaya, Sonny's friend and former VML colleague.[4] Like Sonny, Amaya had been recruited to the VML, starting as a janitor at the Independence Opportunity Center in 1965 and rising eventually to the position of opportunity center director in Dayton, a job he held from 1969 to 1971. Along the way, Amaya earned his GED through the VML and, like Sonny, took some college courses offered by the Oregon College of Education. After leaving the VML, Amaya held positions in several state agencies. In his last state position, with the Bureau of Labor, he came into conflict with the labor commissioner and decided to file a class action lawsuit against the bureau, alleging that it discriminated against minorities. Amaya lost the lawsuit and his job.

Bruised by his experience with the Bureau of Labor, Amaya opted to do something very different. Already active in Mexican American groups, he went to work for the Centro Cultural in Washington County, an organization he had helped to establish. Amaya also took some classes at Linfield College in McMinnville. After the Colegio regained its eligibility for federal financial aid in 1975, he decided to transfer there. By then, Amaya had accumulated about two years of college credit.

Choosing Chicano studies as his field of study, Amaya did some formal course work at the Colegio. In addition, assisted by the members of his *comité*, Amaya documented and got credit for a variety of life experiences: work he had done at the VML and various state agencies; his unsuccessful lawsuit against the Bureau of Labor; projects he had worked on at the Centro Cultural; even his musical compositions. (A serious classical guitarist, who performed

professionally for many years, Amaya had composed scores of songs.)
After two years at the Colegio, Amaya was able to graduate.

Without question, the Colegio was attracting a group of mature,
highly motivated, interesting students. What we don't know is how
many students there were. Two newspaper stories in the fall of 1975
reported that about 100 full-time students were enrolled at the
Colegio—an increase of more than 40 from the troubled spring
quarter of 1975.[5] But that figure of 100, which was provided to
reporters by school administrators, was almost certainly inflated.
Only a few months later, in a document Montes and Romero
submitted to the Northwest Association, the college reported that
57 full-time students were enrolled. Other sources told a similar
story. Enrollment apparently hovered somewhere between 55 and
70 for the remainder of the 1975–76 academic year and for the
entirety of the subsequent one, which was to be Sonny Montes's
last at the institution.[6] Even after the resumption of federal financial
support, therefore, it seems that the college struggled to attract and
retain students.

Warning Signs

Given the fact that HUD had agreed in May 1975 to resume
negotiations with the Colegio if the school gained accreditation
status, it might have been expected that, shortly after the miracle at
Twin Falls, the school's leaders would have focused their energies on
working out a long-term arrangement with the government about
the campus. The press certainly expected that, and HUD expressed
a willingness to talk.[7] But negotiations between the Colegio and
HUD were infrequent over the nine months following the Twin
Falls meeting.

In fact, the only face-to-face negotiations between the two
sides occurred in July 1975, and they were brief and limited in
scope. Now holding title to the Colegio's campus, HUD had no
immediate plans to sell it.[8] That was so not only because HUD
had agreed to discuss a comprehensive agreement with the Colegio
but also because legally it couldn't conclude a sale: under Oregon
law, victims of foreclosure were given a year to redeem the property
by making their overdue payments. But what would happen to the
property in the intervening period? While HUD was willing to

allow the Colegio continued use of the campus, it expected to be paid rent for that privilege. So the Colegio and HUD officials met to work out a short-term lease. In exchange for promised monthly payments, HUD agreed to let the Colegio remain on the campus and also set a deadline of August 15, 1976, by which date the college would have to redeem the property. As it turned out, the Colegio paid HUD nothing of the agreed-upon rent.[9]

But a short-term lease was not the same thing as a long-term solution to the Colegio's foreclosure problem, and on that larger issue there were no talks, primarily because of the continued financial weakness of the Colegio. Even with the restoration of the college's eligibility for federal financial assistance, the Colegio could not possibly come up with the sort of money that HUD demanded in a long-term leasing agreement. Although Jose Romero indicated in an newspaper interview that the school was willing to pay a "reasonable" rental to the government, the truth was that he and Sonny wanted HUD to agree to Willner's proposal, rejected earlier, that the government declare the campus surplus property and donate it to the Mexican American community. HUD was unwilling to consider the idea.[10]

In March 1976, with the redemption deadline getting nearer, the Colegio finally decided to resume negotiations, sending a letter to HUD that offered three proposals for HUD's consideration. Two were familiar—Willner's surplus property proposal and a long-term leasing agreement. The third called for HUD to sell the campus to the Colegio for $250,000–$350,000, with the money coming from a grant the college had applied for. In June 1976, after reviewing the terms of the proposals and the relevant legislation, HUD's legal division determined that none of the three options was worth pursuing. The first was unacceptable because HUD could not simply give the property away, and HUD's legal counsel found inadequate both the payments offered in the second proposal and the sale price discussed in the third.[11] As the 1975–76 academic year came to a close, HUD was losing patience, having not received any payments from the Colegio for nineteen months. "We have given them forbearance until it's coming out of our ears," a HUD official told a reporter. "Sooner or later there is going to have to be an accounting, and someone will have to come up with some money."[12]

In the meantime, relations between the Colegio and the Northwest Association were deteriorating. When the Colegio had been granted candidacy status in June 1975, Sonny had believed that the school's fight for academic legitimacy had been won. "Maybe I was naive in some ways," he recalled. "Maybe it was lack of experience on my part. But I honestly thought that, once they awarded us candidacy status, they gave us six years in which to apply for full accreditation. I assumed that we would be given the opportunity to develop our school."[13]

Sonny realized that, like other candidates for accreditation, the Colegio would be required to demonstrate that it was making progress toward accreditation. There would be periodic reports to file with the Commission on Colleges and periodic reviews by that body. The Colegio would have to get its finances in order. Enrollments would have to increase. The physical plant would have to be upgraded. Various other improvements would have to be made. But that was all. Sonny expected the Commission on Colleges to treat the Colegio like any other candidate for accreditation.[14]

Sonny's understanding was incorrect because it was based on incomplete and, to some extent, inaccurate information about the commission's June 1975 decision on the Colegio's candidacy status. For one, he didn't know that, while a majority of the commission had voted in favor of the Colegio, the debate had been intense, with several members adamantly opposing the Colegio because of its financial deficiencies. He also didn't know that many members of the commission had left the Idaho Falls meeting with the impression that within a relatively short amount of time the Colegio was going to provide the commission with additional information about its financial condition. A few commissioners had derived that impression from statements made in the discussion with the Colegio's representatives. More than a few were influenced by the letter provided to the commission by the Colegio's business manager, Bill Cummings—specifically, by Cummings's assurance that he expected "to have a current financial statement by the end of July 1975" and his qualifying remark that "this will be the annual formal statement before formal audit." In any case, the commission's shared view was that, as one member put it, "the financial statement and an audited report of the Colegio's financial position would be available within a period of months at the latest."[15]

Fast-forward six months to December 1975, when the Commission on Colleges held its next meeting. In the interim, the Colegio had sent no financial statements of any kind to the Northwest Association. Although the commission was not scheduled to hold a formal discussion of the Colegio at the December meeting, informal discussions did take place when two members of the commission who had voted against the Colegio in June, Arthur Kreisman and Robert Coonrod, learned that the institution had not yet filed an audited financial report. They pressed Bemis to get it, maintaining that the Colegio had assured the commission that one would be sent. Bemis agreed to write a letter to the Colegio.[16]

He sent the letter to Sonny on January 26, 1976. Pointing out that, at the time candidacy status had been granted, the commission had understood that an audited statement would be provided shortly afterward, Bemis urged Sonny to send one "at the earliest possible date." In closing, he gave the Colegio a deadline and a veiled warning:

> If you are unable to submit the financial statement . . . to this office by March 1, 1976, please explain the circumstances and indicate when it can be expected. The Commission on Colleges will be meeting in mid-June at which time the matter will be considered.[17]

Sonny admits that, when he received the letter, he failed to appreciate the danger that lay behind Bemis's warning. Still operating on the assumption that the Colegio had been given a six-year window of opportunity to qualify for full accreditation, he had no idea that the Colegio's candidacy status was potentially at risk.[18] But even if he had been aware of the risk, there was little he could have done about complying. The college was no closer to providing an audited financial statement in January 1976 than it had been seven months earlier.

The root of the problem was the monumental mess that was the Colegio's business office. It had been in disarray since 1973, because the college did not have enough money at its disposal to hire a competent, full-time business manager. For several months at a stretch, part-time employees with no background in accounting had run the office. After two years of mismanagement and nonmanagement, many important records could not be located, and no audit was possible. Sonny first became aware of the seriousness of the situation in early 1975, when, having learned that he needed an audited statement in the event that the Colegio applied for candidacy status, he had hired the Salem accounting firm of Aldrich, Kilbride & Naas to conduct an audit of the Colegio's books. After working for about a month, the Salem accountants gave up, telling Sonny that they would only resume the job when the missing files were found. The hiring of Cummings as business manager in April 1975 made a difference. He brought some order to the office, but not enough to warrant inviting back the Salem accountants before the Twin Falls meeting. Nor were they brought back afterward. Despite his best efforts, Cummings was unable to locate all the needed files and generate the promised "current financial statement" before he left the Colegio's employ in September 1975. As of January 1976, no further progress had been made. To make matters worse, despite the fact that the Colegio's renewed eligibility for federal financial assistance had modestly improved the balance sheet, the school did not have sufficient funds to pay for a complete audit. "We had the will and the energy," Sonny told me, "but no money was coming in."[19]

Sonny did what he could to comply with Bemis's request. The Colegio applied to U.S. Bank for a grant to finance the audit, but as of March 1, 1976, the deadline set by Bemis for replying, the bank had not yet made a decision on the school's grant application. On that date, Montes and Romero wrote to Bemis, reporting on their efforts to provide the audited statement. They claimed that, if the college received the grant, the Salem accountants could complete the audit "within a forty-five day period." The bank turned them down.[20]

At that point, even though the Colegio was strapped for money, Sonny decided to proceed with the auditing process anyway. During the month of March 1976, Stephen Tatone, an accountant from the Salem firm, began to examine the Colegio's financial records, putting in a total of 55.5 hours of work. By then, however, the school no longer had enough money to pay Tatone, and he was told to cut back on his work for the Colegio.[21]

In the meantime, having received the Montes-Romero letter about the unfinished audit, James Bemis was not pleased. In another communication to Montes and Romero, he lectured the Colegio's leaders that sound financial management and the preparation of audited reports were "matters of vital importance" to the Northwest Association and reminded them that the Commission on Colleges would be considering the matter of the college's audit at its June 1976 meeting. Bemis wrote again in May, instructing Montes and Romero to submit an audited financial statement by June 1 so that it could be distributed to all members of the Commission on Colleges before the meeting.[22]

Sonny and Jose hoped to meet the deadline. But the accountants, working at a reduced pace since March, could not produce a complete audit of the balance sheet in the time available to them. The Colegio turned over nothing to Bemis on June 1, 1976. Tatone continued working up to June 11, at which point he presented the Colegio with a report of what his firm had done, but not an audit. "It's not that we didn't want to submit an audit," Sonny recalled. "The audit was not ready."[23]

On June 17, 1976, the Commission on Colleges met to consider the Colegio's finances. Virtually all of the members present on that day had attended the meeting a year earlier when the Colegio was granted candidacy status, but their attitude toward the school was much less sympathetic than before. Most were disappointed that the audited statement had not been submitted. Several, like Ellis McCune, the president of California State University at Hayward, felt that the Colegio "had not operated in good faith."[24] Early in the commission's discussion, Arthur Kreisman, the dogged opponent of the Colegio, moved that the association immediately withdraw the school's candidacy status. A few members supported the motion. But others felt that such a step would be premature: the proper action would be to serve notice on the Colegio to "show cause" why its candidacy should not be removed at the commission's December 1976 meeting. A motion to that effect passed unanimously. The commission also set a new deadline for the submission of the Colegio's audited financial statement—October 1, 1976.[25]

After the meeting, Bemis wrote to Montes and Romero, conveying the commission's verdict. When Sonny read the letter, he was shocked. The gravity of the matter at last became clear to him, and he called the Colegio's attorney, Don Willner.[26] The respite the Colegio had enjoyed since Twin Falls was officially over.

212

Peeling Away

Inevitably, everyone who worked at the Colegio, no matter how dedicated, began to think at some point about leaving. It would have been difficult for anyone to avoid having such thoughts. The work was too demanding, even in periods of comparative calm. The pay was too low. The personal costs were too high. Some held out longer than others, but eventually every employee considered resigning. It wasn't necessarily that they had given up on the college. It was rather that, at a certain point, they came to understand that there were limits to what they personally could accomplish and also that there would never be a *right* time to leave. There would always be something more to do.

The process of peeling away from the Colegio was ongoing and untidy. In January 1975, at a time when no staff member was receiving a regular paycheck, Maria Luisa Alaniz decided to take a job at Washington State University. As it turned out, she wasn't yet fully prepared to cut her ties to the college. Later that spring, she returned to Mt. Angel on two occasions to take part in the campus sit-ins. Then, in June 1975, after the Northwest Association had awarded the Colegio candidacy status and money was available for staff salaries, she went back to work at the Colegio and stayed on until late 1977. Joseph Gallegos, who had played a key role in the Colegio's successful struggle to gain accreditation in 1974 and 1975, had begun by late 1975 to consider returning to graduate school. In 1976, he left Mt. Angel and entered a PhD program at the University of Denver. Even so, Gallegos maintained a connection with the Colegio for about a year, writing several evaluation reports in connection with grants received by the institution.[27]

By 1976, the two codirectors started to think about leaving the Colegio. Already thirty-two years of age, with limited savings and a family to support, Sonny needed more income. He had by now accumulated almost enough college credits to graduate from the Colegio; with a degree, he would be eligible for much more remunerative employment. Then an attractive job came to his attention. Since being renamed into existence in 1973, the Colegio had frequent interactions with the Northwest Regional Educational Laboratory ("the Lab," as it was often called), a Portland-based nonprofit organization specializing in contract work on educational issues, with its funding coming primarily from the federal government. Several of the Lab's staff members were Latinos, including Antonio Fernandez, a former employee of the Colegio; Felipe Sanchez Paris; and Francisco ("Cisco") Garcia. All three knew Sonny well, and Garcia, who had been promoted to the position of director of the Lab's Center for Bilingual Education in 1976, was interested in adding Sonny to his staff. Sonny and Garcia discussed the possibility of Sonny joining the Lab. The work interested Sonny, and he was impressed with the projected salary of about $30,000 a year. But, while he was tempted, he eventually decided that, with the Colegio facing renewed assaults from HUD and the Commission on Colleges, he could not leave. Sonny told Garcia that it might be a year before he would be ready to change jobs, and the two of them agreed to resume their discussions at a later date. For Sonny, the peeling away process had begun.[28]

It had begun for Jose Romero too. By 1976, Jose had largely given up the idea of going on for a PhD. Like Sonny, he had conversations with people from the Lab. But Jose had another pressing concern—his wife's education. Before the Romeros had come to Mt. Angel in September 1973, Kathy Romero had been pursuing an undergraduate degree in romance languages at the University of Oregon. Kathy had agreed to put her education on hold so that her husband could take the new job, but she had not anticipated that his involvement would last so long. In the fall of 1976, the Romeros agreed that the time had come to prioritize Kathy's education. They gave up their house next to the Colegio campus and rented a place in Springfield, Oregon, just across the river from Eugene, so that Kathy could resume work on her degree at the University of Oregon. Jose continued to work at the Colegio, commuting each day between Springfield and Mt. Angel, a round-trip distance of about 180 miles, in the family's 1968 Volvo.[29]

Renewal of the Two-Front War

In August 1976, on the eve of a new academic year, hostilities resumed between the Colegio and HUD. The Colegio's redemption period— the grace period it had been granted to pay off its overdue debts to HUD and redeem its property—came to an end on August 15, 1976. Shortly afterward, a HUD regional administrator announced

214

publicly that the organization was planning to offer the campus for sale and an assistant secretary of HUD informed Sonny privately that the government wanted the Colegio's staff and students to vacate the premises before the beginning of the fall semester.[30]

Faced with HUD's stated intention of selling the campus, Sonny expressed optimism to the press that an arrangement with HUD could be worked out. But even behind closed doors, he was not worried, feeling certain that HUD would abandon its course of action if enough pressure were applied to it. He met with his core group of advisors, the college council, and the board, and a collective decision was reached to do whatever was necessary to remain in control of the campus. If possible, they all wanted to avoid public confrontation. "We are not planning anything spectacular like a sit-in or anything like that," Sonny announced.[31]

Events initially followed a familiar script. Colegio officials met with HUD. Prominent political figures such as Al Ullman gave pledges of support. The college initiated a letter-writing campaign, asking supporters to write immediately to HUD, the White House, Oregon's senators, and Governor Robert Straub and request that the government abandon its plans to seize the college campus. None of that appeared to affect HUD's determination to move ahead.[32] Exactly how HUD intended to dispose of the property, however, was unclear. While HUD officials suggested that a public auction would likely be held, they were also considering another possibility. In October 1976, the administrator of the Marion County Housing Authority (MCHA) expressed interest in acquiring the campus and remodeling the buildings to house senior citizens. A month later, HUD and the MCHA secretly held discussions about a sale, and an agreement was tentatively reached, calling for the MCHA to issue bonds to cover the cost of purchasing and remodeling the property, for HUD to buy the bonds, and for the MCHA to pay off the debt over time. HUD officials in the Pacific Northwest felt that this arrangement was preferable to holding an auction. But the final decision about how to dispose of the property would have to be made in Washington, D.C.[33]

By now, Sonny was becoming irritated with HUD. Despite the attempts of allies such as Ullman to reason with the agency, HUD's only concession was to allow the Colegio to occupy the campus for a few additional months, while the government arranged for a sale. In statements to the press, Sonny no longer seemed so confident that a deal with HUD was forthcoming. Had he known about HUD's talks with the MCHA, he might have been even more concerned.[34]

But Sonny didn't have the luxury of devoting all his thinking and working time to HUD-related matters. He was also preoccupied with attempting to save the Colegio's candidacy status and, with it, its eligibility for federal financial aid. The first order of business was to provide the Commission on Colleges with an audited financial statement by the new deadline of October 1, 1976. Although Sonny was intent on meeting that deadline, he also knew, based on his discussions with the Salem accountants, that there was little chance the commission would be satisfied with the Colegio's financial statement. In June 1976, shortly after Tatone had given Sonny an interim report about the Colegio's finances, he and his boss, Kent Aldrich, had met with Sonny and told him that it was not practical for their firm to examine the Colegio's government grant and student loan funds because too many files could not be located. Because of that, the accountants said, they would have to include a "scope limitation" in their final report, stating that they had not been able to examine those funds. By doing so, they would be conveying the unambiguous message that their audit was incomplete.[35]

Tatone resumed his work on the school's balance sheet shortly afterward, and over the course of the summer, completed audits of the Colegio's general fund for the fiscal years July 1, 1974–June 30, 1975, and July 1, 1975–June 30, 1976. Sonny sent the statements to Bemis by the deadline. The audits contained an abundance of data, but there could be no escaping the fact that they were not comprehensive. Indeed, the Salem accountants meticulously listed all the files they had been unable to examine and explicitly stated that, because of those lacunae, "the scope of our work was not sufficient to enable us to express, and we do not express, an opinion on the balance sheet."[36]

With the financial statements finally delivered, the Colegio had to wait two months for the meeting of the Commission on Colleges. In the intervening period, Bemis wrote to Sonny twice about the procedures the commission intended to follow at the

Sonny Montes, September 1976, at a time when the Colegio's struggles with HUD and the Northwest Association were intensifying. Photograph courtesy of the Statesman Journal; *image created from a microfilmed copy.*

December 1976 meeting, emphasizing the point that, unlike in June 1975, a maximum of three Colegio representatives would be allowed to participate.[37] In addition, at Sonny's request, he and two of his colleagues had a face-to-face discussion with Bemis at his Seattle office about the upcoming meeting. Various accounts of that discussion survive, but they provide conflicting views of what transpired. According to Bemis, the group talked mostly about the Colegio's audits, with Bemis offering his opinion that the commission would be "dissatisfied" because they were incomplete. According to Sonny, the session focused on the Colegio's general financial condition, not on the audits.[38]

One direct result of the Seattle discussion was that Sonny and his colleagues understood that the approaching meeting—which was scheduled to take place at the Portland Hilton on December 6, 1976—would touch on a wide range of financial issues. For that reason, the Colegio decided to send seven people to it: Sonny himself; Willner, who knew the most about the college's relations with HUD; two accountants, Aldrich and Tatone, who could answer questions about the audited statements; and three others who were familiar with specific financial questions (two staff members, Laney Kibel and Jan Chavez, and Joe Santana, a member of the board of trustees). While Sonny was aware that only three representatives of the Colegio could be present in the meeting room at any time, he assumed that substitutions would be permitted.[39]

Another Protest March, Another Meeting

By the end of November 1976, the Colegio was in crisis. Its relations with both HUD and the Commission on Colleges were fractured. A loss of the campus appeared to be a distinct possibility, as was a loss of candidacy status. That convergence of precarious circumstances was the occasion for the college community and its allies to reconsider the approach they had adopted in recent months in dealing with HUD and the commission. Sonny held a new round of meetings with the groups he normally consulted—his inner circle, the council, the board of trustees—and a decision was made to go on the offensive. Announcing the change on November 30, he said: "We have been planning to hold back and wait for something to happen, but nothing has. Now we are going to be active. . . . We might not have much money but we do have strong people support."[40]

What Sonny had in mind, and told the press about, was another protest march (he described it as a "solidarity march"), which would be held in Portland on December 6, 1976. Obviously, the date and place were not chosen at random, since on that day and in that city, the Commission on Colleges would be holding its hearing on the Colegio's candidacy status. A display of ethnic unity would send the message to the commission that the state's Mexican American community appreciated the Colegio's educational endeavors. However, the target of the day's march was not to be the Commission on Colleges alone: the organizers also intended to call attention to the actions of its other antagonist, HUD, then in the process of trying to dispose of the campus. In his comments to the press, Sonny revealed that, following the march, he and several other representatives of the Colegio planned to catch a flight to Washington, D.C., to seek support in the college's struggle with HUD from President-elect Jimmy Carter, who was thought to be sympathetic to minorities, and the National Council of La Raza and other organizations that promoted Hispanic causes and defended Hispanic interests. Thus, in this moment of crisis, the Colegio was opting for a combination of tactics—a return, at least for the moment, to collective action and a stepping-up of its lobbying campaign.[41]

As the day of the march approached, Sonny's criticism of HUD escalated. "At HUD, we get passed around like a football," he told a reporter. "They have a personal vendetta against us because we embarrassed them politically. They have been trying to get us out of here since 1973. . . . We filed a discrimination suit with a federal court in 1974. Ever since we did that and spoke up and for our rights and took our campaign nationally they've hated our guts." As before, Sonny was characterizing HUD as both unfair and bullying.[42]

On the morning of December 6, 1976, about 200 people—students, staff, and supporters of the Colegio—set off from Centenary-Wilbur United Methodist Church in the southeastern district of Portland and marched westward toward the Burnside Bridge in the direction of the city's downtown district. A light rain was falling. Some members of the procession carried placards. "Stop the eviction," read one. "Sí, se puede," read a second. After crossing the Burnside Bridge, the marchers proceeded toward the offices of HUD, located in the Cascade Building on S.W. 6th Avenue, and as they did, they began chanting "Viva Colegio Cesar Chavez. Abajo con HUD." HUD had taken precautions for the event, stationing extra security personnel in the building. But the marchers made no attempt to enter. Instead they moved down the street to the Hilton Hotel, where at that very moment Sonny and other representatives of the Colegio were making their presentation to the Commission on Colleges. Some of the protesters shouted words of encouragement that could not have been heard by the people inside. Then, after pausing a few minutes outside the hotel, the procession moved on to its final destination, Portland State University, where a rally and press conference were being held. Sonny, having just finished his meeting with the Commission on Colleges, joined the other protesters at the press conference and spoke a bit about HUD. "This is just the beginning of our struggle," he declared. "We are now going to take the offensive against HUD. We want to say to HUD that the Colegio will never be closed. There are too many people involved. The power of the people will get us what we deserve."[43]

While the solidarity march was generally judged to be a success, allowing the school's leaders and supporters to score verbal points and draw additional public attention to its battles, the same could not be said about the Colegio's meeting with the Commission on Colleges. Problems surfaced even before the Colegio's delegation entered the meeting room to confer with the commission. When the commission's chairman, Robert Coonrod, opened the door to usher the Colegio's representatives inside, he was startled to see, as he later remembered, a group of "ten to fifteen people." He had expected a delegation of two or three, and reminded Sonny that a maximum of three people would be allowed to enter. He also said that no substitutions would be permitted during the hearing. Sonny was taken aback by Coonrod's remark about the impossibility of making substitutions and argued with him about it—to no avail. So on the spot he was forced to make a difficult decision: Who should be selected to enter the room, given Coonrod's insistence that no substitutions would be permitted? He decided to take Willner and Santana with him—Willner, because Sonny thought that the commission would want to know about status of the negotiations with HUD, and Santana, because he was well informed about the school's recent fund-raising efforts. In retrospect, Sonny acknowledges that the meeting would have gone better for the Colegio if he had chosen an accountant. But at the time he was under the impression that the commission was interested in much more than the audits.[44]

The meeting was an extended nightmare. Sonny began by describing the valuable work that the Colegio was doing and the progress that had been made since the granting of candidacy status. After a few minutes of listening impatiently, Coonrod interrupted him. The commission, he told Sonny, was only interested in discussing the Colegio's audited financial statements. Coonrod then turned to Robert Thomas and Janet Hay, two commission members who had been designated to lead the discussion about the audits. The two posed several pointed questions about the documents, which Sonny, with no accountant present to assist him, could not effectively answer. Several members of the commission later described his responses as lengthy and evasive.[45]

Watching the sinking ship from close range, Willner spoke up to say that the Colegio's principal accountant, Kent Aldrich, might be better able to handle the questions that were being asked, and suggested that the commission permit Aldrich to replace him as one of the Colegio's three representatives in the room. The members of the commission discussed that suggestion for several minutes, finally agreeing to permit the substitution. But when Willner went to look for Aldrich, he learned that both accountants, thinking that they would not be allowed to appear before the commission, had left the building. After Willner reported that Aldrich was gone, Sonny made a final appeal to the commission, and then he, Willner, and Santana were excused.[46]

Once alone, the members of the commission talked briefly about the Colegio's fate. There was general agreement that the school's financial statement was unsatisfactory. Someone made a motion to discontinue the Colegio's candidacy status. Twenty commissioners supported it, one opposed it, and one abstained. The Commission on Colleges officially announced its decision on the following day.[47]

In the Midst of Chaos
While the Colegio's leaders and supporters were engaged in a two-front war with HUD and the Commission on Colleges, the college continued to function as an educational institution. As in previous years, a number of classes were held on campus during each quarter, generally in the evenings. One student who attended regularly was Eugenia Torres, a divorcée in her late twenties and a full-time secretary for the Northwest Regional Educational Laboratory. Torres also brought her eight-year-old son, Cameron, along, and she told a Portland reporter that Cameron had accompanied her to "every single class" during the three years she spent at the Colegio. "My son deserves a BA degree, too," Torres quipped. Roberto Gallegos, a nineteen-year-old freshman from Nyssa, Oregon, split his time between formal course work in elementary education and an internship as a tutor/translator at a Hillsboro elementary school. A former farmworker from a family of fifteen children, Gallegos derived great personal satisfaction from his classroom work: "I wish there had been someone around to help me like that when I was a kid."[48]

Rudy Veliz was likewise fully engaged. By the end of 1976, Veliz had come close to completing all the credits needed to receive his degree. The only classes still to be completed were two tutorials with Betty Rademaker, an adjunct faculty member, on "Teaching in the Elementary School." Like many courses at the Colegio, these were to include a practical component. In addition to meeting weekly with Rademaker to discuss assigned readings, Veliz would have to teach a group of second graders in a Salem elementary school how to read, with Rademaker monitoring his performance. Veliz knew that the final two quarters would be difficult, but he was determined to finish up by the spring, aware that the administration and the board of trustees were developing plans to hold graduation ceremonies in June 1977. The school had not held a formal graduation since its name had been changed in December 1973, and there was general agreement that the time had come for one, since at least a dozen current students, including Rudy Veliz, Eugenia Torres, Cipriano Ferrel, Jimmy Amaya, and Sonny Montes, were ready to graduate. Veliz was already thinking about life after the Colegio: he planned next to enroll in Oregon State University and get a teaching credential.[49]

As instructors continued to teach classes and students continued to make progress toward their degrees, Maria Luisa Alaniz, the college's director of admissions, devoted most of her attention to recruiting and retaining students. Her recruiting trips took her to all four corners of Oregon, even to Idaho, and she spent countless hours on the road. The job became even harder in December 1976, when the Commission on College withdrew the Colegio's candidacy status and, with it, the college's eligibility for federal financial aid. Under the circumstances, it was impossible to increase enrollments.[50]

The demands of the job and the stress induced by the college's constant battles took a toll on Alaniz and everyone else on the Colegio's staff. To cope, Alaniz and several colleagues occasionally got together for what she described as "sensitivity sessions." The meetings often included Montes, Romero, Alaniz, Chavez, Gallegos, and Kibel. "Some of us were burned out because of all the problems, all the tension." Alaniz explained. "We helped each other out."[51]

Montes and Romero also found occasional relief in golf.[52] Only about a mile from the Colegio was an inexpensive nine-hole public golf course, Evergreen Golf Club. Not especially long or difficult, it was an ideal place for Sonny and Jose to play, since both of them were hackers, completely self-taught. Oregon being a rainy place, they could not play at Evergreen year round. But they tried to get in a round each week during the spring, summer, and early fall, usually in the late afternoon after work. "It was a way to wind down after a tough day," Romero recalls. "A kind of stress management." He and Sonny were thankful for the opportunity to escape from the office, the phone, and the hassles.

John Little, another hacker, often joined them for a round. The stakes were low—the three of them rarely bet more than two dollars on a round—and good shots were infrequent. Conversation and fellowship appeared to be as important to them as making solid contact with the ball, and they did not necessarily observe the rules of golf etiquette. The three of them talked constantly, even when someone was swinging. Sonny was an especially accomplished kibitzer.

Jose remembers an example of Sonny's talents. The threesome was playing the sixth hole, a short par four that requires players to drive the ball over a pond. Sonny teed off first and hit his shot over the water. Little was next to play. As he addressed the ball, Sonny kept up a nonstop patter. "It's a long drive over the water today, John," he said. "The wind is really kicking up." And then: "You'd better aim more to the right, John. You don't want to land on that mound." And then: "You've really got to belt it today, John. It's a long carry." When Little finally swung, his ball nose dived into the pond. All three of them laughed heartily. "I guess you talked me out of that hole," Little conceded.

Willner and the Legal Option

If the meeting at Twin Falls in June 1975 was the high point of Sonny's tenure as codirector of the Colegio, the one at Portland in December 1976 was the low point. Going into the Portland meeting, Sonny had realized that there was a chance that the Commission on Colleges might vote against the Colegio. Still, he hoped that somehow he could duplicate the miracle at Twin Falls. When things didn't work out, he was disappointed, but not discouraged. He still believed that he could save the college.[53]

223

Sonny was wrong about that. Up to now, he, his colleagues at the Colegio, and his allies in the community had overcome enormous odds and performed extraordinary acts. Without them, the college would have already passed out of existence. But at this stage in the proceedings, there was a limit to what could be accomplished through the techniques heretofore relied on—engaging in negotiations, enlisting powerful allies to intervene on their behalf, broadcasting the college's message, and holding sit-ins, protest marches, and other demonstrations. While the days of engaging in those activities were not over for the Colegio, the major work that remained to be done would have to be done in another arena. Having first lost its campus and now its candidacy status, the school's principal hope for survival lay in taking its battles to the federal and state courts. The key player in that phase of the struggle would not be the Colegio's chief administrative officer, Sonny Montes, but rather its attorney, Don Willner.

Sonny and his Colegio colleagues were extremely reluctant to go to court. They knew from experience that the legal option was costly and saw it as only a last resort. As of late 1976, the college owed Don Willner's firm more than $25,000 as a result of the its past legal difficulties, and Willner was under increasing pressure from his partners to get at least partial payment from the school. For the past three years, whenever Montes and Romero had a meeting with Willner, he would plead with them to give him a token amount, simply to pacify his partners. They gave him mostly promises. Sonny knew, as did Don Willner, that the financial burden of continuing to represent the Colegio would fall on Willner's firm. Because of that, Sonny turned to Willner only when every other conceivable option was exhausted.[54]

On the Northwest Association front, however, Sonny was rapidly running out of options. One by one, they were being eliminated. According to the rules of the Northwest Association, decisions made by the Commission on Colleges on candidacy status or full accreditation could be appealed. Nine days after the commission's verdict on the Colegio, Sonny filed an appeal, alleging injustice and bias. In March 1977, a five-person board of review convened a hearing in Seattle to reconsider the decision, with Sonny and two trustees of the Colegio in attendance. The board voted to sustain the commission's decision.[55] After losing the appeal, the Colegio had only three remaining courses of action: it could apply for reinstatement as a candidate for accreditation—a step that looked unpromising, it could close its doors, or it could turn to the courts for redress. In April 1977, Sonny and Don Willner began discussing the possibility of bringing a lawsuit against the Northwest Association.[56]

Willner filed the lawsuit on June 16, 1977. His principal contention was that the Colegio had been denied due process—that it had not received adequate notice of the reasons for the December 1976 meeting and that the Commission of Colleges had not held a hearing that allowed the Colegio to defend itself properly. Willner sought two things from the court: a preliminary injunction to stop the Northwest Association from revoking the Colegio's candidacy status for the duration of the lawsuit and a permanent injunction to stop the association from revoking candidacy status until a new hearing could be held in which the school was afforded due process of law.[57]

The first phase of the trial took place on July 6, 1977, when the court heard arguments on the Colegio's motion for a preliminary injunction. Presiding was U.S. District Judge Robert Belloni. The question to be decided was essentially financial. The Colegio was asking that its candidacy status be restored temporarily so that its students could apply for federal financial assistance. Deadlines were fast approaching for the submission of applications for federal aid, and, since the Colegio had lost its candidacy status, its undergraduates were not eligible to apply. Willner argued that, unless the court granted the preliminary injunction, the Colegio would suffer irreparable damage, because even if the college prevailed in its lawsuit, it would not be able to get the federal funding it was entitled to.[58] Belloni's decision was not difficult to make, since it was undeniable that the Colegio might be severely damaged if he did nothing. He granted the preliminary injunction. "We're back in business," Sonny commented. Round one had gone to the Colegio.[59]

Round two, though, was the one that mattered, and there was no guarantee about how it would go. The hearing on the permanent injunction was set for August 18, 1977, with Belloni again presiding. Attorneys for both sides assembled relevant documents, spoke to witnesses, and filed several flurries of motions. After reaching an agreement that most of the testimony submitted into evidence would be in written form, with only a few individuals testifying in person at the hearing, Willner and his adversaries, a team of attorneys led by William Hennessey of Seattle, assisted by the staff of the Northwest Association, gathered written statements from witnesses.[60]

Here the Northwest Association's attorneys made crucial errors. To prove their case that the organization had acted fairly, they decided to collect statements from every member of the Commission of Colleges who had participated in meetings with or about the Colegio. Hennessey apparently believed that these statements would support the association's case. That might have been so if the Northwest Association's attorneys had carefully overseen the production of the statements, but they did not. Although the members of the commission received some guidance about what subjects to discuss in their testimony, they wrote the statements themselves. It is unclear how much time the association's attorneys devoted to reviewing those documents. Without question it was not enough.[61]

As the day of the hearing approached, while Willner was looking over the statements written by the members of the commission, he discovered that there were striking discrepancies in their explanations of the purpose of the December 1976 meeting. Willner summarized his findings in a trial memorandum filed on the day before the second hearing. By his count, seven commission members who attended that meeting thought that the issue they were voting on was the "adequacy of the Colegio's financial statements." On the other hand, four of them believed that the issue "included the financial stability of [the] Colegio"; one thought that the "sincerity" of the Colegio was at issue; and still another commissioner contradicted himself, at one time asserting that the issue was the financial statements and at another suggesting that the college's financial condition was under review.[62] Willner's point was that Northwest Association's *own witnesses* supported the Colegio's contention that its representatives went into the December meeting with no clear idea of what to expect. If the members of the commission were confused, how could the Colegio's leaders have been certain about the purpose of the meeting? At the hearing, that simple rhetorical question became the central argument of Willner's case. Several times, he returned to his numerical analysis of the members' explanations of why they had voted to revoke the Colegio's candidacy status, emphasizing their confusion about the issue that was being considered.[63]

Eight days after the hearing, on August 26, 1977, Judge Belloni rendered his opinion. He found that, because the Northwest Association did not provide proper notice to the Colegio about the December 1976 meeting, the Colegio reasonably believed that the subject of discussion on that day was to be the college's "substantive financial condition." He also commented at length on the commission's confusion at the meeting, accepting and echoing Willner's analysis. "The testimony at trial, including the statements of the commission members, made it clear that nothing was clear to the finders of fact. They yet disagree on what the issue was involving Colegio. . . . If the adjudicators did not know, how was Colegio to have known?" Concluding that the Colegio had been denied due process, he ruled in its favor: the Northwest Association had to restore the school's candidacy status, and the accrediting organization could not revoke it until a new hearing was held that afforded due process to the Colegio.[64] Although the Commission on Colleges would later give consideration to the idea of holding another hearing, it ultimately decided against doing so, and the Colegio was able to retain its candidacy status for the remainder of the six-year probation period.

Sonny, his colleagues, and the Colegio's supporters were ecstatic when they heard the news about Belloni's decision. The college now had the external validation that came with candidacy status, and its students would have access to federal financial aid. After learning of the decision, Sonny, John Little, and a large group of Colegio supporters went out to celebrate, traveling to a tavern in Hubbard, Oregon, owned by Juan Ruiz, Sonny's former VML colleague, where they drank, smoked, and enjoyed their victory late into the night.[65]

New Developments on the HUD Front
In the two-front war that Sonny and Jose were forced to fight, the struggle with HUD went on longer. That was so largely because, as of the December 1976–January 1977 period, the list of options

available to the Colegio was still long and recourse to the courts, always seen as the last resort, could justifiably be delayed. It would take time to whittle down the list. In the meantime, Sonny held out hopes—the hope that he could somehow reach an agreement with HUD, the hope that the pressure applied to HUD by its allies would make the agency less intractable, the hope that potential bidders for the campus would not have enough money to satisfy HUD, the hope that foundations could be induced to make large donations, the hope that sizable federal grants could be won, the hope that a white knight would be found to save the school and consequently make it unnecessary to make another telephone call to Don Willner. Until those hopes were exposed as illusion, the Colegio would hold off on turning to the courts.

In the immediate aftermath of the December 6 march in Portland, a number of developments on the HUD front seemed promising. There were continuing indications—one of them being Jimmy Carter's choice of an African American, Patricia Harris, as secretary of HUD—that the Carter administration was going to be more supportive of minorities. In addition, due largely to the lobbying efforts of the Colegio's allies in Washington, D.C., HUD instructed its Seattle office to drop the idea of selling the campus directly to the MCHA, to proceed with the auction, and even to allow the Colegio to participate in the auction if it chose to do so.[66] Then there was the auction itself. HUD had set March 2, 1977, as the deadline for submitting bids for the campus and had set the minimum asking price at $500,000, a substantial amount for a campus in a high state of disrepair. No bids were received. The inflated asking price made it impossible for both the Colegio and the MCHA to submit offers. Others may have been influenced by a different consideration. As Sonny surmised: "I could just imagine the buyers saying to themselves: 'Do we really want to get ourselves involved in this situation? Do we want to buy the buildings and then find out that the Mexicans are not going to leave?'"[67] After the abortive auction, there was another hopeful development. HUD announced that the Colegio would be allowed to occupy the campus until June 15, 1977, and finish out the academic year. Unsure about how to proceed, the department wanted, as one official told the press, "to take a long look at the situation before making any decision."[68]

Still, not all the signs were good. The Colegio, taking advantage of its new reprieve, asked HUD to consider a proposal it had recently developed: that the school would pay HUD $200,000 for the property on the condition that HUD agreed to a two-year payment "moratorium," during which time the Colegio would attempt to raise the money from donors. HUD showed no interest in the new approach. More ominously, HUD revived its talks with the MCHA, which remained interested in acquiring the property on the terms worked out the previous year.[59]

By mid-May 1977, a number of senior HUD officials in Washington, D.C., were anxious to go ahead with a sale to the MCHA, but Secretary Harris was not yet willing to agree. Having promised at the outset of her tenure to be sensitive to the concerns of minority groups, she wanted to see if it was possible to find a solution that left the Colegio in control of its campus. Over the next month, more than a dozen HUD staff members looked into a range of possibilities—a negotiated sale to the Colegio, a long-term lease, a new loan to the Colegio, a sale to the state of Oregon with the state then transferring the property to the college, and several others. In each case, the government officials saw problems, usually legal ones.[70] The Colegio's possible options were beginning to disappear, but because HUD's deliberations were confidential, the school's leaders were not aware of these developments.

On June 15, the Colegio got another reprieve. HUD's most recent deadline for the school to vacate the campus had arrived, but Secretary Harris still had not reached a decision about the disposition of the campus. Spokespersons for HUD announced that, for the time being, the Colegio could stay put, while the agency reconsidered its order to vacate the campus as well as all the other decisions that HUD had made previously about the Colegio.[71]

Over the summer of 1977, HUD was silent about its plans for the campus. But, plans were definitely in the works. In late June, six senior HUD officials, meeting in Washington, D.C., reviewed the department's efforts to find a way to return the campus to the Colegio. Concluding that they could find no legal method of doing so, they recommended that the school be sold to the MCHA. HUD assistant secretary Lawrence Simons endorsed the recommendation in mid-July and Secretary Harris signed on in mid-August, sending instructions to HUD's Seattle office to take possession of the campus.[72] Sonny and his colleagues were aware of none of these decisions.

A Badly Timed Change at the Top

About a year had passed since Cisco Garcia had tried to recruit Sonny to the Northwest Regional Educational Laboratory, and, over the intervening period, Sonny's thoughts had occasionally returned to that job possibility. They did so with greater frequency in the summer of 1977. On June 30, the Colegio held its first graduation ceremony on the front lawn of the college campus. Of the twenty-one students who received degrees, fifteen of them were Mexican Americans. They included Cipriano Ferrel and Rudy Veliz, the campus activists; Jimmy Amaya, Sonny's old VML co-worker; Eugenia Torres, who had brought her son to every class she had taken at the Colegio; and Sonny Montes, the school's director of administrative affairs. Abelardo Delgado, a professor of Chicano studies at the University of Utah, gave the commencement address, and Sonny spoke as well. "We are part of history tonight," he said. "This school should not exist, but it does exist. There is no way that they will ever take this college away from us." With the degree finally in hand, Sonny resumed his discussions with Garcia.[73]

While the fate of the college campus remained unknown, Sonny was becoming more sanguine that an agreement with HUD was in sight. In recent months, there had been promising signs: the failed auction, the reprieves, and the press reports suggesting that, under Secretary Harris's leadership, HUD was reconsidering its past decisions about the Colegio. (He did not know, of course, that the final result of that reconsideration would be a recommitment by HUD to sell the campus.)

Then came Willner's legal victory in August 1977, restoring the school's candidacy status and, with it, the eligibility of its students for federal financial aid. That development improved considerably the Colegio's chances for survival. In Sonny's eyes, with one major problem solved and the second close to resolution, "things seemed to be looking up for the Colegio."[74]

In light of all that, Sonny concluded that the time had come for him to leave. He informed his Colegio colleagues that he planned

Graduation ceremony, Colegio Cesar Chavez, June 30, 1977. Photograph courtesy of The Oregonian.

to resign before the start of the new academic year and to begin work at the Lab in early October. Over the following month, the Colegio chose his successor, Salvador Ramirez, who had joined the Colegio in 1976 as director of planning and research after holding administrative and teaching posts at Washington State University and the University of Colorado.[75]

Sonny made his decision to leave with a certain amount of regret, but also with a realization that, for him, the timing of his departure was as close to right as it was ever going to be. As he later admitted, after having worked overtime at Mt. Angel College and the Colegio for a total of six years, he was, like Mondor and Lopez before him, "totally exhausted." Even if he had wanted to continue, he felt that he could not have. Still, Sonny was not going to cut all his ties to the Colegio. He agreed to join the board of trustees and reached an understanding with the other board members to the effect that, when the Colegio and HUD next sat down together to conduct serious negotiations, he would be included in the Colegio's delegation.[76]

Unfortunately for the Colegio, the timing of Sonny's departure could not have been worse. On September 20, 1977, on the eve of the new academic quarter, HUD broke its summer-long silence. George Roybal, the recently appointed head of HUD's Seattle office, appeared unannounced at a meeting of the Colegio's board of trustees and personally presented Sonny with a letter from HUD assistant secretary Simons informing him that HUD intended to evict the Colegio. The school was given thirty days to leave. The board members gasped when they heard the news. On the following day, Sonny and Salvador Ramirez held a news conference to comment on the eviction notice. "This action by the Department of Housing and Urban Development gives the lie to its expensive publicity campaign aimed at making HUD appear to be the champion of the poor," Ramirez observed acidly. Sonny was predictably defiant. "This is our third annual eviction notice from HUD," he said. "We have no plans for vacating the premises."[77]

This was not an ideal time for the Colegio to announce Sonny's resignation, and the school did not. But reporters somehow got word that he had resigned, and stories about his leaving appeared in the newspapers in the first week of October 1977.[78] The reporters did not discover at the time that Jose Romero was about to leave as well. Like Sonny, Jose had been negotiating on and off with the Northwest Laboratory and had decided to begin work there in November. His replacement would be Peter de Garmo, who held a doctoral degree from the University of California at Berkeley.[79] With Sonny Montes gone and Jose Romero about to depart, others would be in charge during the college's next battle with HUD.

Again, the Legal Option
The Colegio adopted a two-track approach in dealing with the new threat of eviction. On the first track, Ramirez and his supporters, including the approximately thirty students who showed up to register in the first week of October 1977, began organizing a collective-action campaign designed to stop, or at least to delay, HUD's occupation. On the second, Don Willner, operating in the courts, searched for a legal way of retaining the campus. The level of Willner's activity in this period was a measure of how desperate the situation had become: with few options left on the list, the Colegio had to rely on him.

The new round of collective action began at 8 p.m. on October 20, the eviction deadline set by HUD, with a Mass delivered by a Mexican priest at Guadalupe Hall. About a hundred people—college staff members, students, former students, and other members of the college community—were in attendance. Following the Mass, Salvador Ramirez addressed the audience, vowing to resist HUD. "We have prepared ourselves spiritually, legally, and physically for this confrontation," he said. Then, approximately half the participants, a group that included recent Colegio graduate Jimmy Amaya, several current students, and Jose Garcia, president of the board of trustees, occupied one of the college's buildings. A spirit of camaraderie prevailed among the small occupation force. Throughout the night and the following day, they discussed the issues that united them, snacked on sandwiches, and sang *campesino* songs, *corridas*, and other *cantas*, accompanied by Amaya playing his guitar. One thought in all their minds was the possibility that they would be arrested, but they did not seem frightened. A reporter who was with them observed: "Beneath it all, when one person's eyes focused on another's face, there seemed to be an understanding—a shared feeling among the participants that this was the place to be, a final sacrifice against what they called 'government oppression.'"[80]

A few days later, with the building still occupied, the college's collective action campaign received an important endorsement when Cesar Chavez paid an unscheduled visit to the campus. Chavez had by now developed a fondness for the Colegio and was appalled at HUD's determination to dispose of the campus to any qualified buyer. According to newspaper reports, he offered to help the Colegio's leaders in their dealings with HUD, expressing a willingness to participate in any negotiations that might take place between the school and the government and promising to make a call to the Carter White House in support of the Colegio. Shortly afterward, he made the call, urging the president to rein in HUD.[81]

The new collective-action campaign made for good theater, and as it continued over the next two months the press dutifully covered it. But it had no appreciable effect on HUD. Having reached the considered conclusion that no acceptable deal with the Colegio could be worked out, its officials had every intention of pressing forward with their eviction plans, regardless of the public relations consequences. Accordingly, William McAllister, an attorney representing HUD, asked the Marion County Circuit Court for a writ of assistance, which would require the county sheriff to enforce the eviction notice.[82]

From this point forward, the struggle between HUD and the Colegio was to be played out primarily in the courts. Toward the end of October, Marion County Circuit Court judge Richard Barber held a hearing on the writ of assistance and promptly granted it. But when Willner appealed the decision to the Oregon Supreme Court, the judge postponed the eviction while the appeal was pending. That decision insured that the college's educational work could continue for at least a few more months, since it would take that long for the high court to render an opinion.[83]

In December 1977, the Oregon Supreme Court considered the Colegio's appeal of Barber's writ of assistance. Willner, always creative, was ready with a novel argument—to wit, that Barber had erred in granting the writ because, ever since HUD had gained title to the campus, a de facto "landlord-tenant relationship" had come to exist between HUD and the Colegio. To support his argument, he produced documents showing that on three different occasions HUD had agreed to allow the Colegio to remain on the campus until the property was sold. Willner's argument raised questions about Barber's decision, for if a de facto landlord-tenant relationship existed between HUD and the Colegio, the judge had infringed on the Colegio's rights as a tenant when he had granted the writ. Willner also maintained that Barber should not even have held a hearing on the matter, since writ of assistance hearings were to be held only in open-and-shut cases. In this instance, because the college had a reasonable argument, it was entitled to a full hearing, a trial by jury, and the opportunity to cross-examine witnesses.[84]

It took the Oregon Supreme Court slightly more than two months to issue an opinion, and the result was another legal victory for Willner and the Colegio. On February 14, 1978, convinced that HUD had established something approximating a landlord-tenant relationship with the Colegio, the seven justices decided unanimously that Judge Barber had erred in granting the writ of assistance. The bottom line was that there would be no eviction of the college.[85]

Believing that the time was now right to renew the Colegio's efforts to purchase the campus, Willner and Ramirez asked Ullman to arrange negotiations with HUD in Washington, D.C. Over the following weeks, HUD was won over to the idea of restarting talks with the Colegio. Pressure from the school's allies in the nation's capital may have been partly responsible for that decision, but a contributing factor was undoubtedly the realization that pursuing the eviction route would require further legal tangles with Willner. A meeting between the Colegio and HUD was scheduled for March 20, 1978, at the main HUD building. As the day approached, there was another propitious development: for the first time since the Colegio had come into existence, there was a possibility that the Colegio might have enough money at its disposal to conclude a deal with HUD.[86]

The Meeting

The Colegio's delegation at the meeting consisted of four men. One was Sonny, who was included pursuant to his earlier agreement with the board of trustees. He took a flight to Washington, D.C., the day before the meeting with two other members of the negotiating team, Salvador Ramirez and Don Willner. The three of them would be joined in Washington by the fourth member of the delegation, a person with a different kind of connection to the school: it bore his name.[87]

As we know, when he had last visited the college campus in October 1977, Cesar Chavez had offered to take part in negotiations with the HUD. With a settlement now possible, the Colegio's leaders had decided to take Chavez up on the offer. The Colegio's choice of a day for the meeting was actually determined by Chavez's schedule: he had firm plans to be in Washington, D.C., between March 20 and March 22 to receive an award from the Department of Health, Education, and Welfare. The negotiators for HUD apparently had no prior knowledge that Chavez would participate.[88]

Nor was HUD informed that the Colegio would have some other allies in the negotiating room. Before he left for Washington, Sonny had contacted Raúl Yzaguirre, director of the National

Council of La Raza, the Washington, D.C.–based organization that had helped the Colegio in its past battles with HUD, and asked him to invite a group of prominent Latinos in the D.C. area to attend the HUD-Colegio meeting. Over the years, as we have seen, Sonny had learned that, because his people suffered from so many preexisting disadvantages in dealing with Anglo society, it was necessary, whenever possible, to even up the odds. In this case, he wanted to include additional brown faces in the room, feeling that a demonstration of ethnic solidarity might make HUD more receptive to the college's offer.[89]

At about 7:30 a.m. on the meeting day, Chavez, who was staying in the home of one of his supporters in the capital, made a call to Sonny, who was lodged in a downtown hotel. "Can you come over right away?" he inquired. Sonny came and, at Chavez's request, provided a briefing on the Colegio's recent efforts to regain the campus. He reviewed the school's legal battles and then focused on its suddenly more promising financial prospects, explaining that a few weeks earlier, his former co-worker and close friend Pete Collazo had approached him with an intriguing proposition. The proposition involved the Centro Chicano Cultural, the Oregon-based cultural organization that Sonny had helped to establish. In 1970, the Centro had purchased a farmhouse and sixty-three acres of land in Gervais, Oregon, and converted the farmhouse into a facility in which it held cultural events. Three years later the building was severely damaged by fire, and since then the Centro's attempts to build a new structure on the same property had been thwarted by local Anglo farmers, who had never been keen on having a Mexican American meeting place in their small community. Frustrated, Collazo, who had become chairman of the Centro's board, and his fellow board members had decided by February 1978 to relocate the cultural center to the town of Woodburn and dispose of the Gervais property. But Collazo also wanted to do something else. A strong supporter of the Colegio, he suggested to the other board members—and repeated the suggestion to Sonny, who in turn repeated it to the Colegio's board—that part of the proceeds of the sale, which was expected to net about $200,000, should be used to help the Colegio. While there was no assurance that everything would work out exactly as Collazo hoped it would, Sonny, Ramirez, and other leaders of the

Colegio felt that, in all likelihood, the school would at last be able to make an offer that might be acceptable to HUD.[90]

After Sonny had finished, Chavez turned to an aide, and asked him to place three telephone calls immediately. The first was to be to Augustus ("Gus") Hawkins, the influential African American congressman from California; the second to someone at the national office of the AFL-CIO; and the third to a contact at the White House. He explained that, during the HUD-Colegio meeting, he wanted all three of those people to call Patricia Harris and urge her to accept the school's offer. Chavez specified when each of the calls to Harris should be made, insisting that they be spaced precisely thirty minutes apart. Then, as Sonny and Cesar Chavez resumed their conversation, the aide picked up the phone and worked out the arrangements.[91] Chavez had his own ways of improving the odds.

The HUD-Colegio meeting took place in the late afternoon of March 20, 1978. The venue was a large conference room in the HUD building. Sonny, Don Willner, and Salvador Ramirez arrived early, followed by a group of ten to fifteen Latinos assembled by Yzaguirre. Then came Chavez. About half a dozen people from HUD were also present. HUD's spokesman for most of the session was Morton Baruch, acting assistant secretary of the department. Secretary Harris attended briefly while the three groups of participants were getting settled, but left to take a telephone call and never returned to the meeting.[92]

Baruch spoke first. Looking directly at Willner, the only Anglo in the Colegio's delegation, he said: "I assume that you will be negotiating for the college." In fact, Willner wasn't the designated negotiator. Once the Colegio's leaders learned that Chavez would be able to attend the meeting with HUD in Washington, D.C., they had prevailed on him to be the college's principal spokesperson. Willner had concurred with the decision. While he was an accomplished attorney with much negotiating experience, he was no Cesar Chavez, the best known Mexican American in the United States, a man the late Robert Kennedy had described as "one of the heroic figures of our time." It would have made no sense for anyone other than Chavez to speak for the Colegio Cesar Chavez.[93]

Willner deduced at that moment that Baruch and HUD's other representatives had no idea that Chavez was in the room. "They didn't know who he was," he recalled with a chuckle. "They saw a bunch of Mexican faces and assumed that I was in charge." Willner proceeded to correct Baruch. No, he wasn't the spokesman for the Colegio. "Sitting on my right," he said, "is Cesar Chavez. He will be negotiating for the college." As Willner remembered the episode, the HUD delegation was stunned when he made that statement. "They were so scared, they couldn't see straight." For the next two hours, Chavez was in charge.[94]

Sonny has one very vivid memory of the meeting. In the first hour of discussions, one of HUD's attorneys asked him a question. Sonny tried to answer, but, by his own admission, he didn't do well. At that point, Chavez interrupted him, and asked the HUD delegation if it would do him a favor. "Can you guys go get some coffee or something, and just leave us here for ten minutes or so?" Baruch agreed, and everyone except the Colegio's representatives left the room.

During the time-out, Chavez gave Sonny a brief lesson in negotiating tactics. "If you're not sure of an answer," he explained to Sonny, "you don't have to respond. Just say: 'Excuse us. We need to get together for about five, ten minutes.' And then we can get together, and come up with an answer, and reconvene the session." Chavez's point was that a key to negotiating successfully was to set the terms of the discussion. Too often, he told Sonny, when poor people negotiated with representatives of the establishment, they simply accepted the rules set by the establishment. That reduced their chances of getting a favorable result. The representatives of the establishment, generally attorneys, were skilled at posing and answering questions; non-attorneys were not. If poor people were to have any chance of success, it was necessary to change the rules. As Sonny recalls, Chavez called at least one more time-out during the negotiating session with HUD to consult with the rest of the Colegio delegation, and when he did, the group from HUD obediently filed out of the room.[95]

The main item of business discussed at the March 20 meeting was the Colegio's new offer for the college campus. Basically, the offer involved using the anticipated proceeds of the sale of the Centro Chicano Cultural's property in Gervais to finance the purchase of the Mt. Angel campus. The Colegio, operating on the assumption that Collazo would be able to win over the Centro's board, offered to make an initial payment of $50,000, with most of it coming from the money received by the Centro from the future buyer of the Gervais property. After that, over the course of ten years, the Colegio would make regular payments to HUD, with the unpaid balance owed to HUD being guaranteed by future amounts received by the Centro. The grand total paid by the Colegio would be approximately $250,000.[96]

At this point, as the Colegio's representatives realized, they did not have an absolute guarantee of getting the money they were offering to pay. That would depend on the decision of the Centro's board. But they left the negotiating session with the feeling that, if the decision of the board was favorable, their problems with HUD might be solved. "My impression is that [HUD officials] are giving serious consideration to our offer and may well accept it," Willner wrote shortly after the meeting.[97] Just possibly, the efforts of Chavez and Montes to even up the odds had influenced the bureaucrats at HUD to be more accommodating toward the Colegio.

Eventually, a deal was struck. The Centro's board approved Collazo's idea of helping out the college and the sale of the Gervais property went forward. Meanwhile, HUD accepted the Colegio's offer with only minor amendments. In July 1978, at a news conference in Portland, Oregon, HUD secretary Patricia Harris announced that HUD's battle with the Colegio was over. The Mexican American school again held the title to its campus.[98] And because of that, as improbable as it must have seemed, the Colegio, an institution that had seemed to be on the point of extinction on numerous occasions over the past four years, was able to continue operations. As of July 1978, HUD and the Northwest Association had been defeated.

Sonny and the Colegio

Sonny Montes's role in the story of the Colegio is obviously important. He was a key actor—arguably, *the* key one—in the events that transformed Mt. Angel College, a small liberal arts institution catering to middle-class Anglos, into a Chicano-oriented college. He recruited Mexican American students, faculty, and board members, helped to develop a Chicano studies program, lobbied members of

239

the college community to back his Mexican American initiative, and ultimately won enough support to change the college's orientation. In December 1973, twenty-seven months after Sonny arrived there, and due in considerable measure to his efforts, Mt. Angel College officially ceased to exist, and in its place was Colegio Cesar Chavez, one of only a handful of U.S. colleges with a Mexican American administration and a largely Mexican American student body.

After that, except during the brief presidency of Ernesto Lopez, Sonny shared responsibility for directing the Colegio with his good friend Jose Romero. Sonny devoted his attention to administrative matters and Jose to academic concerns. Both of them worked tirelessly for the institution, but because of the division of responsibility, it fell to Sonny to lead the Colegio in its dealings with HUD and the Northwest Association. He attended all the important meetings, presented the college's case to the Commission on Colleges, and directed the collective-action campaign against HUD. His face and words appeared frequently in the press.

This is not to suggest that his contributions to the Colegio exceeded those of others. Romero undoubtedly had a greater impact on the college's intellectual life; Joseph Gallegos, Jan Chavez, Maria Luisa Alaniz, and other staff members and members of the board provided invaluable services. Furthermore, by the spring of 1977, it was clear that, even in the contests with the Northwest Association and HUD, Sonny was no longer the Colegio's most important player. Don Willner had superseded him. All the same, despite some mistakes along the way, Sonny's achievements were impressive. He led the college's successful effort to gain candidacy status in 1975. During the collective-action campaign against HUD, he effectively made his case that HUD was mistreating and bullying the Colegio and mobilized the Colegio's network of supporters to participate in a variety of protest activities. Although in the end it was Willner, not Montes, who scored the decisive legal victories over the Northwest Association in 1977 and HUD in 1978, it was Montes who prolonged the struggle, steadily wearing down the Colegio's opponents, especially the bureaucrats at HUD.

Sonny's success in mobilizing support can be explained in three ways. First, the Colegio benefited from the facts that a Mexican American network was already in place in the region and that Sonny himself was deeply involved in it thanks to his participation in the VML, the grape boycott, the antiwar movement, the Centro Chicano Cultural, and an array of other Mexican American organizations. Second, Sonny ably framed the Colegio's collective-action campaign. Virtually from the outset, in his public statements about HUD, he focused not on the specific issues over which the college and government disagreed but rather on the general, more resonant one of HUD's unjust treatment of Mexican Americans. This framing not only motivated people in the Mexican American community who were already predisposed to favor a Chicano educational institution but also helped the Colegio to gain a certain amount of sympathy from prominent Anglo politicians and the editors of local newspapers. Third, Sonny's knowledge of and reliance on community development techniques played an important part in keeping the "Save Colegio Cesar Chavez" campaign alive. Never the caudillo, ever the catalyst and enabler, Sonny led not by telling people what to do but rather by consulting with them about how best to do it and working with them to develop a strategy. Here was the ultimate paradox: successful leadership in the Chicano struggle in Oregon was built on a foundation of active group participation. What some saw as Sonny's charisma—the sources are filled with references to his "charismatic" qualities—was actually something closer to a mastery of community development techniques. The net result of all these factors was a social movement with a mobilizing structure that was dependable, because the links between the leadership and the support base were strong and resilient.

Finally, it should be recognized that Sonny accomplished all that he did at a time when the structure of political opportunities was inhospitable to Mexican American protest. By the late 1960s the civil rights movement had lost its momentum, and by the early 1970s the Chicano movement, which had always lacked the institutional base that had sustained African American protest, was going through a challenging period of its own. From the outset, then, the "Save Colegio Cesar Chavez" campaign in the mid-1970s was a Sisyphean struggle: there were no compelling reasons for any mainstream political party to speak up for a cash-poor Chicano college in a state with few electoral votes; and, while the Colegio received occasional donations from Catholic organizations, and the National Council of La Raza sometimes lobbied on its behalf, the college (and every other Chicano protest group of the 1960s and 1970s, except for the farmworkers movement) never received anything comparable to the assistance given to African American protesters during the most active days of the civil rights movement. Most of the time, Sonny and the Colegio were forced to rely almost exclusively on the help of the region's Mexican American community, a group of committed Anglo allies such as John Little and Ivo Bauman, and the largesse of Willner's law firm. And when in 1978 a knight finally rode to the college's rescue and provided enough money to finance the settlement with HUD, the knight turned out to be a resident of the neighboring town of Woodburn, and the color of his skin was brown, not white.

The Colegio After Sonny,
Sonny After the Colegio

Having won major legal battles against the Northwest Association and HUD, the Colegio was no longer in immediate danger of closing. But winning battles, even big ones, should never be confused with winning a war. As a new academic year began for the Colegio in late September 1978, there still was no guarantee that the Colegio would remain long in existence.[1]

For one, there was the ongoing problem of very low enrollment. Only eighteen students showed up to register in the fall quarter. Obviously, the bad publicity of recent years and the disheveled state of the campus made recruiting difficult.[2] Meanwhile, old bills remained unpaid, and new ones started to mount up. In the past, there had been some discussion about repairing the campus buildings once the HUD troubles were resolved and then renting out much of that space to other organizations, with the rent money being used to improve the college's balance sheet. The discussion ended soon after the Colegio received estimates of the projected costs—more than $30,000 simply to fix the furnaces and close to $500,000 to repair everything else. With most of the buildings still unusable, the rent income never materialized.[3]

If all that were not enough, there were signs of conflict within the Colegio administration. During the Montes-Romero era, a culture of consultation and cooperation had prevailed at the Colegio. While people disagreed, the disagreements rarely escalated into open conflict, because decisions were deferred until a consensus had been reached. In the post-Montes-Romero era, there was much less discussion, priorities were often set without it, and conflict was more difficult to contain. Ramirez's abilities as an administrator were also at issue. By February 1979, Sonny himself, now a board member, began raising questions at board meetings about how business was being done at the college. He felt that Ramirez needed to direct more of his attention to the preparation of grant proposals.[4]

A more serious challenge to Ramirez's leadership came from another member of the board of trustees, Irma Gonzales. A civil rights compliance officer with the U.S. Civil Service Commission office in Portland, Gonzales had joined the board in 1975. Becoming an active player after the departure of Montes and Romero, she forged an alliance with Romero's replacement, Peter de Garmo. The two of them wanted to make significant changes in the college: to establish a core curriculum of traditional academic courses for all students, provide greater supervision over and structure to the College Without Walls, attract top-flight students (the "cream of the crop," as Sonny put it), and give less attention to recruiting students with farmworker backgrounds. One obstacle they faced was Ramirez, who objected to the pressure they applied on him to carry out their policies. Over time, relations between Ramirez and Gonzales grew acrimonious, and behind the scenes she attempted to oust him. In September 1979, the board forced Ramirez to resign. The college entered a new academic year with no chief administrative officer and an enrollment that, depending on which newspaper story one reads, was either seven or thirty-five.[5]

The internal conflict did not end there. Within the board itself, fissures were developing. Montes, Romero, Little, and others had reservations about the changes favored by Gonzales and de Garmo. They felt that, by favoring a more traditional approach to education and focusing their recruitment efforts on elite students, their opponents were ignoring the needs of the Mexican American community. It made no sense to them to invest so much time and energy in pursuing students who were capable of gaining admission to the University of Oregon or Reed College. It bothered them too that, whereas in the Montes-Romero era the Colegio hosted many community events at no charge, Mexican American organizations now had to pay a fee to use the campus facilities.[6] Their underlying concern was that, by ignoring students from farmworker backgrounds and erecting a financial barrier between itself and the Mexican American community, the Colegio was alienating the groups that had stood by, marched for, and otherwise supported it in its times of troubles.

In this contest between the old guard and the new, it was Gonzales who prevailed, her victory due to her clever (and, according to her critics, sometimes devious) political maneuvers. After Ramirez's departure, the Colegio's board of trustees decided to conduct a national search for a president. With the school lacking an administrative officer, Gonzales volunteered to take the job temporarily and serve only until the president was chosen. In February 1980, the board appointed her acting president, with the understanding that she was to be a caretaker, and a few months later, the presidential search was launched. The search committee identified two finalists, José Angel Gutiérrez, the well-known Chicano activist from Texas, and Reymundo Marin, who had experience in university administration. But when it came time for the board to decide between them, Gonzales, behind the scenes, worked to produce a result that kept her in power. According to Gutiérrez and others, she "rigged" the selection process. In October 1980, by a six to five vote, the board, which now included a number of Gonzales's allies, decided not to offer the position to either of the finalists. Gonzales remained in charge as acting president.[7]

Gonzales was polarizing the Mexican American community as well as the board. In early 1981, a group of Gonzales's opponents formed an organization called the Concerned Community for Colegio Cesar Chavez, which criticized the failure of the presidential search and called for greater community participation in the Colegio.[8] Meanwhile, board members such as Sonny, Jose, and John Little continued to protest Gonzales's policies. Gonzales forced Montes and Little off the board. Romero served out his term but did not seek reappointment.[9]

Even though Gonzales was now in undisputed control of the Colegio, she was not in control of the Colegio's destiny. Ultimately, the Colegio's ability to survive rested on its ability to meet the accreditation standards of the Northwest Association, the organization that had the power to cut off its federal financial assistance. In the spring of 1979, the Commission on Colleges had conducted a review of the Colegio's progress toward accreditation and given the school a passing grade. But it had also indicated that the grade might be lower two years later, when it would have to decide whether or not to grant full accreditation. In particular, the Colegio needed to increase its enrollment. Unless it did so, the accrediting agency might vote against accreditation.[10]

In the spring quarter of 1981, student enrollment was fewer than thirty (one report placed it at twenty-seven, another at seventeen) and the local newspapers carried stories that the college was being mismanaged.[11] Then came the decisive blow. In June 1981, the Commission on Colleges voted unanimously to deny accreditation to the school. Its chief reasons for denial were familiar: low enrollment and the Colegio's inadequate financial base.[12]

That decision sent the school into a tailspin. Gonzales appealed the negative decision, but a review board appointed by the accrediting agency determined that the commission had acted fairly. The school reopened in September 1981 with an enrollment that one newspaper story placed at eleven and another at twenty. In October, in a gesture that confirmed Gonzales's victory in her political battles but had no impact on the college's struggle for survival, a new, more pliable board of trustees changed her title from acting president to president. In February 1982, enrollment was estimated to be "about ten part-time students." The school remained open for the remainder of that quarter, and thereafter ceased operations. In 1983, there were reports that the Colegio had missed a payment to HUD and that Gonzales was offering the campus for sale. Two years later, having not received payments for quite a while, HUD announced that it was going to foreclose.[13]

The final chapter of the Colegio saga was profoundly ironic. In December 1985, with HUD having filed for foreclosure, an anonymous friend of the Benedictine sisters paid approximately $200,000 to HUD to cover the unpaid debts and then donated the property to the Sisters to use as they wished. The sisters decided not to resume their work in higher education.[14]

Large Tracings and Tiny Scratches

The tragedy of the Colegio story is that, after the heroic struggle and collective action of the Montes-Romero era, the Colegio became deeply divided and ultimately closed its doors. Perhaps the closing was inevitable, given the increasingly unfavorable political climate for Chicano (and other minority) causes and the institution's ongoing financial weakness. Even so, more than twenty-five years after the Colegio ceased operations, Sonny finds it difficult to accept that result with equanimity, and, whenever the subject is raised, a flood of "what if" questions sweep over him: what if HUD had treated the Colegio differently from the start? what if he had the contacts then that he has today? what if he and Jose Romero hadn't quit when they had?

That last question is the one that troubles him most. On several occasions, I have heard Sonny discuss the reasons for his stepping down, and every time I have heard the same mixture of sadness and guilt in his voice. He wonders aloud if he accepted too readily the lucrative job offered to him by the Lab. It was, unquestionably, a major turning point in his life. Up to then, despite the undeniable fact that he had undergone a vocational transformation, moving out of the rural labor force into white-collar work and then progressively up the white-collar administrative ladder, his attachment to his rural, lower-class, Mexican American roots had not appreciably diminished. His work had been for the benefit of the poor and disadvantaged. At the VML, he had striven to improve the lives of migrants and former migrants, and at the Colegio, he had tried to provide a college education to Mexican Americans like himself who were not well served by existing institutions of higher education. The job at the Lab was something else—an interesting and important one, to be sure, and also one that he had earned (by finishing his college education and performing well in the workplace), but at bottom, just a job. He was no longer helping out his people and leading demonstrations against any federal agencies that stood in the way. He was no longer a full-time activist. Rather, he was a knowledge worker in a medium-sized nonprofit.

Sonny was hardly the only Mexican American (or African American or Anglo) activist of his era who made this kind of choice. Many did. At a certain point, sometimes after their thirtieth birthday or the arrival of their second or third child, many people of an activist temperament conclude that it is time to move on. In Sonny's case, the stresses of the job and the extraordinary financial sacrifices his family was forced to make contributed to the decision. Intellectually, he understands why he left when he did. But he can't stop wondering whether, if he had stayed on, the college's doors would still be open today.

What will be history's assessment of the Colegio? Most likely it will be mixed. On the one hand, the Colegio can be credited with providing educational opportunities to Mexican Americans, many from farmworker backgrounds, who would not otherwise have received a college education. Furthermore, a Colegio education went well beyond instruction in the classroom. Whenever students or staff members talk about their time there, they invariably comment on the intensity of their experiences—the never-ending discussions about how to cope with the college's problems, their involvement in collective action, the excitement of learning about the real world during internships away from the campus. On the other hand, there is the simple question of numbers: during the Montes-Romero years, the number of full-time students at the Colegio rarely exceeded seventy, and in the years that followed, the student body probably never reached thirty. However intense the Colegio's impact was on its students, the number of students affected was relatively small.

On the issue of the quality of the Colegio education, the views expressed run the gamut from effusive praise to strong criticism. A principal point of contention is the Colegio's nontraditional curriculum, especially its College Without Walls program. At the time, around the United States, College Without Walls programs were both in vogue and under attack. More than a few advocates of a traditional liberal arts education viewed such programs, including those at established schools such as Antioch, Skidmore, and Bard, with skepticism, questioning the intellectual value of apprenticeships and worrying about what those credits were replacing—courses on Chaucer, perhaps. The evaluators sent by HEW in 1975 to report on the Colegio manifested such skepticism, as did some members of the Commission on Colleges, and it may even have been lurking in the mind of a staunch public defender of the Colegio. During an interview several years ago, Don Willner, who received both his BA and law degrees from Harvard, remarked to me matter-of-factly: "You know, the Colegio was not much of an academic institution." For him, the compelling thing about the Colegio was its potential, and his biggest regret about his involvement with the school—he called it "the disaster of my life"—was that the potential was never realized.[15]

The most vocal defenders of the Colegio education are, not surprisingly, the people who were most closely involved with it. Former staff members such as Jose Romero, Jose Gallegos, and Maria Luisa Alaniz attest to the rigor of the Colegio's academic program, as do former students such as Sonny, Jimmy Amaya, Rudy Veliz, and Ramon Ramirez. They maintain that students at the Colegio received far more individual attention and feedback from instructors than was the case in traditional academic settings, that the Colegio encouraged genuinely creative work, and that the portfolio review process was thorough and demanding. In the end, historians, like the surviving historical actors, may never reach a consensus on the question of the Colegio's educational quality, since how one answers the question depends primarily on what the answerer believes to be the acceptable parameters of the college curriculum.

And what about the social movement side of the Colegio story? In retrospect, what was truly extraordinary about the Colegio was the struggle. "Everything was a struggle," Willner recalled.[16] Here, in rural Oregon, a place that had a relatively small Mexican American population at the time, a group of Mexican Americans had taken control of a debt-plagued institution of higher education and come up with a plan to provide a college education to people like themselves. Without question, the cause was laudable: named after a living legend, the Colegio stood as one of the few colleges in the country committed to Mexican American education. But it faced a host of problems, the most notable one being about $1 million of unpaid debts to HUD. So struggle ensued, and the Colegio under Sonny's leadership transformed itself into a social movement. To many people in the region, the Colegio became not a school trying to cope with overdue bills but rather a symbol for much that was wrong with the country's treatment of Mexican Americans.

In the long run, the dream died. Despite an impressive collective-action campaign and some key victories in the courts, the Colegio succumbed to a combination of self-inflicted wounds and ongoing financial and accreditation-related woes. The old leaders left, divisions surfaced within the ranks, enrollment remained low, the bills could not be paid, and the college was forced to close. But that final chapter, however disappointing, should not cause us to lose sight of the struggle and sacrifice of the preceding ones.

Nor we should linger too long on the fact that the social movement that grew up around the Colegio ultimately failed to achieve its objectives. The truth is that most social movements fail in one way or another, usually passing from the scene in relatively short order. A further truth is that failed social movements receive

249

a good deal less attention from historians than successful ones. The social movements discussed at length in our history books are invariably the exceptions; for example, the civil rights movement, which made a good deal of political headway and left undeniably large tracings behind—among them, the March on Washington, Freedom Summer, and the Voting Rights Act of 1965. The failures, by contrast, typically leave behind little to remind us of them—few landmark pieces of legislation or legal decisions, few visual images that are seared into collective memory, and, more often than not, a sparse documentary record. There are no large tracings; at most, tiny regional scratches. But since the failures are typical and the successes are exceptional, are we not likely to learn more about social movements from studying the former than the latter?[17]

The Last Thirty-Plus Years

And what has happened to Sonny Montes and Oregon's Mexican Americans in the thirty-plus years following his departure from the Colegio? In September 2002, during one of my first interviews with Sonny, we discussed at length his life after the Colegio. Sonny's ambivalence was palpable. On the one hand, he recognized that in that period he did some valuable work, but on the other, he regretted the fact that his "level of involvement in continuing the struggles became limited." Although he occasionally participated in protest activities, he did not lead them. The central theme of his life was no longer fighting injustice. Furthermore, the jobs he has held in the post-Colegio years, which have been at mainstream organizations, have had trade-offs: while he has received a respectable salary, he has had to "work within the system" and adopt an essentially assimilationist stance. To effect change, he has had to follow organizational rules, go through channels, and make his case at meetings. When he has succeeded, that success has been achieved primarily by persuasion rather than confrontation and behind closed doors rather than in full public view. Often self-critical, Sonny was particularly so in that early interview.[18] There is a modicum of truth in Sonny's self-assessment, but only a modicum.

Sonny's years since leaving the Colegio can be divided into two unequal parts. In the first, from the fall of 1977 until the fall of 1987, he did essentially the same kind of work for two different

Sonny Montes and John Little at the Texas-Mexico border, August 2003.
Photograph by Glenn Anthony May.

organizations—the Lab, where his immediate supervisor was Cisco Garcia, and Interface Consultants, a small nonprofit founded by Garcia after Garcia had resigned from the Lab. In both organizations, Sonny served as a member of a team of consultants that focused on minority equity issues in education. At the time, the Office for Civil Rights (OCR) of HEW was actively monitoring state educational systems and school districts to determine if they were in compliance with federal legislation and guidelines concerning the education of minority groups. Occasionally it determined that school districts were not meeting the needs of bilingual and limited English–speaking students, and when that happened, it turned to nonprofit organizations that held multiyear contracts with the government to bring noncomplying school districts into compliance. Up to 1981, the Lab's Center for Bilingual Education held that contract for six western states (Oregon, Washington, Idaho, Montana, Alaska, and Hawai'i) and the U.S. possessions in the Pacific (American Samoa, Guam, etc.). After that, the contract was awarded to Garcia's spin-off, Interface Consultants.[19]

From 1977 to 1984, Sonny's principal job on the compliance team was to increase the level of parental involvement in the underperforming schools. His work followed a predictable pattern. Once the OCR had determined that a school district was out of compliance, the team traveled to the district to meet with local educators and begin developing a "voluntary compliance plan" to address the identified problems. Then, working with school administrators, teachers, and parents, the team attempted to execute the plan. For Sonny, that meant repeated visits to the district to create parent organizations in the schools, monitor their performance, and assess their impact on educational outcomes. About halfway through his tenure at Interface Consultants, Garcia promoted Sonny to the position of team director, the promotion bringing him a modest pay increase and the added responsibility of supervising his co-workers. By all accounts, Sonny performed that work well. But there were family-related costs, since he spent at least 50 percent of his time away from home. Sometimes he would be gone for a week, sometimes for more than a month.[20]

In 1987, trouble surfaced in the Interface workplace. Garcia had a falling out with a senior colleague, lost control of the company, and left Interface. Sonny soon followed him out the door. For a while, Sonny mulled over his employment options and then, just as his bank balance was getting low, he learned from Jose Romero, then working for Portland Public Schools (PPS), that the school district had an opening for a "Hispanic resource specialist." Interested in the position, Sonny submitted an application, and after a formal interview, was offered the job. Sonny began work for PPS on November 2, 1988.[21]

Sonny's new job at PPS returned him full time to Oregon—he was no longer obliged, as had been the case when he worked for the Lab and Interface Consultants, to spend weeks at a time away from the state. The new job also forced him to confront daily a new set of educational problems involving the state's Mexican Americans and other Hispanics.[22] To understand the problems, let us focus briefly on developments that had taken place in the decade just past (and ones that were still unfolding) in Oregon's Hispanic communities.

The single most important development was rapid population growth. Due to the combined effects of high birth rates and virtually unregulated immigration, both from other states and from Mexico, the number of Mexican Americans in Oregon was increasing at an astounding pace—from a few thousand in the 1960s, to 45,170 in 1980, to 84,792 in 1990, to 214,662 in 2000. For all Hispanic groups combined, the figures were: 65,847 in 1980, 112,707 in 1990, and 275,314 in 2000.[23] Far from being nearly invisible in Oregon, as they had been during Sonny's first years in the state, Mexican Americans and other Hispanics had become Oregon's largest minority group. As of 1990, Mexican Americans made up 3.0 percent of the populace, and all Hispanics, 4.0 percent. A decade later, the figures were 6.3 percent and 8.0 percent.

But it wasn't population growth alone that would make Sonny's new job so difficult. Complicating the situation were the social, economic, political, and vocational challenges that Mexican Americans and other Hispanic groups faced. The list was long. They experienced much higher rates of unemployment and poverty than did the population at large: in 1990, for example, whereas 12.4 percent of Oregonians lived below the poverty line, the percentage of Oregon's Hispanics who did so was 28.9. They tended to have more menial jobs and earn less income: the median income of all Oregon families in 1990 was $32,336, but for Hispanic families it was $21,871. The fertility level of Hispanic women was higher than that of non-Hispanic women, and Hispanic families were larger. The levels of education of Hispanics were lower than those of non-Hispanics: in the state as a whole, only 1.2 percent of persons twenty-five years and older had less than a fifth-grade education, but for Hispanics the percentage was 15.7. Although some Hispanics (such as Sonny) had made noteworthy social progress, earning college degrees, running businesses, and entering the professions, the vast majority had not. Nor had Hispanics in Oregon yet made a significant mark in state and local politics, as they had in the Southwest. While the lot of Mexican Americans and other Hispanics in Oregon was not uniformly grim, it clearly demanded attention.[24]

At the time Sonny started work with PPS, the school district employed a total of five cultural resource specialists, who were supervised directly by the coordinator of the district's ESL/bilingual program. The specialists were charged with assisting three particular segments of the city's high school students—Vietnamese, Laotians, and Hispanics. Two of the specialists served the Vietnamese population and one the Laotians. The other two worked with the approximately 300 Hispanic students then enrolled in the city's eleven high schools. The resource specialists functioned as mentors and counselors to the students, helped them with academic and family problems, served as advocates for them within the school system, and gave in-service training to the teachers who instructed them.[25]

Soon after starting work at PPS, feeling that the district lacked a plan to meet the needs of the students he was charged with helping, Sonny began introducing changes in the six high schools that had been assigned to him.[26] He developed two types of organizations in each of the schools. One was the Hispanic student support group, which was intended to encourage students to finish their secondary schooling and to pursue a college degree. At the weekly meetings, a variety of activities occurred. For one, students discussed problems they were encountering both in school and at home and searched for solutions. Sonny also used the sessions to do a certain amount of leadership training. He began by asking the students to elect their officers. Once they did, he met with the officers, providing them with guidance about how to run meetings and encourage group participation. Finally, guest speakers were regularly invited to the sessions for the purpose of conveying important information to the students: staff members from the high schools came to talk about school activities and programs, and representatives from local colleges discussed admission requirements, degree programs, and financial aid opportunities.

The second organization was the Hispanic parent support group, which met once a month. It was modeled on the parent groups Sonny had developed during his years as a parental involvement specialist at the Lab and Interface Consultants. At the parent meetings, the attendees addressed a number of core issues—among them, the discrimination experienced by Hispanics in the schools, their low scores on standardized tests, and their high dropout rates. They also brainstormed about how to effect change in the schools. Several times a year, moreover, all the Hispanic parent groups in the district were invited to a plenum session at which they met with school administrators and members of a districtwide organization called Hispanic Parents for Portland Schools, which included some of Sonny's strongest allies in the community.

The program introduced by Sonny was generally considered to be a success, and for that reason, the ESL/bilingual program coordinator instructed the other cultural resource specialists in PPS to adopt it. The only problem was that it placed extraordinary work and time demands on all of them. In the early stages of organization, in order to make certain that the new support groups functioned effectively, Sonny tried to attend as many of the parent and student meetings as he could. That left few free evenings to eat dinner with his family. He was busy with other job-related chores as well—conferences with students, in-service training sessions, the administration of dropout programs.[27]

Another activity consumed a substantial amount of Sonny's time—the creation of an annual Hispanic student leadership conference. The idea of holding such a conference was Sonny's. Heavily involved in leadership training programs during his years at the Lab and Interface Consultants, he believed that they had a powerful community-development effect. The basic approach was to provide individuals with information on important issues and to motivate them to succeed in life, on the assumption that people so trained would then be in a position to lead and represent their communities. "That's where leadership will come from," Sonny told me. "We train the trainers. I have more information than the kids have. I have a greater impact training kids than making presentations to the school board." Sonny also saw the conference as an opportunity for young Spanish-speaking kids in the area to "come together and to network."[28]

The first conference, scheduled for February 1990, was something of a disaster. The plan called for 300 student and teacher participants to assemble at their schools, where they were to board school buses and be delivered to the event site, Montgomery Park, a large building in downtown Portland, at approximately 7:40 a.m. But, on the morning of the conference, snow began to fall in Portland—a rare event in any Portland winter—and that wreaked havoc with the plans. In the end, 158 students attended the conference, many of them making their way to Montgomery Park on their own.[29]

Despite the difficulties, reports about the event were positive. Shortly afterward, several ESL/bilingual program administrators from school districts close to Portland asked Sonny whether their Latino students could attend the next leadership conference. So it was that an event originally held to serve PPS alone was transformed into one serving the entire Upper Willamette Valley. Over the years, the conference (which was renamed the Cesar E. Chavez Hispanic Student Leadership Conference in 1994) has mushroomed in size, as delegations from many other communities in the region began attending, and the organizers found it necessary to cap attendance at about 1,400, allocating a quota of tickets to each of the approximately sixty-five high schools that now participate.[30] As the conference has grown in size, it has grown in complexity. A conference planning committee was established to coordinate activities. Sonny served as chairman for the first few years and as co-chair for most of the following years. The number of committee members has grown to more than thirty. Featured speakers have been invited (Dolores Huerta in 2003, for example), cultural events have been staged, and in recent years close to forty conference workshops have been scheduled. Money is raised for college scholarships, and, over the past decade, between ten and twenty of them have been awarded annually to deserving Latino high school graduates.[31]

While the job of resource specialist has provided much satisfaction, it also has had more than its share of frustrations, many of which have their origins in the diminishing state support

The Mexican American network redux: Jose Romero, Sonny Montes, and John Little receiving awards for their contributions to the Cesar E. Chavez Hispanic Student Leadership Conference, September 2004. Photograph by Glenn Anthony May.

for public education that began in the 1990s. In the November 1990 general election, Oregon's voters passed Ballot Measure 5, which amended the state's constitution by setting limits on property taxes. Given that most of the funding for Oregon's schools came from property tax receipts, Measure 5 posed a direct threat to educational programs throughout the state.[32] One support unit in PPS that came perilously close to elimination as a direct result of Measure 5 was the district's group of resource specialists. In early February 1994, faced with a large budgetary shortfall, the Portland district announced that all the specialist positions would be cut.[33] But the decision outraged the community, which believed that the resource specialists did valuable work. Working together, Hispanic Parents for Portland Schools and MEChA, the country's largest Mexican American student organization, held a rally on February 17 at Pioneer Courthouse Square in downtown Portland to protest the loss of the positions. A newspaper report stated that about 300 parents, teachers, and students were in the crowd. "We are sick and tired of not being taken seriously," said one of the student leaders.[34] Eventually, the PPS superintendent reversed the decision and agreed to retain the resource specialists.[35]

In the years since the rally, Sonny has continued to work overtime to assist Portland's Latino high school students. One constant of the job has been a rapid growth in numbers. In 1988, the year Sonny went to work for PPS, only about 3 percent of the district's students were Latinos. By 1997–98, the figure had grown to 6.14 percent, and by 2006–07, to 11.96 percent.[36] Another constant has been the district's ongoing shortage of money—a shortage that owes much both to Ballot Measure 5 and to a subsequent ballot measure approved by Oregon's electorate in 1997 that further reduced the funding available for public education in Oregon.[37] As a result, more educational cutbacks (especially in support programs) have occurred in Portland while class sizes have grown. In this environment of reduced support, the ESL/bilingual program's small group of cultural resource specialists shrank to three in the first decade of the twenty-first century. But by the close of the decade, thanks to the support of a new superintendent and effective lobbying by community supporters, it had risen again to five—Sonny Montes and Veronica Bañuelos for Hispanics, Huy Hoang for Vietnamese,

Vadim Ruskin for Russians, and Abdi Jamac for Somalis—and the staff members were now known as "equity coordinators."[38]

Despite the ups and downs, Sonny has not succumbed to discouragement or disengagement. "What keeps me going," Sonny explained, "is that I know I'm doing some good. I see lots of kids lost in the system, and I know that I can help them."[39] About that last point there can be no debate. "Sonny has saved so many kids—literally saved the lives of students," Juan Baez, former student retention coordinator for PPS, told me a few years ago. He pointed out that, throughout PPS, Latino students have often received unfair treatment: teachers or principals "throw the book at them" for minor infractions and try to get them expelled. In these situations, Sonny has been very successful at getting a fair outcome for the students. Serving as their advocate, he has argued their case to the teachers or administrators who have been trying to expel them; and if he fails at that, he has represented the students at expulsion hearings. According to Baez, "When Sonny is not present at the hearings, the outcome is vastly different for the students." By keeping the kids in school, he has made it possible for many of them to avoid the clutches of the gangs that have developed in Portland's Latino communities. The only problem, as Baez sees it, is that PPS has not managed to clone Sonny. "We need one Sonny in each high school and middle school in the district."[40]

Anyone who knew Sonny well realized that his marriage to Librada was not idyllic. Like all married couples, their relationship had its ups and downs, but for many years the downs had predominated. By the time Sonny went to work for PPS in 1988, the marriage had broken down, and the couple finally divorced in 1992. Then in 1993, he met Zahidee Henriquez, a native of Venezuela and a Spanish teacher in PPS. They married in 1998, and four years later, their son Leandro was born.[41] After Leandro's birth, Sonny became an active participant in caring for him, taking on parental responsibilities in his new household that he had not assumed in the previous one. It has been a rewarding experience, Sonny's only regret being that he had not played a similarly active parental role when he was a younger man.

Sonny Montes and his son Leandro, July 2007. Photograph by Glenn Anthony May.

Now in his sixties, Sonny has begun to discuss retirement. He had a heart attack in March 2006, a day after the annual Cesar E. Chavez Hispanic Student Leadership Conference. The trauma caused Sonny, like millions of heart attack victims, to reconsider how he lives his life. He wants to be around when his son Leandro goes off to college. He exercises more and has changed his diet. He says that he plans to retire from PPS in the near future.

Perhaps he will. But if he does retire, we should not expect him to spend his days at the senior center. For Sonny, there are always new problems that need addressing. In a telephone conversation in April 2008, he told me of one activity he was involved in, a campaign led by Jose Romero and several other Portland-area Mexican Americans to change the name of Portland's Interstate Avenue to Cesar E. Chavez Boulevard. Launched in late 2007, the effort had started off well, gaining a good deal of support from prominent politicians and gathering momentum. Approval by the city council had seemed likely. Then, however, opponents of the name change had organized, the tide had turned, and the change had been blocked.[42] While Sonny was upset about the result, he was not ready to admit defeat. Nor were Romero and the other leaders of the Cesar E. Chavez Boulevard Committee. "I think we learned some valuable lessons from that experience," he told me. "Next time, we'll be better prepared for what they throw at us."[43]

Conclusion

In this book, I have tried to shed light on the early years of Mexican American community formation in Oregon's Upper Willamette Valley and to explain and assess a social movement. My hope is that the stories told are suggestive of larger truths. But what larger truths do they suggest?

One topic of interest that surfaced in the researching of this book was the impact of external (i.e., non-Mexican American) stimuli on the birth of a Mexican American community in the Upper Willamette Valley. For several decades preceding the creation of the VML, a combination of push and pull factors—the rise of corporate farming and the creation of a labor surplus in the Southwest, the need for migrant labor in the Northwest—had produced a pattern of seasonal migration of Mexican American farmworkers to Oregon and nearby states. Still, up to 1965 the seasonal population movement did not result in large-scale Mexican American settlement in Oregon. One reason for the marked increase in settlement that occurred after 1965 was the creation in that year of the VML, an agency funded with federal War on Poverty dollars that helped Oregon's seasonal migrants to leave the migrant stream.

But it wasn't federal dollars alone that made the difference. While the VML provided assistance to migrants from its first weeks of doing business, it was not until the appointment of John Little as executive director in 1967 that the organization became fully committed to the notion of Mexican American community building. Little gave voice to the Mexican American migrants and seasonal farmworkers in the region, and thereafter they set institutional priorities in the communities served by the VML and held the key positions in the VML hierarchy. The VML thus functioned as a community-building agent in two ways: it provided incentives for migrants (Mexican American and non-Mexican American alike) to settle and served as a kind of leadership-training institute. The result was the nurturing of a group of leaders within Mexican American communities in the Upper Willamette Valley—a group that would play a major role in the nascent Chicano movement in the area.

While the protagonist of the VML story told here is Sonny Montes, the role played by John Little is also significant. Over the course of the twentieth century, a number of Anglos have had a huge positive impact on the course of Mexican American history: Carey McWilliams, Fred Ross, and Jerry Cohen, among others. John Little's name should appear on the list as well. A true believer in community development, he served as an advocate for, a mentor to, and a prodder and friend of the Mexican American people he worked with and for. He also helped to orchestrate the "revolution" of 1968 that put Mexican Americans firmly in control of the organization. But he did so not so much by leading in the conventional way but rather by empowering others—Sonny Montes, David Aguilar, Jimmy Amaya, Frank Martinez, Emilio Hernandez, even Lupe Bustos.

One point worth noting about the history of the VML is that the key moments of Mexican American self-assertion in the organization (the study night of 1967, the revolution of 1968) came at a time when the VML's Mexican American leaders knew relatively little about the course of Chicano protest in other regions. Although Sonny and his co-workers were well aware of Chavez's struggle in the fields, until the Los Gatos conference of 1969, they knew little about Tijerina's Alianza Federal de Mercedes, Gonzales's Cruzada Para La Justicia, and the efforts of groups in East Los Angeles to improve the educational system. In fact, the ideology that informed the early manifestations of Chicanismo in the VML came not so much from the Chicano movement itself but rather from the dogma of mid-twentieth-century community development—essentially, the teachings and practices of Saul Alinsky and Catholic community organizers, as refracted through the lenses and experiences of John Little, a former Papal Volunteer. The underlying principle was a belief that any community had the capacity to make good decisions, and the basic approach was to catalyze the community, never to dictate to it. John Little conveyed the dogma, Sonny and others learned it, and they in turn have conveyed it to others ever since.

The Colegio story is about a noble dream and the social movement that tried to keep the dream alive. This book has given attention to four aspects of that movement—the framing of the Colegio's protest campaign, the forms of contention adopted by the protesters, the movement's mobilizing structure, and the combination of political opportunities prevailing at the time.

Like all social movements, the "Save Colegio Cesar Chavez" campaign began with a grievance—that HUD was threatening to shut down the Colegio because the school had failed to make timely loan payments. As grievances go, this one was problematic, since on the surface, the issue in dispute appeared to be nothing more than the Colegio's failure to live up to its legal obligations. Thus, in framing the protest, the Colegio's leaders chose to downplay those legalities and draw attention instead to HUD's allegedly unfair treatment and bullying of the Colegio. It was a creative approach to a difficult framing problem. What also worked in the college's favor was that HUD's handling of the Colegio was often inept, thereby providing confirmation of the Colegio's characterization of HUD. It is unclear, however, how much impact the Colegio leaders' creative framing had on the course of the movement. It appears to me that their work won more sympathy from newspaper editors and public officials than it did support from the Mexican American community. The latter had other compelling reasons to participate.

One factor that produced a more obvious effect on the movement's development was the familiarity of its leaders with collective action. As we have seen, Sonny's education in the contemporary techniques of contention began at Los Gatos in March 1969 and continued in the streets of Portland, Salem, Hillsboro, and Los Angeles over the following thirty months. Other key participants in the Colegio's campaign with firsthand collective-action experience included Jose Romero, Jimmy Amaya, Cipriano Ferrel, Ramon Ramirez, and John Little. This familiarity with the instruments of contention and experience in using them were significant assets. In the campaign against HUD, Sonny and his allies skillfully employed a mix of techniques, beginning with press conferences and letter-writing campaigns (a variant of the traditional collective-action form of mass petitioning) and moving up the spectrum of contention to more confrontational tactics (rallies, marches, sit-ins).

"Our strength was in organizing." That was Sonny's explanation for the launching of the Colegio's major collective-action offensive in 1975. It was also a fair assessment of the Colegio movement itself, since at the base of any persistent social movement is invariably an effective mobilizing structure. In the case of the "Save Colegio Cesar Chavez" campaign, the structure was the network of social, familial, associational, and vocational connections that I have called the Mexican American network. That structure had its origins in the VML, specifically in the reforms introduced during the Little regime that increased significantly the number of Mexican Americans who participated in the priority-setting and decision-making processes. By the mid-1970s that network had extended considerably beyond the links established in the VML, since new organizations had emerged and new associational connections had been formed. The existence of this now-enhanced Mexican American network was a necessary precondition for the emergence of the social movement that developed around the Colegio. It expedited the task of mobilizing individuals to participate in a collective-action campaign and made it possible to sustain the campaign for several years.

While all the above appears to suggest that the Colegio movement was built on solid foundations, an analysis of the structure of political opportunities at the time leads us to a very different conclusion. Success in many things depends to a large extent on good timing, and unfortunately for its supporters, the "Save Colegio Cesar Chavez" campaign was launched at an unpropitious historical juncture. A very late riser in a cycle of contention that had begun in the late 1950s, the Colegio campaign was forced from the outset to fight its battles with limited assistance from organizations and friends outside its local circle of support. That harsh reality served to offset the advantages of creative framing work, familiarity with collective-action forms, and a well-greased mobilizing structure, and placed definite limits on what could be accomplished by the college's supporters. In the end, the major victories that Colegio leaders were able to achieve in 1977 and 1978 were won in the courts, not in the streets, and even those victories would prove to be insufficient to guarantee the Colegio's ultimate survival. If lessons can be learned from historical episodes, the one that stands out here is that, absent a favorable combination of political opportunities, social movements, no matter how well led, face monumental hurdles.

The VML ceased to exist in the 1970s; the Colegio, in the early 1980s. There are scant physical remains of the latter. While several buildings from the old Colegio campus still survive, they bear few signs of their earlier connection to the defunct Chicano college. Neither organization left behind a large collection of documents or photographs. To reconstruct their stories, the historian is forced to rely primarily on interviews, newspapers, and records scattered in manuscript collections around the country—tiny scratches again. But sometimes even tiny scratches provide clues about deeper meanings.

On March 10, 2003, I attended for the first time the Cesar E. Chavez Hispanic Student Leadership Conference. The principal conference venue on that day was the Chiles Center on the University of Portland's campus, where the university's basketball games are played. The undergraduates were enjoying their spring break at the time, so almost all the faces on the campus were brown. The conference co-chairs were Yolanda Tavera of the Gervais School District and Sonny Montes. The two of them had served as co-chairs for close to a decade and would continue doing so through the 2005 conference. Both were hard at work and very much in evidence. At 7:45 a.m., Sonny greeted the arriving students at the entrance to the Chiles Center, and throughout the day, he guided them to conference workshops and talked constantly to other conference organizers on his walkie-talkie about problems that needed solving. Tavera was stationed at a table in the lobby, handing out programs and T-shirts to participants, supervising a host of teacher volunteers, and answering questions.

After the morning activities, the students ate lunch at University Commons, a student-faculty dining room that is a short walk from the Chiles Center. Meanwhile, the conference planning committee, the featured speakers, and workshop participants assembled in a large dining room at the Chiles Center itself, where they were given box lunches. Although I wasn't hungry at the time, I went to the Chiles Center dining room hoping to make contact with one of the attendees and arrange an interview. When I entered the room, I paused at the doorway, surveying the scene.

There were about sixty people in the room, and I could recognize twenty or so. I saw Sonny, who was talking animatedly as he stood in line and waited to pick up his box lunch, and I spotted several other members of the conference planning committee at the tables—Jose Romero, then an administrator with the Woodburn School District; Tina Garcia, a VML alumna, who at the time was director of the Oregon Migrant Education Service Center; David Loera of Portland Community College, a 1973 graduate of Mt. Angel College and the brother of Pancho Loera, who had helped Sonny to develop the Chicano studies program at the same institution; and John Little, now retired and living in Mt. Angel. Also in the room were two veterans of the Colegio wars: Maria Luisa Alaniz, the coordinator of the Chicano/Latino studies program at Portland State University, and Ramon Ramirez, the president of PCUN. Earlier in the day, both of them had participated in workshop sessions with the conference's featured speaker, Dolores Huerta.

The Mexican American network was still alive and well in March 2003, and it remains so today, even in an era when the term Mexican American has fallen out of favor. Of course, the current version of the network is different from the old one—much larger, less cohesive, and no longer so heavily dominated by the old guard of VML and Colegio veterans. But, it is a potentially powerful force, as was demonstrated by a noteworthy development in Portland. In early 2009, the Cesar E. Chavez Boulevard Committee regrouped, changed its tactics a bit, and succeeded in getting the Portland City Council to approve the renaming of Portland's 39th Avenue to Cesar E. Chavez Boulevard.[1]

It was a satisfying victory, especially to old-timers like Jose and Sonny, who had been battling Anglo opponents for decades and losing a large number of the battles. One reason for this particular success was the effective role played by the Mexican American network in mobilizing support for the street-renaming initiative. That effectiveness was, in part, a function of experience. As this book has shown, a direct connection can be traced from the VML of the late 1960s, with its program of empowering Mexican Americans, to the Colegio Cesar Chavez, with its efforts to educate them, to the "Save Colegio Cesar Chavez" campaign of the 1970s, to the launching of the annual Cesar E. Chavez Hispanic Leadership Conferences in the 1990s, to the Cesar E. Chavez Boulevard Committee of more recent days. The connective tissue that linked these organizations and campaigns was human: a cadre of leaders, the most important of them being Little, Romero, and Montes.

But the network alone was not responsible for the victory—recall that an effective mobilizing structure had been insufficient to save the Colegio. Two additional reasons need to be acknowledged. First, it was far easier to change a street name in 2009 than to pay off a million-dollar debt in 1975: thirty-plus years ago, $1 million was a sizable amount of money. Some battles are simply more winnable than others. Second, and more important, much besides the value of the dollar had changed between 1975 and 2009, and the political odds that were so much against Mexican American protest in Oregon in 1975 had evened up considerably over the next three decades. In 2009, Hispanics made up more than 11 percent of the population of Oregon, and in the country as a whole, approximately 16 percent of the population was Hispanic.[2] The economic and political muscle of the Latinos was also growing, and it was a rare politician indeed, in Oregon or any other state, who could afford to ignore their wishes. In other words, the structure of political opportunities confronting the Cesar E. Chavez Boulevard Committee in 2009 was very much more favorable than that which faced the leaders of the "Save Colegio Cesar Chavez" campaign in the 1970s. Now, at last, the perseverance of the old-timers was paying off.

Notes

Abbreviations Used in the Notes

AU: Al Ullman Papers, Special Collections, Knight Library, University of Oregon (citations take the form AU/box no./folder no.)

CAA: Community Action Agency

CAP: Community Action Program

CCC/NASC-CR: *Colegio Cesar Chavez vs. Northwest Association of Schools and Colleges et al.*, U.S. District Court for the District of Oregon, 1977, Clerk's Record, U.S. National Archives, Seattle

CCC/NASC-TP: *Colegio Cesar Chavez vs. Northwest Association of Schools and Colleges et al.*, U.S. District Court for the District of Oregon, 1977, Transcript of Proceedings, U.S. National Archives, Seattle

CJ: *Capital Journal* (Salem, Oregon)

CMJ/FBI: Celedonio Montes Jr., FBI file (PD 105-3155), provided by FBI pursuant to FOIPA request no.1053630-000

HA: *Hillsboro Argus* (Hillsboro, Oregon)

HEW: Department of Health, Education, and Welfare

HUD: Department of Housing and Urban Development

JPL: John Patrick Little Papers, Special Collections, Knight Library, University of Oregon

MAN: *Mount Angel News* (Mt. Angel, Oregon)

OEO: Office of Economic Opportunity

OJ: *Oregon Journal* (Portland, Oregon)

OLP: *Oregon Labor Press* (Portland, Oregon)

OR: *Oregonian* (Portland, Oregon)

OS: *Oregon Statesman* (Salem, Oregon)

OS/CJ: *Oregon Statesman/Capital Journal* (Salem, Oregon)

PEW/CCC: Paul E. Waldschmidt Papers, Colegio Cesar Chavez folder, University of Portland Archives

RG381: Record Group 381, Records of the Community Services Administration (which includes records of the Office of Economic Opportunity), U.S. National Archives, College Park, Maryland (citations take the form RG381/OEO, agency division/box no.)

SAC: Special Agent in Charge (FBI documents)

SAT: *Silverton Appeal-Tribune* (Silverton, Oregon)

SAT/MAN: *Silverton Appeal-Tribune/Mount Angel News* (Silverton, Oregon)

SJ: *Statesman Journal* (Salem, Oregon)

SMH: Stella Maris House Collection, Oregon Historical Society, Portland (citations take the form SMH/box no./folder no.)

VML: Valley Migrant League

Introduction

1. It would be more accurate to use the phrase "Chicano movements," rather than "Chicano movement," since the Chicano struggle for social justice was so heterogeneous. But I will observe the convention of using the latter.

2. I use the word *asymmetry* (which has become fashionable among historians of colonialism) rather than *inequality* or *oppression*, because it

conveys better the disparity between two groups. *Inequality* appears to suggest that equality is possible. *Asymmetry* gives a better sense of the extent of the difference between one group and another.

3. In the 1970s, a number of scholars—including Rodolfo Acuña and Carlos Muñoz Jr.—likened the subordinate status of Mexican Americans to "internal colonialism." See the first edition of Acuña's survey of Mexican American history—Rodolfo Acuña, *Occupied America: The Chicano's Struggle Toward Liberation* (San Francisco: Canfield Press, 1972), iii, 1–8. That analysis is missing in later editions. Also see the discussion of the "internal colonialism" literature in Carlos Muñoz Jr., *Youth, Identity, Power: The Chicano Movement,* rev. ed. (London: Verso, 2007), 175–78.

4. See, for example, Leonard Pitt, *The Decline of the Californios: A Social History of the Spanish-Speaking Californians, 1846–1890* (Berkeley: University of California Press, 1966); Albert Camarillo, *Chicanos in a Changing Society: From Mexican Pueblos to American Barrios in Santa Barbara and Southern California, 1848–1930* (Cambridge: Harvard University Press, 1979), 6–141; Stephen J. Pitti, *The Devil in Silicon Valley: Northern California, Race, and Mexican Americans* (Princeton: Princeton University Press, 2003), 30–77; David Montejano, *Anglos and Mexicans in the Making of Texas, 1836–1986* (Austin: University of Texas Press, 1987), 15–99; Carey McWilliams, *North from Mexico: The Spanish-Speaking People of the United States,* rev. ed. (New York: Praeger, 1990), 76–96; Manuel G. Gonzales, *Mexicanos: A History of Mexicans in the United States* (Bloomington: Indiana University Press, 1999), 82–112; Rodolfo Acuña, *Occupied America: A History of Chicanos,* 4th ed. (New York: Longman, 2000), 57–155.

5. Oscar J. Martinez, *Mexican-Origin People in the United States: A Topical History* (Tucson: University of Arizona Press, 2001), 7–33, 51–71; Acuña, *Occupied America,* 4th ed., 156–327; Gonzales, *Mexicanos,* 113–90; David G. Gutiérrez, *Walls and Mirrors: Mexican Americans, Mexican Immigrants, and the Politics of Ethnicity* (Berkeley: University of California Press, 1995), 39–58; Montejano, *Anglos and Mexicans,* 103–287; Neil Foley, *The White Scourge: Mexicans, Blacks, and Poor Whites in Texas Cotton Culture* (Berkeley: University of California Press, 1997), 40–201; Zaragosa Vargas, *Proletarians of the North: A History of Mexican Industrial Workers in Detroit and the Midwest, 1917–1933* (Berkeley: University of California Press, 1993); Camarillo, *Chicanos in a Changing Society,* 142–229; George S. Sanchez, *Becoming Mexican American: Ethnicity, Culture, and Identity in Chicano Los Angeles, 1900–1945* (New York: Oxford University Press, 1993); Pitti, *Devil in Silicon Valley,* 78–97; Vicki L. Ruiz, *Cannery Women, Cannery Lives: Mexican Women, Unionization, and the California Food Processing Industry, 1930–1950* (Albuquerque: University of New Mexico Press, 1987), 21–39.

6. On the importance of these variables, see Sidney Tarrow, *Power in Movement: Social Movements and Contentious Politics,* 2d ed. (Cambridge: Cambridge University Press, 1998), 10–25, 91–138. Also see Doug McAdam, John D. McCarthy, and Mayer N. Zald, eds., *Comparative Perspectives on Social Movements: Political Opportunities, Mobilizing Structures, and Cultural Framings* (New York: Cambridge University Press, 1996); Donatella della Porta and Sidney Tarrow, eds., *Transnational Protest and Global Activism* (Lanham, Md.: Rowman & Littlefield, 2005); Sidney

Tarrow, *The New Transnational Activism* (New York: Cambridge University Press, 2006); Charles Tilly and Sidney Tarrow, *Contentious Politics* (Boulder: Paradigm Publishers, 2007). For a thoughtful, suggestive effort to view the Chicano Movement through the prism of social movement theory, see Ian F. Haney López, "Protest, Repression, and Race: Legal Violence and the Chicano Movement," *University of Pennsylvania Law Review* 150 (Nov. 2001): 205–44.

7. I also hope that this book will contribute something to our understanding of social movements in general, if only because its angle of analysis is somewhat different from that of most recent studies of the phenomena. That is, it approaches a social movement more from the perspective of its leaders than from that of the rank-and-file.

Prologue: From Weslaco to Cornelius

1. This discussion of Sonny's years in Weslaco, Fort Worth, and California is based largely on my interviews with Sonny Montes between 2002 and 2010 as well as interviews with the late Celedonio Montes Sr., Margarita Jasso Montes, and Gloria Montes Angulo in La Feria and Weslaco, Texas, Aug. 27–30, 2003. I have also relied on census data and a variety of monographs. On Weslaco, the Lower Rio Grande Valley, and rural Texas, see, in particular, Arthur R. Rubel, *Across the Tracks: Mexican-Americans in a Texas City* (Austin: University of Texas Press, 1966); William Madsen, *The Mexican Americans of South Texas* (New York: Holt, Rinehart and Winston, 1964); Daniel D. Arreola, *Tejano South Texas: A Mexican American Cultural Province* (Austin: University of Texas Press, 2002); Montejano, *Anglos and Mexicans*; Foley, *White Scourge*; Chad Richardson, *Batos, Bolillos, Pochos, and Pelados: Class and Culture on the South Texas Border* (Austin: University of Texas Press, 1999); and Oscar J. Martinez, *Border People: Life and Society in the U.S.-Mexico Borderlands* (Tucson: University of Arizona Press, 1994). While both Rubel and Madsen are viewed by many present-day scholars as ethnocentric, some of the data in their studies are still useful—especially, those in Rubel's book, which is based on his fieldwork in Weslaco from 1957 to 1959.

2. On Weslaco's population, see U.S. Bureau of the Census, *U.S. Census of Population: 1950. Characteristics of the Population* (Washington, D.C.: U.S. Government Printing Office, 1952), vol. 2. part 43 (Texas): 31, 142; and Rubel *Across the Tracks*, 5–7.

3. Rubel, *Across the Tracks*, 13–16.

4. Montejano, *Anglos and Mexicans*, 271–74.

5. *Weslaco, 1919–1969: 50th Anniversary Celebration* (Weslaco, Tex.: Herb Wilt Printing, 1969), 59.

6. The 1960 Fort Worth city directory indicates that the Holiday Inn employed Celedonio Montes as a maintenance man. See *Polk's Fort Worth (Tarrant County, Texas) City Directory, 1960* (Dallas: R. L. Polk & Co., 1960), 780.

7. City of Fort Worth, *Eight Decades of School Construction: Historic Resources of the Fort Worth Independent School District, 1891–1961* (Fort Worth: The City, 2003), 25; "Green B. Trimble Technical High School—School History," http://schools.fortworthisd.net/education/school/schoolhistory.php?sectiondetailid=1422 (accessed May 21, 2008).

8. Permanent High School Record, Fort Worth Public Schools, of Celedonio Montes Jr., Billy W. Sills Center for Archives, Fort Worth Independent School District. On tests: Sonny Montes interviews by the author.

9. Lewis A. McArthur and Lewis L. McArthur, *Oregon Geographic Names*, 6th ed. (Portland: Oregon Historical Society Press, 1992), 205; Metzker's Maps of Washington Co., State of Oregon, Aug. 1964 (Metzker Maps, Tacoma and Seattle, Washington).

10. Secretary of State, *Oregon Blue Book, 1967–1968* (Salem: Oregon Secretary of State, 1966), 212; Oregon State Archives, *Oregon Blue Book*, online edition, City and County Populations, http://bluebook.state.or.us/local/populations/pop01.htm (accessed July 25, 2010).

11. Geri Duyck interview by the author; State Board of Health, *Oregon Migrant Health Service Annual Report, 1964–65* (Portland: Occupational Health Section, Oregon State Board of Health, 1964), 91; *HA*, Apr. 27, 1967, 10; May 8, 1967, 2; and June 22, 1967, 3.

12. This account of the camp meeting in Cornelius and its aftermath is based on my interviews with Sonny Montes. See also Erlinda Gonzales-Berry and Marcela Mendoza, *Mexicanos in Oregon: Their Stories, Their Lives* (Corvallis: Oregon State University Press, 2010), 92.

Contexts: The Upper Willamette Valley, Oregon, and America

1. Secretary of State, *Oregon Blue Book, 1965–1966* (Salem: Oregon Secretary of State, 1964), 115; *Oregon Blue Book, 1967–1968*, 147, 155, 173; William G. Robbins, *Hard Times in Paradise: Coos Bay, Oregon, 1850–1986* (Seattle: University of Washington Press, 1988), 135–36; and *Landscapes of Conflict: The Oregon Story, 1940–2000* (Seattle: University of Washington Press, 2004), 175–77; David Peterson del Mar, *Oregon's Promise: An Interpretive History* (Corvallis: Oregon State University Press, 2003), 221–23.

2. U.S. Department of Agriculture, *Agricultural Statistics 1967* (Washington, D.C.: U.S. Government Printing Office, 1967), 510; U.S. Bureau of the Census, *Census of Agriculture, 1964* (Washington, D.C.: Government Printing Office, 1967), vol. 1, part 47 (Oregon): 7; Peterson del Mar, *Oregon's Promise*, 215–16. In the same 1945–1964 period, nationwide, the number of farms decreased by 46 percent. One additional reason for the decrease was a redefinition of the term *farm* in the 1959 federal census of agriculture.

3. Secretary of State, *Oregon Blue Book, 1967–1968*, 141–42.

4. U.S. Bureau of the Census, *U.S. Census of Population: 1960. Characteristics of the Population* (Washington, D.C.: U.S. Government Printing Office, 1963), vol. 1, part 39 (Oregon): xiv–xvii, 13–14.

5. Bureau of the Census, *Census of Agriculture, 1964*, vol. 1, part 47 (Oregon): 280–83. The much higher statewide average was due primarily to the vast size of farms in eastern Oregon. Many of the landholdings there were cattle ranches, often between 1,000 and 5,000 acres, and cultivated properties in the eastern part of the state were also large, with wheat, barley, and hay being the principal crops. The difference in farm size was, to a large extent, a function of differential soil quality—the drier eastern part of the state was primarily ranch land, but, as I point out in the text, technological developments and human actions also played a role in shaping the regional

landscape. The situation today bears a striking similarity to that of 1964: the current average size of farms is virtually the same, and the differences between east and west persist. See Secretary of State, *Oregon Blue Book, 1965–1966*, 100; and William G. Loy, ed., *Atlas of Oregon*, 2d ed. (Eugene: University of Oregon Press, 2001), 94–95.

6. Elizabeth Keeler, "The Landscape of Horticultural Crops in the Northern Willamette Valley from 1850 to 1920" (Ph.D. diss., University of Oregon, 1994), 7–103, 144–263; Donald O. Johansen and Charles M. Gates, *Empire of the Columbia: A History of the Pacific Northwest*, 2d ed. (New York: Harper & Row, 1957), 231–34; Peterson del Mar, *Oregon's Promise*, 74–75, 160.

7. Bureau of the Census, *Census of Agriculture, 1964*, vol. 1, part 47 (Oregon): 336–51.

8. Secretary of State, *Oregon Blue Book, 1963–1964* (Salem: Oregon Secretary of State, 1962), 129; *Oregon Blue Book, 1965–1966*, 100–101, 119; *Oregon Blue Book, 1967–1968*, 141–42, 173.

9. Keeler, "Landscape," 170–71; Erasmo Gamboa, *Mexican Labor and World War II: Braceros in the Pacific Northwest, 1942–1947*, reprint ed. (Seattle: University of Washington Press, 2000), 1–73; Gamboa, "A Personal Search for Oregon's Hispanic History," in *Nosotros: the Hispanic People of Oregon*, ed. Erasmo Gamboa and Carolyn M. Buan, (Portland: Oregon Council for the Humanities, 1995), 11–16; Gonzales-Berry and Mendoza, *Mexicanos in Oregon*, 31–49.

10. On *bracero* labor after 1947, see, for example, Oregon State Employment Service, *Oregon Post-Season Farm Labor Report 1956* (Salem: Oregon State Employment Service, 1956), 7–8; and *Oregon Post-Season Farm Labor Report 1958* (Salem: Oregon State Employment Service, 1958), 10–11. For the years 1958–1966, the maximum number of interstate migrant farm workers in Oregon during any bimonthly period was as follows: 1958— 16,520 (for the bimonthly period July 16–31); 1959—15,436 (June 16–30); 1960—14,654 (Aug. 1–15); 1961—16,626 (June 16–30); 1962—18,715 (July 1–15); 1963—17,160 (Aug. 1–15); 1964—14,515 (June 1–15); 1965—12,450 (June 16–30); and 1966—19,335 (June 16–30). See Oregon State Employment Service, *Report 1958*, Table C; *Oregon Post-Season Farm Labor Report 1959* (Salem: Oregon State Employment Service, 1959), Table C; *Oregon Post-Season Farm Labor Report 1960* (Salem: Oregon State Employment Service, 1960), Table C; *Oregon Post-Season Farm Labor Report 1961* (Salem: Oregon State Employment Service, 1961), Table C; *Oregon Post-Season Farm Labor Report 1962* (Salem: Oregon State Employment Service, 1962), Table C; *Oregon Post-Season Farm Labor Report 1963* (Salem: Oregon State Employment Service, 1963), Table C; *Oregon Post-Season Farm Labor Report 1964* (Salem: Oregon State Employment Service, 1964), Table C; *Annual Oregon Farm Labor Report 1965* (Salem: Oregon State Employment Service, 1965), Table C; and *Annual Oregon Farm Labor Report 1966* (Salem: Oregon State Employment Service, 1966), Table C. Unfortunately, the Oregon State Employment Service made no effort to calculate the total number of interstate migrants who worked in Oregon during any given year, nor did they provide an ethnic breakdown. In the late 1950s, a few efforts were made by other organizations to provide cumulative totals as well as to determine the percentage of Mexican Americans among them. But they cannot be relied upon, because the methodologies adopted

were nonsensical. My statements about the changing ethnic composition of the migrant army are based on State Board of Health, *Migrant Health Service Annual Report, 1964–65*, 4–5, and interviews with Don Balmer, Tom Current, and Don Willner by the author. See also Gonzales-Berry and Mendoza, *Mexicanos in Oregon*, 52–73.

11. Donald G. Balmer, *Migratory Labor in Oregon* (Portland: Legislative Interim Committee on Migratory Labor, 1958); Tom Current and Mark Martinez Infante, *We Talked to the Migrants* (Salem: Oregon Bureau of Labor, 1958); Tom Current and Mark Martinez Infante, *And Migrant Problems Demand Attention* (Salem: Oregon Bureau of Labor, 1959). Questions were later raised about the last two publications. Mark Martinez Infante, one of the coauthors, turned out to be a fraud and an accused murderer, and doubt was cast on the validity of his contributions to the reports.

12. *OR*, Apr. 9, 1953, sec. 3, 7; and Aug. 11, 1956, sec. 3, 3; Donald G. Balmer, "The Role of Political Leadership in the Passage of Oregon's Migratory Labor Legislation," *Western Political Quarterly* 15 (Mar. 1962): 147–48; *Oregon Laws Enacted and Joint Resolutions, Concurrent Resolutions, and Memorials Enacted*, 49th regular session of the Legislative Assembly (1957), 1343–44.

13. Interviews with Don Willner and Don Balmer; Balmer, "Political Leadership," 151–52.

14. Balmer, "Political Leadership," 149; and *Migratory Labor*, 2, 59.

15. Interviews with Don Balmer, Don Willner, and Tom Current; Balmer, *Migratory Labor*, 2; Current and Infante, *We Talked*; Current and Infante, *Migrant Problems*, 5–9, 157–63. On Catholic groups, see *Catholic Sentinel*, July 10, 1958, 5.

16. Interviews with Don Balmer and Don Willner; Balmer, *Migratory Labor*, 4–72. The bills are reproduced in Balmer, *Migratory Labor*, 61–72.

17. Tom McCall to Friend of Migrant Labor, Nov. 21, 1958, and Minutes of Oregon Committee on Migrant Affairs, Nov. 28, 1958, both in SMH/6/13; Don Balmer interview.

18. Balmer, "Political Leadership," 146–56.

19. Interagency Committee on Migratory Labor, *Report of the Interagency Committee on Migratory Labor: March 1960* (Salem: Interagency Committee, State of Oregon, 1960), section titled "1959 Administration of Migrant Labor Laws" (report is unpaginated); *Report of the Interagency Committee on Migratory Labor: January 1961* (Salem: Interagency Committee, State of Oregon, 1961), section titled "Bureau of Labor Report of Administration of Farm Labor Law"; *1963 Report of the Interagency Committee on Migratory Labor* (Salem: Interagency Committee, State of Oregon, 1964), section titled "Bureau of Labor"; *The 1964 Interagency Committee Report on Migratory Labor* (Salem: Interagency Committee, State of Oregon, 1965), 13–14; *1965 Report of the Interagency Committee on Migratory Labor* (Salem: Interagency Committee, State of Oregon, 1966), 15.

20. Interagency Committee, *Report of the Interagency Committee: January 1961*, section titled "Board of Health Summary of Activities in Relation to Farm Labor Camps and Fields"; *1963 Report of the Interagency Committee*, sections titled "Oregon State Board of Health" and "Bureau of Labor"; *1964 Interagency Committee Report*, 5–13; *1965 Report of the Interagency Committee*, 4–5, 15–16.

21. Aurora Richardson, "The Pilot Program for the Education of Migrant Children, 1959–1960" (History 407 seminar paper, University of Oregon, Spring 2002, copy in Glenn Anthony May's possession); Ronald G. Petrie, *Oregon Pilot Program for the Education of Migrant Children* (Oregon: Department of Education, 1960); Petrie, *The Education of Migrant Children in Oregon: 1962 Report* (Salem: Department of Education, 1962); Interagency Committee, *1963 Report of the Interagency Committee*, section titled "Department of Education"; *1964 Interagency Committee Report*, 15–17; *1965 Report of the Interagency Committee*, 19. Petrie oversaw the summer schools for the first four years of their existence, but after that, the legislature appropriated no money for administration, and the responsibility for management fell to a consultant in the Department of Education.

22. Sarah Hall Goodwin, "Oregon Migrant Ministry," presentation given at Informational Exchange Meeting for Agencies Working with Farm Labor, Portland, May 11, 1964, SMH/5/25.

23. Mary Kay Rowland, memorandum on migrant health, July 11, 1963, SMH/5/5; I. Chauvin, "Health Summary, 1963–1966," ca. 1966, SMH/5/6; *OJ*, May 22, 1964, sec. 2 (Home and Family), 1; *Catholic Sentinel*, Aug. 7, 1964, 12–13; I. Chauvin, "East Multnomah, North Clackamas County Migrant Council—Summary: January 1964–January 1966," SMH/5/21; "Summary of the Migrant Day Care Program," ca. 1964, SMH/1/19.

24. Board of Health, *Migrant Health Service Annual Report, 1964–65*, 2–3; Interagency Committee, *1963 Report of the Interagency Committee*, section titled "Oregon State Board of Health"; *1964 Interagency Committee Report*, 5–7; *1965 Report of the Interagency Committee*, 4–9.

25. Don Willner to Sarah Hall Goodwin and Mary Kay Rowland, Mar. 21, 1963, SMH/6/3; "Volunteer Oregon Citizens for Agricultural Labor," Oct. 10, 1964, SMH/7/13.

26. Bureau of the Census, *Census: 1960. Characteristics*, vol. 1, part 39: 88, 133, 156; U.S. Bureau of the Census, *U.S. Census of Population: 1960. Subject Reports, Nativity and Parentage* (Washington, D.C.: U.S. Government Printing Office, 1965), vol. 2, part 1A: 151. Actually, in both the 1950 and the 1960 censuses there are additional hints about the size of the Mexican American population in a few other states. For the five Southwest states, the census volumes include information about "persons of Spanish surname." On censuses in that period, see Frank D. Bean and Marta Tienda, *The Hispanic Population of the United States* (New York: Russell Sage Foundation, 1987), 36–55.

27. On undercounts, see Bean and Tienda, *Hispanic Population*, 48, 52, 58, 120–21; Martinez, *Mexican-Origin People*, 13; Gonzales, *Mexicanos*, 192; and Guadalupe Friaz, "A Demographic Profile of Chicanos in the Pacific Northwest," in *The Chicano Experience in the Northwest*, ed. Carlos S. Maldonado and Gilberto Garcia (Dubuque, Iowa: Kendall/Hunt, 1995), 36–37, 61.

28. For minority population totals, see Bureau of the Census, *Census: 1960. Characteristics*, vol. 1, part 39: 26. There is a considerable amount of literature on the unhappy history of minorities in Oregon. See, for example, Quintard Taylor, *In Search of the Racial Frontier: African Americans in the American West, 1528–1990* (New York: W. W. Norton, 1998), 75–77, 82,

105, 216, 224, 253–54; Stuart John McElderry, "The Problem of the Color Line: Civil Rights and Racial Identity in Portland, Oregon, 1944–1965" (Ph.D. diss., University of Oregon, 1998), 17–108, 205–42, 309–63; Gordon Dodds, *Oregon: A Bicentennial History* (New York: W. W. Norton, 1977), 54–60, 68–69, 110–13, 16–26, 187–97; and Peterson del Mar, *Oregon's Promise*, 82–83, 108–12, 202–7, 224–32. The excellent bibliography in the last book lists important monographs, articles, and dissertations on the subject.

29. On World War II, see Gamboa, *Mexican Labor*, 112–19. On growers, see chapter 4; Gonzales–Berry and Mendoza, *Mexicanos in Oregon*, 55–59, 67–68.

30. Joseph S. Gallegos interview by the author; Joseph S. Gallegos, "Portraits: Four Hispanic Widows of the Portland Area," *Oregon Humanities* (Summer 1992): 27–29.

31. Kerry Beeaker et al., "Ruben Contreras: Migrant Rights Pioneer Called Hotel Oregon Home," *McMenamins Newsletter* (Dec. 2006–Feb. 2007), 11, 13–16; *OJ*, Aug. 13, 1965, sec. 1, 5.

32. Emilio Hernandez interview by the author.

33. Jimmy Amaya interview by the author; Paul F. Griffin and Ronald L. Chatham, "A Comparative Analysis of the Mexican-American and Russo-American Migrant in the Willamette Valley, Oregon," a study funded by the Office of Economic Opportunity, Sept. 1, 1966, 99–105 (a copy is located in the Oregon Collection, Knight Library, University of Oregon).

34. It is worth pointing out that Mexican-origin people had resided in Oregon in the early twentieth century. The population had declined precipitously in the 1930s, however, when many Mexican-origin people returned to Mexico. See Gonzales-Berry and Mendoza, *Mexicanos in Oregon*, 25–31, and Gamboa, *Mexican Labor*, 5–10.

35. Interviews with Joseph S. Gallegos, Emilio Hernandez, and Jimmy Amaya; Beeaker, "Contreras," 14. For more information on Woodburn and a suggestion that Mexican American communities were slowly emerging in a few places, see Gonzales-Berry and Mendoza, *Mexicanos in Oregon*, 69–72.

36. Milton Viorst, *Fire in the Streets: America in the 1960's* (New York: Simon and Schuster, 1979); Maurice Isserman and Michael Kazin, *America Divided: The Civil War of the 1960s* (New York: Oxford University Press, 2000); John Morton Blum, *Years of Discord: American Politics and Society, 1961–1974* (New York: W. W. Norton, 1991); Allen J. Matusow, *The Unraveling of America: A History of Liberalism in the 1960s* (New York: Harper & Row, 1984); Charles DeBenedetti and Charles Chatfield, *An American Ordeal: The Antiwar Movement in the Vietnam Era* (Syracuse, N.Y.: Syracuse University Press, 1990); Mark Hamilton Lytle, *America's Uncivil Wars: The Sixties Era from Elvis to the Fall of Richard Nixon* (New York: Oxford University Press, 2006).

37. Doug McAdam, *Political Process and the Development of Black Insurgency, 1930–1970*, 2d ed. (Chicago: University of Chicago Press, 1999), 65–116.

38. Ibid., 117–80.

39. On the point that those pieces of legislation were intended primarily to benefit African Americans, see Julie Leininger Pycior, *LBJ and Mexican*

Americans: The Paradox of Power (Austin: University of Texas Press, 1997), 147, 154–57.

40. William H. Chafe, *The Unfinished Journey: America Since World War II*, 6th ed. (New York: Oxford University Press, 2006), 294–332; Doug McAdam, *Freedom Summer* (New York: Oxford University Press, 1988). On the connection between the civil rights movement and Chavez's campaign for farmworker rights, see Marshall Ganz, *Why David Sometimes Wins: Leadership, Organization, and Strategy in the California Farm Worker Movement* (New York: Oxford University Press, 2009), 57–60, 94–98,134–36; and the mountain of source material (including the testimony of many key players in the farmworkers movement) on the magnificent website created by LeRoy Chatfield: http://www.farmworkermovement.us/. Ian Haney López notes that, several years later, there was an important connection between the Black Power movement and the Chicano movement. See Ian F. Haney López, *Racism on Trial: The Chicano Fight for Justice* (Cambridge: Harvard University Press, 2003), 161–67.

41. Tarrow, *Power in Movement*, 142, 145.

42. I am using an estimate of the Mexican American population found in Leo Grebler, Joan W. Moore, and Ralph C. Guzmán, *The Mexican-American People: The Nation's Second Largest Minority* (New York: Free Press, 1970), 605–6. According to those authors, more than 80 percent of the Mexican Americans were concentrated in the two states of Texas and California. The African American population was about 18,900,000 in 1960. On the African American population, see U.S. Bureau of the Census, *U.S. Census of Population: 1960. Characteristics of the Population* (Washington, D.C.: U.S. Government Printing Office, 1964), vol. 1, part 1 (United States Summary): 144.

43. Ignacio M. García, *Viva Kennedy: Mexican Americans in Search of Camelot* (College Station: Texas A & M University Press, 2000), 33–103; Pycior, *LBJ and Mexican Americans*, 116–21.

44. McAdam, *Political Process*, 146–229.

45. Some historians have been critical of these middle-class organizations, labeling them "assimilationist." Mario García has made a compelling case that the charge is unfair. On LULAC, see García, *Mexican Americans: Leadership, Ideology, and Identity, 1930–1960* (New Haven: Yale University Press, 1989), and Guadalupe San Miguel Jr., *"Let All of Them Take Heed": Mexican Americans and the Campaign for Educational Quality in Texas, 1910–1981* (College Station: Texas A & M University Press, 1987). On the American G.I. Forum, see Ignacio M. García, *Hector P. García: In Relentless Pursuit of Justice* (Houston: Arte Público Press, 2002); Carl Allsup, *The American G.I. Forum: Origins and Evolution* (Austin: Center for Mexican American Studies, University of Texas at Austin, 1982); and Patrick J. Carroll, *Felix Longoria's Wake: Bereavement, Racism, and the Rise of Mexican American Activism* (Austin: University of Texas Press, 2003).

46. For example, in the late 1960s, both organizations provided financial support to the Mexican American Youth Organization (MAYO) led by the activist José Angel Gutiérrez. See F. Arturo Rosales, *Chicano! The History of the Mexican American Civil Rights Movement* (Houston: Arte Público Press, 1997), 217–18.

47. For overviews of the Chicano movement, see Rosales, *Chicano!*; Ignacio M. García, *Chicanismo: The Forging of a Militant Ethos among Mexican Americans* (Tucson: University of Arizona Press, 1997); Juan Gómez-Quiñones, *Chicano Politics: Reality and Promise* (Albuquerque: University of New Mexico Press, 1990); George Mariscal, *Brown-Eyed Children of the Sun: Lessons from the Chicano Movement, 1965–1975* (Albuquerque: University of New Mexico Press, 2005); Vicki L. Ruiz, *From Out of the Shadows: Mexican Women in Twentieth-Century America* (New York: Oxford University Press, 1998), 99–126; Yolanda Alaniz and Megan Cornish, *Viva La Raza: A History of Chicano Identity and Resistance* (Seattle: Red Letter Press, 2008), 149–279; Martinez, *Mexican-Origin People*, 174–85; Acuña, *Occupied America*, 4th ed., 328–75; Gonzales, *Mexicanos*, 191–222; Matt S. Meier and Feliciano Ribera, *Mexican Americans / American Mexicans: From Conquistadors to Chicanos* (New York: Hill and Wang, 1993), 198–232.

48. John Gregory Dunne, *Delano: The Story of the California Grape Strike*, 3d ed. (Berkeley: University of California Press, 2008), 51.

49. Ibid., 51–56.

50. Richard Griswold del Castillo and Richard A. Garcia, *César Chávez: A Triumph of Spirit* (Norman: University of Oklahoma Press, 1995), 3–51; Jacques Levy, *Cesar Chavez: Autobiography of La Causa* (New York: W. W Norton, 1975), 3–205; Susan Ferriss and Ricardo Sandoval, *The Fight in the Fields: Cesar Chavez and the Farmworkers Movement* (San Diego: Harcourt Brace, 1997), 3–117; Dunne, *Delano*, 57–136.

51. Reies López Tijerina, *They Called Me "King Tiger": My Struggle for the Land and Our Rights*, trans. José Angel Gutiérrez (Houston: Arte Público Press, 2000), 1–59; Richard Gardner, *Grito! Reies Tijerina and the New Mexican Land Grant War of 1967* (Indianapolis: Bobbs-Merrill Company, 1970), 8–116; Patricia Bell Blawis, *Tijerina and the Land Grants: Mexican Americans in Struggle for Their Heritage* (New York: International Publishers, 1971), 31–48; Rosales, *Chicano!*, 154–59; Meier and Ribera, *Mexican Americans / American Mexicans*, 212–13.

The Valley Migrant League

1. *United States Statutes at Large: 1964* (Washington, D.C.: U. S. Government Printing Office, 1965), 78:508–34. On the evolution of the legislation and the OEO: Michael L. Gillette, *Launching the War on Poverty: An Oral History* (New York: Twayne, 1996), xiv–xv, xix, 73–83, 201–09; Alice O'Connor, *Poverty Knowledge: Social Science, Social Policy, and the Poor in Twentieth-Century U.S. History* (Princeton: Princeton University Press, 2001), 166–95. The CAP program has been much criticized. See, for example, James T. Patterson, *America's Struggle against Poverty in the Twentieth Century*, rev. ed. (Cambridge: Harvard University Press, 2000), 141–45; Michael B. Katz, *In the Shadow of the Poorhouse: A Social History of Welfare in America*, rev. ed. (New York: Basic Books, 1996), 267–69; and Daniel Patrick Moynihan, *Maximum Feasible Misunderstanding: Community Action in the War on Poverty* (New York: Free Press, 1969).

2. Tom Current interview.

3. Ibid.; Tom Current, Prospectus of the Valley Migrant League, ca. Jan. 1965, SMH/6/21.

4. Interviews with Tom Current, Don Willner, and Don Balmer; VML, Minutes of Meetings on Jan. 16, 1965, and Jan. 23, 1965, SMH/6/33; Kent D. Lawrence to Sargent Shriver, Feb. 11, 1965, RG381/OEO, Migrant/Box 222; VML proposal for CAP, ca. Feb.–Mar. 1965, SMH/6/43; VML, Minutes of Meeting on Mar. 19, 1965, SMH/6/21; *OR*, Mar. 20, 1965, sec. 1, 1.

5. VML, Report to Board of Directors, May 5, 1965, and Minutes of Meeting on May 29, 1965, SMH/6/22; *OR*, Apr. 14, 1965, sec. 1, 10; Apr. 23, 1965, sec. 1, 22; May 21, 1965, sec. 1, 25; *OS*, Apr. 22, 1965, sec. 1, 2; and May 30, 1965, sec. 1, 5. Current had been the board's first choice for executive director, but the OEO deemed him ineligible because technically he had been an OEO employee at the time he developed the VML proposal.

6. VML, Board Report, June 25, 1965, and July 16, 1965, and Final Board Report for 1965 Operations, Jan. 21, 1966, all in SMH/6/22.

7. *CJ*, June 23, 1965, sec. 1, 1; *OJ*, Aug. 9, 1965, sec. 1, 2; Aug. 10, 1965, sec. 1, 4; Aug. 11, 1965, sec. 1, 7; Aug. 12, 1965, sec. 1, 6; Aug. 13, 1965, sec. 1, 5; Evaluation Report, Valley Migrant League, Aug. 3, 1965, RG381/OEO, Migrant/222.

8. Final Board Report for 1965 Operations, Jan. 21, 1966, SMH/6/22.

9. Statement of CAP Grant, Jan. 7, 1966; and OEO, news releases, May 24, 1966, and June 6, 1966, all in RG381/OEO, Migrant/Box 222; Evaluation of the Valley Migrant League, Jan. 14, 1966, RG381/OEO, Migrant/213; VML, Board Report, May 1966, SMH/6/23. The article appeared two months later: Robert Morris, "Valley in Transit—Oregon Moves to Help Its Migrant Farm Workers," *Communities in Action* 1 (Aug.–Sept. 1966): 17–20.

10. This account of the Hillsboro opportunity center is based on Emilio Hernandez interview; VML, Report to Board of Directors, May 5, 1965, SMH/6/22; Gary Lansing to Executive Committee, Apr. 13, 1966, SMH/6/26; *HA*, May 12, 1966, sec. 1, 10; June 2, 1966, sec. 1, 2; *OR*, June 10, 1966, sec. 1, 29; Don Willner to Al Ullman, July 15, 1966, with enclosed "Noticia" issued by VIVA, AU/24/29; Eric Biddle, Inspection Report on the VML (Administratively Confidential), Feb. 2, 1967, RG381/OEO, Migrant/213; Gonzales-Berry and Mendoza, *Mexicanos in Oregon*, 79–83, 92–93.

11. Robert Bauman, "The Black Power and Chicano Movements in the Poverty Wars in Los Angeles," *Journal of Urban History* 33 (Jan. 2007): 277–95; Bauman, *Race and the War on Poverty: From Watts to East L.A.* (Norman: University of Oklahoma Press, 2008), 10–68; Susan Youngblood Ashmore, *Carry It On: The War on Poverty and the Civil Rights Movement in Alabama, 1964–1972* (Athens: University of Georgia Press, 2008), especially 253–79; William S. Clayson, *Freedom Is Not Enough: The War on Poverty and the Civil Rights Movement in Texas* (Austin: University of Texas Press, 2010), 65–83; Frank Stricker, *Why America Lost the War on Poverty—and How to Win It* (Chapel Hill: University of North Carolina Press, 2007), 61–82; Noel A Cazenave, *Impossible Democracy: The Unlikely Success of the War on Poverty Community Action Programs* (Albany: State University of New York Press, 2007), 150–66.

12. On Garcia: Priscilla Carrasco interview by the author; VML, Board Report, June and July 1966, SMH/6/23; E-mail communications from Rita Kester (director of communications, Mt. Angel Abbey), Apr. 20, 2004, and

Suzanne McKenzie (library archivist, Mt. Angel Abbey), Apr. 27, 2004, to the author.

13. Sonny Montes interviews; also Sonny Montes interviews by Noreen Saltveit. (In the following notes, *unless otherwise stated*, citations to interviews with Sonny Montes refer to interviews conducted by the author.)

14. Sonny Montes interviews; *HA*, Sept. 5, 1966, 1.

15. Sonny Montes interviews. On the VML's early efforts to provide job counseling: VML, Application to Community Action Program, attachment to CAP 4.6.1, Aug. 1966, SMH/7/1.

16. Statement of CAP Grant, May 30, 1966, RG381/OEO, Migrant/222; George Hamberger et al., *Valley Migrant League Annual Report to the Board for the Period January 1, 1966–March 31, 1967* (Woodburn, Ore.: Valley Migrant League, 1967), 11, 20–22; *OS*, July 7, 1966, sec. 1, 1; *CJ*, Oct. 5, 1966, sec. 1, 1; Tom Current to Noel Klores, Oct. 30, 1967, RG381/OEO, Migrant/215.

17. Sonny Montes interviews.

18. *CJ*, Aug. 27, 1966, sec. 1, 1; *HA*, Sept. 5, 1966, 1.

19. Sonny Montes interviews. On the date of Little's hiring: Tom Current to Noel Klores, Oct. 30, 1967, RG381/OEO, Migrant/215.

20. Sonny Montes interviews; *CJ*, Oct. 5, 1966, sec. 1, 1. On wages, see VML, Meeting with Wayne Morse, Nov. 9, 1967 (and attached materials), SMH/7/11.

21. Sonny Montes interviews; Hamberger, *Valley Migrant League Annual Report January 1, 1966–March 31, 1967*, 22; Report on On-the-Job-Training Program, in VML Proposal for 1967 (detailed), ca. May 31, 1967, SMH/7/2.

22. Tom Current to Noel Klores, Oct. 30, 1967, RG381/OEO, Migrant/215.

23. Sonny Montes interviews.

24. Current, Prospectus of the Valley Migrant League, ca. Jan. 1965, SMH/6/21; VML proposal for CAP, ca. Feb.–Mar. 1965, SMH/6/43; VML, Minutes of Board of Directors Meeting, May 29, 1965, SMH/6/22; Tom Current to Executive Committee, VML, June 10, 1965, SMH/6/25; VML, Executive Committee Minutes, June 17, 1965, SMH/6/33. The VML sometimes referred to the local organizations as "area migrant committees" and "area advisory committees."

25. VML, Executive Committee Minutes, June 17, 1965, SMH/6/33; interviews with Tom Current and John Little by the author.

26. VML, Report to Board of Directors, May 5, 1965, and May 29, 1965, both in SMH/6/22; list of opportunity centers, directors, and assistants, Aug. 10, 1966, RG381/OEO, Migrant/213; interviews with Tom Current and Sonny Montes.

27. On Pape: interviews with John Little and Tom Current; Gonzales-Berry and Mendoza, *Mexicanos in Oregon*, 77–78. On social workers: James Leiby, *A History of Social Welfare and Social Work in the United States* (New York: Columbia University Press, 1978), 280.

28. Tom Current interview; New Programs Committee, Report to Board of Directors, June 29, 1966, SMH/6/40; Tom Current to New Programs Committee, ca. Sept. 1966, RG381/OEO, Migrant/213; New Programs Committee, Evaluation Report to the Board, Sept. 1966, SMH/6/40; VML,

Priorities Adopted by Board of Directors. Sept. 29, 1966, SMH/6/39.

29. Interviews with Tom Current and John Little; John Little interviews by Kay Reid. In the following notes, *unless otherwise stated*, citations to interviews with John Little refer to interviews conducted by the author.

30. John Little interviews; John Little interviews by Kay Reid; *New Catholic Encyclopedia*, 15 vols. (New York: McGraw-Hill, 1967), 10:978.

31. Lee Hoinicki and Carl Mitcham, eds., *The Challenge of Ivan Illich: A Collective Reflection* (Albany: State University of New York Press, 2002), 9–42, 49–51, 129–61, 233–42; John Little interviews.

32. John Little interviews; John J. Considine, ed., *The Missionary's Role in Socio-Economic Betterment* (Westminster, Md.: Newman Press, 1960), 34–55.

33. Considine, *Missionary's Role*, 48.

34. John Little interviews.

35. Will Pape to all staff members, Oct. 19, 1966, SMH/6/34; Ralph Cake to Will Pape, Oct. 27, 1966, SMH/6/26; VML, Board Report, Oct. 1966, RG381/OEO, Migrant/222; Kenneth Vallis to Noel Klores, Nov. 4, 1966, RG381/OEO, Migrant/213; VML, Board Report, Nov. 1966, SMH/6/23.

36. Noel Klores to Kent Lawrence, Nov. 18, 1966, SMH/6/42.

37. Hamberger, *Valley Migrant League Annual Report January 1, 1966–March 31, 1967*, 11; Geraldine Pearson to VML, Executive Committee, Jan. 12, 1967, SMH/6/41; Ray Reusche and Eric Biddle to Edgar May, memorandum on Valley Migrant League (Administratively Confidential), May 8, 1967, RG381/OEO, Migrant/213.

38. Bauman, "Black Power," 277–95, and *Race and the War on Poverty*, 69–136; Clayson, *Freedom Is Not Enough*, 65–83; Cazenave, *Impossible Democracy*, 150–66. It is worth noting that not all the conflict that surfaced during the War on Poverty was between minorities and whites. Both Bauman and Clayson emphasize serious tensions between African Americans and Mexican Americans. See, for example, Clayson, *Freedom Is Not Enough*, 84–99, and Bauman, *Race and the War Against Poverty*, 90–109.

39. In reconstructing the Bustos affair, I relied on: John Little interviews; VML, Board Reports, Jan. and Feb. 1967, SMH/6/24; J. G. Bustos telegram to Sargent Shriver, Feb. 19, 1967, and attached documents concerning Bustos case, RG381/OEO, Migrant/217; VML, Minutes of Board of Directors Meeting, Feb. 23, 1967; VML, Minutes of the Special Board of Directors Meeting, Mar. 16, 1967, and Irene Chauvin, Meeting Report, Mar. 16, 1967, all in SMH/6/35; *OR*, Jan. 28, 1967, sec. 1, 10; Feb. 5, 1967, sec. 1, 34; Feb. 25, 1967, sec. 1, 12; Mar. 8, 1967, sec. 1, 20; *OJ*, Jan. 27, 1967, sec. 1, 1; Feb. 16, 1967, sec. 1, 4; Mar. 7, 1967, sec. 1, 11; *CJ*, Feb. 24, 1967, sec. 1, 1; *OS*, Feb. 25, 1967, sec. 1, 5; Mar. 8, 1967, sec. 1, 1.

40. *OJ*, Feb. 28, 1967, sec. 1, 1, 3; Mar. 1, 1967, sec. 1, 1, 4; Mar. 2, 1967, sec. 1, 1, 4; Mar. 3, 1967, sec. 1, 4.

41. Bob Emond to Edgar May, memorandum on the Valley Migrant League (Administratively Confidential), Mar. 3, 1967, RG381/OEO, Migrant/213; telegram from Al Ullman to Sargent Shriver, Mar. 6, 1967, RG381/OEO, Migrant/217.

42. *CJ*, Mar. 8, 1967, sec. 1, 1; *OS*, Mar. 8, 1967, sec. 1, 1, 3; and Apr. 7, 1967, sec. 2, 13; Will Pape to Kent Lawrence, Mar. 7, 1967, RG381/OEO, Migrant/217; John Little interview.

43. Hamberger, *Valley Migrant League Annual Report January 1, 1966–March 31, 1967*, 14–32.
44. Interviews with John Little and Tina Garcia by the author; VML, Minutes of Executive Board Meeting, June 26, 1968, RG381/OEO, Migrant/216; *McMinnville News-Register*, May 19, 1971, 16.
45. Interviews with Sonny Montes and John Little.
46. My discussion of these incidents is based on my interviews with Sonny Montes and his family.
47. On Chavez in 1962: Ferris and Sandoval, *Fight in the Fields*, 65–77.

The Revolution
1. *OS*, Apr. 7, 1967, sec. 2, 13; *OR*, Apr. 28, 1967, sec. 1, 36; *CJ*, Apr. 28, 1967, sec. 3, 19; Irene Chauvin, VML Meeting Report, Apr. 27, 1967, SMH/6/35; John Little interviews.
2. John Little interviews; Ray Reusche and Eric Biddle to Edgar May, memorandum on Valley Migrant League (Administratively Confidential), May 8, 1967, RG381/OEO, Migrant/213; Comptroller General of the United States, Report on Investigation of Allegations of Abuses in the Administration of Programs Conducted by the Valley Migrant League, July 18, 1967, RG381/OEO, Migrant/213; Audit Division, OEO, Report of Audit, Valley Migrant League, Aug. 31, 1967, RG381/OEO, Migrant/513; Tom Current, Special Problems for VML, Sept. 13, 1967, SMH/6/39; VML, Minutes of Special Board of Directors Meeting, Sept. 13, 1967, SMH/6/35; VML, Task Force Committee Meeting, Oct. 6, 1967, SMH/7/11; VML, Response to GAO Audit, ca. Nov. 1967, and Response to Audit Report No. W-67-57-8, ca. Nov. 1967, both in RG381/OEO, Migrant/214.
3. John Little interviews. On politicking, see Irene Chauvin, VML Meeting Report, Apr. 27, 1967, SMH/6/35.
4. The most intensive of these contacts were to be recorded on special forms (called "contact records") supplied by the OEO. On contacts: U.S. Office of Economic Opportunity, Community Action Program, *Management Information Reporting by Community Action Agencies* (Washington, D.C.: U.S. Government Printing Office, 1967), 59–67.
5. On Granato and counting: interviews with John Little and Sonny Montes; Eric Biddle, Inspection Report on the VML (Administratively Confidential), Feb. 2, 1967, RG381/OEO, Migrant/213.
6. Interviews with Sonny Montes and John Little.
7. VML, Executive Director's Report to the Board of Directors, June 29, 1967, SMH/7/9; John Little to Arthur Fleming, Dec. 1, 1967, RG381/OEO, Migrant/216.
8. VML, Special Study Night Meeting Report, June 29, 1967; and Irene Chauvin, Special Meeting Report, June 29, 1967, both in SMH/7/9. On the reasons for the holding of this session: VML, Minutes of the Board of Directors Meeting, May 25, 1967, SMH/6/35.
9. Interviews with John Little and Sonny Montes.
10. Special Study Night Meeting Report, June 29, 1967; and Irene Chauvin, Special Meeting Report, June 29, 1967, both in SMH/7/9; interviews with John Little and Sonny Montes.
11. On the formation of Los Amigos: VML, Board Report, Oct. 1966, SMH/6/23; VML, Board Report, Jan. 1967, SMH/6/24; *HA*, Apr. 18,

1966, 8; May 12, 1966, sec. 1, 10; Mar. 16, 1967, sec. 1, 3; Apr. 13, 1967, sec. 1, 5; interview with Sonny Montes.

12. Tom Current, Prospectus of Valley Migrant League, ca. Jan. 1965, SMH/6/21; VML proposal for CAP, ca. Feb.–Mar. 1965, SMH/6/43; VML, Board Report, Oct. 1966, SMH/6/23; Hamberger, *Valley Migrant League Annual Report January 1, 1966–March 31, 1967*, 9–11.

13. Special Study Night Meeting Report, June 29, 1967; and Irene Chauvin, Special Meeting Report, June 29, 1967, both in SMH/7/9; interviews with John Little and Sonny Montes.

14. The resolutions were officially approved at the Aug. 23 board meeting (VML, Minutes of the Board of Directors Meeting, Aug. 23, 1967, SMH/6/35), but steps were taken to implement them earlier.

15. Interviews with John Little and Sonny Montes; Tom Current to Noel Klores, Oct. 30, 1967, RG381/OEO, Migrant/215.

16. *Opportunity News*, July 21, 1967, 3. The articles in the newspaper appeared in both English and Spanish. I have slightly altered the English-language quotation in this paragraph to correspond with the Spanish version.

17. Comptroller General of the United States, Report on Investigation of Allegations of Abuses in the Administration of Programs Conducted by the Valley Migrant League, July 18, 1967, RG381/OEO, Migrant/213; Audit Division, OEO, Report of Audit, Valley Migrant League, Aug. 31, 1967, RG381/OEO, Migrant/513. For press reactions, see, for example, *OS*, Sept. 8, 1967, sec. 1, 4; *CJ*, Sept. 8, 1967, sec. 1, 1; and *OJ*, Sept. 8, 1967, sec. 1, 2.

18. David Zarefsky, *President Johnson's War on Poverty: Rhetoric and History* (Tuscaloosa: University of Alabama Press, 1986), 160–86; Katz, *Shadow of the Poorhouse*, 266–67; Irving Bernstein, *Guns or Butter: The Presidency of Lyndon Johnson* (New York: Oxford University Press, 1996), 369–70; Cazenave, *Impossible Democracy*, 154–56. In short order, the war on poverty would suffer another blow when many of the OEO's congressional supporters were defeated in the November 1966 elections.

19. VML, Statement of CAP Grant, Mar. 31, 1967, RG381/OEO, Migrant/218; John Little to Wayne Morse, Feb. 6, 1968, RG381/OEO, Migrant/216.

20. On VML awareness that funding cuts were coming: VML, Minutes of the Board of Directors Meeting, Feb. 23, 1967, SMH/6/35; VML, Executive Director's Report to the Board of Directors, July 26, 1967, SMH/6/24; directions received by staff of Valley Migrant League from Migrant Division, OEO, during the month of August 1967, enclosure in Noel Klores to Kent Lawrence, Sept. 19, 1967, RG381/OEO, Migrant/216.

21. John Little interviews; VML, Minutes of the Board of Directors Meeting, May 25, 1967, SMH/6/35; Gene De la Torre, Evaluation of Valley Migrant League (Administratively Confidential), Aug. 24, 1967; and Noel Klores to Kent Lawrence, Aug. 28, 1967, both in RG381/OEO, Migrant/214.

22. VML, Minutes of the Special Board of Directors Meeting, Sept. 13, 1967, SMH/6/35.

23. Ibid.; Tom Current, Special Problems for VML, Sept. 13, 1967, SMH/6/39; VML, Minutes of the Board of Directors Meeting, Sept. 27, 1967, SMH/6/35; VML, Task Force Committee Meeting, Oct. 6, 1967,

SMH/7/11; Tom Current to Noel Klores, Oct. 11, 1967, SMH/6/42; VML, Response to GAO Audit, ca. Oct./Nov. 1967, and Response to Audit Report No. W-67-57-8, ca. Oct./Nov. 1967, both in RG381/OEO, Migrant/214.

24. VML, Minutes of the Board of Directors Meeting, Sept. 27, 1967, SMH/6/35; VML, Task Force Committee Meeting, Oct. 6, 1967, SMH/7/11; John Little interviews.

25. VML, Meeting with Wayne Morse, Nov. 9, 1967; and Mary Kay Rowland, Special Meeting Report, Nov. 9, 1967, both in SMH/7/11; VML, Report of the Board of Directors Meeting, Dec. 27, 1967, SMH/6/35.

26. Noel Klores to Kent Lawrence, Nov. 27, 1967, RG381/OEO, Migrant/218.

27. VML, Report of the Board of Directors Meeting, Dec. 27, 1967; and VML, Executive Committee Meeting, Dec. 28, 1967, both in SMH/6/35; John Little to Wayne Morse, Jan. 11, 1968, and Feb. 6, 1968, RG381/OEO, Migrant/216.

28. VML, Executive Director's Report, Jan. 24, 1968, SMH/6/24; John Little to Wayne Morse, Feb. 6, 1968; Noel Klores to Kent Lawrence, Feb. 8, 1968; and Noel Klores to John Little, Feb. 13, 1968, all in RG381/OEO, Migrant/216; VML, Executive Director's Report to the Board of Directors, Mar. 27, 1968, SMH/6/24; VML, Statement of CAP Grant, Apr. 4, 1968, RG381/OEO, Migrant/218.

29. John Little interview.

30. Noel Klores to Kent Lawrence, Aug. 28, 1967, RG381/OEO, Migrant/214; VML, Quarterly Report for Quarter Ending Sept. 30, 1967, RG381/OEO, Migrant/216; VML, Executive Director's Report to the Board of Directors, Nov. 29, 1967, SMH/6/24.

31. Ibid.; Noel Klores to Kent Lawrence, Oct. 20, 1967, RG381/OEO, Migrant/218.

32. VML, Minutes of the Board of Directors Meeting, Aug. 23, 1967, SMH/6/35; Noel Klores to Kent Lawrence, Aug. 28, 1967, RG381/OEO, Migrant/214; VML, Task Force Committee Meeting, Oct. 6, 1967, SMH/7/11.

33. VML, Executive Director's Report to the Board of Directors, Nov. 29, 1967, SMH/6/24; VML, Minutes of the Board of Directors Meeting, Nov. 29, 1967, SMH/6/35; VML, Report of Nominations Committee Meeting, Dec. 5, 1967, SMH/6/41; Tom Current to Task Force Committee Members, Dec. 12, 1967, SMH/7/11; John Little to Noel Klores, Dec. 20, 1967, RG381/OEO, Migrant/215; VML, Minutes of the Board of Directors Meeting, Dec. 27, 1967, SMH/6/35.

34. VML, Minutes of Annual Board of Directors Meeting, Jan. 24, 1968; and Mary Kay Rowland, VML Regular Meeting Report, Jan. 24, 1968, both in SMH/6/36; and Mary Kay Rowland, VML Nominating Committee, Overview of Activities in 1967, Jan 30, 1968, SMH/6/41.

35. The writing of job descriptions took some time because an uncooperative OEO nonetheless wanted the entire operations manual to be rewritten. See VML, Minutes of the Board of Directors Meeting, Aug. 23, 1967, Sept. 27, 1967, and Nov. 29, 1967, all in SMH/6/35.

36. VML, Quarterly Report for Quarter Ending Sept. 30, 1967, RG381/OEO, Migrant/216; VML, Minutes of the Board of Directors Meeting, Nov.

29, 1967, SMH/6/35; VML, Quarterly Report for Quarter Ending Dec. 31, 1967, RG381/OEO, Migrant/218.

37. See, for example, the report (VML, Committee Report on Summer Planning, March 1967, SMH/6/39) that the three area directors (Little, Leon Gurney, and Ken Killary) circulated among the VML leadership calling for the organization to be not merely a deliverer of services to the poor but "a catalyst of community development." The report included a discussion of community development techniques, asserting that the VML needed in the future to function primarily as "an advisor and coordinator" and that its principal goal should be empowerment of the people served. "The glory for success belongs to the people we are helping; not to the organization itself or its staff."

38. Interviews with John Little and Sonny Montes.

39. John Little interview.

40. Tom Current to Noel Klores, Oct. 30, 1967, RG381/OEO, Migrant/215.

41. Ibid.; Leon Gurney to Noel Klores, Jan. 12, 1968; and Noel Klores to John Little, Feb. 7, 1968, both in RG381/OEO, Migrant/216.

42. VML, Executive Director's Report to the Board of Directors, Jan. 24, 1968, SMH/6/24; *HA*, Jan. 8, 1968, 1.

43. John Little interview.

44. Interviews with John Little and Sonny Montes.

45. Interviews with Sonny Montes, John Little, and Tom Current; Sonny Montes interview by Noreen Saltveit; VML, Quarterly General Board Meeting, Apr. 28, 1968, SMH/6/36; Farm Worker Proposal to VML Directors, Apr. 28, 1968, included in John Little to Noel Klores, July 19, 1968, RG381/OEO, Migrant/215.

46. This discussion of the April 28, 1968, meeting is based on the transcript of the session and the report of Mary Kay Rowland about it.

47. VML, Quarterly General Board Meeting, Apr. 28, 1968; and Mary Kay Rowland, Regular Meeting Report: VML Full Board Meeting, Apr. 28, 1968, both in SMH/6/36.

48. Ibid.

49. VML, Quarterly General Board Meeting, Apr. 28, 1968; and Mary Kay Rowland, Regular Meeting Report: VML Full Board Meeting, Apr. 28, 1968, both in SMH/6/36; *CJ*, Apr. 30, 1968, sec. 1, 9; *Woodburn Independent*, May 2, 1968, 1.

50. Bauman, "Black Power," 277–95, and *Race and the War on Poverty*, 69–136; Clayson, *Freedom Is Not Enough*, 65–83; Cazenave, *Impossible Democracy*, 151–54; Ashmore, *Carry It On*, 253–79; Stricker, *Why America Lost*, 73–76.

51. VML, Quarterly General Board Meeting, Apr. 28, 1968, SMH/6/36.

Activist

1. Sonny Montes interviews.

2. VML, Minutes of Board of Directors Meeting, May 22, 1968, RG381/OEO, Migrant/216; VML, Staff Orientation and Training Schedule, June 13, 1968, SMH/6/24; VML, Minutes of Executive Board Meeting, June 26, 1968, RG381/OEO, Migrant/216; VML, Executive Director's Report to the Board of Directors, Sept. 4, 1968, and VML, Minutes of the Board of Directors Meeting, Sept. 4, 1968, RG381/OEO, Migrant/213; VML,

Minutes of Quarterly Board Meeting, Sept. 29, 1968, and VML, Minutes of Board of Directors Meeting, Dec. 18, 1968, both in SMH/6/36; and VML, Minutes of Meeting of Board of Directors, Jan. 29, 1969, SMH/6/37.

3. One reason for Hernandez's change in attitude toward the VML was his preference for Little's community development approach. He was also on good terms with Sonny, who had served as area director in Washington County for about six months. Sonny participated in fund-raising events at local churches to help VIVA finance its migrant-assistance projects. Emilio Hernandez interview.

4. VML, Minutes of Board of Directors Meeting, May 22, 1968, RG381/ OEO, Migrant/216; interviews with Emilio Hernandez and John Little. The organization was also known as the "Washington County Farmworkers Board."

5. VML, Minutes of Executive Board Meeting, June 26, 1968, RG381/ OEO, Migrant/216; John Little interview; *OR*, Aug. 19, 1968, sec. 1, 17.

6. Lee P. Brown to Tom McCall, July 14, 1969, Tom McCall Papers, Oregon State Archives, Salem, Admin. Correspondence, 1966–1974, Box 1; interviews with Sonny Montes and John Little.

7. *OR*, Aug. 19, 1968, sec. 1, 17; Sonny Montes interview.

8. *OR*, Aug. 19, 1968, sec. 1, 17; *Washington County News-Times*, Nov. 28, 1968, 4; interviews with John Little, Sonny Montes, and Emilio Hernandez.

9. Sonny Montes interviews.

10. VML, Minutes of Meeting of Board of Directors, Feb. 26, 1969, SMH/6/37; *OS*, Feb. 27, 1969, sec. 1, 2; *OR*, Mar. 8, 1969, sec. 1, 6; interviews with Emilio Hernandez, John Little, and Sonny Montes.

11. *OR*, Mar. 8, 1969, sec. 1, 6; *OS*, Mar. 27, 1969, sec. 1, 2; John Little to Washington County Steering Committee, Mar. 7, 1969, SMH/6/26; interviews with Emilio Hernandez, John Little, and Sonny Montes.

12. John Little to Washington County Steering Committee, Mar. 7, 1969, SMH/6/26; *OS*, Mar. 27, 1969, sec. 1, 2; VML, Minutes of the Meeting of the Executive Board, Mar. 26, 1969, SMH/6/37; VML, Executive Director's Report, Apr. 30, 1969, SMH/6/25; interviews with Sonny Montes and John Little.

13. My discussion of the Los Gatos conference is based on interviews with Jimmy Amaya, Sonny Montes, and John Little; *McMinnville News-Register*, Apr. 30, 1969, 6; and *CJ*, Apr. 23, 1970, sec. 2, 21.

14. The *McMinnville News-Register* (Apr. 30, 1969, 6) described Garcia as a "teacher" at that university, but did not indicate in which department he taught. The university's archives and student records office can find no records indicating that Garcia either served on the faculty or was enrolled as a student. The newspaper article also identified him as president of the "Chicano Institute of California."

15. Griswold del Castillo and Garcia, *Triumph of Spirit*, 51–58, 76–91; Levy, *Autobiography of La Causa*, 206–68; Ferriss and Sandoval, *Fight in the Fields*, 117–48.

16. On Tijerina: Tijerina, *They Called Me*, 59–130; Peter Nabokov, *Tijerina and the Courthouse Raid* (Albuquerque: University of New Mexico Press, 1970); Blawis, *Tijerina and the Land Grants*, 48–172; Gardner, *Grito!*, 117–290; Rosales, *Chicano!*, 159–68.

17. Rodolfo "Corky" Gonzales, *Message to Aztlán: Selected Writings*, ed. Antonio Esquibel (Houston: Arte Público Press, 2001), xvii–xxxviii, 2–34; Ernesto B. Vigil, *The Crusade for Justice: Chicano Militancy and the Government's War on Dissent* (Madison: University of Wisconsin Press, 1999), 30–109; Haney López, *Racism on Trial*, 159–60.

18. Armando Navarro, *Mexican American Youth Organization: Avant-Garde of the Chicano Movement in Texas* (Austin: University of Texas Press, 1995), 80–211; José Angel Gutiérrez, *The Making of a Chicano Militant: Lessons from Cristal* (Madison: University of Wisconsin Press, 1998), 97–192.

19. Muñoz, *Youth, Identity, Power*, 1–4, 61–88; Haney López, *Racism on Trial*, 15–40, 178–86; Ernesto Chávez, *"¡Mi Raza Primero!" [My People First!]: Nationalism, Identity, and Insurgency in the Chicano Movement in Los Angeles* (Berkeley: University of California Press, 2002), 42–51; Acuña, *Occupied America*, 4th ed., 362–65; Rosales, *Chicano!*, 184–95.

20. In August 1968, a month after he had founded the United Farm Workers of Oregon, Ventura Rios held a meeting in Woodburn, where the featured speaker was Sen. Wayne Morse. The master of ceremonies was Sonny Montes, recently returned to Oregon from California. See *OLP*, July 12, 1968, 1, 2; and leaflet titled "Trabajadores Agrícolas" ca. Sept. 1968, SMH/6/19.

21. Sonny Montes interviews. On the boycott campaigns in Portland: *OLP*, Sept. 15, 1967, 5; Sept. 29, 1967, 5; Oct. 13, 1967, 1, 8; Oct. 20, 1967, 1, 8; Oct. 27, 1967, 1; Dec. 15, 1967, 1, 8, July 26, 1968, 1, 5; Aug. 23, 1968, 2; Sept. 20, 1968, 4; Oct. 4, 1968, 5; Nov. 8, 1968, 5; Nov. 22, 1968, 1; Nov. 29, 1968, 2; Dec. 6, 1968, 1, 8; Dec. 13, 1968, 1, 3; Jan. 17, 1969, 8; *OR*, Sept. 5, 1968, sec. 1, 27; Dec. 28, 1968, sec. 1, 7; *OJ*, Nov. 18, 1968, 7; and Dec. 10, 1968, sec. 1, 3.

22. Sonny Montes interviews; Ferriss and Sandoval, *Fight in the Fields*, 148; *OLP*, Apr. 20, 1969, 1; and June 27, 1969, 1, 5; Oct. 3, 1969, 2; *OR*, May 11, 1969, sec. 1, 22.

23. My discussion of Sonny's involvement in the grape boycott is based on my interviews of Sonny Montes.

24. *OLP*, Dec. 12, 1969, 2; Jan. 2, 1970, 1; *OR*, Dec. 17, 1969, sec. 2, 8; interviews with John Little and Sonny Montes.

25. Ferriss and Sandoval, *Fight in the Fields*, 155–57; *OR*, July 31, 1970, sec. 1, 17; *OLP*, Aug. 7, 1970, 1, 2.

26. Sonny Montes interviews; memorandum from SAC, Portland, to Director, FBI, Oct. 21, 1971, CMJ/FBI.

27. Interviews with Sonny Montes and John Little; *OJ*, Aug. 10, 1969, sec. 1, 24; *CJ*, Aug. 30, 1969, sec. 3, 20; *OR*, Sept. 28, 1969, sec. 2, 1; Mar. 11, 1970, sec. 1, 21; Apr. 5, 1970, sec. 1, 31; May 7, 1970, sec. 1, 28; June 13, 1970, sec. 1, 4; Jan. 24, 1971, sec. 1, 1; *CJ*, Aug. 14, 1971, sec. 1, 3.

28. *CJ*, Aug. 30, 1969, sec. 1, 20; *OR*, Dec. 12, 1969, sec. 1, 47; Dec. 25, 1969, sec. 1, 28; Jan. 14, 1970, sec. 3, 6.

29. *OR*, Sept. 28, 1969, sec. 2, 1.

30. This account of the Chicano Moratorium is based on my interviews of Sonny Montes; Jesús Salvador Treviño, *Eyewitness: A Filmmaker's Memoir of the Chicano Movement* (Houston: Arte Público Press, 2001), 135–75; Chávez, *"¡Mi Raza Primero!,"* 61–79; Vigil, *Crusade for Justice*, 110–59; Rosales,

Chicano!, 198–207; Edward J. Escobar, "The Dialectics of Repression: The Los Angeles Police Department and the Chicano Movement, 1968–1971," *Journal of American History* 79 (Mar. 1993): 1483–514.

31. *OR*, May 11, 1971, sec. A, 10; May 29, 1971, sec. A, 7; *OS*, June 17, 1971, sec. 1, 1, 2, and sec. 4, 38; *CJ*, June 17, 1971, sec. 1, 1; *OJ*, June 29, 1971, sec. 1, 1; *CJ*, June 29, 1971, sec. 1, 1; *OS*, July 1, 1971, sec. 1, 1; *CJ*, July 2, 1971, sec. 1, 1; *OS*, July 3, 1971, sec. 1, 1; Sonny Montes interviews; memorandum from SAC, Portland, to Director, FBI, Oct. 21, 1971, CMJ/FBI; Brent Walsh, *Fire at Eden's Gate: Tom McCall and the Oregon Story* (Portland: Oregon Historical Society Press, 1994), 335–36; Riley Gale Peck, "'Veto the Slave Bill': The Struggle Against Senate Bill 677 and the Formation of a Pro–Farm Worker Coalition in Oregon," a prize-winning essay in the University of Oregon Undergraduate Library Research Award Scholarship Competition, 2009, http://hdl.handle.net/1794/10315 (accessed July 10, 2010).

32. *OR*, Aug. 3, 1971, sec. 3, 5; memorandum from SAC, Portland, to Director, FBI, Oct. 21, 1971, CMJ/FBI.

33. On the Brown Berets: Haney López, *Racism on Trial*, 186–204; Chávez, *"¡Mi Raza Primero!,"* 42–60; Muñoz, *Youth*, 102–3; Rosales, *Chicano!*, 184–95, 198–200; Acuña, *Occupied America*, 362–65.

34. Memorandum from SAC, Portland, to Director, FBI, Feb. 1, 1971, and May 4, 1971, CMJ/FBI; interviews with Sonny Montes and John Little.

35. On such records as sources, see, for example, Richard Cobb, *The Police and the People: French Popular Protest, 1789–1820* (London: Oxford University Press, 1970), 3–48.

36. Memoranda from SAC, Portland, to Director, FBI, May 4, 1971, and Mar. 24, 1972; addendum of Apr. 11, 1972, to memorandum of Mar. 24, 1972; and Reclassification Determination, Mar. 28, 1973, all in CMJ/FBI.

37. On techniques and linkages, see Tarrow, *Power*, 29–42, 47–50; McAdam, *Freedom Summer*; Mario Diani, *Green Networks: A Structural Analysis of the Italian Environmental Movement* (Edinburgh: Edinburgh University Press, 1995); Tilly and Tarrow, *Contentious Politics*, 17–23, 120–22.

38. Interviews with John Little and Marshall Lichtenstein by the author; *CJ*, July 4, 1969, sec. 1, 4; Timothy S. Wallace, "State of Oregon v. Estrada: Defending the Right to Support the Rights of Others" (History 407 seminar paper, University of Oregon, Fall 2008, copy in Glenn Anthony May's possession).

39. *OR*, July 31, 1968, sec. 1, 20; Aug. 20, 1968, sec. 1, 14; Sept. 17, 1968, sec. 1, 17; Wallace, "State of Oregon."

40. Interviews with John Little and Marshall Lichtenstein; VML, Minutes of Executive Board Meeting, July 23, 1969, RG381/OEO, Migrant/218. In the previous year, Chuck Harris, a VISTA with a legal background, had been assigned to the VML and done some useful work. But Harris had left.

41. Interviews with John Little and Marshall Lichtenstein; *OR*, Aug. 12, 1969, sec. 1, 11. The Civil Rights Act of 1968 forbade interference with the efforts of government employees to provide services mandated by federal law.

42. Interviews with Marshall Lichtenstein and Charles Merten; *OR*, Apr. 2, 1969, sec. 1, 9.

43. Interviews with Marshall Lichtenstein and Sonny Montes; Sonny Montes interview by Noreen Saltveit.

44. Interviews with John Little, Marshall Lichtenstein, and Sonny Montes; Sonny Montes interview by Noreen Saltveit; *OJ*, Aug. 13, 1965, sec. 1, 5; Mary Ann Casas, "*Moreno v. Tankersley.* The Migrant Class Action of 1969," a prize-winning essay in University of Oregon Undergraduate Library Research Award Scholarship Competition, 2005, http://hdl.handle.net/1794/2513 (accessed Nov. 18, 2008).

45. Interviews with Sonny Montes, John Little, and Marshall Lichtenstein.

46. Sonny Montes interview.

47. This account of the camp entry is based on my interviews with Sonny Montes; *OR*, Aug. 12, 1969, sec. 1, 11; *CJ*, Aug. 13, 1969, sec. 1, 9; *HA*, Aug. 14, 1969, 3; Casas, "*Moreno v. Tankersley*," and Wallace, "State of Oregon."

48. Sonny Montes interviews; Sonny Montes interviews by Noreen Saltveit; *OR*, July 31, 1968, sec. 1, 20; Aug. 12, 1969, sec. 1, 11; Wallace, "State of Oregon."

49. Sonny Montes interview.

50. Interviews with John Little and Marshall Lichtenstein; *CJ*, Aug. 22, 1969, sec. 1, 1; Sept. 3, 1969, sec. 4, 32; Sept. 11, 1969, sec. 1, 6; Jan. 26, 1970, sec. 2, 10; Wallace, "State of Oregon."

51. John Little to Ruth Graves, July 22, 1970; Ruth Graves to Donald Lowitz, July 27, 1970; John Little to Sidney I. Lezak, Oct. 5, 1970; Jerris Leonard to Sidney I. Lezak, Oct. 29, 1970, all in RG381/OEO, Migrant/217; *CJ*, Nov. 3, 1970, sec. 1, 1; *New York Times*, Nov. 8, 1970, sec. 1, 50; VML, Executive Director's Report, Sept. 30, 1970, SMH/6/25.

52. *OS*, Dec. 13, 1968, sec. 3, 28; VML, Minutes of Board of Directors Meeting, Dec. 18, 1968, SMH/6/36; John Little interviews.

53. VML, Minutes of Quarterly Board Meeting, Sept. 29, 1968, and Minutes of Board of Directors Meeting, Dec. 18, 1968, both in SMH/6/36; List of Members, VML Area Advisory Boards, Exhibit I in Report of Evaluation Meeting, Woodburn, Dec. 11, 1968, RG381/OEO, Migrant/214; *OS*, Dec. 20, 1968, sec. 1, 11; *Woodburn Oregon 1968 City Directory* (Eugene: Johnson Publishing Company, 1968), 147, 242; interviews with John Little and Sonny Montes; John Little interview by Kay Reid. Collazo was elected co-chairman of the board in February 1969, and served in that capacity for more than a year before taking a job on the VML staff.

54. VML, Minutes of Meeting of the Board of Directors, Jan. 29, 1969, SMH/6/37; VML application for CAP grant, Mar. 6, 1969, RG381/OEO, Migrant/217.

55. OEO press release on VML grant, Apr. 16, 1969, RG381/OEO, Migrant/514; VML, Executive Director's Reports, July 23, 1969, and Apr. 30, 1970, both in SMH/6/25; VML, Minutes of the Meeting of the Board of Directors, May 28, 1969, and Minutes of Executive Board Meeting, July 23, 1969, both in SMH/6/37; *McMinnville News-Register*, June 4, 1969, 6.

56. On efforts of area directors: VML, Minutes of Executive Board Meeting, July 23, 1969, SMH/6/37; VML, Quarterly Report for the Quarter Ending Sept. 30, 1969, RG381/OEO, Migrant/214. On problems:

VML, Executive Director's Reports, Feb. 25, 1970, Mar. 25, 1970, Apr. 29, 1970, Aug. 26, 1970, Sept. 30, 1970, and Nov. 18, 1970, SMH/6/25. On projects in Independence, Oregon: VML, Minutes of the Executive Board Meeting, Nov. 24, 1969, SMH/6/37; *CJ*, May 15, 1970, sec. 1, 1; *OR*, Dec. 4, 1970, sec. 1, 18; Dec. 6, 1970, sec. 1, 1; *CJ*, Apr. 24, 1971, sec. 2, 15. On later projects: *CJ*, Apr. 10, 1972, sec. 1, 11; Jan. 4, 1974, sec. 1, 9. Also see Erasmo Gamboa, "*El Movimiento*: Oregon's Mexican-American Civil Rights Movement," in *Nosotros*, ed. Gamboa and Buan, 50, 52.

57. On economic development: VML, Executive Director's Report, July 13, 1969, SMH/6/25; VML, Minutes of Board of Directors Meeting, Sept. 28, 1969, SMH/6/37; VML, Executive Director's Reports, Feb. 25, 1970, Mar. 25, 1970, Apr. 29, 1970, Sept. 30, 1970, and Nov. 18, 1970, all in SMH/6/25; John Little to Geraldine Farrell, Nov. 20, 1970, and Little to Antonio Daniel, Dec. 1, 1970, RG381/OEO, Migrant/217; *OJ*, Sept. 29, 1969, sec. 3, 5; *OR*, May 7, 1971, sec. 1, 14.

58. Frank Martinez interview by the author; VML, Executive Director's Report to the Board of Directors, Sept. 4, 1968, RG381/OEO, Migrant/213.

59. Interviews with Frank Martinez and John Little; VML, Quarterly Executive Director's Report, Sept. 29, 1968, SMH/6/24.

60. On Martinez's career advancement: memorandum from Lane Williams to All Staff, Oct. 23, 1968, RG381/OEO, Migrant/218; VML, Minutes of Executive Board Meeting, July 23, 1969, SMH/6/37. On Pablo Ciddio: VML, Minutes of Board of Directors Meeting, Sept. 28, 1969, SMH/6/37; Frank Martinez interview.

61. Special Meeting Report on Mexican American Congress, Dec. 15, 1968, SMH/5/28; *OR*, Sept. 28, 1969, sec. 2, 1.

62. On Martinez's demeanor: interviews with John Little and several anonymous sources. On his attitudes: Frank Martinez interview.

63. On accompanying Little: John Little interview. On the Poor People's Conference: *OS*, May 22, 1970, sec. 1, 2; *CJ*, June 12, 1970, sec. 1, 10; *OS*, Aug. 7, 1970, sec. 1, 10; Sept. 18, 1970, sec. 1, 1, 8; *CJ*, Sept. 19, 1970, sec. 1, 1; *OS*, Sept. 20, 1970, sec. 1, 1, 5; Sept. 21, 1970, sec. 1, 1, 3; Sept. 22, 1970, sec. 1, 4. In fact, McCall became convinced, as a result of the conference and various run-ins with Martinez, that Martinez was a radical. McCall's staff assigned state troopers to spy on follow-up meetings organized by the groups that had sponsored the Poor People's Conference and instructed the troopers to provide lists of the license plates of all the cars parked at the conference sites. See Tom McCall to Charles Williamson, Oct. 2, 1970; McCall to Amanda Kammer, Oct. 7, 1970; Melvin H. Thomas, Report on Meeting of Poor People's Conference Committee, Oct. 17, 1970, Tom McCall Papers, Oregon State Archives, Admin. Correspondence, Box 21, Folder 7; and Oregon State Police to Office of the Governor, Feb. 20, 1971, McCall Papers, Admin. Correspondence, Box 24, Folder 1.

64. VML, Executive Director's Report, Nov. 18, 1970, SMH/6/25; John Little interview.

65. Interviews with Sonny Montes, Jimmy Amaya, and John Little; *OS*, Dec. 10, 1970, sec. 1, 10; Dec. 17, 1970, sec. 1, 1.

66. *OS*, Dec. 18, 1971, sec. 3, 40; *OR*, Jan. 25, 1971, sec. 1, 16; Jan. 28, 1971, sec. 2, 26; Mar. 19, 1971, sec. 1, 28; *OS*, Mar. 31, 1971, sec. 1, 1, and sec. 3, 19; Apr. 29, 1971, sec. 1, 5.

67. On the salary increase: VML, List of Current Personnel, Jan. 19, 1970, RG381/OEO, Migrant/214.

68. Interviews with John Little and Father Christian Mondor by the author.

69. Interviews with Sonny Montes and Father Christian Mondor; Sonny Montes interview by Noreen Salveit. In his 1996 interview with Saltveit, Sonny said that he left the VML in Aug. 1971, but in a 2002 interview with me, he indicated that the date was Sept. 1971. Sonny's FBI file also indicates that he left in Sept. 1971.

70. On health care: *OR*, June 29, 1972, sec. 1, 40; *OS*, Mar. 1, 1973, sec. 1, 6; and Mar. 3, 1973, sec. 2, 13; *OR*, Oct. 25, 1973, sec. 1, 41.

71. See, for example, *OR*, Nov. 10, 1971, sec. 1, 18; *OS*, Aug. 5, 1972, sec. 1, 3; *OR*, Jan. 20, 1973, sec. 1, 8. For a very positive assessment of Martinez's period as director, see Gamboa, "*El Movimiento*," 52–55.

72. On McCall and audits: *OS*, Oct. 19, 1971, sec. 1, 9; Nov. 4, 1971, sec. 2, 19; Apr. 7, 1972, sec. 3, 24; Aug. 25, 1972, sec. 2, 16; Aug. 31, 1972, sec. 2, 13. On Martinez's consolidation of power and subsequent firing: interviews with John Little and Sonny Montes; *OS*, Feb. 1, 1974, sec. 1, 1, and sec. 4, 38.

73. On Bazan and early grants: *CJ*, Apr. 1, 1974, sec. 1, 1; *OR*, June 26, 1974, sec. 1, 21; *OS*, Dec. 19, 1974, sec. 1, 5. On programmatic problems: *CJ*, Feb. 7, 1975, sec. 2, 9; *OR*, July 8, 1975, sec. A, 16; *OS*, Jan. 13, 1976, sec. 1, 10; *CJ*, Jan. 19, 1977, sec. B, 1; *OS/CJ*, Mar. 26, 1977, sec. A, 1, 10; *OS*, May 17, 1977, sec. A, 5. Financial irregularities: *CJ*, Mar. 8, 1976, sec. 2, 13; *OS*, May 25, 1976, sec. A, 6; *OS*, Mar. 15, 1978, sec. A, 8; Mar. 30, 1978, sec. D, 1. Loss of grants: *OS*, Dec. 21, 1978, sec. A, 1, 16; *SJ*, Jan. 20, 1979, sec. D, 2. Resignation: *OS*, May 17, 1979, sec. B, 1.

74. Because there are few archival records for the VML/ORO after 1971, the figures I have provided are only rough estimates. For a statement by Frank Martinez about the services rendered by the VML through 1971, see *OS*, Dec. 30, 1971, sec. 2, 18.

75. Information on the Sanchezes comes from: Esther Sanchez deposition, Sept. 19–20, 2000, in *Esther E. Sanchez v. Philip Morris* (case filed in 2000 in Multnomah County Circuit Court; dropped, 2001); VML, Job Placements, and VML, Contracts Negotiated, attachments to VML, Meeting with Wayne Morse, Nov. 9, 1967, SMH/7/11; *OS*, Jan. 8, 1972, sec. 3, 1, 16; *McMinnville News-Register*, July 1, 1972, 3.

76. U.S. Bureau of the Census, *Persons of Spanish Origin by State: 1980. Supplementary Report, 1980 Census of Population* (Washington, D.C.: Government Printing Office, 1982), 11–12.

From Mount Angel College to Colegio Cesar Chavez

1. U.S. Bureau of the Census, *1970 Census of Population. Characteristics of the Population* (Washington, D.C.: U.S. Government Printing Office, 1973), vol. 1, part 39 (Oregon): 12, 87. The strongest evidence about the size of the Mexican American population in 1970—but it is admittedly problematic—is the count of Mexican-origin people in Mt. Angel in the census of 1980: 421

out of a total population of 2,876. See U.S. Bureau of the Census, *1980 Census of Population. Characteristics of the Population* (Washington, D.C.: U.S. Government Printing Office, 1982), vol. 1, chap. B, part 39 (Oregon): 12.

2. The town's mayor, who also held the position of director of the Mt. Angel Development Corporation, was Joseph Berchtold. Fred Baumgartner, Margaret Hoffer, and William Beyer sat on the city council. The water and sewer commissioner was Philip Meissner, and Peter Meissner served as street commissioner. Leading figures in the chamber of commerce were Leo Traeger, Karl Engel, and Leonard Butsch. On German origins: Sister Ursula Hodes, "Mt. Angel, Oregon, 1848–1912" (master's thesis, University of Oregon, 1932), 44–48. On influentials: Sister M. Alberta Dieker interview by the author; *MAN*, Jan. 7, 1971, 1; Jan. 28, 1971, 1.

3. "Mt. Angel Oktoberfest," http://www.oktoberfest.org (accessed Jan. 3, 2009).

4. Hodes, "Mt. Angel," 67, 70–72, 75–77, 86, 116–19; Mt. Angel Academy and College, *Prospectus of Mt. Angel Academy and College* (Portland: Glass & Prudhomme Company, 1911), 7, 8, 27; Mt. Angel Normal School, *Catalogue 1933–34* (n.p.: n.p., 1933), 7. According to the 1951–52 catalog, the faculty consisted of 27 sisters, one female layperson, and one Benedictine father. See Mt. Angel Women's College, *Catalogue: 1951–52* (Mt. Angel: n.p., 1951), 15.

5. Mt. Angel College, *Announcements for 1960–61, 1961–62* (Mt. Angel: n.p., 1960), 10; Sister M. Alberta Dieker interview.

6. Mt. Angel College, *Announcements for 1960–61, 1961–62*, 23; *Announcements for 1962–63, 1963–64* (Mt. Angel: n.p., 1962), 20; *Announcements for 1964–65, 1965–66* (Mt. Angel: n.p., 1964), 20; *OJ*, Mar. 9, 1965, sec. 1, 8.

7. Sister M. Alberta Dieker interview; *OS*, Dec. 22, 1965, sec. 2, 17; *OJ*, Feb. 3, 1966, sec. 1, 8; *OS*, Dec. 19, 1973, sec. 1, 8; and Jan. 12, 1974, sec. 1, 6; Mt. Angel College, *Announcements for 1966–67, 1967–68* (Mt. Angel: n.p., 1966), 6, 83. On the total amount: *OS*, Dec. 19, 1973, sec. 1, 8; Jan. 12, 1974, sec. 1, 6.

8. *CJ*, Apr. 25, 1967, sec. 2, 15; June 21, 1967, sec. 1, 1; July 25, 1967, sec. 2, 11; Sister M. Alberta Dieker interview.

9. On the handbook: *OS*, Dec. 1, 1969, sec. 1, 1. On curriculum: *OS*, May 1, 1969, sec. 3, 35; *OS/CJ*, Sept. 17, 1969, Oktoberfest section, 14; *OR*, Oct. 9, 1969, sec. 1, 30. On the attitudes of the town and the board of trustees: Sister M. Alberta Dieker interview; *OJ*, Dec. 5, 1969, sec. 1, 6.

10. *OR*, Mar. 5, 1969, sec. 1, 12; Mar. 6, 1969, sec. 1, 15; *OS*, Apr. 23, 1969, sec. 1, 6.

11. On Woelfel: *CJ*, July 25, 1967, sec. 2, 1; *OS*, Apr. 23, 1969, sec. 1, 1, 6. On the management team: *OR*, July 30, 1969, sec. 2, 8; *CJ*, Dec. 1, 1969, sec. 2, 9. On the next president: *OS*, Dec. 24, 1969, sec. 1, 1, 7; Jan. 29, 1970, sec. 1, 1.

12. *CJ*, Feb. 24, 1970, sec. 1, 1; Feb. 28, 1970, sec. 1, 1; and Oct. 18, 1973, sec. 2, 18; *OS*, Feb. 25, 1970, sec. 1, 1, and sec. 3, 13; and Father Christian Mondor interview.

13. *OS*, Feb. 25, 1970, sec. 1, 1; *CJ*, Apr. 30, 1970, sec. 2, 13; *OS*, Aug. 24, 1970, sec. 1, 7; *CJ*, Jan. 13, 1971, sec. 2, 19.

14. Father Christian Mondor interview; *OR*, Aug. 13, 1970, sec. 1, 25.

15. Father Christian Mondor interview; Mt. Angel College, *Announcements for 1966–67, 1967–68*, 83; *OS*, Mar. 9, 1971, sec. 1, 1, 9.

16. Father Christian Mondor interview; *CJ*, Mar. 8, 1971, sec. 1, 1; Mar. 9, 1971, sec. 1, 1.

17. On the letter: *CJ*, Mar. 12, 1971, sec. 1, 1; *OS*, Mar. 13, 1971, sec. 1, 1, 3. Kalberer later provided another explanation (*OJ*, Mar. 24, 1971, sec. 1, 13), but it is not credible. On intimidation: *CJ*, Mar. 19, 1971, sec. 2, 11; Father Christian Mondor interview.

18. Father Christian Mondor interview; *OS*, Mar. 13, 1971, sec. 1, 1, 3; *CJ*, Mar. 16, 1971, sec. 1, 1; Mar. 19, 1971, sec. 2, 11; Mar. 24, 1971, sec. 2, 17; Mar. 30, 1971, sec. 1, 1.

19. *CJ*, May 4, 1971, sec. 1, 1; *OS*, May 28, 1971, sec. 3, 18; *CJ*, June 2, 1971, sec. 1, 1; June 3, 1971, sec. 1, 1; *OS*, June 3, 1971, sec. 1, 2. To get the money to hire the African American professor, Mondor engaged in some creative financing. As president of Mt. Angel, he was entitled to a salary, most of which he dutifully turned over to the provincial of his order, retaining only a modest amount to cover his living expenses. He now suggested to the Jesuit provincial that the excess money be used to pay the salary of the new African American faculty member, and the provincial agreed. The new hire cost the college nothing. Father Christian Mondor interview.

20. Interviews with Father Christian Mondor and Sonny Montes.

21. Mt. Angel College, *Family Album* (Mt. Angel: n.p., 1972), 19; *CJ*, July 10, 1971, sec. 2, 15; *CJ*, Jan. 20, 1972, sec. 1, 8; Interviews with Father Christian Mondor and Sonny Montes.

22. On the behavioral science curriculum, see Mt. Angel College, *Announcements, 1968–1970* (Mt. Angel: n.p., 1968), 32–37. The department was originally called behavioral sciences, but it was renamed behavioral science. Also see Mt. Angel College, *Family Album*, 4, 22.

23. According to Sonny's FBI file, he was still living in Forest Grove in March 1972 (memorandum from SAC, Portland, to Director, FBI, Mar. 24, 1972, CMJ/FBI). On his relocation to Woodburn: Pacific Northwest Bell Telephone Company, *Directory: 1973* (n.p.: Pacific Northwest Bell, 1973), Woodburn-Hubbard Section, 28.

24. Interviews with Sonny Montes and Father Christian Mondor.

25. Father Christian Mondor interview.

26. Richard I. Ferrin, Richard W. Jonsen, and Cesar M. Trimble, *Access to College for Mexican Americans in the Southwest* (Palo Alto, Calif.: College Entrance Examination Board, 1972), 2–15. See also Fred E. Crossland, *Minority Access to College: A Ford Foundation Report* (New York: Schocken Books, 1971), 10–21; and, for a slightly later period, Alexander W. Astin, *Minorities in American Higher Education: Recent Trends, Current Prospects, and Recommendations* (San Francisco: Jossey-Bass, 1982), 32–51.

27. Aurelio M. Montemayor, "Colegio Jacinto Treviño," *The Handbook of Texas Online*, http://www.tshaonline.org/handbook/online/articles/CC/kbc51.html (accessed July 19, 2010); María-Cristina García, "Juárez-Lincoln University," *The Handbook of Texas Online*, http://www.tshaonline.org/handbook/online/articles//JJ/kcj3.html (accessed July 19, 2010); Navarro, *Mexican American Youth Organization*, 178–80; Meier and Ribera, *Mexican Americans / American Mexicans*, 223; Victor Guerra-Garza, "Prólogo";

André Guerrero, "La Cuna: Chicanismo in the Rio Grande Valley"; and Leonard J. Mestas, "Afterward: A Brief History of the Juárez-Lincoln University," in *Hojas: A Chicano Journal of Education*, ed. Victor Guerra-Garza (Austin: Juárez-Lincoln Press, 1976), 1–7, 13–24, 52–53.

28. U.S. Bureau of the Census, *1970 Census of Population. Characteristics of the Population* (Washington, D.C.: U.S. Government Printing Office, 1973), vol. 1, part 39 (Oregon): 137, 324.

29. For the newspaper story: *OR*, Feb. 18, 1970, sec. 1, 12. Most of the students at the University of Oregon were probably enrolled in an HEP (High School Equivalency Program)—hence, they were not college students.

30. Father Christian Mondor interview.

31. Sonny Montes interview. According to Sonny, Mt. Angel College had about twelve African American students in the fall of 1971.

32. This paragraph and the next four are based on interviews with Sonny Montes and Father Christian Mondor.

33. On the FBI considering Montes potentially dangerous: Director, FBI, to Director, United States Secret Service, Oct. 21, 1971, CMJ/FBI. On the Dec. 22, 1971, meeting: interviews with Father Christian Mondor and Sonny Montes; Noreen Saltveit interview with Sonny Montes; and memorandum from SAC, Portland, to Director, FBI, Mar. 24, 1972, CMJ/FBI.

34. Two years later, just before Father Mondor was to leave Mt. Angel, he called Sonny into his office and shared with him the story about the agent's visit. Mondor apologized belatedly for not mentioning it to him earlier, explaining that he did not consider it significant. Sonny, however, was angry. He felt that he should have been informed about the agent's visit at the time. Interviews with Father Christian Mondor and Sonny Montes.

35. *OS*, Jan. 20, 1972, sec. 1, 8. In calculating the drop in enrollment, I am relying on the fall 1971 and winter 1972 figures in the college catalog (Mt. Angel College, *Family Album*, 19).

36. Interviews with Sonny Montes and Father Christian Mondor.

37. Interviews with Sonny Montes, Father Christian Mondor, and Adolfo Blanco by the author; *MAN*, Mar. 23, 1972, 1. On the proliferation of Chicano Studies programs: Muñoz, *Youth*, 153–201.

38. *MAN*, Apr. 13, 1972, 1; Sonny Montes interview.

39. *OS*, June 6, 1972, sec. 1, 6; *CJ*, June 9, 1972, sec. 2, 16; *MAN*, June 15, 1972, 1, 2; Mt. Angel College, *Family Album*, 27. On the state of College Without Walls / University Without Walls programs, see *University Without Walls: First Report* (Yellow Springs, Ohio: Union for Experimenting Colleges and Universities, 1972).

40. *OS*, June 3, 1972, sec. 2, 13; *OR*, June 4, 1972, sec. 1, 54; *MAN*, June 22, 1972, 1. On the new director, *MAN*, Oct. 19, 1972, 1.

41. Interviews with Sonny Montes and Father Christian Mondor; Noreen Saltveit interviews with Sonny Montes; *OS*, July 9, 1972, sec. 1, 12; *MAN*, July, 13, 1972, 1.

42. *MAN*, Nov. 16, 1972, 1; *OR*, Dec. 14, 1972, sec. 1, 54.

43. *OS*, Dec. 8, 1972, sec. 1, 1, 10; *CJ*, Dec. 8, 1972, sec. 1, 1.

44. Father Christian Mondor interview; *OS*, Dec. 8, 1972, sec. 1, 1, 10.

45. Ibid.

46. Father Christian Mondor interview.

47. On the winter quarter: *MAN*, Jan. 11, 1973, 1; Jan. 18, 1973, 1. Concerning the spring quarter, various numbers appeared in the press: *OJ*, Apr. 10, 1973, sec. 1, 3; *OR*, Apr. 11, 1973, sec. 1, 22; *MAN*, Apr. 12, 1973, 1; *OR*, May 29, 1973, sec. 1, 10.

48. Guidelines for Institutional Eligibility for Federal Education Programs, U.S. Office of Education, ca. 1973, a copy of which can be found in AU/208/16.

49. Frank G. Morgan to Jacob Hershman, HEW, June 1, 1973, PEW/CCC; *OR*, Feb. 11, 1973, sec. 3, 9; Apr. 11, 1973, sec. 1, 22; *OS*, Oct. 16, 1973, sec. 1, 3; *OJ*, Dec. 13, 1973, sec. 1, 2; interviews with Father Christian Mondor and Sonny Montes; Sonny Montes interview by Noreen Saltveit.

50. *OS*, Dec. 8, 1972, sec. 1, 1, 10; July 10, 1973, sec. 1, 7; *MAN*, Dec. 14, 1972, 1; Jan. 11, 1973, 1; Jan. 18, 1973, 1; July 12, 1973, 6; *OR*, Feb. 11, 1973, sec. 3, 9; Father Christian Mondor interview.

51. *OS*, Dec. 8, 1972, sec. 1, 1, 10; *MAN*, Dec. 14, 1972, 1; Jan. 11, 1973, 1.

52. *MAN*, Jan. 18, 1973, 1; *OR*, Feb. 11, 1973, sec. 3, 9; interviews with Father Christian Mondor and Sonny Montes.

53. Educational Coordinating Council, Minutes of Meeting of Mar. 15, 1973, and attached exhibits, Oregon Educational Coordinating Council Records, Oregon State Archives, Minutes, Box 4.

54. Interviews with Father Christian Mondor and Sonny Montes; *OS*, Apr. 10, 1973, sec. 1, 1, 13; *OR*, Apr. 11, 1973, sec. 1, 22; *OS*, May 18, 1973, sec. 3, 29.

55. Interviews with Sonny Montes and Father Christian Mondor.

56. Sonny Montes interview; *MAN*, Dec. 20, 1972, 1; Jan. 25, 1973, 1; Feb. 15, 1973, 1; Apr. 5, 1973, 1; *CJ*, Dec. 27, 1972, sec. 2, 14.

57. *MAN*, May 10, 1973, 3; Sonny Montes interview; Sonny Montes interview by Noreen Saltveit.

58. *OS*, May 26, 1973, sec. 1, 1, 10; *OJ*, May 26, 1973, sec. 1, 2. On the College Without Walls: Jose Romero interview by the author; *CJ*, Sept. 15, 1973, sec. 2, 14; *MAN*, Sept. 27, 1973, 1. Another program, outdoor recreation, was added to the list in July 1973 but then dropped. See *OS*, July 10, 1973, sec. 1, 7; *CJ*, Sept. 15, 1973, sec 2, 14; *OS*, Oct. 16, 1973, sec. 1, 3; and *MAN*, Dec. 20, 1973, 1.

59. *OR*, May 29, 1973, sec. 1, 10; *MAN*, May 31, 1973, 1; *OS*, July 10, 1973, sec. 1, 7; interviews with Sonny Montes and John Little.

60. Interviews with Sonny Montes and Jose Romero.

61. This paragraph and the next three are based on my interviews with Jose Romero and Kathy Romero.

62. Jose Manuel Romero, "The Political Evolution of the Farm Workers" (master's thesis, University of Oregon, 1973).

63. On recruitment of Romero: interviews with Jose Romero and Sonny Montes. On the arrival date: interviews with Jose Romero and Kathy Romero; affidavit of Jose Romero, June 10, 1977, in CCC/NASC-CR, 801–3.

64. Father Christian Mondor interview; Frank G. Morgan to Jacob Hershman, HEW, June 1, 1973, PEW/CCC.

65. Father Christian Mondor interview; *OS*, July 10, 1973, sec. 1, 7; *MAN*, July 12, 1973, 6; *CJ*, Sept. 15, 1973, sec. 2, 14.

66. *MAN*, Sept. 27, 1973, 1; *OS*, Oct. 16, 1973, sec. 1, 3; Father Christian Mondor interview.

67. First mentions of the possibility of reapplying to the Northwest Association: *MAN*, Sept. 27, 1973, 1; *OS*, Oct. 16, 1973, sec. 1, 3.

68. Father Christian Mondor interview.

69. Interviews with Father Christian Mondor and John Little.

70. Ibid.

71. Sonny Montes interviews; *MAN*, Sept. 27, 1973, 1; *OS*, Oct. 16, 1973, sec. 1, 3. In December 1973, according to one newspaper account, the number of full-time students had grown to 63; approximately 30 of them were reportedly enrolled in the College Without Walls program. A few days later, the number of full-time and part-time students was said to be 115. But both Montes and Romero admitted to me in interviews that, beginning in the fall of 1973, statements about student numbers were often exaggerated. Relevant sources: *OR*, Dec. 10, 1973, sec. 3, 12; *OJ*, Dec. 13, 1973, sec. 1, 2; interviews with Sonny Montes and Jose Romero.

72. *OS*, Oct. 16, 1973, sec. 1, 3; interviews with John Little and Jose Romero.

73. *CJ*, Oct. 18, 1973, sec. 2, 18; *OJ*, Oct. 18, 1973, sec. 1, 2; *MAN*, Oct. 25, 1973, 1.

74. *CJ*, Nov. 14, 1973, sec. 1, 1.

75. On Romero: *CJ*, Nov. 14, 1973, sec. 1, 1. On Sonny's new title: *MAN*, Oct. 4, 1973, 1.

76. *MAN*, Dec. 20, 1973, 1.

77. *CJ*, Nov. 24, 1973, sec. 2, 13; *OR*, Dec. 10, 1973, sec. 3, 12.

78. *CJ*, Nov. 15, 1973, sec. 1, 1; *OR*, Nov. 16, 1973, sec. 1, 29. The college had paid off about $200,000 of the original loans, which amounted to $1,067,000. But it had missed many payments over the past several years, and thus had accumulated additional liabilities of about $100,000.

79. *CJ*, Nov. 24, 1973, sec. 2, 13.

80. Sonny Montes interviews.

81. *OS*, Apr. 10, 1973, sec. 1, 1, and sec. 2, 13; *OR*, Apr. 11, 1973, sec. 1, 22; interviews with Sonny Montes and Father Christian Mondor; Sonny Montes interview by Noreen Saltveit. On community meetings: *OS*, May 22, 1969, sec. 3, 34.

82. Sonny Montes interviews.

83. Interviews with Jose Romero, Sonny Montes, and Father Christian Mondor; Sonny Montes interview by Noreen Saltveit.

84. Interviews with Sonny Montes and Jose Romero; *OR*, Dec. 10, 1973, sec. 3, 12.

85. *OJ*, Dec. 13, 1973, sec. 1, 2; *CJ*, Dec. 13, 1973, sec. 2, 13; *MAN*, Dec. 20, 1973, 1, 2.

86. *MAN*, Dec. 20, 1973, 2.

The "Save Colegio Cesar Chavez" Campaign

1. "Colegio Cesar Chavez: Philosophy, Goals, History, Faculty, Admissions, Financial, Academic and General Information," PEW/CCC.

2. Ibid.

3. *OR*, Jan. 11, 1974, sec. 1, 16; *OS*, Mar. 6, 1974, sec. 1, 10; William A. Sievert, "Chicano College Sues to Stave Off Foreclosure by H.U.D.," *Chronicle of Higher Education* 8 (June 24, 1974): 3.

4. It is very difficult to estimate the number of students at the Colegio in any specific time period. In his book on the history of the Colegio, Carlos Maldonado appears to accept at face value figures provided by the Colegio in reports submitted to government agencies and the Northwest Association. See Carlos S. Maldonado, *Colegio Cesar Chavez, 1973–1983: A Chicano Struggle for Educational Self-Determination* (New York: Garland, 2000), 88–89. But some of those figures are doubtless inflated. Maldonado indicates, for example, that the college's enrollment exceeded 120 in the 1974–75 academic year. Some documents *do* suggest that the enrollment was that high—for example, a form sent to HEW in January 1975 stating that 126 students were enrolled in the school. (See Institutional Characteristics of Colleges and Universities: Colegio Cesar Chavez, Dec. 20, 1974, in Materials on Cesar Chavez Eligibility, Jan. 23, 1975, AU/208/16.) But assorted newspaper accounts indicate that enrollment was *much* lower—one in Dec. 1974, reporting that there were 25 students at the college; another in Jan. 1975, placing the number at 75; and a third, three months later, stating that 57 students were enrolled. See *SAT*, Dec. 26, 1974, sec. 1, 2; *OR*, Jan. 30, 1975, sec. A, 11; Apr. 21, 1975, sec. C, 8. I refer to the last two newspaper accounts in the text of this chapter. Still, I don't want to convey the impression that newspaper accounts were infallible sources. I raise questions about them in the text of chapter 7. On the question of enrollment, I have also relied on my interviews with Jose Romero, Sonny Montes, and Maria Luisa Alaniz.

5. *Colegio César Chávez* (Mt. Angel, Oregon: The Colegio, 1975), 6–35. Jose Romero and Joseph Gallegos were the main authors of the catalog. Some of the components of the educational approach (the *familia* concept, for example) were discussed in a grant proposal submitted by Gallegos at the beginning of 1975. Relevant sources: interviews with Joseph Gallegos, Jose Romero, and Maria Luisa Alaniz; Proposal to the Fund for Improvement of Post Secondary Education, Jan. 14, 1975, AU/208/16; Maldonado, *Colegio*, 36–41.

6. Jose Romero interview; *OR*, Sept. 14, 1975, sec. C, 5; *CJ*, Sept. 20, 1976, sec. A, 1. For a photograph of a Colegio class: *OR*, Sept. 21, 1976, sec. A, 1.

7. According to an annual report produced by the school's administration in February 1976, all but 5 of the Colegio's 57 full-time students were enrolled in the College Without Walls program. Colegio Cesar Chavez, Annual Report to Northwest Association of Schools and Colleges, Feb. 24, 1976, exhibit N in affidavit of James F. Bemis, July 6, 1977, CCC/NASC-CR, 327–33.

8. *Colegio César Chávez*, 12–13.

9. Ibid., 22–23, 30–31. If a *comité* determined that a student was not making satisfactory progress, the faculty members were expected to provide assistance. If that failed, the core faculty member or the *comité* could negotiate a "probation contract" with the student or, as a last resort, withdraw institutional support.

10. *Colegio César Chávez*, 12–13, 24–25; "Colegio Cesar Chavez: Philosophy," 8; Mt. Angel College, *Family Album*, 24.

11. Interviews with Jose Romero, Maria Luisa Alaniz, and Ramon Ramirez by the author; Sievert, "Chicano College," 3; Maldonado, *Colegio*, 45–47.

12. Sievert, "Chicano College," 3.

13. *SAT*, Apr. 10, 1975, sec. 1, 1.

14. Sievert, "Chicano College," 3.

15. On Veliz: interviews with Ramon Ramirez and Rudy Veliz by the author; *OR*, Mar. 10, 1968, sec. A, 26, and July 1, 1977, sec. A, 11.

16. Comments of Virginia Munsch Nesmith and Abby Flores Rivera, UFW Documentation Project Online Discussion, Dec. 2004–Jan. 2005, 60, 69, http://www.farmworkermovement.us/disc/December%5B1%5D%20 REVISED.pdf (accessed. July 20, 2010); *OS/SJ*, Sept. 26, 1976, sec. A, 14; *OJ*, Feb. 7, 1977, sec. 1, 4; Ramon Ramirez interview; Lynn Stephen, *The Story of PCUN and the Farmworker Movement in Oregon* (Eugene: Department of Anthropology, University of Oregon, 2001), 11–26.

17. Interviews with Jose Romero and Ramon Ramirez; affidavit of Betty Rademaker, June 10, 1977, and affidavit of Jose Romero, June 10, 1977, in CCC/NASC-CR, 31–34, 801–03.

18. Interviews with Sonny Montes, Maria Luisa Alaniz, Jose Romero, John Little, Ramon Ramirez, Rudy Veliz, Jimmy Amaya, and Maricela G. Urzua by the author.

19. Interviews with John Little, Sonny Montes, Jose Romero, and Ramon Ramirez. On similar rumors: *SAT*, May 8, 1975, sec. 1, 2.

20. Ed Hoski to Al Ullman, Mar. 24, 1975, AU/215/12; Mabel Anne Blake to Al Ullman, Apr. 12, 1975, AU/208/15; John H. Bennett to Robert Straub, May 19, 1975, AU/215/10; *SAT*, May 8, 1975, sec. 1, 2; Sept. 30, 1976, sec. 1, 2; Maldonado, *Colegio*, 48–49.

21. *SAT*, May 1, 1975, sec. 1, 3.

22. Sonny Montes interviews.

23. Jose Romero interview.

24. *SAT*, May 15, 1975, sec. 1, 2; *CJ*, Mar. 8, 1974, sec. 1, 4; May 17, 1975, sec. 1, 4; *OS*, Feb. 9, 1975, sec. 1, 4; May 7, 1975, sec. 1, 4; *OJ*, Feb. 14, 1975, sec. A, 8.

25. *CJ*, May 17, 1974, sec. 1, 1; *OR*, May 19, 1974, sec. Forum, 8.

26. Sonny Montes interviews; Sonny Montes interview by Noreen Saltveit.

27. *OR*, May 19, 1974, sec. Forum, 8.

28. Interviews with Don Willner and Sonny Montes; Sonny Montes interview by Noreen Saltveit; affidavit of Ernesto Lopez, June 8, 1974 (in legal action filed against HUD but later dropped), which can be found in AU/208/18.

29. On the early negotiations: affidavit of Ernesto Lopez, June 8, 1974, AU/208/18; *OS*, Jan. 12, 1974, sec. 1, 6; *OR*, Jan. 15, 1974, sec. 2, 6; *SAT*, Feb. 14, 1974, sec. 4, 1; *OS*, Mar. 6, 1974, sec. 1, 10.

30. On the meeting: *CJ*, Mar. 5, 1974, sec. 1, 1; *OS*, Mar. 6, 1974, sec. 1, 10; *CJ*, Mar. 6, 1974, sec. 2, 14; *OR*, Mar. 6, 1974, sec. 3, 8; *OJ*, Mar. 6, 1974, 6; Sonny Montes interview. On attendance: "Representation at Colegio Cesar Chavez News Conference," a document attached to Ernesto Lopez to Friends, Mar. 1, 1974, JPL. On CISCO: *OR*, July 26, 1973, sec. 3, 7; July 28, 1973, sec. 1, 12; and Nov. 9, 1974, sec. C, 10. On the filing of the lawsuit: *CJ*, June 5, 1974, sec. 1, 1; *OR*, June 7, 1974, sec. 1, 40.

31. Tarrow, *Power in Movement*, 21–22, 106–22.

32. Ibid., 117–18.

33. The editorial: *CJ*, Mar. 8, 1974, sec. 1, 4.

34. Another exception: In April, the Colegio's staff and students began a door-to-door fund drive. *OR*, Apr. 18, 1974, sec. 1, 13; *OS*, Apr. 21, 1974, sec. 3, 21.

35. On the breakdown in talks: Don Willner to James T. Lynn, May 17, 1974; Robert C. Odle Jr., to Don Willner, May 24, 1974; Don Willner to James Young, May 30, 1974; and Julian B. McKay to Don Willner, June 4, 1974, all in AU/208/18; *CJ*, June 5, 1974, sec. 1, 1. On Ullman's role: Ivo Bauman to Al Ullman, June 3, 1974, and James Young to Ullman, June 7, 1974, AU/208/16. On renewed negotiations: James B. Kenin to James Young, June 21, 1974; Kenin to Walter Rodgers, June 25, 1974; William C. Paulus to Rodgers, June 26, 1974; Rodgers to Kenin, July 1, 1974, all in AU/208/18.

36. The sticking point in the negotiations was an appraisal that occurred after the Seattle office had worked out the terms. According to the arrangement, the sisters were to convey enough assets to cover the difference between the amount of the unpaid loan balance (approximately $1 million) and the estimated value of the college property, thought to be about $600,000. But the appraisal set the value of the property at about $1.5 million. That meant that the sisters would need to pay nothing. The Seattle office tried to rework the plan, and the sisters agreed to convey some parcels of land. But the administrators in Washington were not satisfied. On the seeming breakthrough: James Young to James Kenin and William Paulus, July 23, 1974; Paulus to Young, July 25, 1974; Kenin to Young, July 26, 1974; and Ivo Bauman to Al Ullman, Sept. 11, 1974, all in AU/208/18. On the appraisal and the reworking of the agreement after the appraisal: Paulus to Young, Aug. 2, 1974; Young to Paulus, Aug. 6, 1974; Paulus to Rodgers, Aug. 19, 1974; and Paulus to Ullman, Sept. 20, 1974, AU/208/18. On rejection: Young to Paulus and Willner, Aug. 23, 1974; and Bauman to Ullman, Sept. 11, 1974, AU/208/18.

37. John R. Proffitt to Ernesto Lopez, May 30, 1974, in "Materials on Colegio Cesar Chavez Eligibility," Jan. 23, 1975, AU/208/16.

38. Don Willner to John R. Proffitt, June 10, 1974, in "Materials on Colegio Cesar Chavez Eligibility," Jan. 23, 1975, AU/208/16.

39. Colegio Cesar Chavez and the University of Portland Pre-Accreditation Arrangement, June 26, 1974; D-Q University and Colegio Cesar Chavez, Affiliate Agreement, June 30, 1974; Michael G. O'Brien, memorandum of meeting of Aug. 29, 1974, with Celedonio Montes Jr. and Lucia Pena; memorandum of telephone conversation with James Bemis, Sept. 3, 1974; and Michael G. O'Brien to Celedonio Montes Jr., Sept. 10, 1974, all in PEW/CCC.

40. Interviews with Sonny Montes and Jose Romero: Sonny Montes interview by Noreen Saltveit.

41. Interviews with Sonny Montes and Jose Romero; Gamboa, "El Movimiento," 56.

42. Interviews with Sonny Montes and Jose Romero; *SAT*, Sept. 12, 1974, sec. 1, 1; *OS*, Sept. 17, 1974, sec. 1, 13.

43. Interviews with Sonny Montes, Jose Romero, Joseph Gallegos, and Maria Luisa Alaniz; Higher Education General Information Survey, Colegio

Cesar Chavez, Dec. 20, 1974, a document in "Materials on Colegio Cesar Chavez Eligibility," Jan. 23, 1975, AU/208/16; Colegio Cesar Chavez, Annual Report to Northwest Association of Schools and Colleges, Feb. 24, 1976, exhibit N in affidavit of James F. Bemis, July 6, 1977, CCC/NASC-CR, 327–33.

44. Interviews with Sonny Montes, Jose Romero, and John Little.

45. Interviews with Sonny Montes and Jose Romero; Gamboa, "El Movimiento," 56.

46. Jose Romero interviews.

47. Sonny Montes interviews.

48. Sonny Montes interviews; Sonny Montes interviews by Noreen Saltveit.

49. Ivo Bauman to Al Ullman, Sept. 11, 1974; Sonny Montes to Fernando C. de Baca, Sept. 9, 1974; Montes to Roberto Olivas, Sept. 16, 1974, all in AU/208/18; William Paulus to Benedictine Sisters, Oct. 15, 1974, AU/208/15; OS, Oct. 10, 1974, sec. 1, 1.

50. CJ, Oct. 10, 1974, sec. 2, 17; OR, Oct. 11, 1974, sec. 1, 20.

51. "Additional Notes of Site Visit of Dr. J. Bemis," Oct. 15, 1974, in "Materials on Colegio Cesar Chavez Eligibility," Jan. 23, 1975, AU/208/16; interviews with Joseph Gallegos and Sonny Montes; affidavit of James Bemis, July 6, 1977, CCC/NASC-CR, 265–66.

52. Guidelines for Institutional Eligibility for Federal Education Programs, U.S. Office of Education, ca. 1973, a copy of which can be found in AU/208/16; interviews with Sonny Montes and Joseph Gallegos.

53. [Joseph] Gallegos to Terrel Bell, Oct. 15, 1974, in "Materials on Colegio Cesar Chavez Eligibility," Jan. 23, 1975, AU/208/16; interviews with Sonny Montes and Joseph Gallegos.

54. John R. Proffitt to [Joseph] Gallegos, Nov. 6, 1974, "Materials on Colegio Cesar Chavez Eligibility," Jan. 23, 1975, AU/208/16.

55. For example, they included a letter from the state's superintendent of public instruction, Verne Duncan, affirming the Colegio's degree-granting status. "Colegio Cesar Chavez," Duncan asserted, "is still the same corporation as it was in 1965 and the same school as it was in 1920 and earlier." According to Duncan, since Mt. Angel College had been authorized to grant degrees, the Colegio was authorized to do so as well (Verne A. Duncan to [Joseph] Gallegos, Jan. 7, 1974, in "Materials on Colegio Cesar Chavez Eligibility," Jan. 23, 1975, AU/208/16).

56. On the deadline: James Allen to Ernesto Lopez, Oct. 25, 1974, in "Materials on Colegio Cesar Chavez Eligibility," Jan. 23, 1975, AU/208/16; Celedonio Montes and Jose Romero to Al Ullman, Jan. 10, 1975, AU/208/16. In place of the self-study, the Colegio's leaders offered assertions—their own assertions that they were working on the self-study and intended to finish it shortly. They also asked both Bemis and Father Paul Waldschmidt, the president of the University of Portland, who had given them advice about the preparation of the self-study, to write letters to HEW, confirming the fact that work on the self-study was under way and explaining why the Colegio had been unable to produce a self-study earlier. Both men did so. (See Paul E. Waldschmidt to John R. Proffitt, Dec. 4, 1974, and James F. Bemis to John R. Proffitt, Dec. 23, 1974, in "Materials on Colegio Cesar Chavez Eligibility," Jan. 23, 1975, AU/208/16.)

57. [Joseph] Gallegos to John R. Proffitt, Jan. 7, 1975, with enclosures; Celedonio Montes and Jose Romero to Al Ullman, Jan. 10, 1975; and Al Ullman to John Proffitt, Jan. 16, 1975, all in AU/208/16. As the day of the meeting approached, Ullman continued to press HEW to come to a favorable decision. In addition, at Sonny's request, another Oregon congressman, Les AuCoin, wrote several letters to HEW officials in support of the Colegio's efforts to restore its funding eligibility. See, for example, Les AuCoin to John R. Proffitt, Jan. 22, 1975, AU/208/16.

58. On the meeting: *CJ*, Jan. 24, 1975, sec. 2, 13; and Jan. 28, 1975, sec. 2, 9; interviews with Sonny Montes and Joseph Gallegos.

59. *OR*, Jan. 30, 1975, sec. A, 11; *CJ*, Feb. 4, 1975, sec. 1, 1; *OS*, Feb. 5, 1975, sec. 1, 5; Robert Straub to Terrel Bell, Feb. 4, 1975, and Jose Romero to Al Ullman, Feb. 10, 1975, both in AU/208/16; *CJ*, Feb. 21, 1975, sec. 1, 1; Terrel Bell to Al Ullman, Mar. 3, 1975, AU/208/15. Some newspaper accounts initially indicated (incorrectly) that the amount placed in escrow was $200,000.

60. Sonny Montes interview.

61. Ibid.; *CJ*, Mar. 26, 1975, sec. 1, 1; *OR*, Mar. 27, 1975, sec. A, 1, 16.

62. Interviews with Sonny Montes and Jose Romero.

63. This paragraph and the following two are based on interviews with Sonny Montes, Jose Romero, Joseph Gallegos, and Rudy Veliz; Gamboa, "El Movimiento," 56; *SAT*, Apr. 10, 1975, sec. 1, 1; Sept. 4, 1975, sec. 2, 5.

64. On Chavez's problems: Griswold del Castillo and Garcia, *Triumph of Spirit*, 116–38. On Tijerina: Rosales, *Chicano!*, 167–70. On the Brown Berets: Rosales, *Chicano!*, 205–07; Chávez, *"¡Mi Raza Primero!,"* 51–60. On the failure of political organization: Armando Navarro, *La Raza Unida Party: A Chicano Challenge to the U.S. Two-Party Dictatorship* (Philadelphia: Temple University Press, 2000); Chávez, *"¡Mi Raza Primero!,"* 80–97; Vigil, *Crusade for Justice*, 160–305; and Gutiérrez, *Chicano Militant*, 215–41.

65. Aldon D. Morris, *The Origins of the Civil Rights Movement: Black Communities Organizing for Change* (New York: Free Press, 1984), 120–38; Martinez, *Mexican-Origin People*, 178–80.

66. Sonny Montes interviews.

67. *CJ*, Mar. 26, 1975, sec. 1, 1; *OS*, Mar. 27, 1975, sec. 1, 1; *CJ*, Mar. 27, 1975, sec. 2, 9; *SAT*, Mar. 27, 1975, sec. 1, 3; press conference release, Mar. 26, 1975, enclosure in Colegio's request for support, Mar. 31, 1975, AU/208/15.

68. *CJ*, Mar. 27, 1975, sec. 2, 9; *OS*, Mar. 28, 1975, sec. 4, 36; *OR*, Mar. 30, 1975, sec. A, 22.

69. Colegio's request for support, Mar. 31, 1975, AU/208/15.

70. Jose Romero interviews.

71. Sonny Montes interview; Sonny Montes interview by Noreen Saltveit. Sonny also recalls one incident that was discussed in the Oregon press. Fairly early in the Colegio's struggle with HUD, a newspaper reported that an FBI agent had stopped a car full of Mexican Americans from California just outside the town of Mt. Angel and arrested one of its occupants, who had an outstanding warrant issued against him. The implication of the newspaper account was that the arrested man was associated with the Colegio. Sonny had never seen the fellow in his life and was sure that he had no connection to

the Colegio. "What would an FBI agent be doing right outside Mt. Angel?" Sonny asked rhetorically.

72. This paragraph and the next are based on Jose Romero interviews. On minority hiring in the FBI: Federal Bureau of Investigation, *FBI History*, section titled "Aftermath of Watergate," http://www.fbi.gov/libref/historic/history/text.htm (accessed July 21, 2010).

73. *CJ*, Mar. 27, 1975, sec. 2, 9; Apr. 1, 1975, sec. 1, 1.

74. "Support Colegio Cesar Chavez" leaflet, attachment to the Colegio's letter requesting support, Mar. 31, 1975, AU/208/15; *OS*, Apr. 26, 1975, sec. 1, 1, 12; *OR*, Apr. 26, 1975, sec. D, 5.

75. On Willner's proposal: Sonny Montes to Diane Armpriest, ca. Apr. 21, 1975, and Robert Straub to Al Ullman, Apr. 29, 1975, AU/208/15; *OS*, Apr. 26, 1975, sec. 1, 12. On negotiations: *CJ*, Apr. 28, 1975, sec. 1, 1; *OS*, Apr. 29, 1975, sec. 1, 2; *OR*, Apr. 29, 1975, sec. A, 1; *CJ*, May 5, 1975, sec. 1, 1; *OS*, May 6, 1975, sec. 1, 1, 18.

76. *CJ*, May 6, 1975, sec. 1, 1; May 8, 1975, sec. 1, 1; *OS*, May 8, 1975, sec. 2, 19; *OR*, May 8, 1975, sec. B, 1.

77. *OS*, May 10, 1975, sec. 1, 8; May 14, 1975, sec. 1, 1, 17; *CJ*, May 14, 1975, sec. 2, 25; *OR*, May 14, 1975, sec. E, 4; May 17, 1975, sec. A, 8; June 19, 1975, sec. A, 1, and sec. B, 2; and Al Ullman to Robert Straub, May 19, 1975, AU/208/15.

78. Interviews with Sonny Montes and Joseph Gallegos; Sonny Montes interview by Noreen Saltveit.

79. *CJ*, Apr. 23, 1975, sec. 2, 13; *OR*, May 17, 1975, sec. A, 8; *SAT*, June 19, 1975, sec. 1, 3.

80. *OR*, June 8, 1975, sec. C, 1. HEW's decision to deny accreditation to the Colegio was announced in mid-May 1975. At the time, Sonny and several colleagues from the Colegio were in Washington, D.C., meeting with HUD officials. Unhappy about the rejection, Sonny asked to speak to the committee and a meeting was arranged. Sonny appealed to the committee to reconsider, but the chairman flatly turned him down. "They were extremely rude to us," Sonny recalled in an interview. Incensed, he told the chairman that, despite the setback, he was sure that the Colegio was going to regain its eligibility for federal funding. The chairman's response was to laugh at him.

81. [Joseph] Gallegos to James Bemis, Apr. 28, 1975; James Bemis to Celedonio Montes and Jose Romero, May 5, 1975; and James Bemis to Charles J. Flora and Theodore Murguia, May 5, 1975, exhibits E, F, and G in testimony of James F. Bemis, Aug. 8, 1977, CCC/NASC-CR, 539–43; Sonny Montes interviews; Sonny Montes interview by Noreen Saltveit.

82. Charles J. Flora and Theodore I. Murguia, Candidate for Accreditation Report—Colegio Cesar Chavez, June [4,] 1975, exhibit H in testimony of James F. Bemis, Aug. 8, 1977, CCC/NASC-CR, 544–50.

83. Interviews with Sonny Montes and Jose Romero; testimony of Charles J. Flora, Aug. 8, 1977, CCC/NASC-CR, 413.

84. Ibid.; testimony of Paul E. Waldschmidt, Aug. 8, 1977, Shirley B. Gordon, Aug. 8, 1977, Robert J. Coonrod, Aug. 8, 1977, Arthur Kreisman, Aug. 8, 1977, Robert G. Leonard, Aug. 8, 1977, and Ellis S. McCune, Aug. 10, 1977, CCC/NASC-CR, 470–71, 478–79, 495–96, 617–18, 673–74, 735–36; W. H. Cummings to whom it may concern, June 16, 1975, exhibit K in testimony of James F. Bemis, Aug. 8, 1977, CCC/NASC-CR, 557–58.

85. On the commission's discussion: testimony of Charles Flora, Aug. 8, 1977; Paul E. Waldschmidt, Aug. 8, 1977; Shirley B. Gordon, Aug. 8, 1977; Robert K. Thomas, Aug. 8, 1977; Robert W. Coonrod, Aug. 8, 1977; James F. Bemis, Aug. 8, 1977; Arthur Kreisman, Aug. 8, 1977; Janet S. Hay, Aug. 8, 1977; Fred L. Esvelt, Aug. 8, 1977; James L. Taylor, Aug. 8, 1977; Roy E. Huffman, Aug. 8, 1977; Robert G. Leonard, Aug. 8, 1977; Barbara S. Iten, Aug. 8, 1977; and Ellis S. McCune, Aug. 10, 1977, CCC/NASC-CR, 413, 470–71, 478–79, 483–84, 495–97, 509–10, 617–18, 635–36, 652–53, 660–61, 667, 673–74, 680–81, 735–36.

86. *CJ*, June 18, 1975, sec. 1, 1; *OR*, June 19, 1971, sec. A, 1; sec. B, 2; Jose Romero interview.

87. Sonny Montes interview.

Under Siege

1. *CJ*, Sept. 11, 1975, sec. 2, 14.

2. *OR*, Sept. 14, 1975, sec. C, 5.

3. Ramon Ramirez interview; Stephen, Story of PCUN, 11–34.

4. On Amaya: Jimmy Amaya interview; *OR*, Oct. 16, 1973, sec. 1, 25; Sept. 14, 1975, sec. C, 5.

5. *CJ*, Sept. 11, 1975, sec. 2, 14; *OS*, Oct. 18, 1975, sec. 2, 18.

6. Colegio Cesar Chavez, Annual Report to Northwest Association of Schools and Colleges, Feb. 24, 1976, exhibit N in affidavit of James F. Bemis, July 6, 1977, CCC/NASC-CR, 327–33; OJ, Nov. 20, 1976, sec. 1, 3; CJ, Mar. 2, 1977, sec. A, 1; OS, Oct. 25, 1977, sec. A, 1; Maria Luisa Alaniz interview.

7. *OS*, June 19, 1975, sec. 1, 1, 11; *OR*, June 21, 1975, sec. A, 14; *CJ*, June 21, 1975, sec. 1, 1; July 23, 1975, sec. 1, 1; *OR*, July 25, 1975, sec. A, 11.

8. Initially, a procedural obstacle stood in the way of negotiations between HUD and the Colegio: the campus first had to be put up for auction so that the government could acquire the title. Although theoretically the auction might result in the sale of the campus to a third party, it was generally thought that the only bidder would be the government. Once the government acquired the title to the campus, the college and HUD would be free to work out an arrangement. In July 1975, the auction was held at the Marion County courthouse. As expected, the federal government submitted the only bid, an offer to purchase the Colegio for slightly more than $1 million. On the auction: *CJ*, July 23, 1975, sec. 1, 1.

9. On the redemption period: *SAT*, May 20, 1976, sec. 2. On the short-term lease: *OS*, Sept. 3, 1976, sec. A, 1; *OR*, Sept. 3, 1976, sec. A, 1.

10. *OR*, Sept. 14, 1975, sec. C, 5; *OS*, Oct. 18, 1975, sec. 2, 18.

11. Robert E. Elliott, memorandum to James L. Young, June 18, 1976, and James L. Young to Celedonio Montes, Aug. 31, 1976, both in AU/208/15.

12. *CJ*, May 14, 1976, sec. A, 1.

13. Sonny Montes interview.

14. The documentary record appears to support Sonny on this point. In a June 1975 letter sent to Sonny officially informing him that the Northwest Association had awarded candidacy status to the Colegio, Bemis wrote not a word about the college being obligated to provide an audited statement, despite the fact that he mentioned other future obligations of candidates for accreditation, such as the filing of an annual report. See James F. Bemis to

Celedonio Montes Jr., June 23, 1975, exhibit L in James F. Bemis testimony, Aug. 8, 1977, CCC/NASC-CR, 559–60.

15. On the views of the commissioners, see the testimony of Charles Flora, Aug. 8, 1977; Paul E. Waldschmidt, Aug. 8, 1977; Shirley B. Gordon, Aug. 8, 1977; Robert K. Thomas, Aug. 8, 1977; Robert W. Coonrod, Aug. 8, 1977; James F. Bemis, Aug. 8, 1977; Arthur Kreisman, Aug. 8, 1977; Janet S. Hay, Aug. 8, 1977; Fred L. Esvelt, Aug. 8, 1977; James L. Taylor, Aug. 8, 1977; Roy E. Huffman, Aug. 8, 1977; Robert G. Leonard, Aug. 8, 1977; Barbara S. Iten, Aug. 8, 1977; and Ellis S. McCune, Aug. 10, 1977, CCC/NASC-CR, 413, 470–71, 478–79, 483–84, 495–97, 509–10, 617–18, 635–36, 652–53, 660–61, 667, 673–74, 680–81, 735–36. On Cummings's letter: W. H. Cummings to whom it may concern, June 16, 1975, exhibit K in testimony of James F. Bemis, Aug. 8, 1977, CCC/NASC-CR, 557–58. The commissioner quoted in this paragraph is Paul E. Waldschmidt (CCC/NASC-CR, 471).

16. Testimony of Robert W. Coonrod, Aug. 8, 1977, and Arthur Kresiman, Aug. 8, 1977, CCC/NASC-CR, 497, 619. On the requirement to file reports: James F. Bemis to Celedonio Montes Jr., June 23, 1975, exhibit L in testimony of James F. Bemis, Aug. 8, 1977, CCC/NASC-CR, 559–60.

17. James F. Bemis to Celedonio Montes, Jan. 26, 1976, exhibit M in testimony of James F. Bemis, Aug. 8, 1977, CCC/NASC-CR, 561.

18. Sonny Montes interview.

19. CJ, Sept. 11, 1975, sec. 2, 14; testimony of Stephen M. Tatone, Aug. 15, 1977, and testimony of Celedonio Montes, Aug. 15, 1977, CCC/NASC-CR, 773–74, 781–82; courtroom testimony of Stephen M. Tatone, Aug. 18, 1977, CCC/NASC-TP, 87–88, 91; Sonny Montes interviews.

20. Testimony of Celedonio Montes, Aug. 15, 1977, CCC/NASC-CR, 782; Celedonio Montes and Jose M. Romero to James F. Bemis, Mar. 1, 1976, exhibit N-2 in testimony of James F. Bemis, Aug. 8, 1977, CCC/NASC-CR, 569.

21. Testimony of Stephen M. Tatone, Aug. 15, 1977, CCC/NASC-CR, 774.

22. James F. Bemis to Celedonio Montes and Jose M. Romero, Mar. 12, 1976, and May 12, 1976, exhibits N-3 and O-1 in testimony of James F. Bemis, Aug. 8, 1977, CCC/NASC-CR, 570–71.

23. Celedonio Montes and Jose Romero to James F. Bemis, May 17, 1976, and Bemis to Montes and Romero, May 21, 1976 (with a handwritten notation by Bemis on his carbon copy, dated June 4, 1976), exhibits O-2 and O-3 in testimony of James F. Bemis, Aug. 8, 1977, CCC/NASC-CR, 572–73; testimony of Celedonio Montes, Aug. 15, 1977, CCC/NASC-CR, 780; Sonny Montes interview.

24. Northwest Association of Schools and Colleges, Agenda for Closed Session of Summer Meeting, June 16–18, 1976, exhibit E in affidavit of Barbara S. Iten, July 6, 1977; testimony of James F. Bemis, Aug. 8, 1977; and testimony of Ellis. E. McCune, Aug. 10, 1977, CCC/NASC-CR, 234–36, 512–15, 736–38.

25. Testimony of Charles J. Flora, Aug. 8, 1977; and Northwest Association of Schools and Colleges, Summer Meeting Minutes, ca. June 18, 1977, exhibit G in Flora testimony; testimony of James F. Bemis, Aug. 8, 1977;

testimony of Arthur Kresiman, Aug. 8, 1977; testimony of Ellis E. McCune, Aug. 10, 1977, all in CCC/NASC-CR, 414–15, 466, 619, 736–38.

26. James F. Bemis to Celedonio Montes Jr., June 22, 1976, exhibit P in testimony of James F. Bemis, Aug. 8, 1977, CCC/NASC-CR, 574; Sonny Montes interview.

27. Interviews with Maria Luisa Alaniz and Joseph Gallegos.

28. Interviews with Sonny Montes and Francisco Garcia; Sonny Montes interview by Noreen Saltveit.

29. Interviews with Jose Romero and Kathy Romero.

30. *CJ*, Aug. 9, 1976, sec. A, 1; Aug. 24, 1976, sec. A, 1; *OS*, Sept. 3, 1976, sec. A, 1; *OR*, Sept. 3, 1976, sec. A, 1; James L. Young to Celedonio Montes, Aug. 31, 1976, AU/208/15.

31. *OR*, Aug. 27, 1976, sec. B, 1; Sept. 3, 1976, sec. A, 1; *OJ*, Sept. 4, 1976, sec. 1, 3; *SJ*, Sept. 11, 1976, sec. A, 4; *CJ*, Sept. 20, 1976, sec. A, 1; Sonny Montes interview.

32. Interviews with Sonny Montes and Jose Romero; Sonny Montes, "Urgent Appeal," ca. October 1976 (which includes copies of Al Ullman to Carla Hills, Sept. 22, 1976, and Jim Weaver to Carla Hills, Oct. 6, 1976), AU/208/15.

33. *OS*, Dec. 3, 1976, sec. A, 14; *SAT/MAN*, Dec. 12, 1976, sec. 1, 2; *OR*, Nov. 3, 1977, sec. B, 2; *OS*, Nov. 3, 1977, sec. A, 1, 2; Nov. 4, 1977, sec. C, 1; Dec. 6, 1977, sec. B, 1.

34. *OR*, Sept. 21, 1976, sec. A, 1; Al Ullman to Carla Hills, Sept. 22, 1976, AU/208/15; *OS*, Sept. 24, 1976, sec. A, 11; *CJ*, Oct. 13, 1976, sec. A, 1; *OS*, Nov. 17, 1976, sec. A, 2; Nov. 30, 1976, sec. C, 1; *OR*, Dec. 1, 1976, sec. D, 1; Sonny Montes interview.

35. Courtroom testimony of Stephen M. Tatone, Aug. 18, 1977, CCC/NASC-TP, 87–93; testimony of Stephen M. Tatone, Aug. 15, 1977, and Celedonio Montes, Aug. 15, 1977, CCC/NASC-CR, 774–75, 780–81; Sonny Montes interview.

36. Celedonio Montes to James F. Bemis, Oct. 1, 1976, and Aldrich, Kilbride & Naas, Colegio Cesar Chavez, Balance Sheets, June 30, 1975, June 30, 1976, and Aug. 31, 1976, exhibits Q and T-1 in testimony of James F. Bemis, Aug. 8, 1977, CCC/NASC-CR, 575, 578–600; Sonny Montes interview.

37. James F. Bemis to Celedonio Montes, Oct. 11, 1976, and Nov. 8, 1976, exhibits R and S in testimony of James F. Bemis, Aug. 8, 1977, CCC/NASC-CR, 576–77. It seems that, in the period since the Colegio had won accreditation status, the commission had changed its way of doing business, due primarily to what had transpired in Twin Falls. Up to then, the commission had set no limit on the size of delegations sent by schools applying for accreditation or candidacy status. Schools had sent at most two or three representatives. At Twin Falls, however, Sonny and six others had entered the meeting room. The commission decided to pass a new rule, setting a limit on the size of delegations in order to avoid a repetition of that experience.

38. Courtroom testimony of Celedonio Montes, Aug. 18, 1977, CCC/NASC-TP, 33–35; testimony of James F. Bemis, Aug. 8, 1977, Barbara S. Iten, Aug. 8, 1977, and Celedonio Montes, Aug. 15, 1977, CCC/NASC-CR, 518–20, 682–83; 782–84; Sonny Montes interview.

39. Courtroom testimony of Celedonio Montes, Aug. 18, 1977, CCC/ NASC-TP, 35–37; testimony of Celedonio Montes, Aug. 15, 1977, CCC/ NASC-CR, 784; Sonny Montes interview.

40. *OS*, Nov. 30, 1976, sec. C, 1; Sonny Montes interview.

41. *OS*, Nov. 30, 1976, sec. C, 1; *SAT/MAN*, Dec. 2, 1977, sec. 1, 2.

42. *OR*, Dec. 1, 1976, sec. D, 1; *OS/CJ*, Dec. 5, 1976, sec. A, 1, 15.

43. *OS*, Dec. 7, 1976, sec. C, 1; *CJ*, Dec. 7, 1976, sec. B, 1; *OR*, Dec. 7, 1976, sec. C, 1.

44. Courtroom testimony of Celedonio Montes, Aug. 18, 1977, CCC/ NASC-TP, 36–37; testimony of Robert W. Coonrod, Aug. 8, 1977, CCC/ NASC-CR, 498–99.

45. Courtroom testimony of Celedonio Montes, Aug. 18, 1977, CCC/ NASC-TP, 38–39; testimony of Robert W. Coonrod, Aug. 8, 1977; Janet S. Hay, Aug. 8, 1977; and Ellis E. McCune, Aug. 10, 1977, CCC/NASC-CR, 499–501, 637, 738–40.

46. Don Willner interview; affidavit of Kent L. Aldrich, June 16, 1977; and testimony of Robert W. Coonrod, Aug. 8, 1977; Janet S. Hay, Aug. 8, 1977; and Stephen M. Tatone, Aug. 15, 1977, CCC/NASC-CR, 25–26, 501, 637–38, 775–76.

47. Testimony of James F. Bemis, Aug. 8, 1977, CCC/NASC-CR, 523–24; *OS*, Dec. 8, 1976, sec. A, 1.

48. *SAT/MAN*, Jan. 27, 1977, sec. 1, 3; *OJ*, Feb. 7, 1977, sec. 1, 4; *OR*, July 1, 1977, sec. A, 11.

49. On Veliz: interviews with Rudy Veliz and Ramon Ramirez; affidavit of Betty Rademaker, June 16, 1977, CCC/NASC-CR, 31–34. On discussions about graduation ceremonies: *OS*, Jan. 3, 1977, sec. D, 1; *OS/CJ*, Jan. 22, 1977, sec. D, 6; Feb. 19, 1977, sec. A, 5.

50. Maria Luisa Alaniz interview.

51. Ibid.

52. My source for this golf story: Jose Romero interview.

53. Sonny Montes interview.

54. Interviews with Sonny Montes, Jose Romero, and Don Willner; Sonny Montes interview by Noreen Saltveit; *CJ*, Apr. 20, 1977, sec. B, 2; *OS/CJ*, Apr. 23, 1977, sec. A, 4; Celedonio Montes and Jose Garcia to Don Willner, May 9, 1977; enclosure in Willner to Salvador Ramirez, Oct. 4, 1977, JPL.

55. James F. Bemis to Celedonio Montes, Dec. 14, 1976; Celedonio Montes to George E. Erickson, Dec. 16, 1976; Special Board of Review to Erickson, Mar. 30, 1977; and Erickson to Montes, Apr. 4, 1977, exhibits U, W, X, and Z, in testimony of James F. Bemis, Aug. 8, 1977, CCC/NASC-CR, 601–602, 605–12, 615.

56. Interviews with Sonny Montes and Don Willner; *OS/CJ*, Apr. 23, 1977, sec. A, 4.

57. Complaint of Colegio Cesar Chavez, June 16, 1977, and Memorandum in Support of Preliminary Injunction, June 16, 1977, CCC/NASC-CR, 1–17, 61–79; *OR*, June 17, 1977, sec. C, 1.

58. Memorandum in Support of Preliminary Injunction, June 16, 1977; affidavit of Celedonio Montes, June 29, 1977; Memorandum of the Northwest Association of Schools and Colleges in Opposition to the Preliminary Injunction, July 5, 1977; and Memorandum of Northwest

Association of Schools and Colleges, July 6, 1977, CCC/NASC-CR, 61–79, 100–102, 178–90, 197–203.

59. Preliminary Injunction Order, July 8, 1977, CCC/NASC-CR, 383–84; *OR*, July 7, 1977, sec. B, 2; *OS*, July 8, 1977, sec. C, 1.

60. On the procedures adopted in collecting the testimony of witnesses: James F. Bemis to Paul E. Waldschmidt, July 21, 1977, and Paul E. Waldschmidt to James F. Bemis, July 25, 1977, PEW/CCC.

61. James F. Bemis to Paul E. Waldschmidt, July 21, 1977, and Paul E. Waldschmidt to James F. Bemis, July 25, 1977, PEW/CCC.

62. Trial Memorandum of Plaintiff, Aug. 17, 1977, CCC/NASC-CR, 843–48.

63. Transcript of Proceedings, Aug. 18, 1977, CCC/NASC-TP, 6–7, 21–22, 138–42.

64. Opinion of Robert Belloni, Aug. 26, 1977, and Judgment of Robert Belloni, Sept. 2, 1977, CCC/NASC-CR, 899–903, 969–70. Belloni also specified that the association would be required to give the Colegio ninety days' advance notice of the hearing and a clear statement of the charges against it, and that any new hearing, unlike the past one, would have to provide adequate safeguards of the college's rights.

65. Interviews with Sonny Montes and John Little.

66. *OS*, Dec. 14, 1976, sec. A, 2; *OR*, Dec. 14, 1976, sec. B, 1; *OS*, Dec. 16, 1976, sec. A, 1, 8.

67. *CJ*, Mar. 2, 1977, sec. A, 1; *OS*, Mar. 3, 1977, sec. A, 5; Sonny Montes interview. On the MCHA not bidding: *OS*, Dec. 16, 1976, sec. A, 1, 6.

68. *OS*, Mar. 3, 1977, sec. A, 5.

69. On the new Colegio proposal: Celedonio Montes Jr. to Patricia Harris, Feb. 11, 1977, AU/208/15; *OS*, Mar. 3, 1977, sec. A, 5; *OS/CJ*, Apr. 2, 1977, sec. A, 8. On the MCHA: *CJ*, Oct. 21, 1977, sec. C, 1.

70. HUD's interest in a sale to the MCHA: *OS*, Oct. 25, 1977, sec. A, 2; Oct. 26, 1977, sec. A, 7. Harris: *CJ*, June 15, 1977, sec. C, 2. HUD's exploration of various options: Ruth T. Prokop, Memorandum to Lawrence B. Simons, June 9, 1977, and Edward W. Norton, Memorandum to W. K. Cameron, June 14, 1977, both in AU/208/17. In discussing the Colegio's purchase proposal, for example, Prokop pointed to an earlier opinion by HUD's general counsel that stated: "No legal authority exists for departing from the requirement that disposition [of the property] must be made on the basis you determine would have the greatest likelihood of minimizing loss to the Government."

71. *OS*, June 14, 1977, sec. A, 7; *CJ*, June 15, 1977, sec. C, 2; *OS*, June 16, 1977, sec. C, 5.

72. Memorandum from Lawrence Simons to W. K. Cameron, Lawrence Simons, etc., July 12, 1977, and W. K. Cameron to Marilyn Melkonian, Aug. 17, 1977, exhibits in "Amended and Supplemental Answer, Affirmative Defenses, Request for Declaratory and Injunctive Relief and Demand for Jury Trial of Defendant Colegio Cesar Chavez," Apr. 25, 1978, in *U.S.A. vs. Colegio Cesar Chavez* (District Court for the State of Oregon, County of Marion), a document found in AU/208/17.

73. On graduation ceremonies: *OS*, July 1, 1977, sec. C, 1; *CJ*, July 1, 1977, sec. B, 2; *OR*, July 1, 1977, sec. A, 11. On Sonny's thoughts about the

job possibility and his discussions with Garcia: interviews with Sonny Montes and Francisco Garcia by the author.

74. Sonny Montes interviews; *OS*, Sept. 21, 1977, sec. A, 1; *OR*, Oct. 7, 1977, sec. C, 3.

75. Interviews with Sonny Montes and Francisco Garcia; Sonny Montes interview by Noreen Saltveit; *OR*, Oct. 7, 1977, sec. C, 3. On Ramirez: Maldonado, *Colegio*, 42.

76. Sonny Montes interviews; Sonny Montes interview by Noreen Saltveit.

77. Lawrence B. Simons to Celedonio Montes, Sept. 20, 1977, AU/208/17; *OJ*, Sept. 21, 1977, sec. 1, 1; *OR*, Sept. 22, 1977, sec. B, 9. On Roybal delivering the letter on Sept. 20: Don Willner to Patricia Harris, Oct. 6, 1977, AU/208/17.

78. *OS*, Oct. 4, 1977, sec. C, 1; *OR*, Oct. 7, 1977, sec. C, 3.

79. Interviews with Jose Romero and Sonny Montes.

80. *CJ*, Oct. 21, 1977, sec. C, 1; *OS*, Oct. 21, 1977, sec. A, 1; *OS/CJ*, Oct. 22, 1977, sec. A, 1, 2; Jimmy Amaya interview.

81. *OS*, Oct. 28, 1977, sec. A, 1, 7; *OR*, Oct. 28, 1977, sec. B, 1; *SJ*, Nov. 5, 1977, sec. B, 8.

82. *CJ*, Oct. 20, 1977, sec. C, 1; *OR*, Oct. 22, 1977, sec. A, 10; *OS/CJ*, Oct. 23, 1977, sec. C, 1; *CJ*, Oct. 24, 1977, sec. A, 1.

83. *OS*, Oct. 25, 1977, sec. A, 1, and sec. C, 1; Oct. 27, 1977, sec. A, 7; Nov. 9, 1977, sec. B, 1; Nov. 19, 1977, sec. A, 1. Barber agreed to the postponement only after the Colegio had posted a $50,000 bond, secured by the personal assets of nine Colegio supporters. One was Sonny.

84. *CJ*, Dec. 9, 1977, sec. A, 1; *OS/CJ*, Dec. 10, 1977, sec. C, 1; *OR*, Dec. 15, 1977, sec. D, 1; Maldonado, *Colegio*, 76–77.

85. Opinion of Supreme Court of the State of Oregon in *United States National Bank of Oregon and Patricia Harris vs. Colegio Cesar Chavez*, Feb. 14, 1978, found in AU/208/17; *CJ*, Feb. 14, 1978, sec. A, 1.

86. Don Willner to Al Ullman, Feb. 14, 1978, Feb. 28, 1978, and Mar. 1, 1978; Salvador Ramirez to Al Ullman, Feb. 15, 1978; and Don Willner to Patricia Harris, Mar. 3, 1978, all in AU/208/17; *SAT/MAN*, Feb. 16, 1978, sec. 1, 4. The other favorable development, the Colegio's suddenly improved financial situation, is discussed in the next section of this chapter.

87. Interviews with Sonny Montes and Don Willner.

88. Actually, on Feb. 1, 1978, Salvador Ramirez had written to HUD Secretary Patricia Harris, informing her that Chavez would be in Washington, D.C., between March 20 and March 22 and suggesting that a new round of HUD-Colegio negotiations involving Chavez be held then to discuss a proposal Ramirez had come up with. At the time, HUD was playing hardball with the Colegio and dismissed the suggestion. Harris likely never saw the letter. The situation changed later in the month when HUD lost its court case with the Colegio and Ullman put pressure on it to hold negotiations. At that point, HUD was more willing to talk and intermediaries were able to arrange the meeting. But those intermediaries evidently didn't convey the information to HUD's negotiating team that Chavez would be a member of the college's delegation. My explanation is based on my interviews with Montes and Willner and documents in the Ullman papers, such as Salvador Ramirez to Patricia Harris, Feb. 1, 1978, AU/208/17.

89. Interviews with Sonny Montes and Don Willner; Sonny Montes interview by Noreen Saltveit.

90. On the meeting with Chavez: Sonny Montes interviews; Sonny Montes interviews by Noreen Saltveit. On the travails of the Centro: *OS*, July 21, 1973, sec. 1, 1; Aug. 15, 1973, sec. 1, 5; Nov. 7, 1973, sec. 1, 5; *CJ*, Nov. 22, 1973, sec. 2, 23; *OS*, Mar. 13, 1975, sec. 1, 8; May 9, 1975, sec. 1, 5. Regarding Collazo's plan: Colegio Cesar Chavez, Minutes of Board of Trustees Meeting, Mar. 10, 1978, and Pete Collazo to Jose Garcia, Mar. 17, 1978, enclosure in Don Willner to Patricia Harris, Mar. 20, 1978, JPL.

91. Sonny Montes interview; Sonny Montes interview by Noreen Saltveit.

92. Interviews with Sonny Montes and Don Willner; Sonny Montes interview by Noreen Saltveit; Don Willner to Al Ullman, Mar. 24, 1978, AU/208/17.

93. Don Willner interview.

94. Ibid.

95. Sonny Montes interviews; Sonny Montes interview by Noreen Saltveit.

96. On the terms of the HUD proposal: Pete Collazo to Jose Garcia, Mar. 17, 1978, and Don Willner to Patricia Harris, Mar. 20, 1978, both in JPL; *OS*, Apr. 13, 1978, sec. A, 1, 2. Some money for the down payment made by the Colegio was to come from two donations promised the school (one from the Tektronix Corporation of Portland and the other from the Presbyterian Synod). On the donations: *OS*, July 5, 1978, sec. A, 1, 2.

97. Interviews with Sonny Montes and Don Willner; Don Willner to Al Ullman, Mar. 24, 1978, AU/208/17.

98. On Centro approval: Agreement between Colegio Cesar Chavez and Centro Chicano Cultural, Apr. 10, 1978, AU/208/17; *OS*, Apr. 13, 1978, sec. A, 1, 2. On the sale of the Gervais property: Don Willner to Marilyn Melkonian and Ed Norton, May 5, 1978, with attached documents (including a copy of the land sale contract, dated April 24, 1978), AU/208/17. HUD-Colegio agreement: *OR*, July 5, 1978, sec. A, 1; *OS*, July 5, 1978, sec. A, 1, 2.

The Colegio After Sonny, Sonny After the Colegio

1. By design, this account of the college's demise is brief. Although it is tempting to write more, since the details of the story are so extraordinary (the battles between the various players, the activities of Gonzales), I have resisted the temptation for two simple reasons. First, it would be hard to make the case that, except for the interesting details, the story merits extended treatment since enrollment at the Colegio had dropped by 1978 to fewer than 20 students. Second, the book is not about the college alone, but about Sonny Montes, the birth of a community, and a social movement.

2. *OS*, Sept. 26, 1978, sec. C, 2.

3. General Fund Bank Account, Colegio Cesar Chavez, Aug. 31, 1978, attachment to Colegio Cesar Chavez, Minutes of Board of Trustees meeting, Oct. 20, 1978; Ruben A. Flores to [Roberto] Gutierrez, Aug. 29, 1978; Colegio Cesar Chavez, Minutes of Board of Trustees meeting, Sept. 8, 1978; Salvador Ramirez, Chief Administrator's Report, July 6, 1979; Joan Cook to Board, Dec. 20, 1979, all in JPL. Also see *SAT/MAN*, July 8, 1978, sec. 1, 1, 8.

4. Colegio Cesar Chavez, Minutes of Board of Trustees meeting, Feb. 13, 1979, JPL; Sonny Montes interview; Maldonado, *Colegio*, 80–81.

5. On Gonzales's appointment: *OR*, Nov. 9, 1975, sec. C, 11. On the academic changes: Peter de Garmo, memorandum to Colegio Board, Aug. 7, 1979; Colegio Cesar Chavez, Student Handbook, ca. March 1980, JPL; interviews with Sonny Montes and Jose Romero. On the firing: Maldonado, *Colegio*, 80–81. On enrollment: *OS*, Dec. 12, 1979, sec. B, 1; *OR*, Mar. 16, 1981, sec. B, 1.

6. Interviews with Sonny Montes and Jose Romero; Sonny Montes interview by Noreen Saltveit; Gamboa, "*El Movimiento*," 57.

7. On the search: Reymundo Marin to Jose Garcia, Dec. 18, 1979; Jose Romero to Reymundo Marin, May 8, 1980; Felipe Sanchez Paris to Board of Directors, June 20, 1980, all in JPL. On Gonzales's allies on the board: Colegio Cesar Chavez, Board of Trustees Meeting, Agenda, May 16, 1980, JPL; Gutiérrez, *Chicano Militant*, 273–74; Maldonado, *Colegio*, 83–88.

8. Agenda of the Concerned Community for Colegio Cesar Chavez, ca. March 1981, JPL; Maldonado, *Colegio*, 87. On earlier criticism of Gonzales: *SJ*, Dec. 12, 1980, sec. A, 1.

9. Maldonado, *Colegio*, 87–88; interviews with Sonny Montes, Jose Romero, and John Little.

10. James F. Bemis to Salvador Ramirez and Peter de Garmo, June 19, 1979; and Salvador Ramirez, Chief Administrator's Report, July 6, 1979, JPL.

11. *OR*, Mar. 16, 1981, sec. B, 1; and June 3, 1981, sec. A, 17; *SJ*, June 4, 1981, sec. A, 1.

12. *SJ*, June 30, 1981, sec. A, 1; *OR*, June 30, 1981, sec. B, 1; Maldonado, *Colegio*, 87; Irma Gonzales to "Friend" [of the Colegio], June 30, 1981, JPL.

13. On the unsuccessful appeal: Gonzales to "Friend," June 30, 1981, JPL; *SJ*, July 6, 1981, sec. B, 1; July 21, 1981, sec. B, 3; Aug. 4, 1981, sec. B, 3; Oct. 1, 1981, sec. C, 10. On fall 1981 enrollment: *SJ*, Oct. 9, 1981, sec. B, 1; *OR*, Oct. 25, 1981, sec. A, 33. On Gonzales's change in title: Maldonado, *Colegio*, 87–88. On Feb. 1982 enrollment: *OR*, Feb. 2, 1982, sec. B, 1. On developments in 1983 and 1985: *SJ*, Apr. 18, 1983, sec. A, 1; Mar. 17, 1985, sec. A, 1, and sec. C, 1; *OR*, Apr. 21, 1983, sec. A, 19.

14. *OR*, Dec. 19, 1985, sec. C, 7; *SJ*, Dec. 19, 1985, sec. A, 1.

15. Don Willner interview.

16. Ibid.

17. Not all social scientists privilege winning social movements in their studies. Sociologists and political scientists tend to look at losers, too, apparently operating on the belief that there is something to be learned from the typical as well as the exceptional.

18. Sonny Montes interview.

19. On the Center for Bilingual Education: Northwest Regional Educational Laboratory, *Northwest Report*, May 1978, 1; April 1979, 2; Oct. 1980, 1; *Annual Report to Members*, 1975, 17; 1976, 19, 30; 1977–78, 4, 10, 13; 1978–79, 10–11, 22, 35; 1979–80, 11, 22, 34; 1980–81, 1, 19, 43; interviews with Sonny Montes, Jose Romero, and Francisco Garcia. On Interface: interviews with Sonny Montes and Francisco Garcia.

20. Interviews with Sonny Montes and Francisco Garcia; Northwest Regional Educational Laboratory, *Annual Report to Members*, 1976, 19; 1977–78, 4.

21. Interviews with Francisco Garcia, Jose Romero, and Sonny Montes; Sonny Montes interview by Noreen Saltveit.

22. The designator "Hispanic," referring to all Americans of Spanish cultural background, was first used by the U.S. Bureau of the Census in 1970 and came into common usage later in the decade, when all U.S. government agencies and programs were required to use the term in the collection and presentation of data on race and ethnicity. In Oregon in 1990, approximately 80 percent of all Hispanics were Mexican-origin people.

23. Bureau of the Census, *1980 Census of Population. General Population Characteristics*, vol. 1, chap. B, Part 39 (Oregon), 32; U.S. Bureau of the Census, *1990 Census of Population. Social and Economic Characteristics: Oregon* (Washington, D.C.: Government Printing Office, 1993), 11; Betsy Guzmán, *The Hispanic Population: Census 2000 Brief* (Washington, D.C.: U.S. Census Bureau, 2001), 4.

24. Bureau of the Census, *1990 Census of Population. Social and Economic Characteristics: Oregon*, 70, 71, 75, 77, 78, 84, 102, 114, 121, 126. For valuable overviews of Mexican American/Hispanic social issues in the 1980s and 1990s, see Martinez, *Mexican-Origin People*, and Bean and Tienda, *Hispanic Population*. On Oregon, see Gonzales-Berry and Mendoza, *Mexicanos in Oregon*, 102–73. There are also useful chapters in *Nosotros*, ed. Gamboa and Buan.

25. On the responsibilities of the resource specialists and the evolution of the ESL/bilingual program: Scott Montanaro, "Finding a Role for Bilingualism: Language Minorities in Portland Public Schools, 1975–2005," a prize-winning essay in the University of Oregon Undergraduate Library Research Award Scholarship Competition, 2008, http://hdl.handle. net/1794/2910 (accessed Jan. 3, 2009); interviews with Sonny Montes; and *OR*, Apr. 14, 1986, sec. B, 4. On the number of Hispanic high school students: PPS, 1988 October Enrollment Report, PPS Records Management Office.

In the Elementary and Secondary Education Act of 1968, also known as the Bilingual Education Act, the U.S. Congress had acknowledged for the first time the special needs of "Limited English Proficiency" students in U.S. public schools. Title VII of that act helped to fund school districts around the country in developing programs, including bilingual programs, which assisted those students. After its passage in 1968, the Bilingual Education Act was reauthorized several times, with a host of amendments. At first, Title VII was interpreted largely as a means of redressing civil rights violations, but over time it was used to provide needed services to groups that were not victims of segregation or racial discrimination. To get Title VII funding to support bilingual education programs, school districts were obliged, at periodic intervals, to submit grant proposals to the federal government. In Portland, a small portion of the funding for the ESL/bilingual program came from the federal government in the form of Title VII grants, but most of the money came from the district itself. Relevant sources: Montanaro, "Finding a Role"; Pycior, *LBJ and Mexican Americans*, 184–87; Carmen West interview by the author.

26. This paragraph and the next are based on my Sonny Montes interviews and Sonny Montes interviews by Noreen Saltveit. There were 11 high schools in the district at the time. In addition to ten "regular" high schools (Benson, Cleveland, Franklin, Grant, Jefferson, Lincoln, Madison, Marshall, Roosevelt, and Lincoln), there was an alternative high school called Vocational Village. Sonny was responsible for six, and another resource specialist, Judith Garcia-Lilly for the other five. When Garcia-Lilly left, she was replaced by Sylvia Baradas-Everson.

27. Sonny Montes interviews; on one dropout program, *OR*, April 25, 1989, sec. B, 11.

28. Sonny Montes interviews.

29. Interviews with Sonny Montes and Jose Romero; Sonny Montes interview by Noreen Saltveit.

30. Interviews with Sonny Montes, Jose Romero, Yolanda Tavera, and David Martinez by the author; *1995 Annual Conference: October 10, 1995, University of Portland, Chiles Center, Portland, Oregon* (Portland: César E. Chávez Hispanic Student Leadership Conference, 1995), 3; *16th Anniversary Conferencia de Liderazgo* (Portland: César E. Chávez Hispanic Student Leadership Conference, 2006), 2.

31. *1995 Annual Conference; Thirteenth Annual Conferencia de Liderazgo* (Portland: César E. Chávez Hispanic Student Leadership Conference, 2003); *14th Annual César E. Chávez Hispanic Student Leadership Conference* (Portland: César E. Chávez Hispanic Student Leadership Conference, 2004); *15th Annual César E. Chávez Hispanic Student Leadership Conference* (Portland: César E. Chávez Hispanic Student Leadership Conference, 2005); *16th Anniversary Conferencia de Liderazgo.*

32. *Voter's Pamphlet, State of Oregon General Election, November 6, 1990* (Salem: Oregon Secretary of State, 1990), 32–43. For 1991–1992, the measure capped property taxes intended for funding public schools at 1.5 percent of the property's assessed value, and provided further that, over the next four years, the cap would be lowered to 0.5 percent. (Hence, the rate was set at 1.25 percent for 1992–1993; 1.0 percent for 1993–1994; 0.75 percent for 1994–1995; and 0.5 percent for 1995–1996.) Taxes targeted for other purposes could not exceed 1 percent of assessed value.

33. *OR*, Feb. 2, 1994, sec. C, 2; Sonny Montes interviews; *Willamette Week*, Dec. 13, 1995, 25–26; Montanaro, "Finding a Role."

34. *OR*, Feb. 18, 1994, sec. C, 1. The number of specialists had increased to 6 by 1994.

35. Sonny Montes interview; Montanaro, "Finding a Role."

36. For 1988 figures: PPS, 1988 October Enrollment Report, PPS Records Management Office. For 1997–1998 figures: PPS, Enrollment Report, October 1997, PPS Records Management Office. For 2006–07 figures: Oregon Department of Education, "Student Ethnicity 2006–2007, Portland SD 1J," http://www.ode.state.or.us/sfda/reports/r0067Select2.asp (accessed Sept. 10, 2007).

37. Actually, there were two ballot measures. The first, Measure 47, passed in 1996 but had legal flaws. In 1997, Measure 50 replaced it. See Measure No. 47, proposed by initiative petition to be voted on at the general election, November 5, 1996, http://www.sos.state.or.us/elections/nov596/voters.

guide/MEASURES/MEAS47/M47.HTM (accessed May 9, 2008); and Measure No. 50, House Joint Resolution 85—referred to the electorate of Oregon by the 1997 legislature to be voted on at the special election, May 20, 1997, http://www.sos.state.or.us/elections/may2097/voters.guide/M50/M50.HTM (accessed May 9, 2008).

38. Interviews with Sonny Montes, Huy Hoang, and Vadim Ruskin by the author.

39. Sonny Montes interview.

40. Juan Baez interview by the author.

41. Sonny Montes interviews.

42. On the controversy, see the compilation of news stories about the street-renaming effort on the website of the César E. Chávez Boulevard Committee, http://www.cesarechavezboulevard.com/news.html (accessed Jan. 3, 2009).

43. Sonny Montes telephone conversation with the author, Apr. 7, 2008.

Conclusion

1. Anne Saker, "New Cesar E. Chavez Boulevard Brings Change for Postal Service, Too," *OregonLive.com*, Nov. 30, 2009, http://www.oregonlive.com/portland/index.ssf/2009/11/new_cesar_chavez_boulevard_b.html (accessed July 24, 2010).

2. U.S. Census Bureau, "State and County QuickFacts: Oregon," http://quickfacts.census.gov/qfd/states/41000.html (accessed July 24, 2010).

A Note about Sources

In writing this book, I have relied heavily on primary sources—mostly interviews with historical actors, newspaper reports, and documents in government archives and other manuscript repositories.

I conducted interviews with thirty-three people: Maria Luisa Alaniz (Portland, Oregon, July 2003), Jimmy Amaya (Hillsboro, Oregon, Nov. 2003), Gloria Montes Angulo (La Feria and Weslaco, Texas, Aug. 2003), Juan Baez (Corvallis, Oregon, Oct. 2007), Don Balmer (Portland, Oregon, April 2002), Adolfo Blanco (telephone interview, Mar. 2006), Priscilla Carrasco (telephone interview, May 2004), Tom Current (Portland, Oregon, May 2002), Sister M. Alberta Dieker (Mt. Angel, Oregon, Feb. 2006), Geri Duyck (Cornelius, Oregon, Nov. 2003), Joseph Gallegos (Portland, Oregon, Aug. 2003), Francisco Garcia (Washington, D.C., July 2006), Tina Garcia (telephone interview, Dec. 2008), Emilio Hernandez (Cornelius, Oregon, Nov. 2003), Huy Hoang (Portland, Oregon, Oct. 2003 and Aug. 2005), Marshall Lichtenstein (telephone interview, June 2005), John Little (ten formal interviews in several locations in Oregon and Texas, and eighteen telephone interviews, May 2002 to July 2010), David Martinez (Portland, Oregon, Mar. 2005), Frank Martinez (Bothell, Washington, June 2003), Charles Merten (telephone interview, June 2005), Father Christian Mondor (two telephone interviews, Dec. 2005), Celedonio Montes Jr. (nineteen formal interviews in several locations in Oregon and Texas, and sixteen telephone interviews, Aug. 2002 to July 2010), the late Celedonio Montes Sr. (La Feria and Weslaco, Texas, Aug. 2003), Margarita Jasso Montes (La Feria and Weslaco, Texas, Aug. 2003), Ramon Ramirez (Woodburn, Oregon, May 2006), Jose Romero (six formal interviews in several locations in Oregon and seven telephone interviews, Aug. 2003 to July 2010), Kathy Romero (Portland, Oregon, Sept. 2004), Vadim Ruskin (Portland, Oregon, Oct. 2003 and Aug. 2005), Yolanda Tavera (Portland, Oregon, Mar. 2005 and Mar. 2006), Maricela G. Urzua (Portland, Oregon, Mar. 2006), Rudy Veliz (telephone interview, Dec. 2008), Carmen West (telephone interview, Aug. 2007), and Don Willner (Portland, Oregon, May 2002). I also benefited from interviews conducted by others—in particular, the interviews of Sonny Montes by Noreen Saltveit McGraw (identified at Noreen Saltveit in the notes), which took place in Dec. 1996, and the interviews of John Little by Kay Reid, conducted between Dec. 1995 and Mar. 1997. (I am grateful to McGraw and Reid for providing me with transcriptions of those sessions.) All these interviews have proved to be invaluable, often providing material about which the documentary record is silent and occasionally correcting that record. I have donated all my taped interviews to the Special Collections Department at the University of Oregon, where they are available to researchers.

I have derived much information from newspapers as well, particularly about the VML, Mt. Angel College, and the Colegio. All of my newspaper research took place in the University of Oregon's Knight Library, which has a comprehensive collection of microfilmed Oregon newspapers. The papers that proved to be most useful were the *Capital Journal* (Salem), the *Hillsboro Argus*, the *Mount Angel News*, the *Oregon Journal* (Portland), the *Oregon Labor Press* (Portland), the *Oregon Statesman* (Salem), the *Silverton Appeal-Tribune*, and the *Statesman Journal* (Salem, a title that came into existence after the merger of the *Capital Journal* and the *Oregon Statesman*). While newspapers cannot be counted on to provide a complete, nuanced picture of any historical development, they serve a particularly vital function in a research project such as my own—one in which the organizations under examination have passed out of existence and did not deposit a collection of their records in a library or any other manuscript repository.

What then about surviving manuscripts—personal corres-pondence, interoffice memoranda, unpublished reports, transcripts of meetings, and the like, the types of documents historians often use to tell their stories about the past? Fortunately, a few relevant collections of such sources exist. In the case of the VML, the most valuable are the records of Stella Maris House, a Portland-based Catholic organization engaged in social work, which are held by the Oregon Historical Society (Portland), and the files of the Office of Economic Opportunity, which are included in the Records of the Community Services Administration (Record Group 381), housed in the U.S. National Archives, College Park, Maryland.

Stella Maris House performed its good works primarily in the Portland area, focusing on the indigent and minority groups. Several of the staff members at Stella Maris House were deeply involved with the VML from the outset, and two of them served on the board of directors. Both scrupulously collected all documents provided them at board meetings, took detailed notes of the meetings themselves, and wrote regular reports about the progress of the VML. Many such documents are included in the Stella Maris House holdings at the Oregon Historical Society. However, while the collection is very rich for the first five years of the VML's operations, it holds little on developments in the 1970s. Also rich are the files of the Office of Economic Opportunity, the federal agency that funded the VML and other CAAs. Although some of the documents found in that collection duplicate those in the Stella Maris House records, the OEO holdings also include a mountain of correspondence between the VML and OEO administrators, periodic reports by VML employees about operations, periodic evaluations of the VML by OEO, and additional materials. Unfortunately, like the Stella Maris House records, the OEO files are extensive for the 1960s and fragmentary for the 1970s. Finally, it is worth noting that the papers of Oregon governor Tom McCall contain items of interest on the VML.

Two major manuscript collections contain important documents relating to the Colegio's struggles with HUD and the Northwest Association of Schools and Colleges. The first is the papers of Al Ullman, the influential Oregon congressman who was a staunch supporter of the Colegio and received regular updates from Colegio officials about HUD's efforts to foreclose. That collection, housed in the Special Collections Department of the University of Oregon's Knight Library, includes an impressive number of documents from the office files of HUD, sources that came into Ullman's possession by a circuitous route. During the course of the Colegio's litigation with HUD in 1977 and 1978, Don Willner, the college's legal coun-sel, filed a Freedom of Information Act request for all documents bearing on the HUD-Colegio relationship. The U.S. government quickly complied, turning over the documents, and the Colegio in turn sent a copy of the lot to Ullman. They provide information about HUD's actions as well as insights into the thinking of HUD administrators. Unfortunately, the huge collection of HUD records (Record Group 207) that are located at the U.S. National Archives, College Park, Maryland contain almost nothing on the Colegio's battles with HUD.

The second important source on the Colegio's struggle is the trial record of the Colegio's lawsuit against the Northwest Association: *Colegio Cesar Chavez vs. Northwest Association of Schools and Colleges et al.*, U.S. District Court for the District of Oregon, 1977. The entire trial record, including affidavits, supporting documentation, and the transcript of proceedings, can be found in the Seattle branch of the U.S. National Archives. It provides a fascinating view of the challenges faced by the Colegio's leaders, Sonny Montes and Jose Romero—the heavy debt load, the difficulty of producing an institutional self-study and an acceptable financial statement, the constant pressure of deadlines. It also helps to explain the views of the members of the Commission on Colleges.

The papers of Paul E. Waldschmidt, the president of the University of Portland, a rich collection of documents located in the University of Portland Archives, complement the aforementioned trial record. Waldschmidt, who served on the Commission of Colleges, initially supported the Colegio in its battles, providing advice on preparing the institutional self-study and showing a willingness to write a letter in support of the Colegio to the Department of Education, but he later soured on the institution. Last but not least, I found useful a small collection of documents recently deposited by John Little in the Special Collections Department of the Knight Library. While the collection has almost nothing on Little's involvement with the VML, it is very informative on the Colegio's final years, a period during which Little served as a member of the board of trustees. Anyone interested in telling the full story of the Colegio's demise will need to consult it.

Index

Montes, Armando (SM's son), 8, 17

Montes, Celedonio Armendadez
(SM's father), 9, *10*, 11, 12-15, 17,
18, 72, 73, 74

Montes, Celedonio, Jr. *See* Montes,
Sonny

Montes, David (SM's son), 100

Montes, Diana (SM's sister), 14

Montes, Estella (SM's sister), 11,
12-13, 72

Montes, Gloria (SM's sister), 11, 12-
13, *12*, 72

Montes, Javier (SM's son), 141

Montes, Leandro (SM's son), 258,
259

Montes, Librada Arce (SM's wife),
8, 17, 18, 19, 57-58, 60, 99-100,
141, 183, 258

Montes, Lupe (SM's sister), 14

Montes, Margarita Gonzales Jasso
(SM's mother), 9, *10*, 12-13, 14-
15, 17

Montes, Maria Armendadez (SM's
grandmother), 10-11

Montes, Olivia (SM's daughter), 60

Montes, Raquel (SM's daughter), 58

Montes, Sonny:

Childhood: birth, 8; childhood
in Weslaco, 8-11; contact
with Anglos, 9, 16, 72-74;
elementary school, 9, 71; family
relationships, 10-11; high school
years, 14-17, 72-73; migrant
field work, 1, 3, 5-6, 12-13,
14-15, 17, 71, 72, 73-74, 110;
move to Fort Worth, 10, 14

Early Years and Valley Migrant
League: antiwar activism, 113,
116, 241; as area director for
Forest Grove, 104, 123, 130; as
area director for Hillsboro, 83-
85, 90-93, 181; as area director
for Woodburn, 93; as assistant
job counselor, 56-57, 58-60, 61,
71, 181; births and adoption of
children, 17, 58, 60, 100, 141;
and Centro Chicano Cultural,
112, 116, 241; Chicano

activism apart from VML, 6,
109-17, 262; engagement and
marriage to Librada, 17-18; FBI
surveillance, 114-15; Garcia
as mentor for, 54, 55-56; on
Governor's Advisory Committee
on Chicano Affairs, 112, 177;
grape boycotts, 110-12, 116,
175, 241, 262; introduction to
Valley Migrant League, 19-20;
job at Farm Workers Home,
100-104; job at Reedley grape
farm, 8, 17, 18, 181; job offer
from VML, 1-2, 3, 20-21,
53-54; Little as mentor for, 4,
6, 58, 59-60, 69-72, 74, 75,
91-92, 223, 227, 261; Los
Gatos conference, 104-10, 115,
116, 262; newspaper profiles of,
84-85, 112-13; Portland State
University protest, 114, 143,
262; as program aide, 6, 21, 50,
54-56, 61, 181; resignations
from VML, 98, 131; role in
VML "revolution," 93-98;
self-help housing program,
123-25; Senate Bill 677
protest, 114, 175; Tankersley
farm confrontation, 119-22;
transition to activism, 1-2, 6,
74-75, 79, 98, 109-17, 262

At Colegio Cesar Chavez/Mt.
Angel College: and Cesar
Chavez, 174-75, 233, 235-
39; Chicano studies program,
147-49, 155-56, 239, 265; co-
directorship with Jose Romero,
2, 6, 181-82, 183-84, 240;
college coursework and degree,
6, 141, 213, 222, 230, 248-49;
as director of ethnic affairs, 130-
31, 140-41, 181-82; as director
of student services, 161, 182;
FBI surveillance, 146, 194-95;
Jose Romero hired by, 155-57;
as member of board of trustees,
231, 243, 244, 245; Mondor

Woelfel, La Salle, 137, 138
women's movement, 40, 178
Woodburn Opportunity Center, 49,
  51, 62-63, 66, 69-71, 93, 131
World War II, and *bracero* program,
  26-27, 34, 35, 43
Wynia, Bob, 62, 67, 76-77, 78, 86,
  93-94

Yamhill County, Ore., 23, 24, *25*, 26
Yamhill County Farm Workers
  Organization, 80
Young Citizens for Community
  Action, 108
Yzaguirre, Raúl, 235-36